GW00777566

Early Modern Literature in History

General Editor: **Cedric C. Brown**
Professor of English and Head of Department, University of Reading

Within the period 1520–1740 this series discusses many kinds of writing, both within and outside the established canon. The volumes may employ different theoretical perspectives, but they share an historical awareness and an interest in seeing their texts in lively negotiation with their own and successive cultures.

Titles include:

Anna R. Beer
SIR WALTER RALEGH AND HIS READERS IN THE SEVENTEENTH CENTURY
Speaking to the People

Cedric C. Brown and Arthur F. Marotti (*editors*)
TEXTS AND CULTURAL CHANGE IN EARLY MODERN ENGLAND

Martin Butler (*editor*)
RE-PRESENTING BEN JONSON
Text, History, Performance

Jocelyn Catty
WRITING RAPE, WRITING WOMEN IN EARLY MODERN ENGLAND
Unbridled Speech

Danielle Clarke and Elizabeth Clarke (*editors*)
'THIS DOUBLE VOICE'
Gendered Writing in Early Modern England

James Daybell (*editor*)
EARLY MODERN WOMEN'S LETTER-WRITING, 1450–1700

John Dolan
POETIC OCCASION FROM MILTON TO WORDSWORTH

Henk Dragstra, Sheila Ottway and Helen Wilcox (*editors*)
BETRAYING OUR SELVES
Forms of Self-Representation in Early Modern English Texts

Pauline Kiernan
STAGING SHAKESPEARE AT THE NEW GLOBE

Ronald Knowles (*editor*)
SHAKESPEARE AND CARNIVAL
After Bakhtin

James Loxley
ROYALISM AND POETRY IN THE ENGLISH CIVIL WARS
The Drawn Sword

Anthony Miller
ROMAN TRIUMPHS AND EARLY MODERN ENGLISH CULTURE

Arthur F. Marotti (*editor*)
CATHOLICISM AND ANTI-CATHOLICISM IN EARLY MODERN ENGLISH
TEXTS

Mark Thornton Burnett
CONSTRUCTING 'MONSTERS' IN SHAKESPEAREAN DRAMA AND EARLY
MODERN CULTURE

MASTERS AND SERVANTS IN ENGLISH RENAISSANCE DRAMA AND CULTURE
Authority and Obedience

Early Modern Literature in History
Series Standing Order ISBN 0-333-71472-5
(*outside North America only*)

You can receive future titles in this series as they are published by placing a standing order.
Please contact your bookseller or, in case of difficulty, write to us at the address below with
your name and address, the title of the series and the ISBN quoted above.

Customer Services Department, Macmillan Distribution Ltd, Houndmills, Basingstoke,
Hampshire RG21 6XS, England

Constructing 'Monsters' in Shakespearean Drama and Early Modern Culture

Mark Thornton Burnett

© Mark Thornton Burnett 2002

All rights reserved. No reproduction, copy or transmission of this publication may be made without written permission.

No paragraph of this publication may be reproduced, copied or transmitted save with written permission or in accordance with the provisions of the Copyright, Designs and Patents Act 1988, or under the terms of any licence permitting limited copying issued by the Copyright Licensing Agency, 90 Tottenham Court Road, London W1T 4LP.

Any person who does any unauthorised act in relation to this publication may be liable to criminal prosecution and civil claims for damages.

The author has asserted his right to be identified as the author of this work in accordance with the Copyright, Designs and Patents Act 1988.

First published 2002 by
PALGRAVE MACMILLAN
Houndmills, Basingstoke, Hampshire RG21 6XS and
175 Fifth Avenue, New York, N.Y. 10010
Companies and representatives throughout the world

PALGRAVE MACMILLAN is the global academic imprint of the Palgrave Macmillan division of St. Martin's Press, LLC and of Palgrave Macmillan Ltd. Macmillan® is a registered trademark in the United States, United Kingdom and other countries. Palgrave is a registered trademark in the European Union and other countries.

ISBN 0-333-91434-1

This book is printed on paper suitable for recycling and made from fully managed and sustained forest sources.

A catalogue record for this book is available from the British Library.

Library of Congress Cataloging-in-Publication Data

Burnett, Mark Thornton.
    Constructing 'monsters' in Shakespearean drama and early modern culture / Mark Thornton Burnett.
        p. cm. – (Early modern literature in history)
    Includes bibliographical references (p.) and index.
    ISBN 0-333-91434-1 (cloth)
    1. Shakespeare, William, 1564–1616 – Characters–Monsters
2. Monsters in literature. 3. Marlowe, Christopher, 1564–1593.
Tamburlaine the Great. 4. Jonson, Ben, 1573?–1637. Bartholomew Fair.
5. Timur, 1336–1405 – In literature. 6. Body, Human, in literature.
7. Villains in literature. I. Title. II. Early modern literature in history
(Palgrave (Firm))

PR2992.M65 B87 2002
822.3'3 – dc21   2002072630

10   9   8   7   6   5   4   3   2   1
11   10   09   08   07   06   05   04   03   02

Printed and bound in Great Britain by
Antony Rowe Ltd, Chippenham and Eastbourne

Contents

List of Figures

Acknowledgements

I owe primary thanks to four institutions which have generously funded my research, made available precious time and provided material resources. Queen's University, Belfast, granted me a semester of study leave, and the British Academy provided an additional semester away from teaching and administration under its one-year research leave scheme. The Huntington Library appointed me to a Andrew W. Mellon Foundation Fellowship, while the Harry Ransom Humanities Research Centre at the University of Texas at Austin granted a Pforzheimer Fellowship. Were it not for the backing of these institutions, *Constructing 'Monsters'* would, indeed, still be at the stage of construction rather than completion.

Colleagues have been equally forthcoming with expertise and comment. At Queen's, Belfast, I would like to thank the splendid Renaissance team of Ewan Fernie, Clare McManus and Ramona Wray. They have given nurturing suggestions and constructive advice, and the book is much the richer for their input. To Ramona Wray there goes a special debt of thanks. She provided invaluable reflections on, and insights into, how the manuscript might be improved: without her the book could not have been written. Also at Queen's, Brian Caraher, Kevin De Ornellas, Ellen Douglas-Cowie, Ivan Herbison and Hugh Magennis have been importantly supportive. Further afield, I am fortunate to have benefited from the collegiality and friendship of, variously, Michael Dobson, Arthur Kinney, Kate McLuskie, James Shapiro, Rick Waswo and Stanley Wells. All have either heard versions of the book or have facilitated my continuing investigations into matters 'monstrous' – to them many thanks.

Versions of *Constructing 'Monsters'* have been given as papers in Belfast, Chicago, Dublin, Florence, Glasgow, Groningen, Leeds, Paris, St Andrews, San Francisco and Stratford-upon-Avon. I would like to thank the audiences on those occasions for their informed attention, the organizers of the conferences at which I spoke, and the colleagues who invited me to address their staff and students. In particular, I am greatly obliged to Peter Holland, François Laroque, Andrew Murphy, Nick Roe and Helen Wilcox for the warm reception they extended to me.

The wider academic community has also been generous in reading drafts of chapters. Pertinent, timely and wise feedback came from, among others, John Archer, Emily Bartels, Crystal Bartolovich, Dympna Callaghan, Fran Dolan, Charles Edelman, Neil Kenny, Laura Lunger Knoppers and Diane Purkiss. No less significantly, as I was chasing 'monsters' across far-flung libraries and archives, the following, as well as fruitful conversation, offered welcome hospitality: Doug Bruster (who also read parts of the book in an initial manifestation), Patricia Fumerton, Bernth Lindfors, Judy Wells Lindfors and Elizabeth Scala. Three collectors – Peter Jackson, Carla Raymond and Warren Raymond – were cordial and enthusiastic, kindly taking the time to introduce me to the world of their own 'cabinets of curiosity'.

At Palgrave Macmillan, I have profited from the patience and guidance of Eleanor Birne, Charmian Hearne and Becky Mashayekh. Cedric Brown has been a model series editor, and I am also in the debt of Anon., one of the readers of the manuscript. Meanwhile, at Planet Wild, Mat Fraser, Daniel Gooding and Paul Sapin gave me the opportunity to test out my ideas in a larger documentary domain.

An earlier (now almost unrecognizable) incarnation of Chapter 5 was published in *Shakespeare Survey*, 50 (1997), pp. 187–99. I am grateful to Cambridge University Press for permission to reprint an amended version of that material.

Introduction

What have we here – a man or a fish? – dead or alive? . . . A
strange fish! Were I in England now . . . and had but this fish
painted, not a holiday-fool there but would give a piece of
silver. There would this monster make a man – any strange
beast there makes a man. When they will not give a doit to
relieve a lame beggar, they will lay out ten to see a dead Indian.

The Tempest (1611)[1]

What Moon-calf has she got with her? . . . What, this Harti-
choke? A Childe born with a beard on his face? . . . why sister
this is monstrous, and shames all our kindred. . . thou art horri-
bly deceived sister, this Urchin cannot be of thy breeding, I
shall be asham'd to call him cousin . . .

[William Shakespeare and William Rowley],
The Birth of Merlin (*c.* 1620)[2]

> Let him take thee,
> And hoist thee up to the shouting plebeians –
> Follow his chariot, like the greatest spot
> Of all thy sex; most monster-like be shown
> For poor'st diminutives, for dolts . . .

Anthony and Cleopatra (1606–7)[3]

In the opening quotations, Trinculo in *The Tempest* and the Clown in
The Birth of Merlin find themselves confronting an apparent anomaly of
nature. As is implied in their adoption of the interrogative mode, both
are unsure how to classify the phenomenon facing them. 'What have
we here – a man or a fish?' asks Trinculo, his question indicating an

urgent need to determine Caliban's genus. Likewise, the Clown's opening references attempt to situate the hirsute Merlin as a 'Moon-calf' (an 'abortive birth' and a 'shapeless substance produced in the uterus') and an artichoke respectively.[4] The enlisting of both human and vegetable categories works to suggest the classificatory inadequacy of each. Merlin, like Caliban, fits into no easy arrangement.

In order to resolve the interpretive problems thrown up by these 'extraordinary bodies', Trinculo and the Clown introduce a third category – 'monster'.[5] The term 'monster' derives from at least one noun and two inter-related verb forms. In Latin, *monstro* means to show, demonstrate and reveal; a *monstrum* is a portent, prodigy or sign as well as an 'unnatural thing'; and *moneo* translates as to give warning of or presage.[6] With its associations of alterity and inexplicability, the label 'monster' provides for Trinculo and the Clown a way of understanding physical difference while simultaneously confirming it as 'other'. The label's classificatory power is reflected in each speaker's movement from question to statement, and from bewilderment to psychological composure.

The 'monstrous' designation is particularly useful, it might be suggested, because of its amorphous, subsuming quality. In the reflections of the first two speakers, 'monster' emerges as a term that can simultaneously encompass a preternaturally hairy child, a fish-like human, a 'strange beast' and a 'dead Indian'. Moreover, the final quotation suggests that the term's descriptive utility might be expanded to embrace not only the physically 'different', but also a host of perceived cultural deviations. Cleopatra, of course, is immediately 'monstrous' in being a captive who is ethnically 'other' – a dramatic version of those sixteenth- and seventeenth-century native Americans shipped to England and installed on the Thames for Londoners to wonder at.[7] But it is also her status as a woman ruler that defines Cleopatra as 'monster': her threatened 'monster-like' future is directly related to her appropriation of male power. For Anthony, then, 'monstrosity' is the way in which Cleopatra's flouting of dominant gender expectations will be conceptualized by a hostile Roman public. His comment points up the fact that a society's conventions are often as narrowly demarcated as its physical norms, enabling 'monstrosity' to signal a range of personality and behavioural traits which fall outside prescribed perimeters.

In positing 'monstrosity' as a quality that will be identified in Cleopatra by the Romans, Anthony alerts us to the constructed nature of the 'monstrous' designation. Cleopatra becomes 'monster-like' only upon her arrival in the Italian capital, suggesting a reading of her status that shifts according to geographical locale. *The Tempest* can be seen as similarly self-conscious in its foregrounding of the construction process. Trinculo's comment that, in England, a 'dead Indian' might be regarded as no less a 'monster' than a 'strange fish' or a 'strange beast' points up the xenophobic mindset that places on a par all such unfamiliar phenomena. The 'monstrous' designation, it seems, has less to do with what the 'monster' actually possesses and more to do with the manner in which it is perceived. Like Anthony's speculative remodelling of Cleopatra, Trinculo's reflections work to deflect responsibility away from the inherent characteristics of the 'monster' and onto the subjectivity of the spectator.

It might not be coincidental, therefore, that the idea of audience plays a disproportionate role in all three passages. Thus Anthony dwells upon the particular interest that Cleopatra will have for Rome's 'shouting plebeians', and Trinculo is fired to imagine how Caliban will excite the 'holiday-fool'. Crucial to such an encounter is the motif of display. Cleopatra, Anthony predicts, is to be 'hoist[ed] . . . up' and 'shown', the detail of the physical movement indicating her elevation above the other captives. The oppositions rehearsed in Anthony's speech, moreover – the 'greatest' is on show before the 'poor'st' – illuminate the peculiarly inversive power dynamic that characterized the early modern exhibition of the 'monster'. At the same time, his contemptuous evocation of the unruly mob marks out Cleopatra's display as mass entertainment. Publicity rhetoric – Cleopatra is the 'greatest spot / Of all [her] sex' – links the Egyptian queen to the projected display of Caliban in *The Tempest*. As a fairground attraction, Caliban will be 'painted', his image copied and circulated and his professional exposure marketed to guarantee a large audience. The potential profit of display is such that Trinculo's fantasies of self-aggrandizement are easily stimulated: 'any strange beast . . . makes a man'. No commercial imperatives are evoked in *The Birth of Merlin*, but even here a display situation seems to be anticipated. In the Clown's fear that the bearded child will shame 'all our kindred' can be glimpsed the shadowy prospect of exhibition. The other passages suggest that such a fear of public presentation is well founded, since it is in display that the alterity of 'monsters' is ultimately confirmed. Cleopatra has her 'monster-like' credentials finalized when she is 'shown'; Caliban is stamped 'monster' only after his exhibition has been contemplated.

All three passages (in their terms of reference, in their use of the language of discovery and wonder, in their attention to motifs of exhibition and display, in their emphasis upon classification, in their compulsion to assimilate 'difference', and in their self-conscious privi-leging of audience response) demonstrate their investment in one of the most intriguing and least understood discourses of the period – the discourse of 'monstrosity'. By the time Shakespearean representations were circulating, the 'monstrous' had become a focus of intense fascination. In a range of guises, 'monsters' and their associations found a sure place in the early modern psyche. The appeal of the 'extra-ordinary body' was attested to in ballads, diaries, proclamations and satirical verses, as well as in plays.[8] Wonder-books and their generic relatives flourished, thanks in large part to their ability to draw upon and commemorate the most celebrated 'monsters' of the day. In the same moment, 'monster' exhibitions, which assumed a range of forms, were cultivated by the populace across the country. The fairground, the market, the tavern and the private house were all spaces where various types of 'monstrosity' were elaborated. Chapter 1 investigates these locations, beginning with a discussion of the fairground 'freak show'. A 1601 Marstonian satire refers to 'our monstrous penny-showes', and this ascription of a one-penny admission price is con-firmed by a number of later writers, making a visit to a fairground 'monster'-booth within reach of the majority of wage-earners in the period.[9] Discussion here centres on the type of encounter such wage-earners might have experienced in the early modern 'monster'-booth. It analyses material conditions, thematic preoccupations and perfor-mative choreographies in order to trace the facility with which this site fractured into a spectrum of other display venues, including the court and the 'cabinet of curiosities'.

'Monstrous' exhibition sites had a dynamic relation to a wide range of philosophical writings. At this time, medical explorations, moral treatises and a deluge of pamphlets lent intellectual credence to a growing debate about questions of 'monstrous' significance and status. Addressing these materials, Chapter 1 argues that the 'monstrous' body produced anxieties about singleness and doubleness, autonomy and dependency, sameness and otherness, and civility and savagery, which were discharged through that work. In at least some cases, such a textualization of anxieties was prompted by a 'monstrous' exhibit; indeed, in a number of explorations with a philosophical orientation, explicit connections are forged between the author's wonderings and the exhibition stage. The very same writings might also be regarded a another kind of 'monstrous' performance. Combining narratives about the significance of the 'monster' with lengthy passages of physical description and often detailed woodcuts, these texts constituted a more rarefied and intellectual substitute for the sensational experience of the 'monster'-booth.

'Monstrous' performances of yet another sort, the chapter concludes, found a convenient home in the theatre. Within the walls of the play-house one expected to witness marvellous tales, miraculous transfor-mations, fantastic creatures and, in a limited number of cases, 'actual' 'monsters'.[10] The irony of all three opening quotations is that, by the time the prospective exhibitions of Caliban, Cleopatra and Merlin are anticipated, they are, of course, already well under way. The theatre, it might be suggested, was itself a display-site for the showing of 'mon-strosity', one in which the 'monstrous' qualities of its protagonists are on show from the earliest scenes.

Indeed, it is possible that the plays owed at least some of their appeal to costume decisions and presentation details which stressed the char-acters' unusualness. One might speculate that the boy actor cast as Cleopatra wore a spectacular Egyptian costume and 'blacked up' to indi-cate the queen's 'tawny' complexion, and that Merlin was played with an exaggerated false beard. Certainly, in the case of Caliban, an unusual amphibian outfit was a crucial property. Michael Baird Saenger has recently argued that the actor taking the part of the 'monster' in early performances dressed in 'green sleaves and trousers with fins attached to them', a costume which, with its human and fish-like appendages, drew a heightened notice to Caliban's peculiar physical condition.[11] Without doubt, such staging strategies gained energy from popular con-structions of the 'monstrous', with the two feeding into each other to bestow upon an individual 'monster' an even more distinctive theatri-cal presence. When Trinculo mocks the 'holiday-fool' who pays 'ten doits' to see a 'dead Indian', and when Anthony scorns the 'shouting plebeians' who are 'shown' Cleopatra for 'dolts' (small sums of money), they metatheatrically invoke another economic transaction, one which has already taken place – the monetary exchange required to enter the playhouse. Their reflections upon the admission price charged for beholding a 'monster' jokingly remind playgoers that they, too, have parted with money to watch 'monsters' perform.

To that performance crucial implications are attached. The last twenty years of literary criticism have singled out Renaissance drama as a privileged site for understanding and contesting the preoccupations and priorities which animate society and culture as a whole. Through the interactions of dramatic 'monsters' – in their voices, questions and quandries – we can see the drama posing the kinds of interpretive dilem-mas that mark it out as an important use of the 'monstrous' discourse

and place it at the centre of the philosophical project. For an understanding of the 'monstrous' in all of its cultural guises, then, it is to a
contextualized reading of theatrical representation that we need to turn.

The book's architecture is organized so as to mime the various stages
of the exhibition of the 'monster' in Shakespearean culture. Chapter 1
and the Epilogue form the flaps of a 'monster'-booth. Advancing into
the booth itself, one encounters internal curtain chapters on Marlowe
and Jonson. In Marlowe's *Tamburlaine the Great* (1587–88), Chapter 2
suggests, success is measured via the ways in which the discourses of
'monstrosity' are appropriated: Tamburlaine emerges as victorious when
he puts rhetoric into practice, reducing his enemies to the level of
'actual' 'monsters' and supervising a series of 'monstrous' events. By
contrast, as Chapter 6 argues, Jonson's *Bartholomew Fair* (1614) shows a
less obvious debt to to the discourses of 'monstrosity'. However, tropes
of display and demonstration, a concern with enormity and reproduction, an anxiety about the unstable identities of the fairground
participants and representations of an urge to define mean that the play
extends and diversifies the more specific discussions of 'monsters' initiated elsewhere. The play's comic genre, moreover, brings a parodic and
even interrogative dimension to its particular project, which is Jonson's
rivalry with Shakespeare. Inserted between these assessments of
Marlowe and Jonson are Chapters 3, 4 and 5, which, focusing on Shakespeare, reflect not so much a final confrontation with the 'monster' displayed at the heart of the booth as an effort to tease out the various
representational uses of 'monsters' across a single professional career.
Thus *Richard III* (1591) finds in the shape of Richard's 'monstrous'
proportions a commentary on England's uncertain political fortunes,
Chapter 3 contends. Because Iago is realized as a fairground-type impresario who shows 'monsters', and Othello as a sort of Baconian 'rationalist' who requires 'proof' of their existence, Chapter 4 asserts, *Othello*
(1601–2) can be most profitably regarded as a work in which two rival
cultural traditions interlock and compete for prominence. Chapter 5
posits *The Tempest* (1611) as Shakespeare's most searching exposition
of 'monstrosity', since the play brings together in a unique combination a competition between a 'monster' (Caliban) and an impresario
(Prospero), a plethora of local investigations and a charged sensitivity
to the effects of reproduction, which is mediated through metaphorical
constructions of parthenogenesis. In so doing, *The Tempest* establishes
itself as a disquisition on the redemptive power of art and the properties and potentialities of the theatre itself. By situating 'monstrosity' at
the centre, and in its discussion overall, therefore, this study discovers

'monsters' not only as a mechanism whereby the dramatist was empowered to address his own craft, but also as key contributory elements to early modern cultural, political and social debate.

In arguing for the importance of the 'monster', this book engages with the period's characteristic interplay between what might loosely be termed 'rationalism' and 'superstition'.[12] Throughout the period, a fresh interest in instrumentation and technology, a new enthusiasm for classificatory systems and a growing reliance on observation and experiment compete and merge with established systems of belief and older notions of 'truth'.[13] As a property which pushed mechanisms for understanding to their very limits, the theatrical body of the 'monster' was a crucial site on which theories collided, hypotheses were tested and the battle for 'science' was waged. The process was not explicit or monolithic, and the chapter outlines should have indicated the relevance of 'monsters' to less metaphysical enquiries. Nevertheless, tensions resulting from the messy overlap of contemporary ideological systems form the backdrop for a gallery of arguments which might appear otherwise unconnected: a myriad of smaller, more localized discussions enters into and draws power from the larger debate. At a time when a spirit of rationalism was shaping the cultural *mentalité*, the discourses of 'monstrosity' found a metaphorical utility considerably beyond their immediate frames of reference.

'Monsters', of course, are not merely an early modern phenomenon. An additional argument of the book is that many of the ideas, formulations and prejudices circulating with 'monsters' in the Shakespearean theatre have helped to determine modern reflections on the display and reproduction of the body. The Epilogue, which closes the book and the booth, elaborates this thesis. Tracing connections between Renaissance discourses of 'monstrosity' and late twentieth-century and early twenty-first-century debates surrounding exhibition, the 'body beautiful' and disability, it argues that the anxieties of recent decades have illuminating precursors in an earlier historical moment. If Caliban, Cleopatra and Merlin seem rooted in the past, then they also have a shaping influence on the present.

1
Mapping 'Monsters'

At the height of a busy exchange in Jonson's *Bartholomew Fair* (1614), the watchman Bristle reprimands his partner Haggis for neglect of duty. The cause of the dereliction – Haggis' enthusiasm for a particular fairground attraction. Complains Bristle: 'You . . . met the man with the monsters, and I could not get you from him.'[1] The reference is not elaborated on, but this chapter posits 'the man with the monsters' – the entrepreneur behind what might be usefully understood as an early modern 'freak show' – as a crucial constituent of the imaginative landscape of early modern England. Exploiting through exhibition a contemporary fascination with those people and properties that stood outside existing taxonomies and systems of knowledge, this figure represented the most clearly defined entrance point to the 'monstrous' experience.

Examining the early modern 'freak show', and resurrecting a sense of its scope and rationale, this chapter explores a culture anxious about measuring perceived deviations against inherited standards of 'normality'. Beginning with this process, it goes on to trace the 'monstrous' – and particular 'monsters' – through a range of exhibition spaces (material, ideological, social and textual), demonstrating that the fairground site was capable of fracturing into a range of other performative spaces, one of which was the theatre. Forceful links are thereby suggested between what are often taken to be divergent discursive fields and endeavours, restoring to the theatre and its productions something of their polymathic cultural intensity. Interconnections are grounded first in the metaphorical tropes favoured by anti-theatricalists and then in the performative conventions that pushed the fairground and the theatre into a similar semantic field. As a whole, the argument prepares the ground for a reading of the drama as an important space in which 'monstrous' debates unfolded.

I

By positing a connection between fairgrounds and theatres, this chapter suggests a material underpinning for the oft-cited anti-theatrical analogies between the stage and the 'monster'-booth. Within the Renaissance itself, links between theatres and 'monsters' were common currency. There are numerous examples of commentators citing areas of correspondence, invariably to condemn the playhouse and to bolster the censorship programme that may have inhibited its progress. 'And they that neuer goe out of their houses,' remarked puritan pamphleteer Stephen Gosson in 1579, 'wil neuer beleeue that [there] . . . are . . . such horrible monsters in playing places.'[2] The prospect conjured up here – that a playhouse could be taken for a species of 'monster'-booth – not only enjoyed constant repetition but was expanded to brand as 'monstrous' not only playhouses but also all of their productions and appurtenances. For, as a later argument maintained, if playing spaces summoned into consciousness the fairground's most disturbing demonstrations, then so could the performances they accommodated, which were also deemed to possess 'monstrous' characteristics. Plays are *'infernal'* and 'prodigious Stage-abominations', an early seventeenth-century anti-theatrical vituperation claimed, so *'crooked, and distorted in themselues, that no Art can make them straite'*.[3] Drawing on Latinate diction (as 'abominations', plays lie beyond the kith and kin of 'mankind') and prophetic utterance (the 'monstrous' origins of the drama are implicitly the harbingers of its damnable fate), this criticism is animated by its adaptation of an established philosophical identification.

Many of these criticisms, of course, hinged on a belief in the inherent 'monstrosity' of the actor's profession. 'I . . . terme . . . Players . . . Monsters . . . Bicause vnder colour of humanitie, they present nothing but prodigious vanitie,' wrote William Rankins in 1587, in a formulation that was echoed by another anti-theatricalist, William Prynne, in 1633: players, he wrote, 'vncreate themselues' to *'metamorphose . . . into . . . Monsters'*.[4] These identifications were instructive in two vital respects. To label the player a 'monster' was to warn against the immoral fictions and deceitful vacuity that his craft disseminated. It was also to alert audiences to the shape-shifting strategies whereby he muddled God-given identifications, unmaking himself, turning 'monstrous' and becoming, in the process, worryingly unclassifiable. Often associated with actors, inappropriate or inordinate dress was also 'monstrous', a vocal and wide-ranging group of critics held. The implicit objection was that such dress collapsed gender divisions, eradicated class markers and propelled treasured taxonomies into chaos.[5] Transgressions of the sumptuary order could also signal the possibility of a more frightening dissolution – the apocalypse. As a 1600 satire asserted, 'cutting sutes portend . . . wracte [destruction] vnto our weale and vs'.[6] Judged against this anxiety, the actor presented a tricky ontological problem. Less of a prodigy portending the end of the world, the actor was a 'monster' in a double sense – 'monstrous' in constantly changing his attire and 'monstrous' in the commercial profit that he reaped from making a spectacle of his own body.

If, in the contemporary puritan sensibility, fairground 'monsters' and playhouse actors traversed a comparable ideological terrain, this may have been at least in part because they worked within similar material arenas. Jeffrey D. Mason has argued that 'the street fair, as a site or venue, is comparable to a theatrical stage', emphasizing the parallel behaviours of the participants at each event.[7] Other points of contact between the fairground and the theatre are quick to suggest themselves. At the most obvious level, both institutions staged plays and both cultivated a recognizable dramatic repertory. When the diarist Thomas Crosfield attended a fair in Oxford in July 1635, for instance, he mentioned 'the witches of Lancashire over ag*ainst* y^e *Kings* Head', a reference to Brome and Heywood's celebrated supernatural drama.[8] Some of the plays discussed in individual chapters of this book had notable fairground histories. *Bartholomew Fair* (1614) was listed as an attraction at Bartholomew Fair at the Restoration; *The Tempest* (1611) was presented there during the late seventeenth century; and productions of *Tamburlaine the Great* (1587–88), whether staged by players or puppets, were popular at fairs well into the eighteenth century.[9] More suggestive still is the interchangeability of the entertainers involved. In his commentary on the papers of Henry Herbert, the Master of the Revels, N. W. Bawcutt remarks that licences to 'use *Interludes*, and *masques*' and 'to exercise *the quality of playing*' were not infrequently granted to druggists and apothecaries – fairground 'mountebanks', to adopt a contemporary term – which suggests that the dividing lines between the Smithfield impresario and the Southwark actor were not as pronounced as it might initially appear.[10] It is not inconceivable indeed that the 'Monster-Master' could double as the interpreter of a stately tragedy or a boisterous comedy, and would have been expected to do so by a seasoned, well-travelled audience.

Over and above their performative correspondences, theatres and 'monstrous' display sites engaged in exchanges of energy at a practical level. As S. P. Cerasano reminds us, the contemporary dramatic experi-

ence was regularly enacted alongside the fairground-type animal spectacles of the Bear Garden, which involved the skills of performing apes
and horses or the conflicts of baited bears, mastiffs and even tigers.[11]
Not only practically linked, these entertainments were also institutionally integrated in 1604, when, as Matthew Bliss points out, 'Philip
Henslowe purchased the office of the bearward and wholly controlled
the sport for the next seven years'.[12]

However widely the performative interests of the impresario might
have ranged, in a fairground setting, he brought together under the title
of 'monster' a gamut of non-normative types. These 'monsters' ranged
from animals distinguished by an unfamiliar species location or a physical anomaly to humans whose bodies marked them out as 'different' –
in the words of Rosemarie Garland Thomson, 'extraordinary'.[13] Likely
to be encountered at the fairground were such human 'monsters' as
those delineated in Beaumont's *The Knight of the Burning Pestle* (1607)
and Jasper Mayne's *The City-Match* (1637–38?). In the former, the
Citizen's wife recalls a visit to 'the little child that was so fair grown
about the members ... and the hermaphrodite'.[14] In the latter, the
'hairy wench', the 'woman with dead flesh' and the armless mother are
the attractions on offer.[15]

The lure of the differently furnished body – one that has either
developed beyond conventional limitations or has been arrested in its
progress – is obvious here, and these dramatic details have numerous
historical points of contact. A preoccupation with incompletion animates the 1580 exhibition of a 'boye ... w[hi]che ... had no [nipples]'
at the 'abbey fayre' in Shrewsbury, and the appearance of a 'child borne
without Armes' in Coventry in 1637.[16] By contrast, many advertisements, chronicles, diaries and satirical verses testify to the astonishing
impact of excess – the spectacle of a superfluous development or enlarge-
ment.[17] In 1656, the main draw at a Leatherhead fair was a 'Monster
[who] ... was all belly ... [and] could not stirre', and in 1660, a 'German
giant', who reputedly stood at 'nine foot', toured England to considerable acclaim.[18] These exhibition details suggest that some among the
'monstrous' *homo sapiens* may not have confined themselves to a single
fairground appearance; instead, visits to a number of fairs were included
on a larger itinerary. In the Midlands, the South-West and the developing conurbation of the capital was a paying clientele, and the variety of
fairground locations associated with the exhibition of 'monsters' signals
a widespread responsiveness to that commercial opportunity.

If the record of 'monstrous' human exhibits is substantial, that of
'monstrous' animals is generally more sketchy, suggesting that different

exhibitions stimulated different reactions. Possibly, the human 'monster' was to prove more enduring because the exhibition touched more closely upon the viewer's experiential sense of self. Certainly, the contexts invoked in Jonson's *The Alchemist* (1610) posit the crowd-pulling potential of a non-normative animal display. Amazed at the crowd about his house, Lovewit wonders: 'What should my knave advance, / To draw this company? He hung out no banners / Of a strange calf with five legs to be seen, / Or a huge lobster with six claws?'[19] His comment bears out the ways in which some animals with non-typical physical features – such as the pig with claws, the ram with four horns and the sow with six legs – received mention not only in dramas, but also in ballads and legal pronouncements.[20] Also displayed in increasing numbers in the period were baboons, birds from Peru, beavers, camels, dromedaries, tropical fish, elks, lions and possums.[21] Invariably publicity material labelled such animals as 'outlandish' or 'straunge', reinforcing the notion that it was their unfamiliarity that authorized the 'monstrous' designation.[22] One might also suggest that spectacles involving strange species worked to secure a sense of national superiority: to capture a foreign 'monster' and to reduce it to the level of a fairground curiosity was to push back the boundaries of the 'known' and to domesticate an otherwise alien environment. On occasions, it seems that the alien environment was purposefully produced and that specious animals were created to satisfy the demand for exoticism. When a clerk in Thomas Nabbes' play *Covent-Garden* (1632–3) jokes about having a 'Baboone . . . kill'd . . . stuff't' and shown 'at countrey Faires . . . for a *Ginney Pigmie*' (a Guinea pygmy), he opens up the possibility that at least some 'monstrous' animals on display were elaborate deceptions.[23] It is tempting to speculate that, in such cases, two species were surgically fused into one, as in the case of Barnum's 'Fejee Mermaid', or that a stuffed assemblage of fur and feathers might have sufficed for more gullible spectators. Other sources lend support to the hypothesis, suggesting that, at times, dissimulation fed the early modern appetite.[24] In this connection, the real/unreal binary often seen as separating fair and theatre quickly dissolves.

Whether a differently formed human or animal, an exotic specimen or a manufactured marvel, all 'monsters' benefited from performative conditions that steered theatres and 'monstrous' display sites towards comparable ideological arenas. Prominent at the fairground were such entertainments as magic demonstrations, puppet performances, waxwork shows and rope-dancing presentations, fencing matches, tumbling and vaulting contests, and pike-tossing and gun-firing competitions, many of which migrated from, or gravitated to, the theatre.[25] As well as animal spectacles, the theatre was a display space for all manner of extraordinary human demonstrations, and not only those restricted to the dramatic actor. William Vincent, an entertainer skilled in 'Legerdemain [and] . . . other feates', danced on the ropes at the Fortune Theatre in March 1635, and his exhibition was typical of the ways in which tumblers and acrobats invariably took to the stage to introduce or conclude a performance.[26] As William Cartwright wrote in 1634 of the annual Oxford fair, 'Rare Works and Rarer Beasts do meet; we see / In the same street *Afrik* and *Germany* . . . These cry the Monster-Masters, Those the *Dutch*: / All arts find welcome, all men come to do / Their tricks and slights'.[27] The passage constitutes a rich evocation of exhibitions jostling for prominence, of audiences and shows crowded together in a uniquely cosmopolitan collective.

Competing foci of interest meant that 'monstrous' staging, both in the theatre and the fairground, evolved into a multi-levelled aural, visual and textual experience. Potential customers of the fairground were alerted to its 'monstrous' contents via the circulation of bills and pictures, carefully positioned in fields and thoroughfares.[28] Once inside the fair, 'monster'-booths solicited the public's attention through sound: drums, trumpets and even bagpipes struck familiar notes to signal a particular exhibit or the commencement of a performance.[29] More than mere appeals to sensory perception, these accompaniments to the fair constituted choreographic, acoustic and rhetorical strategies, codes that tempted the public to place a visit to the 'monster' at the top of the list.

Chief among the rhetorical weapons of the 'Monster-Master' or exhibition manager was the 'spiel', the address to the assembled throng concerning the attraction just beyond the flaps of the tent. The 'Monster-Master' exploited various inducements in his speech, none more persuasive than the promise of unheard of wonder. ' "Here within this place, is to be seen the true, rare, and accomplished monster, or miracle of nature",' exclaims Edward Knowell in Jonson's *Every Man in His Humour* (1598) in the earliest dramatization of the impresario.[30] In a 1649 diatribe against parliament, such a figure is parodied through the announcement of Toby Tell-Troth, the 'presenter of the properties':

> *Gentlemen, pray come in, and doe not thinke* Sir,
> *'Tis* Gerbier's *Puppet-play or th'* Water-drinker:
> *This is a reall* Monster, *bred in this Ile*,
> *No* Trundles *Dragon, nor made* Crocodile,
> *To cheat good people with: no juggle, gull*,
> *And yet 'tis all, a* Cheat, *a juggle, Bull*.[31]

In this representation of parliament as a fearsome beast on display, the formulaic elements of the 'spiel' are evident. The direct personal appeal and the use of imperatives aim to capture the interest of passers-by. The accumulation of negative emphases and the hyperbolic language work to build excitement, while the trope of comparison serves to draw attention to the speaker's moral integrity.[32] At some poetic remove from an 'original', the passage nevertheless highlights the competitive contexts out of which the rhetorical shifts of the 'Monster-Master' took shape.

Verbal appeals took energy from the 'monster'-booth's eye-catching paraphernalia (many of which had theatrical associations). About or above the booths were draped canvas banners or flags featuring pictorial interpretations of the 'monster' described in the impresario's address.[33] These worked to foster tension between the external representation and the imagined internal 'reality': only by penetrating the booth could the consumer's sense of anticipation be resolved. Visual messages were sometimes augmented by a textual announcement, which in turn opened up another set of interpretive dimensions. It is precisely such a dynamic that Macduff anticipates when, in *Macbeth* (1606), he plans to have his nemesis 'as our rarer monsters are, / Painted upon a pole, and underwrit / "Here may you see the tyrant" '.[34] Like Cleopatra and Caliban, Macbeth is baited with a 'monster-like' fate that reifies him into spectacle, although here the transformation relies on a textual summary that replaces an individual psychology with a universal epitaph.[35] The sensational tenor of 'tyrant' alerts us to the fact that some banners appear to have used artistic licence. In the *c*. 1604 play of the same name, Bussy d'Ambois describes 'a monster . . . paint[ed] . . . in . . . cloth / Ten times more monstrous than he is in troth', a hyperbolic practice which, we might assume, was fairly common.[36] Making a 'monster' as 'monstrous' as possible made sound business sense.

With the fairground's deployment of material resources in mind, payments made by the Master of the Revels during the 1570s for 'Canvas for A Monster' and 'the wax and woorkmanshipp of vj personages' take on a special importance.[37] Truncated as they are, these references introduce two possibilities. The first is that the artifice on display at the theatre excited admiration in the same way that the dissimulating arts available at the fairground provoked amazement. The second is that the stages of contemporary theatres, as accompaniments to the dramatic action, were periodically draped with images or representations of 'monsters'. To advertise the characteristics of an 'extraordinary body', and to announce the main attractions of a play, it seems, were practices that commented on each other in a mutually enabling dialectic.

A deeper connection manifests itself in the use of the curtain. On entering the 'monster'-booth, the customer faced a fabric divider. By separating 'monster' from client, this worked to increase expectation (only when the divider was removed could one indulge in the freedom to gaze), to provide additional opportunities for rhetoric and to protect the exhibit that the 'presenter of the properties' would shortly reveal.[38] Surveying the stage directions of contemporary dramas suggests that curtains also functioned, as in the 'monster'-booth, as the final boundary between the unknown and the known, the familiar and the wonderful. In *The Winter's Tale* (1611), Paulina draws a curtain to show in the 'discovery space' the 'statue' of Hermione. Clearly, Hermione is no 'monster', but her exposure does induce Leontes' 'wonder', and the strange events carried in her train are the stuff of fairground fantasy. 'Such a deal of wonder is broken out within this hour, that ballad-makers cannot be able to express it,' exclaims the second gentleman, as if imagining the processes whereby news of a 'monster' emerges and advertisements about its professional appearances circulate.[39] Material resources in *The Winter's Tale* build a bridge between the ballad-makers and the 'Monster-Masters'; they suggest that forms of revelation constitute each other via common codes; and they show that, through a romantic construction of divine judgement, forgiveness can be won and new relations can be created. To reveal the 'extraordinary body', and to mount and maintain a theatrical production, constituted jointly reinforcing activities.

The theatre and 'monster'-booth were further linked through the increasingly performative and interactive nature of the latter's exhibitions. Giving particular value for money was a Dutch 'dwarf' on show with a 'lame giant' in London in 1581. He tossed a cup, shot a bow and arrow, brandished a rapier, blew a trumpet, threw a ball, flourished a hammer, wielded an axe and danced a galliard with a member of the audience.[40] Similarly, a French woman 'w[i]thout hands' who toured the country in the early 1630s encouraged inspection of the diverse 'workes' (sewing, washing and writing) 'done w[i]th her feete'.[41] It seems that, in many cases, a theatrical component was introduced in order to underscore the particular exhibit's physical disability. The antics of the Dutch 'dwarf' function to emphasize his shortness and to place his condition in a comic light, while the pedalian agility of the French woman serves to stress her lack of manual dexterity. Through performance, these 'monsters' were able to carve a place for themselves in the public memory. These accounts of their exhibitions indicate that their actions provoked wonder long after the fairground had relocated.

Theatrical elements allowed an audience to enjoy a sense, however illusory, of a performer's quotidian existence. Often the fairground's utilization of advertisements, banners, bills and pictures fostered this process, in their most successful incarnation, enabling a monster to establish a popular persona, which rivalled that of any player celebrity. Among these more extensively commemorated examples were men and women who cast into confusion normative modes for understanding the body and its operations. Almost all were 'hybrids' – body types that combined seemingly incongruous elements.[42]

A first group of 'hybrids' merged in a human frame characteristics conventionally associated with the animal kingdom. During the late 1580s, the English curiosity-seeking public was captivated by Margaret Vergh Griffith, an elderly Welsh woman who 'had an horne foure inches long moste miraculously growing out of her forehead downe to her nose' (Figure 1).[43] The fact that the occasions on which she appeared prompted a rush of commentaries offers a telling measure of her impact. Seeing her in the flesh seems to have pushed many into print. Typical of this process is a 1588 pamphlet containing the testimony of a 'learned Preacher', who, having 'diligently examined the party her selfe', found 'the thing to be true'.[44] Through such reports, presumably, Griffith intrigued audiences who had never experienced the fairground encounter. No less well known was Mary Davis, the horned woman from Great Saughall in Cheshire (Figure 2). Born in 1594 or 1596, she was, like Griffith, exhibited to the public in old age; unlike her Elizabethan predecessor, she appealed not only to the investigator but also the collector. The field of circulation in which her shed horns participated – a 1670 pamphlet argued that one was passed on by an 'English Lord . . . to the *French* King', another was obtained by 'Sir *Willoughby Aston*', who 'reserves it as a Choice Rarity' – points up the rich currency of Davis' name and body in a number of circles as well as the extent to which, even during the course of her life, she was reified into a museum-piece.[45] From a run of appearances, it seems, a horned woman could be transformed from a 'monster' into a celebrity.

A second group of 'hybrids' gained widespread attention not for the possession of a single animal attribute but for the spectacular illusion of an almost complete absorption within an animal identity. With this group, interest centred on the coming together in one individual of what appeared to be two separate species. A material manifestation of the hirsute child described in *The Birth of Merlin* (*c.* 1620), Barbara Urselin (or Van Beck), sometimes known as the 'hairy-faced woman' from Augsburg, was shown in England from the 1630s onwards (Figure 3). On initial inspection, it was Urselin's fur-clad figure that impressed, and this was publicized via the associations of her name, which was probably created for performance purposes: 'Barbara' and 'Urselin' bring to mind an arresting conjunction between barbarity, beards and bears. In particular, a publicity machine focused on a construction of Urselin as a paradoxical combination of the 'wild beast' and the lady of accomplishment. She was, for instance, engraved in 1653 and 1658 at play on a harpsichord, a move that advertised her as a performative attraction while simultaneously highlighting a unique mixture of feminine graces and bestial appearance.[46] A measure of the appeal of such a construction was the survival of Urselin's persona during her lengthy absence from England during the civil war. Her return in the late 1650s with Michael Van Beck, her husband, was immediately popularized in a ballad (now lost) and led to a celebrated London appearance.[47] Possibly, the ballad made mention of Urselin's new marital status; certainly, her union could have been used to emphasize further the dichotomy between the respectable female instrumentalist and the hairy animal exterior. This may even have been its rationale: if some nineteenth-century commentators are to be believed, the marriage was engineered by Van Beck solely to exploit Urselin's commercial potential as a 'frightful creature'.[48]

Whereas Urselin provoked notice partly because she had secured a spouse, Tannakin Skinker, the Dutch 'hog-faced gentlewoman', achieved notoriety as a 'monster' searching for a mate (Figure 4). Constructed as resembling a pig and communicating only in grunts, Skinker and her ill-fated quest for a husband were marketed from the late 1630s via a chain of publicity exercises. The first of these, as with Urselin, was the purposeful deployment of the associations embedded in her name: 'Tannakin' was a diminutive form of 'Anne' and a mocking synonym for Dutch women in general, while 'Skinker' was an amalgamation of terms connoting liquor, lizards and foul odours, demons alike in the popular mind. (Even before her exhibition commenced, therefore, Skinker had been objectified and marked out as unsettling.) The second was a sustained literary campaign designed to bring Skinker to the cultural forefront. In no less than two dramas, four pamphlets and five ballads, contemporary reports assert, Skinker played either a major part or was targeted for ribald comment.[49] Some of these materials were oriented towards stimulating interest in a forthcoming professional appearance. A 1653 pamphlet about a 'great giant' bound for a London show declares that 'the *Hoggs-fac'd Gentle-woman* is sent for out of *Holland* to be his god-mother', a statement that is as much a promotion for Skinker's possible arrival in the capital as it is an attempt to work out her new godchild's genealogy.[50] Others were instrumental in establishing for Skinker an unflattering reputation. A 1639 ballad, for instance, enlists contemporary xenophobic sentiments to reinforce Skinker's hopeless marital prospects. 'Although she haue a golden purse', it runs, 'She is not fit to be a nurse / in England', a remark which shifts Skinker away from national soil and the prospect of an unholy, 'monstrous' alliance.[51]. The presence of Skinker in popular materials across a fourteen-year period illuminates not so much the proverbiality of her name, I would suggest, as a long and successful exhibition history. Like Urselin, Skinker owed her prominence to the ways in which a fictional identity was made commercially viable through public relations.

Even this second group of 'hybrids', however, was overshadowed by a third and final 'monstrous' combination. 'Parasitic ectopy', the phenomenon of a host body attached to, and providing nourishment for, a weaker, imperfectly formed sibling, first impressed itself on the English public when Lazarus Colloredo, a young Genoese joined at the navel to John Baptist, his blind, vestigial twin, arrived in London in the winter of 1637 (Figure 5). The celebrity status of this 'man monster', as he was termed, was apparent in his sophisticated staging techniques and accompanying retinue. For his frequent appearances, Lazarus was accompanied by two employees: one blew a trumpet to announce the performance, the other collected money from the customers. On another occasion, he commissioned a local artist to reproduce his 'portraiture' on a banner, again indicating his skill at self-promotion.[52] Contemporary reports were responsive to Lazarus' entrepreneurship, and he was invariably described as a 'Gentleman well qualifide' who had a refined 'Deportment', was 'well clad' and 'gallantly attir'd'.[53] Commercial success, the class-inflected details suggest, enabled Lazarus to present himself as a man of breeding and distinction, not so much a common 'monster' as a court fop.

II

The display histories of Lazarus Colloredo and his ilk confirm that exhibitions occurred outside the fairground, and that a range of spaces was developed to bring the 'monstrous' body before the public eye.

Exhibitions, it might be suggested, created appetites and audiences for 'monsters' that 'Monster-Masters' who confined themselves only to the fairground may not always have been able to assuage. Unfortunately, it is often difficult to ascertain precisely where an exhibition took place. Some references, such as those to Bartholomew Fair, are unambiguous: Barbara Urselin was there in 1640 and Tannakin Skinker in 1654, when a 'Signe' identified her booth.[54] But such definite citings are rare, and contemporary discourses about the display of 'monsters' more often frustratingly vague. Phrases such as 'brought foorth to publike view', 'brought vp to London', 'carried up and downe the country', 'in London . . . to be seen' and 'seen . . . at a publick Show' may indicate a fairground appearance, but they may also indicate an alternative venue.[55] When in the 1580s, Margaret Griffith, the horned Welsh woman, travelled 'to be seene aswell in London as in other places of this Realme', it seems reasonable to suppose that a fair would not have featured at every point.[56] Similarly, Barbara Urselin's tour of the country in the 1630s, organized for her by her father while she was still a child, can hardly have depended merely on fairground opportunities.[57] The exhibition history of Lazarus Colloredo confirms such an hypothesis. Following a successful gallop through the European capitals and his 1637 London appearance, Lazarus relocated to Norwich in 1638 and Aberdeen in 1642.[58] At this final stage of his journey, he hired a 'lodging' in the town where he was able to put on his show and accommodate himself and his servants.[59] Here is evidence of one show at least which stood wholly independent of the fairground circuit.

While an exclusively hired city residence would have been beyond the means of many performers, it is likely that those wishing to display the 'monster' found potential in a whole range of metropolitan situations. The exhibition of 'monsters' took place in markets, taverns and private houses. For instance, a child 'with ruffes' was 'to be seene' in a private house in 'Glene Alley in Suthwark' in 1566; a 'marueilous straunge fishe' caught between Calais and Dover in 1569 was first unveiled in Billingsgate; and in 1653 it was reported that a 'rich *Jew*' intended to show a nineteen-foot native American in no less splendid a venue than St Paul's Cathedral ('because the *Mouth Inn* . . . is . . . too little').[60]

At each level of society, and in every cultural cranny, the lure of the 'monster' could be discerned. Even a 'monstrous birth' ran the risk of becoming a public occasion, although the impetus was not commercial.[61] A local anomalous delivery, as sixteenth- and seventeenth-century pamphlets suggest, might draw neighbours, parish priests and gentry alike, suggesting a culture well versed in gazing at the 'monstrous'.[62] In these scenarios, the first exhibition site of the 'monster' was not so much the holiday tent as the mother's lying-in chamber.

It was arguably because the fairground was capable of diluting into other spaces, and because its practices proved infinitely adaptable, that 'monsters' came to the attention of a host of contemporary authorities. As in the case of a theatrical performance, for a 'monster' exhibition to take place, permissions had to be sought and licences obtained. Nor was this necessarily a straightforward process. In 1571, the Liverpool council threatened with imprisonment 'wandrang people bryngyng into this towne any monstruous or straung[e] beastes', an indication, perhaps, of a puritan sensibility opposed to popular entertainment.[63] Nor was this an isolated instance. In 1622 in Norwich, one 'Iohn ffinlason', wishing to 'shewe a monster haveinge six toes on a foote & six fingers on his hand', was 'inioyned to depart this Citty', and in 1632, Barbara Urselin was turned away from Hull, possibly because her father had lied about her age on his 'patent'.[64] A reaction against the ribald behaviour and commercial interference associated with the fairground may have been at the heart of these objections. If 'monsters' placed on display a preter-natural incompletion or excess, then they might also foster imbalances in the social equilibrium. Alternatively, spectators flocking to exhibi-tions may have been feared as carriers of infection, particularly when plague was afflicting other parts of the country. Materially and meta-phorically in these formulations, a space which was 'monstrous' was constructed as contagious.

One exhibition space existed beyond the censorship of local author-ity. This was the court, at which the sovereign's sponsorship inevitably took precedence over the approval or disapproval of a state official. To adopt Henri Lefebvre, who argues that 'social spaces interpenetrate one another and/or superimpose themselves upon one another', the court was the fairground in miniature.[65] English monarchs had long enjoyed access to strange beasts via the menagerie at the Tower of London, but they also delighted in the experience and possession of an extensive list of more obviously 'monstrous' productions, as the example of the 'monstrous chylde' from Chichester, presented to Elizabeth I in 1562 embalmed in a box, demonstrates.[66] James I set up a park of exotic creatures, part of his fascination with the 'freaks and monstrosities of nature', and, in view of his links with the Bear Garden and the King's Men, indicative of the cross-fertilizing influences between theatrical animals and royal menageries.[67] Curiosity about 'monsters' under the Tudors continued under the Stuarts, and in 1633, a '*man-Childe, born in old Bridewell . . . having two distinct Heades, two Hearts, two armes & the*

Stump of another' was *'shewn to King Charles &* y^e *Queen'*: as the description of the child suggests, some form of dissection may also have accompanied the demonstration.[68] Visits by celebrated luminaries of the exhibition circuit, similarly, became a regular feature of court life. When Margaret Griffith, the horned Welsh woman, was sent up to London aged 60 in 1588, it was 'to the end she might be seene of the Lords of the Queenes maiesties most honorable priuie Councell', and when Lazarus Colloredo appeared before the capital's public in 1637, it followed hard upon a presentation before an exclusive royal assembly.[69]

Out of this royal investment in all things 'monstrous' several implications emerge. First, 'monsters' were not limited in terms of their social appeal; on the contrary, the conditions of their exposure permitted them to range between classes and institutions at one and the same time. Second, taking up Marcel Mauss' theory that gifts or 'prestations' set up binding obligations among the members of particular social organizations, it can be argued that 'monsters' sometimes functioned as tokens, as offerings designed to win patronage.[70] Third, it would seem that royal interest interacted dynamically with public interest, with the two spheres of activity coming together to bestow upon a particular 'monster' a heightened curiosity value. Between the fairground and the court, it seems, were well-established lines of communication. Finally, the court constructed itself as a permanent and exclusive exhibition site to which a 'monster' could turn. Such is the inevitable conclusion if we consider the fondness for populating royal households with non-normative employees. Among the ladies-in-waiting of Elizabeth I, Thomasina, the queen's sumptuously dressed 'dwarf', held a special place.[71] Under Charles I and Henrietta Maria, the court was often diverted by Jeffrey Hudson or 'Jeffriedos', who stood at three feet, nine inches: his particular trick on state occasions was to be drawn with a loaf of bread from the pocket of Charles' 'giant' porter, William Evans.[72] As with more popular exhibitions, the antics of Evans, Hudson and others borrowed from a familiar repertoire of devices, combining elements of surprise, contrasts of scale, interactions with guests and performative interludes. At the entertainments of the Tudor and Stuart monarchs, the echoes of Bartholomew Fair were never very far away.

But if Whitehall evolved into an exclusive location for the exhibition of 'monsters', there was one final venue where the public accessibility of the fairground and the private selectivity of the court found a convenient meeting-place. More obviously than other institutions, the 'cabinet of curiosities' bridged the display spaces within which the 'monster' was witnessed, since it drew a variety of audiences and operated both as a commercial and a non-commercial enterprise. Also termed *kunstkammern* or *wunderkammern*, 'cabinets of curiosities' were brought together in the sixteenth and seventeenth centuries by members of the English and European aristocracies eager to house on one site nature's wonders (Figure 6). Their collections boasted, as well as other 'monstrous' miscellanea, strange fruits, plants and metals, stuffed chameleons, dragons and fish, New World costumes and artifacts, and even, in one instance, 'Blood that rained in the *Isle of Wight*', a property resonant with apocalyptical implications.[73] As Anthony Alan Shelton states in his recent study of the 'cabinets': 'What the collector sought . . . were not common or typical items, but rare, exotic and extraordinary testaments to a world subject to Divine caprice'.[74]

At an immediate level, the 'cabinet of curiosities' brought together in a spirit of nostalgia articles with which court 'monsters' had formerly been linked. In the 1620s in Lambeth, John Tradescant founded the 'Ark', a botanical and natural history collection which was subsumed into the Ashmolean Museum in 1683. Among its treasures were the boots belonging to William Evans, the 'giant' porter, and Jeffrey Hudson's tiny 'Masking-suit'.[75] If Tradescant was unable to secure the 'originals' for his 'Ark', he seems to have been content with seizing upon fragments and representations, souvenirs that flattered the owner through their connotations of an august lineage. But the 'cabinet of curiosities' imitated the court's fascination with 'monsters' in a more vital respect. As well as mortal remains, these bizarre assemblages accommodated living persons who were permanently installed for domestic edification. In their accommodation of living persons, the 'cabinets' displayed a performative leaning. The Bologna collection of Ferdinand Cospi featured a 'dwarf' as both curator and study piece, while in the wonder-cabinet of Peter the Great of Russia a hermaphrodite could be encountered who was employed at a stipend of 20 roubles a year.[76] Small wonder, then, that the immediate descendant of the 'cabinet of curiosities', the museum, was commonly termed the *theatro*.[77] When the 'cabinet of curiosities' was able to unite the inanimate and the animate, the quick and the dead, the lord's mastery of monarchical example, and standing in the eyes of his peers, were dramatically augmented. The histories of his possessions, coupled with the constant availability of his 'monstrous' servants, established his space as a worthy rival to any royal household.

At a deeper level, 'cabinets of curiosities' took energy from, and found a defining rationale in, the ephemeral activities associated with the fairground. The menu of 'monstrous' human and animal attractions revealed at the fair formed a significant basis for the extraordinary accumulations of the private collectors. On occasions, there is a direct link between the properties of the cabinets and particular fairground exhibits. For example, one of the excrescences shed from the head of Mary Davis, the horned woman from Great Saughall in Cheshire, was acquired by the Ashmolean in 1685, presumably in the wake of a unique London appearance.[78] More broadly, the fairground's menu of 'monstrous' human and animal attractions formed a significant basis for the accumulations of the private collector. Thomas Platter, a Swiss medical student, visited the London apartment of Walter Cope, a politician and antiquary, in 1599, and marvelled at his gallery of 'queer foreign objects': the 'twisted horn of a bull seal', a 'unicorn's tail' and a 'flying rhinocerus'.[79] A contemporary verse about the 'strange . . . bounty' on show at the fairground has much in common with this catalogue.[80] The seventeenth-century 'cabinet' of the Coventry anatomist Nehemiah Grew included 'the entire skin of a Moor', while the early eighteenth-century museum of the naturalist John Morton displayed among its '*Northamptonshire* rarities' a 'monstrous young *Quail* . . . a Four-legg'd Bird'.[81] In these combinations, as with early modern 'monster' exhibitions, a fascination with racial alterity and 'unnatural' multiplicity is clearly evident.

Like the fairground demonstrations to which they were related, 'cabinets of curiosity' borrowed from a parallel interest in the unfolding 'natural' wonders of the New World, dissolving boundaries between the animal and the human, and instances of unfamiliar species. The *wunderkammer* originated in interchanges between monarchs and magnates; it sustained itself by bringing the display-case and the 'monster'-booth into a new and unexpected partnership. Poised on the cusp of a crucial historical juncture, it gathered into itself the forces that were to create the museum of modernity.

III

Such exhibition sites had a dynamic relation to a wide range of variously descriptive and interpretive writings. From wonder-books and medical treatises through to moral reflections and dramatic forms, texts posed the kinds of interpretive dilemmas that mark them out as vital interventions in a larger intellectual project. Philosophical explorations either concentrated on 'monsters' alone or combined with related discussions, but all offered insights into the hold of the 'monster' on the social imaginary. In many ways, such texts acted as a substitute for the material exhibition of the 'monster': such an imperative finds support in the number of illustrations accompanying analysis and in the fact that wonder-books, which so fervently elaborated 'monstrous' histories, not infrequently advertised themselves as '*Cabinet*[s] . . . of *Curiosities*'.[82] It is even possible that some of these may represent the formal equivalent of an exhibition audience's vernacular responses. But such texts had a further imperative in common – a drive to explain the 'monster', to provide a rationale for its existence, to decipher its significance and to demystify its status as cultural anomaly.

The project often began by furnishing 'monsters' with definitions and classifications. Perhaps because 'monsters' encompassed so many types, and were experienced so widely across the social spectrum, the first task of many writers was to narrow down the field of enquiry. Definitions were arguably additionally attractive in that they lent the philosopher a cloak of authority, confining 'monsters' to the bounds of contemporary knowledge. 'Monsters' were thus brought within a sphere of control, even if this was to prove eventually illusory.

Most writers drew on one of two complementary definitions proposed in the period. The first highlighted the perceived link between the 'monster' and 'unnaturalness'. 'Monsters' in this formulation were measured against normative standards, which were blessed with the stamp of divine approval. Thus the theologian Lewes Lavater and surgeon Ambroise Paré, in 1572 and 1573 respectively, equated 'monsters' with occurrences 'which hapneth agaynst nature' and with '*things . . . brought forth contrary to the common decree and order of nature*'.[83] 'Decree', 'order' and 'nature' – all are terms that, for Lavater and Paré, when applied to the 'monster', betray its transgressive potential.

A second definition in contemporary circulation seized on 'disproportion' as a defining feature. In a 1565 thesaurus, Thomas Cooper designated as a '*monster*' that which '*excedeth, lacketh or is disordred in . . . forme*', while the medical practitioners Helkiah Crooke in 1631 and John Sadler in 1636 constructed 'monsters' in relation to a flouting of the rules of 'Figure, Magnitude, Scituation and Number'.[84] Nature's law is here as fixed as a mathematical principle: because 'monstrosity' can be tabulated, it can also be identified.

Beyond their classificatory utility, such approaches to the 'monster' were discursively productive. The ways in which the 'monster' was defined by Lavater, Paré and their compatriots facilitated its metaphorical usage. From Paré's definition of the 'monster' as 'unnatural', it is only a small step to the colloquial use of the term 'monster' to indicate a broader spectrum of 'unnatural' acts, peoples and social practices. Examples of this usage of 'monster' can be found beyond the drama in other texts of the period. In popular pamphlets and official pronouncements, for example, the term is variously adopted to characterize drunkenness, idleness, ingratitude, the Irish, lust, the multitude, murder, prostitution, rebellion, self-seeking, sexual indeterminacy, treason and vagabondage.[85] Because definitions pivoted on normative constructions, the derogatory force of 'monster' could be brought to bear on all manner of departures from the status quo.

No less influential in the philosophical construction of the 'monster' was the effort to determine its causes. Texts offered a multiplicity of possibilities, all of them directed towards explicating the 'monstrous' body. The number of texts suggests the urgency of this imperative: it also suggests that to write about a 'monster' may have been as lucrative as staging the 'monster' exhibition itself. The 'monster', many contemporary writers maintained, was solely the product of godly interference. 'It is most certaine, that these monstrous creatures . . . do proceede of . . . God', noted Pierre Boaistuau, the author of a wonder-book, in 1569, and comparable assertions circulated well into the seventeenth and even eighteenth centuries, suggesting the durability of the deity as an interpretive instrument.[86] The myriad arguments that 'monsters' were the result of bestiality, copulation during menstruation, devilry, incest, sectarianism, sodomy, unions between men and women of different religious persuasions and unlawful lust may be seen as elaborating this theme, since they posit a relationship between a transgression of godly injunctions and the precipitation of dire parturient consequences.[87] 'Monsters', according to this schema, owed their conception to 'sin', with the 'monstrous' actions of the parents being reproduced in the 'monstrous' shapes of their progeny.

Other writers cast their theoretical nets more widely. Originally writing in 1573, for instance, Ambroise Paré listed eleven possible factors behind 'monstrous births', and endeavoured to strike a balance between such matters as the 'glory of God', the 'straightnesse of the wombe', a 'fall, straine or stroake' and 'hereditary diseases'.[88] The cataloguing of such a plethora of factors could be read as a reluctance to be intellectually straitjacketed. More likely is that the equal weight given to heavenly arbitration, biological complication, intellectual speculation and supernatural visitation in contemporary discourses reveals a system in tension with itself, one in which few of the positions entertained were mutually exclusive. On the 'monstrous' body, then, it might be argued, battled the competing claims of God and science.

It is notable that, even inside more mystical interpretations, humoral, physiological and temporal theories of causation were attended to with a growing urgency. Among such theories, which might broadly be described as 'secular', those highlighting an anomaly in the reproductive system were increasingly popular. For the pamphleteer Thomas Bedford, writing in 1635 about the birth of conjoined twins, there was but one determinant: the 'indisposednesse' of the parents' 'Vessells'.[89] For the physician Robert Basset, commenting in 1637, 'the super-aboundance of Seede . . . the insufficiency of the *Materia*, the weakness of the seminall vertue [and] the defect of the wombe' were the factors behind the '*generation of Monsters*'.[90] The medical practitioner Nicolaas Fonteyn averred in 1652 that 'in the wombe . . . monsters are bred . . . according to the variety of the humour, which floweth into the *Matrix*'.[91] Despite the moral flavour of terms such as 'weaknesse' and 'vertue', aspired to in these formulations is an ideal of rational objectivity. A 'monstrous birth' is recognized as having a biological aspect, one that can be traced back to the body's generative interstices.

However, challenging evolutionary notions of progress was the simultaneous circulation of the theory of maternal impressions. This theory insisted that the pregnant woman was capable of transferring to her foetus an imprint of the psychological and visual stimuli which she herself had experienced. Thus the pamphleteer Thomas Lupton in *c*. 1590 was of the opinion that a woman with child, crossed in her path by a hare, would produce a 'monster' with a 'Hare-lippe'.[92] ''Tis thought that the hairie Child that's shewn about,' exclaims an intelligencer in Cartwright's comedy, *The Ordinary* (1635), 'Came by the Mothers thinking on the Picture / Of Saint *Iohn Baptist* in his Camels Coat' – a reference to the exhibition of Barbara Urselin, but also a theatrical attempt to explain the mystery of hirsutism.[93] Clearly, these evocations of an extraordinary generative capacity take on contrasting guises, but common to them both is the central role of the female imagination in the creation of the 'monstrous'. The susceptible and dangerously mimetic nature of female reproductive power singles women out to be as puzzling and as disturbing as 'monsters' themselves. Given this identification, it is hardly surprising that, on the contemporary exhibition circuit, female 'monsters' were to prove so prominent.

Most worryingly, the drive to explain 'monsters' could be used as one justification behind the policing of women's social intercourse. If the woman's imagination operated at such a refined degree of receptiveness, a contemporary argument ran, then she needed to be restrained from experiencing harmful influences. A select group of writers, indeed, explicitly associated the increase in 'monstrous births' with the popularity among women of visits to fairground 'monster'-booths.[94] A similar trajectory is glimpsed in a 1600 translation of a Spanish wonder-book. It delineates the narrative of an actor in Germany, who, having 'played the deuill' with a touring company, returns home while still in costume and 'vse[s] the company of his wife without changing [his] deformed habite'. The recipient of the actor's attentions promptly 'conceaued childe, and came to be deliuered of a . . . deuill, in forme so horrible, that no deuil of hell could be figured more lothsome or abhominable'.[95] In this displaced dramatic scenario, the puritan objection that the theatre is a lust-enkindling influence is lent added force by a reformulation of the theory of maternal impressions: merely gazing at the player is enough to generate infernal progeny.

Fundamentally, of course, the theory of maternal impressions found its animating rationale in an anxiety about ensuring proof of paternity: the woman who produced a child that did not resemble the father threatened to imperil a whole series of contemporary codes of maidenly conduct as well as the system of primogeniture. Fuelled by apprehensions about the fragility of individuation, this anxiety in turn connected with fears of the visual distinctions between humans and animals dissolving into an irredeemable ontological confusion. Both ideas, however, are overshadowed by the suggestion that all those who come into contact with the drama will end up in thrall to its 'monstrous' properties. Of course, similar anxieties are articulated about other forms of recreation, offering a forceful realization of the perceived threat of popular performative pastimes in general. In Chapman's *Bussy d'Ambois* (*c.* 1604), for example, a courtier-soldier recalls the following story: 'I have heard of a fellow, that by a fixed imagination looking on a bull-baiting, had a visible pair of horns grew out of his forehead'.[96] Such is the potency of the spectacle he witnesses, the 'fellow' is cuckolded by the bull-baiting, thereby emerging both as a dramatic male version of Mary Davis and Margaret Vergh Griffith (those other horned 'monsters' who frequented the contemporary exhibition circuit) and a devil incarnate. As with the example of the devilishly dressed actor, one 'monster' is capable of bodying forth many others. The anecdotes thus concatenate fairground animals, human exhibitors and satanic productions in warnings about the thrill of audience involvement and the perils of inordinate excitement.

As the points of contact between dramatic examples and contemporary celebrities suggest, 'monster' shows may have constituted an inspirational resource for theatrical representation. Certainly, the determinants bridging an individual 'monstrous' exhibition and a subsequent textualization are, in some cases, unavoidable. The display of Lazarus Colloredo, whose imperfect twin dangled at his breast, for instance, generated a plethora of intellectual reflections. Lazarus exploded the binaries that separated one human from another and, in so doing, was quickly taken up as a key discussion-point. First, Lazarus' appearance recalled the image of a mother caught in mid-delivery, and thus gave rise to enquiries into the gendered nature of reproduction and the possibilities of parthenogenesis: a 1637 verse represented him as 'bear[ing] and foster[ing]' John Baptist, his twin, 'at his tender wombe'.[97] Second, the spectacle of two bodies locked in one prompted rumination upon individual responsibility. The question posed in a 1640 pamphlet – 'whether [the brothers] ... are possessed of two soules; or have but one imparted betwixt them both' – was a significant falling-block to contemporary attempts to arrive at a coherent view of the self.[98] Independently of the advertising mechanism that he himself controlled, therefore, Lazarus spawned an epistemological crisis. Similarly, a 1670 pamphlet used the body of Mary Davis, the horned woman from Cheshire, to reflect upon medical ethics and intellectual responsibility. It concluded that further enquiries into Davis' condition are 'proper for a Colledge of Physitians', 'and no question but it will be esteemed worthy to employ the *Ingenious Vertuosos* of the Age'.[99] A reference to the activities of the Royal Society, which received its charters in 1662 and 1663 to record and analyse the 'strange facts' of natural history and philosophy, the comment registers one move to understand the phenomenon of the differently made body according to a 'rational' scheme.

Broader explorations concentrated on the meanings inscribed on the 'monstrous' frame. In the explorations of the period, God is represented as using the 'monster' as an instrument either for conveying displeasure or for encouraging reformation. For example, children born with a 'monstrous' verbal facility are seen as the channel through which an indignant deity communicates.[100] Likewise, divine retribution is detected in the birth of conjoined twins: a 1609 ballad declares the infants to be an angry verdict on their German mother's vanity and pride.[101] Such 'monstrous' children were also interpreted as warning signs from above. 'Children monsterously borne prouoke vs to bridle our vntamed flesh', argued popular pamphleteer Thomas Churchyard in 1580; a 'Monster' delivered without 'lippes' was sent to 'teach . . . that we want sanctified lippes to glorifie the powerfull name of our gratious God', a 1613 meditation on a devastating Southamptonshire fire concluded.[102] In the 'monstrous' body, then, the unregenerate could find the key to salvation. Via such formulations, deciphering 'monsters' took on a vital importance: correct interpretation revealed no less than the missive of the divine. It was a small step to the argument, growing out of the etymological derivations of the monster, that the anomalous body was predictive of things to come.

In 1572, Lewes Lavater argued that 'monsters' manifested '*shewing[s] or warnyng[s] [of] some thyng to happen afterward*', confirming for 'monsters' a prodigious power.[103] Lavater was one of an influential group of writers who read the 'monstrous' body to reveal not only the infractions of the present but also the shape of things to come. Thus it was the view of William Bullein in 1573 that 'when [monsters] doe come, euer commeth either the alteration of kingdomes, destruction of Princes, greate battaile, insurrection, yearthquakes, honger, or Pestilence after them', indicating a direct link between the appearance of the 'monster' and desolation ahead.[104] 'Monsters' were worrying, then, not only because of their heavenly associations, but also because of their connections with the instability of the terrestrial world. Bullein's traversing of local, national and natural disasters suggests the ease with which the body of the 'monster' could be enlisted to signal a wide range of social and political changes.

As symbolic properties which foreshadowed future events, 'monsters' lent themselves well to a variety of appropriations. Discussion with a more local orientation unravelled the connections between the 'monster' and key controversies of the period. 'Because of its ontological liminality, the monster notoriously appears at times of crisis,' remarks Jeffrey Jerome Cohen, and his observation is borne out by the facility with which crucial contemporary developments and 'monsters' are discovered as familiar bedfellows.[105] A 1636 recommendation that Charles I respect the ancient privileges of parliament took the form of a meditation on Jeffrey Hudson, the diminutive court favourite: '*Dwarfes,*' the writer maintained, 'are as a voice crying . . . *O King remember how thou art little.*'[106] The statement positions the 'monster' as a repository of foreknowledge in order to issue a political reprimand. In contrast to the Hudson meditation was the 1642–3 royalist comment on a two-headed child. Its birth in London was seen as a judgement on recent events: '*The sinnes of Heads, in government abus'd, / The sinnes of hearts, opinions false infus'd, / And broacht abroad to raise up foes and factions, / And Armes and Armies to confound with fractions.'*[107] Here the 'monstrous' child concatenates in its confused corporeity the infractions of its political moment. Made 'monstrous' by its contexts, it is seen to stand as a singular instance of the seventeenth century's most significant historical impasse: each appendage is a code, and the whole speaks ominously of the revolution imminent.

At a historical moment marked by an upsurge in millennial apprehension, perhaps the most regularly utilized resource for enquiring into the significance of 'monsters' was the book of Revelation. The centrality of its 'monsters' made Revelation an obvious touchstone for investigators, while the illusiveness of its rhetoric allowed it to be the sub-text beneath very different philosophical endeavours. In its apocalyptic positioning of the 'monster' alongside bloody rains, comets, earthquakes, eclipses and tempests, for instance, Revelation could be used to lend authority to contemporary attempts to link the 'monstrous' body with the end of the world.[108] A hermaphrodite and a bird-like child born in 1615 to a Faversham woman were greeted in apocalyptic terms: 'hereupon will follow the iudgement day' opined the pamphlet in which the 'monsters' were described.[109] At a deeper level, narratives employed the episodes of Revelation to explore in detail the significance of sixteenth- and seventeenth-century 'monstrous' phenomena. In 1608, Edward Topsell had recourse to Revelation when he turned to the Whore of Babylon's delivery of a plague of frogs and locusts in order to account for a recent series of 'monstrous births' in Italy. Paralleling the two events, Topsell argues that the interpretation of one must inform the other. His marshalling of evidence to suggest that the Whore's delivery in Revelation represents 'the depravation of Christian religion' thus permits a similar point to be made about the Italian 'monsters', which are revealed as encapsulating the 'pride & vanity of the *Romish* faith'.[110]

Where analogy was the primary tool wielded by Topsell, other interpreters favoured fresh scriptural exegesis. Several commentators argued for a figurative understanding of Revelation's 'monstrous' creatures (dragons and hydra-headed beasts), which would recognize a new positioning of the 'monstrous' in early modern culture. Discussing the 'conflate[d]' creatures of the apocalypse in 1619, Samuel Purchas stated that 'Man himselfe is this Monster' and thereby facilitated a location of Revelation's seventeenth-century equivalents among the Englishmen of his day. Rather than identify the 'monstrous' by outward appearance ('that which Nature hath by necessity imposed'), Purchas suggests that the abortive Gunpowder Plot reveals the 'Monsters of mankind'.[111] From a contrasting standpoint, a 1656 verse elaborates this movement by positioning parliament as 'that *Beast of eyes* in th' *Revelations'*. Here a linguistic dependency on Revelation combines with more secular 'monstrous' associations to create a parodic trajectory in which the vision of Saint John is rewritten as a fairground exhibition. The poet's lengthy description of the 'monster' 'fore-stall[s] the Show', and he implores his readers to pay a 'pence apeece' to 'Enter and see' the 'monster' for themselves.[112] Such a recasting of scripture as popular entertainment may be unusual, but it typifies the ways in which a diverse range of texts attempted to underscore the seriousness of their subject through the invocation of the final book of the Bible. In such texts, Revelation stands in the place of sustained scientific or philosophical enquiry, its 'monstrous' contexts bolstering an often opportunistic and politically expedient imperative.

IV

Such an excited reaction to 'monstrous' entertainments takes us back to the responses of Haggis in Jonson's *Bartholomew Fair* (1614). As we will recall, Haggis reacted in a similarly enthralled manner to fairground 'monsters', which, as this chapter has claimed, shared correspondences with the theatre via a maze of connecting routes. Between the events and exhibits unfolded to the playgoing audience, the clientele of the cabinet, the court's hangers-on and the carnival crowd can be detected self-conscious borrowings and determining interrelations. Today the fairground is a shadowy version of its former self, and the 'man with the monsters' has long since moved on; in the early modern period, however, as the foregoing discussion has argued, it was a vibrant and influential centre for popular pastime, with its 'monstrous' qualities and 'monstrous' performers spilling out to embrace the culture at large. By acknowledging the generic slippages between popular and high-cultural exhibition spaces, this chapter both insists on the interactive energy of the theatre's anomalous subtexts and makes a case for the drama's unique place in debates conducted around the 'extraordinary body'.

As I have suggested throughout this chapter, plays both rehearsed and challenged many of the concerns about 'monsters' articulated in the non-dramatic material of the period. Moreover, subsequent chapters in this book argue that a number of contemporary dramas played lengthy variations on 'monstrous' themes, weighing up problems of spectacle, causation and judgement alongside visual displays reminiscent of the fairground and other exhibition locales. Marrying two cultural imperatives (the desire to gaze at the 'monster' and the move to comprehend it), the theatre *demonstrates* its investment in the strangely licensed and licentious ephemera of the fairground in the same moment as it uniquely mobilizes the major constitutive markers of 'monstrosity' – material, discursive and performative. It is to the theatre's own 'monstrous' productions that we now turn.

2

'The strangest men that ever Nature made': Manufacturing 'Monsters' in *Tamburlaine the Great*

The Prologue to the first part of Marlowe's *Tamburlaine the Great* (1587–88) features a pledge to change the course of Elizabethan theatrical practice:

> From jigging veins of rhyming mother-wits,
> And such conceits as clownage keeps in pay,
> We'll lead you to the stately tent of war,
> Where you shall hear the Scythian Tamburlaine:
> Threat'ning the world with high astounding terms
> And scourging kingdoms with his conquering sword.
> View but his picture in this tragic glass,
> And then applaud his fortunes as you please.[1]

Two comparisons are at work here, the first elevating Marlovian drama above the meaner business of contemporary 'clownage', the second paralleling a distinction between the action of the stage and the higher rhetoric of the playwright's 'tent of war'. Both, however, harbour a more pressing function – the imperative to seduce the paying customer – and, in this sense, the Prologue functions as no simple choric commentator. Rather, the Prologue's dependence on a provocative invitation, a hyperbolic inauguration and the promise of a unique attraction means that Marlowe's rousing announcer is closer in spirit to the carnival barker. Similarly, the 'tent of war', to which interested parties will be guided, draws energy from the 'monster'-booth of the contemporary fairground; in the same way that the fairground 'monster' unsettles and amazes, so too will *Tamburlaine the Great*, here prefigured as the source of an 'astounding' linguistic experience, be judged extraordinary.

A further glimpse of the fairground is afforded by the Prologue's 'tragic glass'. As well being displayed in 'cabinets of curiosity', mirrors, in a range of guises, were staple features of early modern popular shows and exhibitions.[2] In this sense, Marlowe's mirror might best be understood not by tracing its *de casibus* connections but by attending to its etymological origins.[3] According to Anthony Alan Shelton, because '*mir*, the root of *mirabilis* (marvellous, wonderful) and *mirari* (to wonder at), is from where our word "mirror" derives', a close correlation between 'visual images and the idea of the marvellous' can be established.[4] Part of the 'astounding' stylistic impact of *Tamburlaine the Great*, one might argue, is the play's capacity to arouse wonder in a fashion akin to the mirror's production of the same aesthetic response. By enticing the audience into its popular frame of reference, the Prologue throws other sixteenth-century entertainments into sharp relief, even as it points up the crucial importance of its 'View' of the Scythian Tamburlaine. In so doing, it posits a spectacular basis to the marvellousness of the titular protagonist.

Marlowe's 'tragic glass' makes a second metaphorical appearance towards the end of Part One, neatly framing the narrative and pushing further a sense of Tamburlaine's preternatural abilities. Pointing to the signs of destruction and discord around him, the Marlovian juggernaut celebrates the 'sights of power [that] grace [his] victory' (I:V.i.475). '[S]uch are objects fit for Tamburlaine,' he continues, 'Wherein as in a mirror may be seen / His honour' (I:V.i.476–8). Imagined in the mirror in this climactic scene are 'bloody purple showers' and a 'meteor that might terrify the earth' (I:V.i.461–2), phenomena which operate not only as analogies for Tamburlaine's success, but also as prodigious occurrences of 'monstrous' extraction. The subtexts animating the Prologue are now elaborated in the suggestion that the mirror stages the 'monstrous'. Whether what is 'monstrous' manifests itself as heavenly disruption or the extraordinary rise to greatness of a commoner, Tamburlaine is represented as controlling the experience. Having appropriated the Prologue's 'glass' analogy and subsumed to himself its authority, it is he who determines the quality of his onlookers' reactions. Such a manoeuvre has a twofold effect. It broadens and complicates the spectrum within which designators of 'monstrosity' might operate. But it also facilitates the hero's construction of himself as the supreme showman: by wielding a demonstrative rhetoric, Tamburlaine comes to dictate the theatrical encounter.

In this chapter, I argue that *Tamburlaine the Great* is intimately concerned with the processes whereby 'monsters' are created, deployed and contested. This can be seen particularly keenly in those scenes where Tamburlaine and his enemies vie not so much for the ownership of kingdoms and crowns as for the most persuasive interpretive understanding of the 'monsters' of classical antiquity. Traditionally, Marlowe's absorption in classical learning has been seen as integral to the dramatist's portrayal of Tamburlaine either as an expression of Protestant moral philosophy or as a manifesto for the Herculean hero.[5] More recent assessments have turned away from Marlowe's narrowly intellectual contexts to the wider colonial and geographical networks in which *Tamburlaine the Great* is implicated, arguing for the phenomenon of the protagonist as an ethnicized other, an alien stranger who, despite social shortcomings, fashions himself to command centre stage.[6] By introducing 'monsters' to these readings, this discussion aims to complicate current assessments of the play's historical embeddedness and to show that the play's contextual locations are simultaneously more circumscribed and and more extensive.

Divided into two parts, the chapter first addresses the various deployments of the 'giant', the 'cannibal', the 'hydra' and the 'devil'. Because the 'monsters' are already inscribed with histories either of victory or defeat, a combative element is introduced, as the principal players rewrite mythic archetypes to advance their respective projects. Dominating the process is Tamburlaine who, in demonstrating himself and in being demonstrated, emerges as the central participant in a system in which 'monstrosity' is manufactured at a number of interrelated levels. But *Tamburlaine the Great* simultaneously destabilizes a straightforward application of 'monsters' through acts of appropriation and parody. In its second section, the chapter thus considers Tamburlaine's attempts to 'monsterize' not only his opponents and consort but also the appearances and forms of his natural environment. Nowhere is this better illustrated than in the play's closing stages in which the protagonist appoints himself chief architect of Revelation, the apocalyptical discovery through 'monsters' of final judgement. *Tamburlaine the Great* thus represents no easy demonstration of Protestant historiography. Nor does it struggle only with the ideological import of a parvenu who habours territorial ambitions. Instead, the play animates the 'picture' of Tamburlaine by privileging 'monsters' as the most crucial element of its operative mode. In manufacturing 'monsters' at the level of language or via stage business, moreover, Marlowe's drama becomes itself a site of investigation, a laboratory where questions about the 'monstrous' implications of artistic production can freely circulate.

I

'Monsters' are first directly invoked not in relation to Tamburlaine but to Cosroe, brother to the King of Persia. In what is the play's first example of a relocating rhetoric, Mycetes reprimands Cosroe, exclaiming: 'What, shall I call thee brother? No, a foe, / Monster of Nature, shame unto thy stock, / That dar'st presume thy sovereign for to mock' (I:I.i.103–5), the charge being that to threaten sovereignty is to be discovered as a 'monster'. A revealing reversal of that 'monstrous' imputation occurs in the scene where the dying Cosroe labels his tormentors 'The strangest men that ever Nature made' (I:II.vii.40). Cosroe's comment underscores the earlier construction of 'Nature' and its non-normative generational capacities, but it functions this time to position Tamburlaine as the 'monstrous' type. Having usurped Cosroe's monarchical seat, Tamburlaine inherits his 'monstrous' mantle, the smooth transference indicating the shifting quality of 'monstrosity' in this play. The new alignment is fitting for a figure who will become the most extended exemplar of a movable 'strangeness' that stands outside existing taxonomic arrangements. From the opening stages of *Tamburlaine the Great*, the protagonist has posed a challenge to the descriptive categories favoured by the forces of officialdom. Zenocrate leaves her captor in a class limbo because of her uncertainty over whether he is a 'shepherd' (I:I.ii.7) or a 'lord (I:I.ii.33), while Theridamas finds traditional racial markers stretched when he is suborned by 'resolvèd noble *Scythians*' (I:I.ii.224; my emphasis). An ethnically marginalized figure and a social upstart who nevertheless secures compelling martial triumphs, Tamburlaine constitutes an intractable problem for contemporary representational practices. It is not to be wondered at, therefore, that the play abounds in attempts to situate Tamburlaine in a traditionally restrictive classificatory paradigm. As Emily C. Bartels states, drawing on colonial contexts, Tamburlaine's enemies impose 'their own constructions of difference upon him [so that] . . . he becomes . . . an . . . imperialized object, a convenient other'.[7]

The assessment is enabling, but it neglects the extent to which Tamburlaine is active in the elaboration of his own 'monstrosity'. Confronted by a number of alienating tags, Tamburlaine contributes to the manufacture of 'monsters' by simultaneously embracing and rejecting his enemies' identifications. The hero both embroiders the markers attached to him and erects counter-pictures to those sketched by his opponents, continually fixing himself, in the words of David H. Thurn, in 'specular relation to his objects' and placing 'the image of his triumph before the eyes of the audience'.[8] Even as Cosroe excoriates Tamburlaine's bewildering alterity, for instance, Marlowe's renegade builds on the label of 'strangeness' to put himself on display as a fascinating attraction. Anticipating the day when he and his followers will be 'view[ed]' as 'emperors' (I:I.ii.67), Tamburlaine lays out his stolen gold like a trophy and tears off his shepherd's 'weeds' (I:I.ii.41) to reveal himself as a knight in armour. Taken together, such demonstrative moments operate to establish Tamburlaine's mastery of his world. More specifically, these intensely theatrical gestures are managed to support a classificatory system that endows Tamburlaine with 'marvellous' and 'wondrous' attributes. In similarly projecting forwards, Tamburlaine imagines that the reflections of his 'golden wedges' (I:I.ii.139) will 'amaze the Persians' (I:I.ii.140), and the victory parade in which he participates is specifically designed to trigger a concomitantly awe-struck response:

> . . . [K]ings shall crouch unto our conquering swords
> And hosts of soldiers stand amazed at us,
> . . . with their fearful tongues they shall confess,
> 'These are the men that all the world admires.'
> (I:I.ii.219–22)

One meaning of the verb 'to admire' is 'To view with wonder or surprise; to wonder or marvel at', and, for Tamburlaine, the production of this response is vital.[9] In complementary discussions of the aesthetic, James Biester has argued that 'wonder . . . conditioned, established, and maintained internal political and social relations', while Peter G. Platt writes that 'wonder and the marvellous' form the '*telos*' with which 'a comprehension of God's word' might be achieved.[10] One might suggest, then, that Tamburlaine, as part of his aspiration for dominion, dresses himself in conventional clothes, in the not so much 'strange' as familiar image of the divinely sanctioned ruler. Wonder will furnish Tamburlaine with the means of showing himself a successful leader; at the same time, it leaves open the possibility of aggrandizement and immortalization through his association with the godhead.

The sensation of wonder, in turn, feeds from and is a cousin to the early modern idea of 'curiosity'. An informing principle behind the collections of contemporary 'cabinets', 'curiosity', as Katie Whitaker points out, 'involved wonder and admiration at whatever was rare or outstanding, whether in size, shape, skill of workmanship, or in any other respect. Such rarities formed the curiosities whose unusual and outstanding qualities *curiosi* admired and wondered at.'[11] Certainly, 'curiosity' would seem to be rooted deep in Marlowe's play, the impulse revealing itself most obviously in the perception of Tamburlaine as 'extraordinary'. Both 'curiosity' and wonder inhere in the figuration of Tamburlaine as a production of the 'curious sovereignty of art' (I:II.i.13) – an arresting rarity and a prize artifact. Menaphon describes a personage

> Of stature tall, and straightly fashionèd,
> Like his desire, lift upwards and divine;
> So large of limbs, his joints so strongly knit,
> Such breadth of shoulders as might mainly bear
> Old Atlas' burden; 'twixt his manly pitch
> A pearl more worth than all the world is placed,
> Wherein by curious sovereignty of art
> Are fixed his piercing instruments of sight,
> Whose fiery circles bear encompassèd
> A heaven of heavenly bodies in their spheres . . .
> His lofty brows in folds do figure death,
> And in their smoothness amity and life;
> About them hangs a knot of amber hair . . .
> On which the breath of heaven delights to play . . .
> His arms and fingers long and sinewy,
> Betokening valour and excess of strength:
> In every part proportioned like the man
> Should make the world subdued to Tamburlaine.
>   (I:II.i.7–16, 21–3, 25, 27–30)

Detailed here is a species of 'giant': Tamburlaine is of a 'tall' stature; his 'limbs' are 'large'; his 'shoulders' resemble those of Atlas (the Titan condemned to carry the world); his 'arms' and 'fingers' are 'long'; his desire strives 'upwards'; the hairs on his head are touched by the heavens; his eyes are 'fiery' (in the exegetical tradition, the giants' appearance is 'distinguished by a glowing face and eyes from which shines an eerie light'); and he is possessed of superhuman strength.[12] Like a 'presenter of the properties', or even an in-play Prologue, Menaphon itemizes the bodily features of the Scythian in a catalogue that utilizes the strategies of the poetic blazon, a descriptive tradition devoted to inscribing, in Elizabeth Cropper's words, 'ideal types . . . composed of every individual perfection'.[13] Because it inverts a male convention of representing female beauty in which the speaker possesses the addressee by siting her in a masculine economy, Menaphon's address might be seen as a poetic means of controlling the 'strangeness' of Tamburlaine and exorcizing his 'curious' aspects. If so, the strategy backfires, with Tamburlaine exceeding the descriptive frame and, through the inquisitive gaze directed at him, ascending to a form of empowerment. Cosroe has but one response to the extended summation of the protagonist's qualities: in language that echoes closely the wonder motifs employed in fairground accounts of displays of 'giants', he accepts that Tamburlaine is 'a wondrous man' (I:II.i.32) who, 'in [his] forehead' (I:II.i.3), 'Bears figures of renown and miracle' (I:II.i.4).[14] The potential of Tamburlaine's 'giganticism' to evoke wonder is reinforced by Cosroe's reaction, and the hero accrues to himself a greater 'curiosity' through being so marvellously judged by two leading members of Persian authority.

Implicit in Menaphon's privileging of certain attributes is the conviction that Tamburlaine is possessed of superior, warrior-like attributes. Viewed through a 'gigantic' lens, Tamburlaine is understood to own both physical strength and soldierly ability. The move reflects the contemporary logic whereby early modern 'giants' were invariably constructed, a mode of thought exemplified by the recurrent siting of the 'gigantic' body in court employment practice. Under Elizabeth I, the royal guard-chamber was dominated by the 'gigantic' Dutch porter, who reputedly stood at seven feet, six inches, his high stature presumably being read as an indication of his seeming invincibility.[15] Other 'giants' featured prominently in the armed forces. Apparently no less than seven feet, four inches in height, Anthony Payne, known as the 'Cornish giant', fought for Cornwall with Charles I during the Civil War, was appointed chief Yeoman of the Guard by Charles II and served as halberdier of the guns under Sir John Grenville at the Plymouth garrison: his various offices are testimony to a high-profile career.[16] By seeing in Tamburlaine a 'valiant soldier' (II.iii.61) who might play a vital and visible role as 'general lieutenant' of his 'armies' (I:II.v.9) and, later, as standard-bearer, Cosroe thus acts in keeping with a prevailing perception of 'giants' while simultaneously mimicking royal example. At the same time, Cosroe's choice of Tamburlaine to be his 'natural' representative has a controlling directive. Where Menaphon's device for situating the 'wondrous' Tamburlaine is literary, Cosroe's is cultural – an attempt to confine the Scythian within the parameters of a familiar military convention.

The mystique arising from the manufacture of Tamburlaine as a 'wondrous' and 'gigantic' phenomenon is enhanced by a dialogic process.

One of the play's concerns is the way in which its leading personalities depend and borrow from each other to secure rhetorical mastery. In a striking manipulation of the 'giant' metaphor, for instance, Tamburlaine fictionalizes his imperial endeavour in a prediction of global supremacy. He plans to 'extend his puissant arm' from 'the east unto the furthest west' (I:III.iii.246–7), an image that equates the 'gigantic' size of his limbs with the vast expanse of his projected territorial possessions. The body, in this stolen formulation, becomes both the sign and the guarantor of geographical conflation, with Tamburlaine, a new Colossus, collapsing empires beneath his all-consuming form. In the same moment, the play offers ample precedent for the construction of the hero as an index of a future narrative, underlining the idea that Tamburlaine's fictions, and the projections of his allies/adversaries, reinforce each other through rhetorical exchange. Here, the signifying role embraced by the Scythian is actually established at a relatively early stage – namely, in Menaphon's estimation that Tamburlaine enjoys a status of prophetic consequence. (The protagonist's brows 'figure' [I:II.i.21] or prefigure life and death, and his members 'Betoken' [I:II.i.28] or portend inevitable victory).

The process, however, is not simply reinforcing. Even as Tamburlaine's gargantuan proportions are perceived as paving the way for events still ahead, they are also the record of histories past. According to Menaphon, Tamburlaine's 'giant' size points to an earthly and heavenly reciprocity, an ideal equilibrium, leading Jonathan Crewe to argue that the protagonist 'can appear . . . to be no monster but rather the figure in which the human form divine manifests itself after a degrading interregnum'. But the idea that the Asiatic brigand re-establishes 'a "lost" or eclipsed state of perfection' neglects at least one contemporary 'gigantic' development.[17] When so-called 'giants' bones' were disinterred in the English Renaissance, contemporaries rushed to commemorate them as proof of a sorry diminution in the height of the human frame, identifying more precise locations for the claim that Tamburlaine represents a harmonious fusion of forces.[18] It was partly as examples of a present corruption that such bones were exhibited in 'cabinets of curiosity', churches and popular entertainment spaces: to cite a 1587 translation of a discussion about 'giants', 'the offspring of our time, beeing corrupted by succession growing out of kinde, hath through ye decrease of them that are now borne, lost the comlinesse of the auncient beautie'.[19] Tamburlaine is 'wondrous', then, at least in part because he displays in a living embodiment the magnitude of a gallery of 'gigantic' predecessors. Perhaps more important than his predictive pertinence is his connection to a juncture marked by unadulterated lineage and a resistance to inter-familial unions ('succession growing out of kinde'): in Tamburlaine is enshrined the prospect of decontamination. For Cosroe, whose interest in the monarchical seat is condemned as a form of defilement (I:I.i.99–105), Tamburlaine can thus be seen as exerting a symbolic appeal.

Precisely because of the 'gigantic' image created for him and exploited by him, Tamburlaine is enabled to entertain ever more extravagant ambitions. The importance of rhetoric to success is demonstrated in the ways in which the 'rogue of Volga' (I:IV.i.4) builds on earlier projections to imagine himself as the star player in his own gigantomachia. The lances and bullets of his armies, he promises:

> Shall threat the gods more than Cyclopian wars;
> And with our sun-bright armour as we march
> We'll chase the stars from heaven and dim their eyes
> That stand and muse at our admirèd arms.
>
> (I:II.iii.21–4)

Presenting himself in the mould of his 'giantly' equivalents, Tamburlaine summons and conflates a collective memory of the Titans, who fought with Zeus (and were, in some accounts, thrown into Tartarus as a punishment), and the Cyclopes, 'giant' 'cannibals' imprisoned by their brother, Cronus, and later freed by Zeus' agency.[20] Laurence Coupe points out that there is 'an intimate connection between "mythography", the interpretation of myth, and "mythopoeia", the making of myths', and his comment bears out the ways in which Tamburlaine, through selective reading, creates for himself a mythology in which in his own achievements will be paramount.[21] In grounding his actions in terms of classical precedent, Tamburlaine simultaneously lends reinforcement to the notion that his rise to power is inevitable, for, as Coupe states, 'myth . . . carries with it a promise of another mode of existence, to be realized just beyond the present time and place'.[22] Tamburlaine's brand of 'mythopoeia' thus allows him to write himself into future history. Equally importantly, it furnishes him with a means of deflecting those mythic features that might be construed as contentious. No mention is made here of the presumption of the 'giants' in challenging the godhead; instead, it is the reception of the aspiration that commands attention. As the recurrence of the trope of admiration suggests, the focus, in line with related aesthetic strategies, centres only on the 'wondrous' effects that 'gigantic' actions generate. According to Richard

Levin's survey of Elizabethan responses to Tamburlaine, moreover, the protagonist seems to have been viewed with 'amoral wonder' and 'admiration' rather than moral condemnation by contemporary audiences.[23] One might conjecture, then, that with both on-stage onlookers and playhouse spectators, 'mythopoetic' adaptation worked to confirm Tamburlaine's grandeur in the eyes of the collective imagination.

The 'giants' are evoked for a final appearance at the end of Part One. 'As Juno, when the giants were suppressed / That darted mountains at her brother Jove,' states Tamburlaine of Zenocrate, 'So looks my love, shadowing in her brows / Triumphs and trophies for my victories' (I:V.i.511–14). The switch from 'mythopoeia' to 'mythography' here is of interest: his victories assured and on the point of marriage, Tamburlaine elects to eschew the upstart elements of the myth; rather, he privileges a narrative of political restitution and consolidation. About to take truce with the world, and remodelling himself as a law-maker and not a law-breaker, Tamburlaine aligns himself with the instruments of authority as opposed to the agents of transgression, burying with his freshly manufactured identity the ghosts of 'monsters' past.

As an enemy to the state, however, Marlowe's potentate cannot consistently be accommodated within a manipulable category of 'wonder' or simple 'giganticism'. What the play reveals is the process whereby the rhetoric of 'wonder' cedes place to a more interpretively capacious taxonomy of 'monstrosity', and it is through the bridging mechanism of race that the transformation is effected. The use of such an instrument need not seem surprising, for, as numerous cultural theorists have pointed out, differently perceived bodies invariably appeared, in Rosemarie Garland Thomson's words, 'not just as monsters, but as . . . racialized monsters'.[24] Ethnicity brands Tamburlaine through the summoning of his 'Scythian' and 'Tartarian' origins. He is labelled by his opponents a 'sturdy Scythian thief' (I:I.i.36), a 'Scythian slave' (I:III.iii.68) and typical of 'Scythians rude and barbarous' (I:III.iii.271). By the same token, he is one of a number of 'base-born Tartars' (I:II.ii.65) and heads a 'Tartarian rout' (I:I.i.71). Critics have tended to see in such racial designations metaphors for nations colonized by or traded with by the Elizabethans: Roger Sales finds in Tamburlaine's Scythian identity an echo of the native Irish, while Richard Wilson draws a parallel between Marlowe's Tartar and the Russian Emperors courted by the English Muscovy Company.[25] Certainly, the joint attachment – both 'Scythian' and 'Tartarian' – of Tamburlaine has its place in the period's larger debates about a developing national identity. But Marlowe's ethnic detailing comes alive, I would suggest, not only in material and trading connections but also via the mythic 'monstrous' inhabitants peopling Scythia and Tartaria in the social imaginary. According to Stephen Bateman in 1581, in '*Scythia* . . . are men called *Hippopodes*, the vpper part of whose bodies are like men, but the nether part like to horses'; 'the *Scithians* . . . are reported to haue but one eye a peece', a 1590 geographical compendium asserted; and the view of a 1600 translation of a Spanish work was that 'men in . . . Scithia [have] so little mouthes, that they cannot eate, but maintaine their liues with sucking in onely the substance and iuice of flesh and fruites'.[26] Bodily difference was apparently no less common in Tartaria. 'Among many valleys in *Tartaria* are . . . straunge Monsters: they haue a long necke aboue their breastes, and a head in manner of a Grype or Griffin', a collection published in the 1580s stated, while Donald Lupton observed in 1636, summing up the climate of opinion: 'The *Tartarians* are [the] most deformed of all men.'[27] Animating the behavioural and class implications of the play's language of ethnicity – Tamburlaine is imagined as both unruly and plebeian – are thus 'monstrous' associations conjured by a Scythian and Tartarian frame of reference. Together, these allusions offer a negative inversion of the 'gigantic' narrative that places Tamburlaine at the peak of physical development, for they locate the protagonist on one of the lowest rungs of an evolutionary chain. The implied taint of contamination sharpens the critical edge: both Scythians and Tartarians are represented as collectively imperfect, revealing disorderly differences even from each other and their own kind. The effect is to augment a sense of the protagonist's menace. Not only a singular 'monster', Tamburlaine also stands for a much larger and more unpredictable body of racial 'inferiority' and 'monstrous' deviation.

 Growing out of the play's stress upon 'giganticism' and its suggestive application of topographical danger is the dramatic preoccupation with the 'cannibals' or *anthropophagi*. These particular 'monsters', whose heads grew beneath their shoulders and who were sometimes confused with the Scythians and the 'dog-headed' *cynocephali*, constituted a site of vexed fascination for Renaissance writers, thinkers and cartographers.[28] Lear's reference in *King Lear* (1605–6) to the 'barbarous Scythian, / Or he that makes his generation messes / To gorge his appetite' brings together some of these concerns, crystallizing, as it does, a sense of ethnic alterity, destructive hunger and familial upset.[29] While the *anthropophagi* do not explicitly feature in *Tamburlaine the Great*, they are rhetorically implicit in the play's stress on, to adopt Fred B. Tromly's words, 'figurative feeding' and 'unnatural appetite'.[30] Tamburlaine constructs himself as a 'fiery thirster after sovereignty' (I:II.vi.31) who will 'glut . . . the dainties of the world' (II:I.iii.220) in a formulation that, via a typical manoeuvre, is later manipulated and embellished by his enemies. Amasia identifies the hero as a 'monster that hath drunk a sea of blood / And yet gapes still for more to quench his thirst' (II:V.ii.13–14), twisting Tamburlaine's trope into an accusation of glut-tony. Given the ways in which myths are simultaneously made and interpreted in the play, it is not to be wondered at that Tamburlaine's 'monstrous' body is soon visited with 'cannibalistic' traits. Indeed, for Tamburlaine's enemies, spotlighting the cannibal in the conqueror becomes the vehicle with which they distinguish themselves from his escalating attrocity. In suggesting that Tamburlaine will share the fate of Tereus, Zabina threatens her tormentor with the narrative of the mythological father who ate his own son (I:IV.iv.23–5) and expresses horror at the scene's manifestation of the protagonist's domestic politics.[31] By building on 'monstrous' subtexts, these registrations of 'monstrous' appetite institute lines of demarcation codified in terms of food and flesh, civility and savagery. They establish norms of famil-ial behaviour in contrast to the non-normative, quasi-incestuous and ingestive charges laid at the Scythian's door. And they lend approval to notions of control and restraint over and above Tamburlaine's geo-graphically worrisome form of insatiable consumption.

Perhaps the most frequently invoked 'cannibals' in the English Renaissance were the 'giants' of antiquity. Orality and greed were the traits that linked these two 'monstrous' species, notably as they were demonstrated in the Titan, Cronos, who devoured his own children to prevent them usurping his monarchical seat.[32] Coupled with pride and ambition, such qualities stamped 'giants' with a particularly troubling and multivalent strain of 'monstrosity', as Cosroe's condemnation of Tamburlaine's defection from Persia abundantly illustrates.[33] 'Wonder' having been compromised in its descriptive utility, Cosroe reaches beyond aesthetics to mythic parallels, asking:

> What means this devilish shepherd to aspire
> With such a giantly presumption,
> To cast up hills against the face of heaven
> And dare the force of angry Jupiter?
> But as he thrust them underneath the hills
> And pressed out fire from their burning jaws,
> So will I send this monstrous slave to hell
> Where flames shall ever feed upon his soul.
>
> (I:II.vi.1–8)

Here Cosroe manufactures Tamburlaine as another type of Titan, in this case Enceladus (or, as he was sometimes known, Typhon or Typhoeus), the 'giant' trapped by Zeus under Etna for daring to aspire to divine power. Typhon was employed in Renaissance historiography as an emblem of both hybridization and rebellion, no doubt because he traced his mixed descent to Gaia (the Earth) and Pontus (the Sea), combined human and reptilian features, sported a hundred heads and breathed fire.[34] A will to racial differentiation and cultural elevation is thus enacted in Cosroe's speech; as Ginevra Bompiani observes, the battle with Typhon displays 'the superiority of Zeus over the primitive monster . . . a . . . subtle superiority . . . of a more highly evolved civilization'.[35] At the same time, one might highlight the levelling tendencies at work in Cosroe's exclamation. A 'Fascination with the monstrous is testimony to our tenuous hold on the image of perfection,' writes Elizabeth Grosz, adding, 'The freak confirms the viewer as bounded, belonging to a "proper" social category.'[36] There is more than a whiff of Cosroe in Grosz's assessment, for the Persian monarch's positioning of himself betrays once again a desire to normalize, to inculcate a system of 'natural' values and to belong to the 'right' interpretive community. As part of that urge, Cosroe refigures appetite. There is a kind of poetic justice in the prediction that 'flames shall . . . feed upon [Tamburlaine's] soul': the treacherous 'cannibal' will now himself be consumed by a force powerful enough to restore a desecrated social order.

Embedded in Cosroe's normalizing is another 'monstrous' echo, one that, because domestic in form, may have struck a chord with some Elizabethan audiences. As we have seen, Cosroe manufactures himself as Zeus reincarnate, rewriting Olympian history and making of the myth a moral vanquishing of a 'monstrous' interloper. But Cosoe is simultaneously a cousin to Brute, the original 'settler' of England, which suggests an additionally intricate level of contextual suggestiveness. Before the Trojan Brute 'civilized' 'Albion', Anthony Munday claimed in 1605, the country was 'a vast Wildernes, inhabited by Giants, and . . . Monsters'.[37] Brute's success in ridding this newfound land of its native inhabitants and founding its capital became an integral part of ritual and historiography, with chronicles detailing the victory and annual processions re-enacting the encounter.[38] In *Tamburlaine the Great*, therefore, the promise to send the 'monstrous slave to hell' might be seen as a mode of racial cleansing. Itself implicated in the period's anxieties about 'foreigners' and 'strangers', the pledge of Marlowe's Persian potentate flatters the sensibilities of an expansionist age and highlights in the play's Asiatic conflicts a native provenance. Through Cosroe, the struggle with the Scythian is made to accommodate a local colouring, a reminder of the nation's inception and the dawning of its civic *communitas*.

Jeffrey Jerome Cohen suggests that 'representing' a 'culture as monstrous justifies its displacement or extermination by rendering the act heroic'.[39] This assessment certainly accords with the ways in which all of the play's characters practise forms of 'mythography' to lend an intrepid edge to their respective disputes. In this way, a further 'monstrous' dialogue emerges not from rhetorical competition between an 'other' and his opposite but from shared strategies of appropriation between the members of similar social groupings. Evoking the huge animal sent by a wrathful Artemis, the Soldan of Egypt states, 'Methinks we march as Meleager did, / Environèd with brave Argolian knights, / To chase the savage Calydonian boar' (I:IV.iii.1–3), his confident use of the plural 'we' throwing into stark relief the singular boar's isolation. In this equation, while his enemies are ennobled through the association with the hunt, Tamburlaine, imaged as swine, is pushed off the human register. A comparable mythic borrowing is staged when Bajazeth likens the strength of his sons to that of Hercules, who overthrew 'all the brats y-sprung from Typhon's loins' (I:III.iii.109). He refers, of course, to the snake-like dog, Orthrus, the beast of Lerna and the chimera, 'monsters' dispatched by Hercules as part of his labours. Eugene M. Waith has argued that such allusions in *Tamburlaine the Great* culminatively underscore the hero's 'colossal individuality' and 'god-like superiority', and it is not difficult to support his claim.[40] If Tamburlaine is the 'Calydonian boar', for instance, he is also an agent of divinity; and if the Soldan is Meleager, the analogy hints at a grim destiny, for the King was killed during the 'chase'. In other ways, however, Waith's reading passes over the ambiguous effect of the drama's allusions. At least in Bajazeth's manipulation of the 'Herculean' narrative, Tamburlaine is stripped of authority; overcome as a 'monster' by the legitimate offspring of the Turk, the Scythian will also have to endure the defeat of his illegitimately 'monstrous' progeny. Even if Tamburlaine occupies the rhetorical centre of his world and commands the 'mythopoetic' process, therefore, spaces emerge for alternative narratives that seek to justify his cultural genocide.

The idea is extended in the conjuration of a peculiarly resonant 'monster'. In its composite and contradictory anatomy, the hydra lent itself with an apt plenitude to invention. Engendered between Typhon and Echidna (a 'monster' with the upper body of a woman and the lower body of a snake), this multi-headed creature was slain by Hercules, came to exemplify pride, ingratitude, self-seeking and the

multitude, and wound up exhibited (apparently stuffed) as a 'rare Mon-
umente' in the Duke of Venice's treasury.[41] A diverse spectrum of fictions, conventions and institutions is thus encoded in the Soldan of
Egypt's outcry:

> A monster of five hundred thousand heads,
> Compact of rapine, piracy, and spoil,
> The scum of men, the hate and scourge of God,
> Raves in Egyptia, and annoyeth us.
> My lord, it is the bloody Tamburlaine,
> A sturdy felon and a base-bred thief . . .
> That dares control us in our territories.
>   (I:IV.iii.7–12, 14)

The familiar trajectory of the Greek and Roman story is bolstered in
the ways in which the Soldan becomes a new Hercules bringing to
boot the 'presumptuous beast' (I:IV.iii.15) of Tamburlaine. Enlivening
the adaptation is the admixture of more contemporary archetypes.
Because the phrase 'study felon' mimes language enlisted in Elizabethan
statutes against social mobility, it casts Tamburlaine in the mould of
the vagabond, who was not infrequently represented as a 'monster'
in popular polemic: generic and class details unite in a repressive
combination.[42] In addition, the holy militarism circulating at this
point takes energy from the means whereby the hydra was put to
work to analogize those nations deemed hostile to Reformation ideology. A 1588 pamphlet by Laurence Humphrey held that the '*Hydra* . . .
of many heades' is the 'Monster of *Rome*', and early seventeenth-century
attacks against Irish rebels similarly tied them to the 'beast compact'
of 'many heads'.[43] In a curious metaphorical turnabout, the Egyptian
Soldan emerges here as an exemplar of Englishness set in opposition to a Scythian who incorporates the worse traits of Italian
and Irish Catholicism. Judged in this manner, the speech confirms
Tamburlaine's candidacy for a 'monstrous' identity by linking him
with idolatrous and dissenting forces closer to home. It has the effect
of simultaneously consigning Tamburlaine to spiritual oblivion while
vindicating the ascendant religious power of his enemies, and
amply bears out Walter Stephens' suggestion that one of the antitheses
that the unregenerate 'monster' dialectically underscores is 'piety'.[44]
If Tamburlaine is the 'the hate . . . of God', it is because the Soldan of
Egypt is the spokesperson for a Protestant triumphalism. The hydra,
Tamburlaine, can only ever be annihilated, the speech would seem to

suggest, for he is combated by nothing less than the endeavours of the elect.

Identifying Tamburlaine as a devil made manifest concatenates the associations of mythic infraction and typological difference written into other species of 'monster' and gives clarificatory reinforcement to the bridge dividing the Scythian from the establishment. In a similar way, the move to trace Tamburlaine back not to 'Nature' but to a hellish point of origin represents the play's most searching enquiry into his 'monstrous' unorthodoxy. The Governor of Babylon, for instance, arraigns the Tartarian tyrant as a 'Vile monster, born of some infernal hag' (II:V.i.110): a sort of Caliban delivered by an unnamed Sycorax, Tamburlaine here is fatherless. Even his imagined mother is demonized through the anxious construction of her reproductive powers. Quick to support a related hypothesis is Meander; musing on Tamburlaine's treachery, he declares: 'Some powers divine, or else infernal, mixed / Their angry seeds at his conception' (I:II.vi.9–10). Possibly alluded to here is the Judeo-Christian view that 'giants' were produced when fallen angels (*filii dei*) coupled with the daughters of Cain (*filiae hominum*): the miscegenation embodied in the explanation is equally reflected in the speaker's critical attitude toward the intermingling or 'mix'ing of different kinds.[45] More likely is that Meander's rationalization intervenes in long-standing beliefs about coitus between humans and evil spirits. Writing in 1569, Pierre Boaistuau commented on 'women of . . . *Goathes* [who] . . . wandring by the desertes of *Scythi[a]*, were got with childe of Diuels, whereupon one of them brought forth a monster'.[46] The statement figures Scythia as a place of 'monstrous' contamination while also outlining the dangers of national (and arguably ethnic) hybridization; framed in the context of Marlowe's play, it demonstrates the extent to which, the moment Tamburlaine shows himself recalcitrant, a fantasy of pure 'gigantic' lineage is overtaken by a conviction of diabolic adulteration. Similarly suggestive of a movement away from such idealizations was the 1635 voice of Thomas Heywood. He explains how a 'barbarous woman' in Brazil, 'accompanying with one of these Daemons, brought forth a Monster . . . with eyes staring, and seeming to sparkle fire'.[47] While adumbrating 'barbarity' and 'monstrosity' as mutually constitutive, Heywood's description erects itself on the most frequently mentioned defining characteristic of the 'monstrous birth' – the fiery eyes of the differently formed infant.[48] In Menaphon's earlier paean to Tamburlaine as a 'wondrous' 'giant', we recall, the 'fiery' eyes of the hero also received emphasis, implying that, in the same moment that his marvellousness is celebrated, the hint of an unspeakable nativity is contemplated. Certainly, by dwelling upon the demonic colour of Tamburlaine's arrival in the world, his detractors convince themselves of his infernal caste. The Soldan of Egypt is persuaded that Tamburlaine is 'As monstrous as Gorgon, prince of hell' (I:IV.i.18); the King of Jerusalem agrees that he is a 'damnèd monster, nay, a fiend of hell' (II:IV.i.171); and Ortygius concludes he is a 'fiend, or spirit of the earth, / Or monster turnèd to a manly shape' (I:II.vi.15–16). Insisting upon a consistent theory of interpretation, and making available a common grammar, this 'monster' incorporates into itself and supersedes all other efforts to pin down the irredeemable protagonist. Stigmatized as a fiend from a number of quarters, Tamburlaine appears, for this moment at least, overwhelmed by the weight of a shared rhetorical arsenal.

II

'Monsters' in *Tamburlaine the Great*, then, exist in a creative war zone, a competitive field in which the 'extraordinary body' is moulded to communicate tussles over possession, exposition and ethics. This is seen with peculiar intensity in the ways in which ideas of 'monstrosity' are played out across the Tamburlainean anatomy in the same moment that the hero strategically discovers his own 'strangeness'. Crucially, however, Tamburlaine does not only put his own form on display; he also creates a range of other 'monsters', spectacles in which the opponents of his régime feature as the chief exhibits. In this way, the marauding warlord seeks to reject his detractors' accusations and to transform them to his own advantage, not so much giving birth to 'monsters' as manufacturing them to bear his unique signature. Stamped with Tamburlaine's meanings and owing their genesis to his powers, such 'monsters' become, in one instance, a forceful signifier of his march to ascendancy and, in other examples, a clue to his inexorable deterioration. As part of this process, the play enacts the performative modes of a fairground, with Tamburlaine gravitating between object and subject positions, between the 'monster' on display and the impresario who manages its professional exposure.

It is through Bajazeth that the transformation of the accusatory rhetoric of Tamburlaine's opponents is initially effected. Because confined, Bajazeth is treated as a vagabond and forced to submit, in M. J. Power's words, to a 'further deterrent to the unruly and the rogue' – the 'setting up' in Elizabethan London 'of street cages as temporary prisons'.[49] By confining Bajazeth, Tamburlaine seeks to reapply the vagrant label to his Turkish foe, divesting himself of a recurrent charge. But Bajazeth's vagabond status arguably impresses less than his captive position, and, in this regard, he is opened to the extended 'monsterizing' of Marlowe's *übermensch*. 'The monster,' states Meredith Anne Skura in a discussion of Shakespearean dramaturgy, 'was the obverse of the successful hunter or warrior . . . He was one of the prisoners or slain animals at the back of the parade, a souvenir or trophy, a deflated enemy.'[50] Viewed in this way, Bajazeth might be seen as a palimpsest for the 'Hermaphrodites' displayed in the triumphal procession of Tamar Cam in the lost 1602 play of the same name, or for the defeated Cleopatra in *Anthony and Cleopatra* (1606–7), threatened with being 'shown' in Rome 'most monster-like' for 'poor'st diminutives'.[51] Because he is 'kept' (I:IV.ii.85) in a cage to be 'drawn' in 'triumph' (I:IV.ii.86), Bajazeth is forced to stand as a 'monstrous' manifestation of an incarcerating régime. Whatever power resided in Bajazeth now attaches itself, through the Turk's embodiment as 'monster', to Tamburlaine, who appropriates from his captive not only kingdoms but charisma.

The process of Bajazeth's 'monsterization' is fuelled by the injection of increasingly spectacular ingredients. Once caged, Bajazeth enters upon a period of self-imposed starvation. In the order of orality to which he is subjected, Bajazeth has his initial resistance turned against him, as he is taunted with 'scraps' (I:IV.ii.87) by his gaoler. A more permanent marker of 'monstrosity' is here brought into play, for Bajazeth, in a humiliating gender reversal, is made to assume some of the properties of young women, like Jane Balan of '*Constans*', who was described in 1603 as having lived for three years without any 'foode or sustenance'.[52] Such 'starving maids' were popularized in the period as 'monstrous' phenomena and were reported to be 'taken' about by parents to 'get vnto themselues profite', rather as Bajazeth, as a malnourished feature of Tamburlaine's touring caravan, is used by the Marlovian bandit to win for himself additional kudos.[53] Bajazeth is 'monster', indeed, precisely because he is 'taken' about. As Robert Hobson noted in 1631, Bajazeth is notable for having been 'carried up and downe by the *Conquering Tamberlaine*' like a 'wilde Beast' or 'an *Affrican Monster*', for having been colonized, 'monsterized' and mobilized all at the same time.[54] Like the 'strange' and 'monstrous' animals exhibited by contemporary impresarios, the Turkish emperor is advertised as a theatrical event. Brought 'forth' (I:V.i.194) as a 'goodly show' (I:IV.iv.63) to 'strain his voice' (I:IV.iv.69) in a song at Tamburlaine's banquet, Bajazeth represents both a 'sight of strange import' (I:V.i.469) and a 'spectacle'

(I:V.i.340). Signifying and theatricalizing elements join here to under-gird Bajazeth's role as a body in performance and an object at which to gaze. With Tamburlaine managing the proceedings, Bajazeth, now exoticized, is also ethnicized, illuminating both the tit-for-tat nature of rhetorical construction in the play and the ways in which the Scythian acts upon internalized racial assumptions. Thus created non-native, Bajazeth functions as the yardstick with which the limits of Tam-burlaine's empire will be measured: the Turk's enfleshment demon-strates the reaches of his victor's geographical achievement. All of these meanings cohere in the summation of Bajazeth's misery in which the term 'monstrous' is chosen to encapsulate the nature of the experience: unable to tolerate his 'loathèd life' (I:V.i.304), the emperor dashes his brains out in the hope of release from his 'monstrous slaveries' (I:V.i.241). Disgust, class frustration and self-laceration unite in one of the play's most explosively unnerving moments.

With the captive kings, the idea of a body in performance is taken to a further stage. Imitating Celebinus' success in training his 'steed' (II:I.iii.38) to 'trot' (II:I.iii.39) and 'curvet' (II:I.iii.41), Tamburlaine binds the kings to his chariot and seeks to force them, in turn, to execute circus-like tricks. Before they established themselves as permanent fixtures at the circus in the eighteenth century, performing horses, and even horse-races, were a central component of fairground enter-tainments and touring demonstrations.[55] From the 1590s to the 1600s, the most celebrated horse was Marocco: according to contemporary accounts, this bay gelding continually astounded with his feats, such as dancing, distinguishing a crucifix, pissing on command, responding to monarchs' names and supposedly climbing the spire of St Paul's Cathe-dral.[56] Not surprisingly, Marocco's exhibition was quick to be labelled a 'monstrous sight', and the horse was also linked with 'monsters' in a number of late Elizabethan dramatic allusions.[57] Via a comparable logic, Tamburlaine's instruments of transportation are tainted with such an imputation of 'monstrosity'. Not only will the kings exhibit dietetic grotesquerie through having to eat 'human flesh' (II:IV.iii.13), thereby taking on themselves the cannibalistic traits of their captor's imputed appetite, they will also be shown up as 'pampered jades' (II:IV.iii.1): in Tamburlaine's reference to these 'horses of inferior breed', associations of admixture and bastardization abound.[58] But perhaps the most reveal-ing point about the captive kings is their failure to be marvellous. They 'draw but twenty miles a day' (II:IV.iii.2), Tamburlaine com-plains; they need 'bits . . . To bridle their contemptuous cursing tongues' (II:IV.iii.43–4); and their 'coltish coach-horse' behaviour smacks of 'blasphemy' (II:IV.iii.52). These, then, constitute neither the sleek mounts of the chase nor the 'woonderfull and strange' creature of the exhibition chamber; rather, the kings appear performative mishaps, possessions that have confounded manufacture and the transformation to another category.[59] Tamburlaine's frustration with his human charges points up a representational failure and a lapse in the hero's signifying autonomy. As 'mirrors', Jerusalem, Natolia, Soria and Trebizond reflect not so much the hero's command of his theatrical space as the increasing mania of his projections. Having invested in a culture of 'monstrous' demonstration, Tamburlaine must now aspire to ever more fantastic (and eventually unrealizable) modes of communicating his ability. One residual element in the chariot scenes clarifies these suggestions. In II:IV.iii, Tamburlaine announces his intention to ride to Babylon, urging his human calvacade forward at line 97 but not actually leaving until 36 more lines have elapsed. The implication, as Johannes H. Birringer observes, is that, on the narrow boards of the Elizabethan stage, Tamburlaine's chariot can move around only in a series of circles.[60] In this image of constriction and limitation, the audience is granted a forceful optic embodiment of Tamburlaine's waning hold on his world.

If Tamburlaine is unable to confine the captive kings through 'monsterization', he is more successful with the members of his inner circle. Paradoxically in the plays, Zenocrate is 'monsterized' as obviously as the Tartar's opponents, although via alternative methods and with stasis rather than movement as the defining characteristic. After discovering the first dying and then deceased Zenocrate, either behind a curtain or in a booth placed upon the stage, Tamburlaine preserves her body:

> Where'er her soul be, thou shalt stay with me,
> Embalmed with cassia, ambergris, and myrrh,
> Not lapped in lead but in a sheet of gold,
> And till I die thou shalt not be interred.
>
> (II:II.iv.129–32)

Critics such as Sara Munson Deats, Simon Shepherd and Lisa S. Starks helpfully understand Tamburlaine's treatment of Zenocrate in these scenes in terms of the 'fetish'.[61] However, attention to the broader contextual issues that the queen's embalming arouses is additionally productive. In being stuffed, in fact, Zenocrate is manufactured as a 'mummy', a property familiar to the contemporary public consciousness as a standard fairground attraction. In Beaumont and Fletcher's *Cupid's Revenge* (1607–12), Bacha, a murderous widow, is imagined 'tyde to a post', 'dryde ith sunne' and subsequently 'carryed about and shone at fayres for money', while Artesia, a state enemy in *The Birth of Merlin* (*c.* 1620), sometimes attributed to Shakespeare and Rowley, is taunted with a similar fate.[62] As the Earl of Chester states:

> stake her carcase in the burning Sun, till it be parcht and dry, and then fley off her wicked skin, and stuff the pelt with straw to be shown up and down at Fairs and Markets, two pence a piece to see so foul a Monster . . .[63]

Clearly, Zenocrate is neither punitively identified as a 'monster' nor exhibited for commercial profit. Her body, however, packaged and paraded, is reified via its points of contact with the petrified corpses of Smithfield. Because Zenocrate 'shalt stay' with Tamburlaine, for instance, she becomes part of his roving geographical peregrinations. Marlowe's overreacher also erects a special 'royal tent' (II:III.ii.37) where the dessicated remains are installed to be 'gaze[d]' (II:III.ii.33) at. This, in turn, is adorned with a 'hanging' (II:III.ii.28) 'Sweet picture' (II:III.ii.27) of Zenocrate, and complemented both by a 'streamer . . . To signify she was a princess born' (II:III.ii.19, 21) and a 'table' (II:III.ii.23) on which her 'virtues and perfections' (II:III.ii.24) are extolled. It may not be too fanciful, in short, to suggest that Tamburlaine constructs a typical Elizabethan 'monster'-booth, complete with banners, images, emblems and textual advertisements.

In a discussion of death and the feminine aesthetic, Elisabeth Bronfen states that the 'image of the embalmed feminine body [indicates] not just the power of the survivor and/or the masculine gaze but also a form of vision that places the viewed object and its viewer outside temporality and that allows a triumph over any vacillating energies'.[64] These arguments have a direct bearing on Tamburlaine's conservation strategies, since, in many ways, the shepherd-bandit acts to to stay time, to slow mutability and to cheat death, perhaps his most intransigent opponent. The protagonist turns to Zenocrate's remnants to determine the pace of his own narrative. To these tactics for derealizing mortality important class dimensions are attached. Growing out of the interplay between the theatre and the fair is a dramatic reminder of the hero's plebeian beginnings. Because confirmed through Zenocrate as an itinerant showman, Tamburlaine appears once again socially and ethnically identified. Not so much the transcendent potentate, Tamburlaine seems, by this point of the play, more akin to the wandering entertainers of his day, to the 'gypsies', 'Spaniards' and 'Turks' who, in popular representations, juggled, rope-danced, tumbled, puppeted and exhibited 'exotic' animals.[65] In this sense, death takes Tamburlaine not forwards in his odyssey but backwards to its inception. But the 'mummification' of Zenocrate simultaneously discovers, I would suggest, Tamburlaine's will to manufacture for himself an alternative self-image. Despite the distance of its historical subject, Edward L. Schwarzschild's discussion of Charles Willson Peale, taxidermy and the early American museum is relevant here. He observes: 'For Peale, death was . . . an inscrutable if unavoidable freak of nature . . . Peale would colonize death, making it his territory . . . [his] pictorial, chemical and curatorial efforts were part of a larger attempt to . . . empower his self and his nation'.[66] Working in a post-Enlightenment moment, Peale offered his public displays of the natural world that, as well as demonstrating evolutionary principles, testified to the growing power of American imperialism.[67] Marlowe's Tamburlaine might be seen as the forerunner of such an aesthetic. For he now strives to show that, if his enemies are 'monsters', so, too, is the larger order that determines the shape of all human endeavour. To manufacture death as the ultimate 'monster', one that can be overcome through preservation and accumulation, will enable Tamburlaine to go beyond mere earthly accolades to proclaim himself a celestial conqueror.

In his display of Zenocrate, then, Tamburlaine is inserted even more surely into the role of impresario. In that he simultaneously memorializes her form, he takes on some of the qualities of the collector and curator. Among the 'better sort' in the English Renaissance, collecting 'mummies' was a specialist pursuit. In 1586, John Sanderson, a gentleman and merchant, was so taken by the 'mummies' he encountered at the Pyramids that he 'broke of[f] all parts of the bodies . . . and brought home divers heads, hands, arms, and feete for a shewe'. He adds: 'One . . . hand I brought into Ingland to shewe, [I] presented . . . to my brother, who gave the same to a doctor in Oxford'.[68] 'Mummified' fragments, it seems, circulated among *cognoscenti* as souvenirs and rarities, tokens that could be traded, exhibited to friends and relatives, and experienced in private gatherings. Given their appeal to the upper classes, it is not surprising that 'mummies' also came to occupy pride of place in 'cabinets of curiosity', those privileged assemblages of 'monstrous' miscellanea brought together in an encyclopaedic spirit. When Thomas Platter, the Swiss medical student, visited Walter Cope at his London 'cabinet' in 1599, he saw an 'embalmed child (Mumia)', and during a 1638 trip to the 'Ark' in Lambeth, Georg Christoph Stirn was shown 'the hand of a mummy', displayed, with 'monstrous' appropriateness, next to 'the hand of a mermaid'.[69] Judged against this set of practices, the 'royal tent' accommodating Zenocrate might appear not so much a 'monster'-booth as a *wunderkammer*.

The connection is forcefully revealed in Part Two's final stages. First, Tamburlaine indulges in a litany of priceless materials, mentioning 'Inestimable drugs . . . precious stones . . . [and] rocks of pearl that shine as bright / As all the lamps that beautify the sky' (II:V.iii.153, 157–8). On the one hand, this might appear merely as an inventory of his treasure-chest; on the other, it can be read as a type of natural history collection, an encyclopaedic roll-call of rarities: to appreciate the contents of the metaphorical museum of the 'monarch of the East' (I:I.i.43) is to acknowledge the scale of Tamburlaine's accomplishments. Second, Tamburlaine orders the 'hearse of fair Zenocrate' to be 'fetch[ed]' (II:V.iii.211) and 'placed by [his] . . . chair . . . as parcel of [his] funeral' (II:V.iii.212–13). Interestingly, a stress upon showing now recurs: Tamburlaine agitates to engineer a 'sight' (II:V.iii.226) of the 'mummy', while his lines 'Pierce through the coffin and the sheet of gold / And glut your longings with a heaven of joy' (II:V.iii.227–8) would seem to invite a prising open of the lid of Zenocrate's resting-place.[70] At once, Tamburlaine here bespeaks an eroticization of the 'monster'; not surprisingly, therefore, critics have glossed his actions as 'penetration', 'consummation' and even 'necrophilia'.[71] But Tamburlaine also behaves, I would suggest, in line with a collector's compulsions. The shadow of John Sanderson's private unveilings hangs over the Scythian's organization of an exclusive exhibition before a select viewing audience. The fact of making Zenocrate the crowning glory of his territorial advances, moreover, structures Tamburlaine as an expression of particularly aristocratic colonial interests. And the successful colonialist, we recall, can claim even death as a subject. Via the 'monsterizing' of Zenocrate, then, Tamburlaine comes to inhabit an uncertain terrain that touches upon both a sideshow at Bartholomew Fair and the corridors of the Royal Society. The despot's demonstrative enterprise reveals not so much his wife as his own fraught location in history – betwixt and between an 'English' antiquarian and a 'foreign' performer, a commoner and a gentleman. In this way, Tamburlaine's final act of bodily manufacture ultimately deflects attention away from his climbing after immortality to the phenomenon of his irreconcilably divided social identity.

A further illustration of such division emerges in the parallel parts Tamburlaine assumes throughout – both conqueror of death and its arbiter or representative. By deploying the colours of his armour and tents as indicators of his mood, for instance, he agitates to dispense mortality. Although his 'tents' (I:IV.i.49) and costumes, initially 'White [in] ... hue' (I:IV.i.50), indicate 'the mildness of his mind' (I:IV.i.52), they quickly turn 'scarlet' (I:IV.i.55) and 'Black' (I:IV.i.59) if the enemy does not yield. This final colour 'menace[s]' (I:IV.ii.61) the complete annihilation of Tamburlaine's 'foes' (I:IV.i.63), suggesting the crucial importance of visual interpretation to the protagonist's military encounters. Tamburlaine's changing palette might be read inside the mechanisms of spectacular publicity manipulated by contemporary fairground stallholders. But his play with white, red and black can also be unpicked inside a scriptural perspective. In a 1642–3 account of the outbreak of the Civil War, John Vicars likens Tamburlaine's predictive colour sequence to God's use of 'portentious' and 'ocular Emblemes': the 'flags' of 'that famous Warriour', he writes, forewarn just as force-fully as the deity's 'signes and wonders' (which are interpreted as 'fearfull apparitions in the ayre, monstrous births, [and] heart-frighting-voyces and exclamations').[72] Vicars may be responding here to the play's textual links between signs and their consequences. Certainly, Tam-burlaine can be seen to be taking on a godly role in matters of prodi-gious anticipation. The Tartarian aspirant imitates heavenly authority in mobilizing his stagecraft as a proleptic instrument. In so doing, it is as if he adopts one of the traditional responsibilities of divinity in seeking to determine the course of human destiny. Via a move which simultaneously privileges Tamburlaine's agency and the inevitability of a decreed path, the future becomes a puzzle to be ascertained by the correct interpretation of the protagonist's revelatory accoutrements.

Such a dual imperative may find its rationale in contextual pressures. From 1572, competing theories circulated in learned circles about a great northern conqueror who was to introduce a golden, messianic age, and, from the early 1580s onwards, thanks to a new star, a comet and an earthquake, 1588 was feared as a 'yeere of wonder' and great calami-ties.[73] Changes in reigns, religions and estates were looked forward to; strange heavenly conjunctions were prophesied; and the overthrow of monarchies was forecast.[74] Probably composed in 1587–88, *Tamburlaine the Great* coincides with, and reflects on, these trends in astrological and philosophical speculation. Not only does the hero defy the godhead by harnessing 'signes and wonders' for purposes of rhetorical aggrandize-ment; he also brings to completion his 'monsterizing' appropriations, manufacturing 'monstrous' occurrences and orchestrating the fre-quency of their appearances. Marlowe's 'scourge of God' (II:V.iii.249) thus imagines transfiguring the events of his natural universe into addi-

tional mirrors that refract his magnificence, casting himself as a producer of prodigies, a begetter of new 'monstrous' creations. At moments
such as these, the signifying emphasis begins to reside less with
Tamburlaine than with a world at the mercy of his own exegesis.

Given the prominence of earthquakes in the predictive literature of
the 1580s, it is perhaps not be wondered at that *Tamburlaine the Great*
should highlight these types of preternatural disturbance. Although
some commentators entertained prosaic explanations, most argued that
earthquakes, preludes to further upset, were sent as tokens of God's
wrath.[75] 'Let vs remember . . . the fairest Cities in Asia sunk for sinne,'
wrote Anthony Munday in 1580, reminding his readers of the great
earthquake that had recently rocked London.[76] In its representational
concerns, *Tamburlaine the Great* might be seen as a dramatic re-
enactment of Munday's warning; of greater interest, however, is the
bypassing of contemporary theories in favour of a framework that
plays up the part of Marlowe's 'earthly god' (II:I.iii.138) in earthquake
manufacture. Tamburlaine claims that he will 'have the leading of so
great a host / As with their weight shall make the mountains quake'
(I:I.ii.48–9), a boast which by Part Two has broken free even of this
hyperbolic mould: the 'inferior world [will] quake' merely with his
'looks' (II:I.iii.139), it is asserted. Via these formulations, Tamburlaine
threatens to make the earth itself suffer from a 'monstrous' displacement, an indication, perhaps, of the play's adjudication between, and
collapsing of, forces of human and divine intervention. In a piece of
typically provocative stagecraft, the dramatist equates godly indignation and the practices of Tamburlaine as his self-elected scourge, establishing the hero as a key player in the imminent *annus mirabilis*.

Cosmological and planetary movements, a central component of the
prognosticating lore into which Marlowe's play inserts itself, figure as
even more strident testimonies to Tamburlaine's dominion. But Tamburlaine, rather than scrutinizing the skies' effects to map the trajectory
of his victories, treats them as rhetorical confirmation of a power that
has already been achieved. In this sense, the play rewrites the predictive convention, moving from events to signs rather than from signs
to events and further unsettling a godly ownership of premonitory
machinery. An eclipse, for instance, described in a 1580 pamphlet as
a 'monstruous . . . diminishing of light', will, Tamburlaine insists, be
generated by his grief for Zenocrate's 'absence' (II:II.iv.51).[77] Here Tamburlaine indulges in a sort of emotional parthenogenesis, externalizing
his condition by seizing upon its metaphorical equivalent. His statement also reveals an increasingly impassioned edge to his exclamations,

as he moves from terrestrial vibration to cosmic reorganization. The theme is elaborated when, in a related figurative application, he imagines the 'swords . . . lances and . . . shot' (I:IV.ii.51) of his army filling the upper element in an extravaganza of the skies. Such is the puissance of their general, it is implied, that Tamburlaine's forces supersede divinely produced heavenly apparitions to become themselves a prodigious point of reference.[78] The suggestion finds its most extreme articulation in the Scythian's later promise to place not only military equipment in the air but entire battalions: he can, he maintains, conjure 'armèd men' to 'march upon the towers of heaven' and 'Run tilting round about the firmament' (II:IV.i.204–6). Casting a glance at the meterological phenomenon known as 'armies in the clouds', described as 'monstrous formes' in a 1602 treatise, the play now refines into open confrontation Tamburlaine's progenitive audacity.[79] For the Asiatic 'Emperor of the world' (II:III.v.22) can at this point contemplate colonizing even heavenly territory. And he will do so, notably, in the guise of the entertainer, with his troops staging acrobatic accomplishments and a vertiginous celestial spectacle.

But 'signes and wonders' in the upper element do not remain the rhetorical province of the Scythian alone. In the same way that contemporaries argued about the precise form that the year of calamities would take, so do Tamburlaine's enemies read into the signifying capabilities of the natural environment a variety of interpretive possibilities. Yet it is not so much another incarnation of 'mythography' or 'mythopoeia' that is staged as a species of meterological militarism, the martyrs and victims of Tamburlaine's rule wrestling with him for a stake in the prodigious power-game. Typically for a drama enmeshed in a multiplicity of predictive appurtenances, *Tamburlaine the Great* abounds in rival rhetorical realizations of extraordinary showers. Drawing from the wounds of his foes, Tamburlaine argues, the clouds have shed 'bloody purple showers' (I:V.i.461), symbolic accompaniments to his rule over the African territories. In this figure, the heavens become the barometer of the magnitude of the warlord's earthly massacres. The potency of the Marlovian protagonist is arguably sapped, however, when his metaphor is reinvented as an imprecation by the forces of officialdom. '[H]eaven' (I:IV.ii.5), Bajazeth exclaims, in a pert reversal of Tamburlaine's bombast, will 'pour' poison down 'this glorious tyrant's throat' (I:IV.ii.7). The King of Jerusalem elaborates, imagining 'heaven' (II:IV.i.143) pouring 'down blood and fire on [Tamburlaine's] head, / Whose scalding drops will pierce [his] seething brains' (II:IV.i.145–6).

Miraculous rain was a frequent port of call in the wonder- and prodigy-books of the period, with the majority of writers agitating for augural explanations. 'Wonderfull . . . signes', such as falls of milk, flesh, worms, frogs, fish, wool, iron and tiles, discovered the 'threatnynges of the Gods', argued pamphleteers in 1583 and 1602, while a rain of blood in 1620 was a forewarning of the invasion of *'Polonia'*, a 1638 publication advised.[80] The interpretive positions of forewarning described here accord with those open to Tamburlaine's adversaries as they mass together to contemplate the potential meltdown of his empire and, by implication, to approve a faith in divine retribution. Culminatively, their interventions mean that the play appears less a site for prodigious appropriation as an arena of predictive contest: the Scythian's world is unhinged when its marvellous operations are buffeted by conflicting constructions. Tamburlaine does not remain the undisputed impresario, and the complexion of his omnipotence is compromised by the promise of fresh spectacles, alternative performances.

One crucial factor lent a feverish intensity to the prophetic hysterics of late sixteenth-century England – the conviction that the explosion of prodigious productions exciting the populace spelled the imminence of the apocalypse. Such a possibility was raised in a German digest of ancient predictions published in 1553, in a Latin verse version composed in the same year by Regiomontanus (Johann Müller of Königsberg) and in a 1577 English rendition of the narrative released by Thomas Rogers, the Anglican theologian.[81] The state of play was encapsulated by the astrologer, Richard Harvey, in a 1583 examination: once 'That yeare' of 1588 had been reached, he stated, 'an utter and final overthrowe, and destruction of the whole world shall ensue'.[82] Of course, apocalypse could take many forms, but central to it, commentators argued, were sequences of natural disaster – storms, darkened skies, floods and mass destruction.[83] Interestingly, it is through the conjuration of such happenings and the vitalizing energy of Revelation that the play, too, aspires to the status of an apocalyptic statement. Only when the sun falls 'from [its] sphere' (I:I.ii.175), states Tamburlaine, will he be defeated, going on to argue that his 'overthrow' (I:IV.ii.11) will be marked by the burning of 'the glorious frame of heaven' (I:IV.ii.10). With Zenocrate's passing, similarly, the earth will be apocalyptically darkened with 'endless night' (II:II.iv.7), a prognostication that finds its apotheosis in Tamburlaine's brag that his career is intimately entwined in the lead up to the 'dissolution of the world' (II:III.v.82). Some critics, such as Roy W. Battenhouse, R. M. Cornelius and Henry W. Wells, have taken such claims to imply that Tamburlaine might represent a version of the Antichrist.[84] It would be a mistake, however, to understand Tamburlaine in these scenes simply as an anti-Christian force in a disintegrating global system. Nor might it be profitable to read apocalyptical invocations only as a further example of Tamburlaine's mythic appropriations. Crucially, despite its investment in the 'end', the play never reveals to us the final conflagration. Instead, what is privileged is the preparatory business to judgement, the struggle but not the resolution. In this sense, *Tamburlaine the Great* constructs itself to fit a model of eschatological interpretation which focuses on the 'here and now'. Laurence Coupe argues that 'all *Apocalypse* is *now* . . . The tension we are interested in is not that between present and future, but that between present and present. It is between the present of the already and the present of the not yet'.[85] In apocalyptical terms, then, the drama emerges as a rehearsal rather than an enactment precisely because the 'overthrowe' of the world unfolds even in the events that herald its arrival.

This suggestion sits easily with the scriptural readings of some critics, which recognize that, in Eugene Hill's words, '*Tamburlaine* . . . contain[s] Apocalyptic allusions'.[86] Hill's conclusion, however (that 'the play *is itself* an Apocalypse'), underestimates the drama's temporal relation to an apocalyptical perspective.[87] Critics have similarly skirted over the metatheatrical role played by 'monsters' in the concluding stages.[88] In Part One, Tamburlaine summoned death into representation with a typically demonstrative gesture, warning the Virgins of Damascus, 'there sits imperious Death, / Keeping his circuit by the slicing edge' (I:V.i.111–12). The 'circuit' reference establishes death as a judge who will pronounce punishment on the resistant citizens: the implication is that Tamburlaine's league with the law enables him to put into play his own executionary practices. But Part Two is witness to the hero's loosening hold on deathly instruments, and, ironically, it is at Babylon, the city condemned in Revelation for its fleshly indulgences, that a sense of his frailty first impresses itself.[89] Earlier a 'fleshless body' that 'feeds' (I:V.i.115) on spears, death is now described as an 'ugly monster' (II:V.iii.67), 'an eyeless monster that torments [Tamburlaine's] soul' (II:V.iii.218). At once the 'monsterization' of an unseeing death offers powerful corroboration of Tamburlaine's failing specularity.[90] A further index of decline is glimpsed in the suggestion that, through death, the 'cannibalizing' Tamburlaine has met his appetitive match. Such are the limits of the protagonist's theatrical sovereignty: the 'monster', who made 'monsters' of people and possessions, is unable to master the 'monster' of mortality, highlighting the fact that Tamburlaine's rhetoric has reached the furthest point of its transformative capacities. Nor can Tamburlaine muster the directorial authority to control the body in performance, for, in his metaphorical fancy, death 'flies away' and 'comes stealing on' (II:V.iii.70–1) in a disobedient rejection of the *impresario's* injunctions.

Amidst its closing constructions of falling stars (II:V.iii.2) and discandying heavens (II:V.iii.26), the play conjures the apocalypse in one final but transfigurative invocation. In a characteristically mythographic manoeuvre, Tamburlaine summons the examples of Phaethon (II:V.iii.232), who wrought havoc when he rode the sun's chariot too close to the earth, and Hippolytus (II:V.iii.241), whose horses dragged him to death when they were frightened by a sea-bull. Addressed to Amyras, Tamburlaine's lines reinforce an impression that his son is inadequate to the task of inheriting and running the empire. One might even conclude that Marlowe is here gesturing to the source narratives in which Tamburlaine's two surviving sons quarrel, divide their father's territories and eventually lose them to Bajazeth's descendants. In this respect, *Tamburlaine the Great* assumes a gloomily selective stance towards the prophetic cultures informing its outlook. There is, in Laurence Coupe's words, no 'new cosmos' that emerges from the 'catastrophe' of Tamburlaine's passing, no 'promised land or . . . kingdom'.[91] Still less does the play strive to usher in a sense of a messianic age, golden or otherwise. Instead, it draws attention only to the theme of fallen estates and monarchies overthrown. In what is arguably one of the most nihilistic endings in Renaissance drama, an audience wakes up to the fact that only some of the drama's signs have been fulfilled, that Marlowe has presented a misleadingly mythopoetic version of doomsday. For the most terrifying aspect of the Tamburlainean apocalypse is that it fails to take place: the awaited revolution remains just that, a devoutly feared hour that is still to come.

III

In their wide-ranging study of wonders and the order of nature, Lorraine Daston and Katharine Park sort 'monsters' into three main types, each of which excites a particular response:

> As portents signifying divine wrath and imminent catastrophe, monsters evoked horror: they were *contra naturam*, violations of both the natural and moral orders. As marvels, they elicited wondering

pleasure: they were *praeter naturam*, rare but not menacing, reflecting an aesthetic of variety and ingenuity in nature as well as art. As deformities or natural errors, monsters inspired repugnance: they were neither ominous nor regrettable, the occasional price to be paid for the very simplicity and regularity in nature from which they so shockingly deviated.[92]

As a test case for the sorts of 'monstrosity' characterizing early modern England, *Tamburlaine the Great* amply bears out Daston and Park's identifications. Devils and 'giants', exotic beasts and bodily remnants, signs and wonders – all circulate in the play as constructions of 'monster' and all assume a variety of prophetic, singular and physically anomalous guises. The forms adopted, moreover, are never consistent. At any moment, one 'monstrous' species can blur into, or be confused for another, suggesting both the extent and potential of the 'monster' as a descriptive vocabulary. The play simultaneously illustrates a rich spectrum of presumed responses to 'monsters'. Among other dramatic reactions, Marlowe's 'monsters' trigger, at one and the same time, receptions that range from curiosity (the workmanship of Tamburlaine's body) to terror (the implications of his prognosticating projections), from astonishment (the play's language) to disgust (Bajazeth's taking of his own life). In many ways, then, *Tamburlaine the Great* represents an enactment of the interpretive possibilities of 'monstrosity' at work in the period, standing as testimony to the ways in which the 'monster' manifested itself as well as to the aesthetic structures into which it could be guided. As a performative utterance, it might be suggested that the play functions rather like an animated wonder-book, both putting flesh on the text's contents and subjecting them to critical scrutiny.

Given such an engagement, it is not surprising that 'monsters' in *Tamburlaine the Great* confront and translate contemporary anxieties both within the scope of the play world and beyond its perimeters. Outside the playhouse, social and political spectres such as civic unrest and bipartite propaganda could well be construed as an amalgamation of 'monstrous' otherness, deviant forms from which the country needed to purify itself. The concern in *Tamburlaine the Great* with classification and taxonomy, and with species distinctions and the adulteration of lineage, surely struck a particular chord in the minds of some Elizabethan audiences. Inside *Tamburlaine the Great*, 'monsters' also address dominant preoccupations, but here they are manipulated as tools with which empowerment can be secured or dislodged. For

Tamburlaine, both 'monsterizing' the self and 'monsterizing' others provides a temporary route out of his racial and social deadlock. One might also suggest that the Scythian's command of his environment begins to slip when he loses his performative hold on 'monsters' and on the manufacturing process that brings them into theatrical prominence. In this sense, 'monsters', tokens of a transformative utility, function in the play not so much as tangible objects but, rather, as symbolic goods and counters, items of intellectual property and examples of cultural practice, all of which can be exchanged, bartered for, earned and accumulated.

The notion that 'monsters' might be manufactured introduces an additionally complicating dimension to Daston and Park's analysis by highlighting the multivalent ways in which the 'monster' is forever slipping free of a categorizing framework. For 'monsters' in *Tamburlaine the Great* fail to constitute an essence that has its genesis only in biology or divinity. Rather, 'monsters' emerge from theatrical applications or linguistic borrowings as the products of a society's invention and experiment. By underscoring the idea of manufacture, in fact, *Tamburlaine the Great* playfully suggests an alliance with a quasi-scientific desire for enquiry. Dramatic reflections upon Tamburlaine's conception and seventeenth-century embryological explorations conducted by the Royal Society inhabit mutually constitutive territory.

Such connections can be suggested, I think, because of the theatrical innovations characterizing Marlowe's dramaturgy. Insofar as they can be manufactured, 'monsters' in *Tamburlaine the Great* bear witness to the play's new aesthetic, to the impact of a stagecraft so extraordinary that it, too, might be deemed 'monstrous'. Through the 'monsters' of his first major play for the public amphitheatres, Marlowe announces his unique arrival. In this sense, the dramatist, like the Tamburlainean impresario, puts his attributes on display. From the early 1590s, when the details of his grisly demise first began to circulate, the supposedly intemperate Marlowe has been biographically linked with his protagonists. But, in his own day, Marlowe as a curious 'monstrous' mixture exercised no less fascination as a construction than the hot-headed desecrator of Elizabethan orthodoxies. On the one hand, Thomas Kyd, when he vituperated 'marlowes monstruous opinions' in his 1593 deposition to Sir John Puckering, assumed a *contra naturam* attitude, equating 'monsters' with a transgression of horrific proportions.[93] On the other hand, Gabriel Harvey, when he wrote in 1593, possibly recollecting the language of *Tamburlaine the Great*, of 'Magnifique Mindes, bred of Gargantuas race' and Marlowe's 'wondrous selfe', endorsed a *praeter naturam* position: the 'monster' is notable because it is astonishing, singular, marvellous and remarkable.[94] If the playwright's career mirrored that of his characters, it was because he was able to stimulate responses that ran the whole gamut of the 'monstrous' aesthetic. In so doing, Marlowe was to find that it was from the same 'monstrous' infusions that filled his fictions that his own cultural identities were created.

3
'Monsters' and 'Molas': Body Politics in *Richard III*

A 1658 English translation of a treatise by the sixteenth-century Dutch physician, Levinus Lemnius, relates the following episode:

> a woman . . . married a Sea-man, and conceived by him, her belly began to swell to such a vast magnitude, that one would think it would never hold to carry the burden. When nine Moneths were past . . . the Midwife was cal'd; first with much a do she was delivered of a rude lump . . . there were fastned to it on both sides two handles, like to arms for the length and the fashion of them; It panted and seem'd to be alive, as sponges and Sea-fish . . . After this a Monster came forth of the Womb with a crooked back, and a long round neck, with brandishing eyes, and a pointed tail, and it was very nimble footed. So soon as it came to the light, it made a fearful noyse in the room, and ran here and there to find some secret place to hide itself: at last the women with cushions fell upon it and strangled it. This kind of Monster, because like a Leech it sucks the blood from the child, they call it a Leech, commonly a Sucker. At last this woman extreamly tired and almost ready to die, brought forth a Man-child, of which the Monster had so eaten up the flesh; that soon as it was christened, it had very little life remaining in it.[1]

Animating the passage is the evocation of three 'extraordinary' productions – a partly consumed infant, a 'monster' (the so-called 'leech') and what was described in the period as a 'mola', an essentially shapeless composition of flesh that frequently appeared before a 'natural' term was completed. This is, then, a birth of multiple 'monstrous' proportions.[2] As part of his adjudication between the three deliveries, Lemnius avails himself of a theoretical paradigm that equates physical appearance with behavioural traits. The non-normative shape of the 'mola' is directly linked to its sub-aquatic responsiveness, while the distorted frame, fiery look and scampering mobility of the 'monster' are read as evidence of its aural destructiveness and annihilatory tendencies.

Such an interpretive move lies at the heart of *Richard III* (1591) in which Shakespeare's anti-hero continually capitalizes upon his anomalous anatomy. Before displaying himself in public, Richard grants the theatre audience a private viewing of his 'deformity', theatricalizing both classical authority and the early modern 'monster' pamphlet in seeing as mutually constitutive bodily difference and a damaged moral outlook.[3] His 'rudely stamp'd' (I.i.16) and 'shap'd' (I.i.14) body, he tells us, determines that he will prove a 'villain . . . subtle, false, and treacherous' (I.i.30, 37). Similarly, in a 1585 discussion, William Clowes argued that 'a deformed and ill favored bodie . . . is a liuely representation of a vitious and ill disposed nature . . . as [the] bodie is crooked, Crabtree lyke, and growne out of all order, so [the] minde is monstrous', while a 1614 pamphlet, *Deeds against nature, and monsters by kinde*, contains the supposed lament of John Arthur, a crippled man executed for strangling his wife: 'For heauen had markt me out for shame, / Whereto I did my courses frame: / And as I was mishapt by kind, / Deformed also was my mind'.[4] The language of marking, moulding and 'monstrous' development deployed here suggests the extent to which Richard, in his envisioning of himself, appropriates popular physiological conceptions. It also illuminates the ways in which Richard is represented as scripting his history from the shards of other 'monster' texts, becoming, in the process, a dramatic concatenation of prevailing views about 'monstrosity' in its inner and outer manifestations.

If Richard explains his 'monstrosity' as a sign of his irredeemability, Lemnius is of an opposite opinion, arguing that 'monsters' can form part of a reformatory programme. His treatise's gloss is that 'monsters' stress the need for restraining lustful urges and avoiding copulation during menstruation: 'these . . . things should teach all men and women to use all decency, and orderly proceedings in their mutual embracings, lest Nature should be wronged thereby,' he states.[5] But Lemnius' description remains plagued by the anxieties attendant on the 'monstrous' body even as it seeks to silence them by investing in a schema of physical denial. Both the 'monster' and the 'mola' are troubling creations that vex the author's descriptive instruments. As they test the limits of existing approximations and identifications, so, too, do they promise to disrupt a properly sequential progression of time. Because the 'mola' is uncommonly prior and the 'monster' is exceptionally advanced, 'Nature' has been disoriented. The cannibalistic ingestion of the 'Man-child' by the 'monster', moreover, symbolizes a dislocation of the paternal line and a threat to systems of inheritance: with the 'monstrous birth' comes the potential overturning of both temporal and familial arrangements. The prospect is localized in the Duchess of York's admission that her son's 'birth' was a preternaturally 'grievous burden' (IV.iv.168). According to the Duchess, Richard 'cam'st on earth to make the earth my hell' (IV.iv.167), a claim that accommodates the protagonist's 'monstrous' emergence from the womb within an infernal frame of reference. With its 'crooked back' and 'pointed tail', the 'monster' in the Dutch description appears modelled from comparably devilish material, even standing as an infantilized version of the humped Duke of Gloucester. Indeed, Lemnius is at some pains to distinguish between the spiritual conditions of his female subject's deliveries. Both the 'mola' and the 'monster' are refused baptism, which points up their exclusion from institutionally sanctioned identifying ceremonies. By contrast, the 'Man-child' is 'christened', thereby becoming, despite its mutilated state, an index of social incorporation among otherwise abandoned 'monstrous' siblings.

In this chapter, I shall argue that *Richard III* follows the contours of an account such as Lemnius' in staging the processes whereby a lineal order is grotesquely upset. Discussion will suggest that an unsettling significance clusters about Richard in that he cannot be confined to one 'monstrous' type: both in *Richard III* and the tetralogy as a whole, the protagonist is imagined as a combination of partially developed and grotesquely well-defined traits. On the one hand, Richard is akin to the 'mola' – an 'unlick'd bear-whelp / That carries no impression', a 'foul indigested lump' and an 'indigest and deformed lump' that is 'un-finish'd, sent before . . . time / Into this breathing world scarce half made up' (I.i.20–1).[6] On the other hand, he is an intimate relation of the 'monster' already equipped with features and movement: 'Teeth hadst [he] in [his] head when [he] wast born', he 'could gnaw a crust at two hours old' (II.iv.28) and 'had . . . teeth before his eyes, / To worry lambs, and lap their gentle blood' (IV.iv.49–50).[7] The conventional explanation for children born with teeth was that they were sent as warnings from above, as divine prognosticators of such calamities as pestilence and famine.[8] In the play, however, such 'monstrous' tropes are invoked only to be reworked, a recurring example being the ways in which Richard's association with a range of temporal 'monstrous' signifiers is invariably politicized. *Richard III* is a drama obsessive about the end of eras, as the opening, which celebrates a culmination to the Wars of the Roses, implies. To Richard's construction of a combative relationship between his fluctuating form and the cessation of the martial conflict, I maintain, specifically Tudor implications are attached. As Richard is poised between finished and unfinished states, so was late sixteenth-century England in the throes of discontinuing the Elizabethan dynasty and making plans for its replacement. Alternating between a number of different bodily categories, Richard emerges as a fraught national metaphor. In Richard's lack can be glimpsed the absent legacy at the centre of the kingdom (the incompletion of the Tudor line or the miscarriage that signifies the non-reproductive body of Elizabeth I); in his precocious development are the traces of a narrative that has exhausted itself (a winding down of the political machine that the Tudors had created and a final negation of hopes that the royal womb would be progenitive).

In keeping with these arguments, the chapter begins with a discussion of the Elizabethan succession struggle. It is within the context of an insecure monarchical inheritance, the first and second sections suggest, that one can understand the play's representation of women concerned about genealogy, parturition and the ownership of the prophetic voice. Attending to the overlapping areas between the gendered rhetoric of *Richard III* and the most pressing political predicament of the Elizabethan nation-state also permits a reappraisal of the play's 'spectacularization' of the protagonist an a 'monster', a strategy orchestrated as part of a confrontation with a linguistically empowered female community. Nowhere is such bodily exploitation made more apparent than in Richard's appearance before the city's oligarchy, which the drama ironically stages as a historically resonant version of a fairground demonstration. The third and fourth sections pursue the fairground connection, notably through an exploration of the ways in which the pig and the contortionist are put to work as ciphers for the condition of a country in crisis. In this context, the association of both types with Richard (and with the figure of Proteus) enables a more nuanced understanding of the drama's topical reworking of 'monstrous' *topoi*. Uniquely poised in the shifting terrain between the 'monster' and the 'mola', over the course of the play Richard's body can be made to perform a range of metaphorical functions. It is only at the close that bodily entanglements are unravelled and that a 'Man-child' unharmed by Richard and 'christened' with an affirmative agenda – Richmond – can emerge.

I

A critical commonplace in writing on *Richard III* is that the protagonist's body can be read in politically analogous terms. Thus Linda Charnes comments that 'Shakespeare's audience would immediately have recognized Richard's physical deformity . . . as a synecdoche for the state'; Richard Marienstras, in an essay on the play, argues that the 'king's body as well as the body politic were supposed to symbolize the natural order of things'; and Michael Torrey asserts that 'Richard's misshapen body reveals . . . [the] condition . . . of . . . the world'.[9] What has not received attention is the extent to which the political embeddedness of Richard's 'monstrous' anatomy is informed by the polemic of the contemporary succession. Throughout the 1590s, as Susan Frye comments, Elizabeth's 'ageing made her vulnerable . . . she was anxious that she might be left outside her own government's decision-making process' as she declined.[10] As leading statesmen in the Privy Council were engineered by Robert Cecil into a political consensus, James VI of Scotland – 'male, protestant and available', in the words of one recent historian – emerged as the most plausible candidate to take over from the ailing female sovereign.[11] The Scottish monarch, however, was by no means a generally recognized choice. Nor did his credentials guarantee the likelihood of a peaceful accession. From the beginnings of her reign, Elizabeth was exercised by the factional implications of definitively naming her replacement, and, as a consequence, succession speculation was subjected to increasingly prohibitive legislation. A pronouncement of 1571 imposed severe punishments on those who broadcast claims to the throne, while a 1581 statute forbade astrological reflections on the consequences of the Queen's demise.[12] It was precisely the bringing into play of such rulings that spelled the downfall of Peter Wentworth's celebrated attempts to precipitate a resolution to succession questions. Following up the circulation of a petition to Elizabeth in 1587 and an aborted address to parliament in 1589, Wentworth directed a disastrous speech about the succession to the Commons in 1593, an unwittingly self-destructive move which resulted in a state examination, the summoning of his confederates and his own incarceration and eventual death in the Tower.[13] Notwithstanding the policing of Wentworth's agitations, the period was rife with debates about and tracts on the succession, many of which make a crucial contribution to the varieties of 'monstrosity' *Richard III* investigates.

Of immediate interest in the succession materials is the extent to which the body is reified into a site of political consequence. Between the play's dramatized bodies and the Elizabethan period's political bodies, there are fruitful points of contact. As early as 1566–67, a parliamentary plea urging the Queen to nominate an heir had recourse to a metaphor of bodily wholeness ('the prince and commonwealth ioyned together make a perfect man consisting of head, bodie and members, and cannot be separated'), and it was followed in 1594 by Robert Parsons' 'conference' in which he argued that the replacement of 'blood succession' by other systems such as 'election' precipitates 'vniuersal destruction & desecration of the whole body'.[14] Perhaps the most forceful elaboration of the theme came with Peter Wentworth's 'exhortation' to Elizabeth, which, following a period of protracted drafting, was eventually published in 1598. By appealing to the Queen directly, it took the arguments of its predecessors onto a more dangerous stage: 'As therefore you are our head, shew your self to haue dutifull care and loue to your bodie, that if you may help it . . . you leaue it not headles, as a dead trunk . . . Otherwise you see . . . that al your noble acts done in your lifetime are not onlie blemished, but also clearly defaced.'[15] Together, these configurations of mutilated or separated bodies, blemished acts, dying growths, general defacement and universal desecration bear a striking resemblance to comparable linguistic clusters in *Richard III*, suggesting that the play assembles its national preoccupations through the discursive matrix of its political determinants. The idea of a 'noble isle' (III.vii.124) in eclipse, which, in Buckingham's archly self-conscious peroration, it is Richard's duty to restore to 'glory' (III.vii.120), is similarly a manoeuvre characteristic of succession polemic: viewed inside a constitutive rhetoric, *Richard III* becomes itself an intervention in a broader argument about the country's uncertain fate.

II

At issue in reflections on the succession, of course, is the need for a clear 'line' linking one sovereign to the next. As early as 1580, Henry Howard, Earl of Northampton, in an account of English royalty, drew a parallel between an undecided monarchical legacy and civil strife: 'the only cause of all these mutations and alterations in government hath manifestly appeared to be the want of a lineal and natural successor in the prince's governing.'[16] Interestingly, the idea of an unambiguous 'lineal' connection, and the principle of a 'natural' succession, both of which are highlighted here, are redeployed when Buckingham states that

Richard, because he bears the exact imprint of his father's likeness, is the undisputed claimant to the throne (III.vii.13). Since it echoes a familiar *topos*, the announcement suggests that to refuse Richard's royal rights is to plunge the country into a political maelstrom: in so doing, it builds up a powerful case for the protagonist's candidacy. The extent to which the play discharges 'lineal' preoccupations is further illustrated in the frequency with which the reign of Richard III became a point of reference for contemporary commentators. More than one political analyst used the monarch as an example of a blot on, and a divergence from, otherwise healthy royal family connections. Writing on the Yorkists in 1602, Sir John Harington sees as inextricably inter-twined Richard's anomalous appearance, his 'monstrous' behaviour and a ravaged succession system: 'one degenerate Prince of that lyne . . . deformed by nature, did unnaturalie and like a vyper bite out his mother's owne bowels by defamacion, and murder his nephews to make sure their deprivation'.[17] In this formulation, 'unnaturalness' is empha-sized by Richard's refusal to wait 'naturally' in 'lyne' for his proper historical placement. Certainly, in the play, Richard goes to extreme lengths to remove others from the royal pecking-order. Already at the start his intrigues cause Edward to worry that 'His issue disinherited should be' (I.i.57). Elsewhere, Richard labours secretly to have his name sent to the top of the pile of succession contenders. As Robert N. Watson states, 'When he is not reshuffling the order of succession, as he does with Clarence, Richard is often engaged in obstructing, tangling, or eradicating the lines of hereditary connection.'[18] For Richard, these genealogical manoeuvrings are an intricate part of his endeavour to make fast his 'success', a term that the play highlights on no less than three occasions.[19] To further the chances of his takeover, Richard has broadcast the rumour that the 'monstrous' taint of 'bastardy' has put 'Edward's children' (III.v.74) out of the running for the crown; instead, the emphasis now needs to fall, his publicity machine argues, on his own recuperative and perfecting 'lineaments' (III.v.90). The protago-nist's quest for sovereignty is of a piece, I would suggest, with a politi-cal culture immersed in reflection upon the shapes of its future prospects. In Richard's own 'monstrous' actions, moreover, is encoded a related scenario – the possibility that royalty, through injury to mothers and the obliteration of youth – may be altogether annihilated. In its darkest moments, *Richard III* can imagine not only the fracturing of the line but its irrecoverable disappearance.

  Perhaps unsurprisingly, therefore, *Richard III* is a work intensely absorbed both in theorizing about origins and in ruminating on reproduction in its non-normative incarnations. Nowhere do these pre-occupations receive a more strident articulation than in the scenes devoted to female conference. A focus for women's disappointment is that they are able to deliver only unwelcome emotions. 'I am not barren to bring forth complaints' (II.ii.67), observes Elizabeth, to which the Duchess of York adds, 'I am the mother of these griefs' (II.ii.80). In their antiphonal character, these formulations suggest that psychological extremity has crushed the capacity to give birth to flesh-and-blood offspring. An elaboration of women's anxieties about a denaturalized maternal function is graphically encapsulated in animal metaphors. The Duchess of York, for instance, laments that she has 'hatch'd' a 'cockatrice . . . to the world' (IV.i.54). Queen Margaret concurs, adding to this realization of a 'monstrous' Richard her own embellishment: 'From forth the kennel of thy womb hath crept / A hell-hound that doth hunt us all to death' (IV.iv.47–8). Death and the womb in *Richard III*, indeed, are close associates. The Duchess of York wishes that she might have 'intercepted' Richard by 'strangling [him] in her accursed womb' (IV.iv.138) in an exclamation that builds on one of her earlier remarks: 'O my accursed womb, the bed of death!' (IV.i.53). A contradictory imperative is at work here, the Duchess representing herself as simultaneously taking control of, and in thrall to, her reproductive capacities. In its mantra-like concern with the 'accursed womb', moreover, these lines form an alliance with late Elizabethan succession treatises in which a mother's deadly inheritance is vigorously debated. 'And seeing God hath ordayned you our nursing mother,' wrote Peter Wentworth, drawing in the 1598 published version of his treatise upon the symbolic mythology of Elizabeth's mothering of the nation, '[do not] vnnaturallie leaue vs . . . doe not . . . leaue vs your people . . . to the rage & furie of hell & helhounds . . . as you are [a] naturall daughter and true heir in the one, so shewe your selfe to be as naturall also in the other.'[20] The passage works by negative example to suggest that Elizabeth, in not having reproduced, is an 'unnatural' mother, one whose unfruitful womb threatens to put England in peril. Wentworth's argument plays a political variation on the parturient frustrations Shakespeare's play delineates. For, like her dramatic female counterparts, Elizabeth is also, in some senses, responsible for a 'monstrous' legacy: in both Shakespeare's play and Wentworth's tract, women stand accused of releasing hell-hounds into their realms. As women's wombs in *Richard III* provide a nursery for the devilish protagonist, so does Elizabeth's womb threaten her country with an infernal destiny.

At one and the same time, Richard's body is seen as the product of alternative 'monstrous' beginnings. Margaret's account of his entry into the world ranges widely over a number of possibilities:

> Thou elvish-mark'd, abortive, rooting hog,
> Thou that was seal'd in thy nativity
> The slave of Nature, and the son of hell;
> Thou slander of thy heavy mother's womb,
> Thou loathed issue of thy father's loins . . .
>   (I.iii.228–32)

The mixed lineage Richard's physical differences betray – he is a product of an animal, elves, hell, 'Nature' and a human parent – marks him out as a hybridized creature with no one defining familial attachment. Clearly, such a construction associates Shakespeare's anti-hero with the debased and 'unnatural' successor who haunted Elizabethan political reflections, and this is stressed in the ways in which the play's women strive to distance themselves from the process of Richard's genesis. As the word 'slander' implies, Richard is 'imputed to' or 'put upon' women, a move that permits Margaret to claim for his mother and the female sex as a whole a disassociation of responsibility. Additional absolution for women is provided when Margaret states: 'Sin, death, and hell have set their marks on him, / And all their ministers attend on him' (I.iii.293–4). Here human parents cede place to a conjunction of three infernal shaping influences, a blasphemous trinity that, significantly, displays no obviously gendered identification. Via such alienating strategies, women manage briefly not only to confirm Richard's generic differences, but also to adopt an empoweringly detached attitude toward his alterity.

Marjorie Garber has written that Richard delights in 'projecting and displacing [the] characteristics' of his 'deformity . . . onto others'.[21] This is an arresting observation, but it needs to be supplemented by an engagement with the ways in which the protagonist's defence strategies frequently identify women as objects of critical arraignment. Faced with a vocally hostile female solidarity, Richard strives to prevent women escaping the effects of his influence. In particular, he rewrites the notion that he is less an intra-uterine 'monster' (affected during pregnancy or at birth) than an extra-uterine 'monster' (physically changed later in life). Promulgating the theory enables Richard, in an explanation of his 'monstrosity', simultaneously to introduce women as dangerously shaping instruments while depriving them, in Jean E. Howard and

Phyllis Rackin's words, of 'theatrical power and agency'.[22] In his condemnation of Queen Elizabeth, for instance, he reconceptualizes
his body as a site of affliction and a target of conspiracy, pushing
the demonic accusations levelled at him into a female arena. Transference is initiated when Richard reveals his 'deformity', suggesting that
his arm has previously been veiled to elicit the interest of a curious
public:

> Then be your eyes the witness of their evil.
> See how I am bewitch'd! Behold, mine arm
> Is like a blasted sapling wither'd up!
> And this is Edward's wife, that monstrous witch,
> Consorted with that harlot, strumpet Shore,
> That by their witchcraft thus have marked me.
>
> (III.iv.67–72)

At once here Richard's self-presentation contests the womb-centred
interpretations of his female relations, promoting a construction of
himself as singular ('I . . . mine . . . me') in contrast to a plurality of
women ('their . . . their') massed to ensure his torment. And, by representing himself as living testimony, he once again theatrically exploits
the conventions of the 'monster' pamphlet in which reliable 'witnesses'
(invariably clergymen) feature to vouch for the 'truth' of the phenomenon described.[23] This rhetorical procedure permits him to begin to
undermine the valency of Margaret's charge that his 'marked' frame
betokens an infernal nature: of course, Richard finds a determining logic
in a theory of mind/body congruity when alone, but the more open circulation by women of a similar physiological philosophy requires his
repressive intervention. Instrumental to Richard's project is the suggestion of an unholy connection between Queen Elizabeth, the King's wife,
and Jane Shore, his mistress. Attacking at the level of a same-sex
alliance, the protagonist is able to vilify not just woman but women:
an individual sexual dereliction becomes synonymous with the entire
female sex. Because Richard directs his own 'monstrosity' at that 'monstrous witch', moreover, he is able to reconfigure early modern concepts
of bodily difference, to complicate, in Michael Torrey's words, deformity's 'semiotic status': 'monstrosity' shifts to signifying a destructive
action rather than an anomalous appearance.[24] By the end of the scene,
Richard has not only converted previously wavering supporters, but
has also gained an intellectual superiority in matters of 'monstrous'
accountability.

A ruler without an heir, Elizabeth steered much of her political effort towards reproducing, through pageantry or performance, likenesses of herself, all of which stressed her unique status. As a sovereign with limited family connections, Elizabeth delighted in, and profited from, her singleness. Whether she was compared with Astraea or Diana, Venus or the Virgin Mary, the cultural machine surrounding Elizabeth was devoted to celebrating her exceptional virtues. Declared by the Act of Supremacy to be 'the only supreme governor', Elizabeth took pleasure in having her customary motto – *semper eadem* – occasionally trans- formed to *semper una*. 'Una' (or 'One') was, of course, a cult name for Elizabeth, as the first three books of Spenser's *The Faerie Queene*, first published in 1590, demonstrate.[25] With Richard, too, one encounters a carefully worked concentration on a single personality. Absorption in the self is elevated into a philosophy. 'I am myself alone', he com- ments in *Henry VI, Part III* (1591), concluding, as his end in *Richard III* approaches, 'What do I fear? Myself? There's none else by; / Richard loves Richard, that is, I and I' (V.iii.183–4).[26] But because Richard, like Elizabeth, is also in the position of having no immediate descendant, he is impelled, contrary to Ian Frederick Moulton's view that the pro- tagonist 'gives no thought to progeny', to consider the ways in which he might become progenitive.[27] Typically, for Richard, reproduction will have a 'monstrous' flavour. To Edward's widow, who queries how her children died, he states: 'But in your daughter's womb I bury them, / Where, in that nest of spicery, they will breed / Selves of themselves, to your recomforture' (IV.iv.423–5). Multiply suggestive, the remark reveals the extent to which the monarch will retain his indivisibility by putting into circulation facsimiles of himself, avoiding the imprint of women only by using the womb as a temporary home for the next Ricardian generation. The audacious appropriation of an animal motif (part of a terminology usually wielded by women) demonstrates the confidence with which Richard plots this next metaphorical victory. No less arrest- ing here is the allusion to the phoenix, the mythical self-impregnating bird so favoured by Elizabeth in her iconography.[28] As the Queen's iden- tification with the bird participated in related reflections on her suc- cessor, so does Richard invoke the phoenix to set the seal on his own perpetuation. If Richard is decided on authoring additional Richards, he is, at least metaphorically, pregnant, and, in this regard, a final set of 'monstrous' characteristics falls into place. According to Margaret, Richard is a 'bottled spider' (I.iii.242) and a 'bunch-back'd toad' (I.iii.246). It is as if Richard's misshapen body – bloated and extended – parodies the image of a woman with child. Both a continued tyranny and a political regeneration are encoded as possibilities in Richard's physical outline.

Intricately interrelated in the play are suggestions about unborn progeny and women's predictive powers. From the start, Richard aims to establish himself via a variety of behind-the-scenes stratagems. 'Plots have I laid, inductions dangerous, / By drunken prophecies, libels, and dreams' (I.i.33–4), he states, highlighting a link between dark presentiments and the portentous significance of his 'monstrous' anatomy. A notable feature of 'monster' literature was the prophecy, with apocalyptical predictions, scriptural exegeses and tales of extraordinary happenings all boasting foreknowledge of great wars, universal cataclysms or the arrival of a saviour.[29] At this point, of course, Richard has had prophesied only that ' "G" ' (I.i.39) will be the 'murderer' of 'Edward's heirs' (I.i.40). However, once this possibility is put into play, Clarence is thrown into gaol and Richard is free of a potential political rival, empowered via the languages of extraordinary phenomena to ascend ever more surely to his self-appointed goal. Interestingly, one of the additional ways in which women seek to counter Richard is by speaking in a predictive vein, not so much rewriting the past as prophesying the future. Nowhere is this more obvious than in the scene where Anne, to damn Richard's part in the death of her husband, imagines his paternal prospects as 'monstrous':

> If ever he have child, abortive be it:
> Prodigious, and untimely brought to light,
> Whose ugly and unnatural aspect
> May fright the hopeful mother at the view,
> And that be the heir to his unhappiness.
>
> (I.ii.21–5)

Critics have noted that Anne describes a type of Richard and maps out for herself a role in which she plays his mother and the mother of his child at one and the same time. As Marjorie Garber writes: 'The fantasy child who is to be the only offspring of Richard and Anne is Richard himself.'[30] A psychological stress on these lines, however, would seem to pass over their deeper political and rhetorical implications. For instance, set alongside the succession anxieties of the 1590s, Anne's expostulation might be seen to take on a self-conscious responsiveness to the question of the nation's 'unhappy' inheritance. By exploiting 'prodigious' curses and hinting at maternal rejection, moreover, Anne comes briefly to subsume Richard's 'monstrosity' to her own perspective. Thus she can proceed to designate Richard a 'lump' (I.ii.57), a 'dreadful minister of hell' (I.ii.46) and a 'Foul devil' (I.ii.50), while simultaneously disallowing him from using these terms to his own advantage. In her imaginative facility and determining grasp on futurity, Anne poses an unsettling threat to Richard's construction of a strategic self.

With Queen Margaret, too, an ability to authorize 'monstrous' events is celebrated. The female reliance on modes of rhetorical resistance receives a spectacular emphasis in her denunciation of Richard's activities. For 51 lines Margaret waits in the wings, vilifying Richard with her asides and tantalizing spectators' sensibilities. Her climactic entrance – 'Which of you trembles not, that looks on me?' (I.iii.160) – vividly directs the audience gaze to her self-elected status as a prodigious embodiment of vengeance:

> If heaven have any grievous plague in store
> Exceeding those that I can wish upon thee,
> O, let them keep it till thy sins be ripe,
> And then hurl down their indignation
> On thee, the troubler of the poor world's peace . . .
> No sleep close up that deadly eye of thine,
> Unless it be while some tormenting dream
> Affrights thee with a hell of ugly devils.
>
> (I.iii.217–21, 225–7)

Here she threatens to undermine one of the visual edifices whereby Richard constitutes himself, causing him to see in unwelcome ways. The 'monster' that subdues others to his looks will, in Margaret's formulation, have his sight plagued by mirror-images of his own infernal derelictions: her anticipated dreamscape thus plays an arresting variation on Richard's theory that the the reproduction of likenesses of himself will dissipate female hostility. It is when she is in a predictive vein, in fact, that Margaret is at her most authoritative. Appointing herself 'prophetess' (I.iii.301), Margaret speaks of the 'sorrow' (I.iii.300) that Richard will bring to England in lines that bristle with multiple significations. Beyond the play, her language brings to mind the situation of a female monarch who elected not to publicize her kingdom's future; within the play, the more overt manipulation of the prophetic art promises both to reveal Richard's own subterfuges and to establish women as the only reliable political commentators.

Perhaps the most direct challenge comes when Anne encodes the deceased Henry VI as a spectacle of 'monstrous' potential. She appeals to both Richard and the on-stage 'gentlemen' (I.ii.55) who are her audience:

> Behold this pattern of thy butcheries.
> . . . See, see dead Henry's wounds
> Open their congeal'd mouths and bleed afresh . . .
> Thy deed inhuman and unnatural
> Provokes this deluge most unnatural . . .
> Either heav'n with lightning strike the murderer dead,
> Or earth gape open wide and eat him quick . . .
>
> (I.ii.53–6, 60–1, 64–5)

Taking on the role of presenter, Anne demonstrates a corpse which is miraculous because it newly bleeds. This is, then, a stigmatic body, a speaking anatomy that is a 'witness' (I.ii.238) not of the supposed afflictions visited on Richard, but of his dissimulating criminality. By the same token, the body is 'monstrous' because of the ways in which the term 'stigmatic' is equated with physical 'deformity' elsewhere in the tetralogy: by implication, the inner/outer logic exploited by Shakespeare's anti-hero is here contested, with the King's remains becoming a sign less of their own 'monstrosity' than that of Richard himself.[31] When Anne, in her interpretation of the bloody 'deluge', summons an apocalyptical register, signs feature even more prominently, for earthquakes, floods and lightning were the precursors of final judgement. (In this connection, a further dimension of the succession question can be glimpsed, Henry's body marking the passing of an older order and the prospect of future calamity.) In a Tamburlainean vein, Anne ventriloquizes a wrathful deity, bidding natural forces to direct their energies against Richard's malefactions. As God in contemporary pamphlets opens the ground to correct a blaspheming citizenry, so does Anne command the earth to swallow up a Richard who has desecrated and made 'monstrous' his Christ-like sovereign: now it is Anne's discourse, rather than Richard's, that theatricalizes its popular cultural contexts.[32] Perhaps the most powerful part of her argument is Anne's hint of a metaphorical alliance between herself and Henry: she would, she states, to avoid attracting Richard, with her 'nails . . . rend that beauty from [her] cheeks' (I.ii.130). The line suggests that Anne is capable of evolving, by her own art, into an authentic speaking picture, a mutilated exhibition as dramatic as the 'monstrous' corpse she makes her subject. It shows, too, the ideological distance travelled by Anne from the scene's inception. At the start, Anne is represented as seeing the royal form as a conduit for the divine. At the culmination of her exchange with Richard, she can contemplate becoming herself a godly instrument, an embodiment of the belief later popularized by seventeenth-century religious sects that the woman prophet's body was, in Diane Purkiss' words, a 'true icon of God' and a vehicle of 'semiotic significance'.[33]

When Richard later invites Anne to stab him with his sword (I.ii.177–82), he opens out the possibility that he, too, can be made a punctured body, a signifying corpse. By the logic of the scene, Anne would thereby become, like Richard, the 'monster', leaving Richard to take on the mantle of a miraculous stigmatic. If Richard elsewhere in the play works as a construction of an 'unnatural' successor, therefore, here he is distinctive for freeing himself of the taint of difference. Linda Charnes observes that Anne and Richard 'enact a shared voyeurism, a perverse ocular communion over and through a shared body that they have both "entered" and appropriated', and her comment is helpful in placing the ways in which Richard campaigns to take over Anne's visuality, in the process discovering her as as the 'monstrous' persecutor and himself as Christ-like substitute.[34]

Overturning the balance of rhetorical power sets the scene for what is to be Richard's most direct onslaught on the country's political defences. By involving the members of his party in a performance staged for the officials and citizens of London, he manages both to continue campaigning against women and to initiate a powerful self-image – that of a new Messiah whose task is to lead England to salvation. It is via this ironically stylized civic drama, moreover, that the play's concern with the succession receives its fullest statement. At the start, the protagonist assumed the parts of both showman and exhibit. As he prepares for his début before the capital, however, theatrical responsibility is divided between a number of associates, suggesting Richard's tightening hold on the state's affairs. Now it is Buckingham, for instance, who plays the 'Monster-Master', dealing, in the process, a harmful blow to Anne's earlier execution of the role of 'mistress of ceremonies'. For Richard's benefit, Buckingham recollects his initial address and popularization of the Ricardian cause:

> Withal, I did infer your lineaments –
> Being the right idea of your father,
> Both in your form and nobleness of mind –
> Laid open all your victories in Scotland,
> Your discipline in war, wisdom in peace,
> Your bounty, virtue, fair humility;
> Indeed, left nothing fitting for your purpose
> Untouch'd, or slightly handled in discourse.
>   (III.vii.12–19)

Teasingly unveiling and anticipating through disclaimers and denials, Buckingham enlists images of sexual decadence and the 'unsatiate greediness of [Edward's] desire' (III.vii.7) as a prelude to the final revelation of Richard himself. But it is not Richard who will be the 'monster' at the centre of the 'monster'-booth, for he has already reconfigured for the on-stage audience how 'monstrosity' might be identified. Thus Buckingham can introduce into the imaginative conception of Richard 'form' and a 'fair humility', which, in the context of the 'oratory' (III.vii.20), suggest bodily wholeness and integrity. Richard's physical anomalousness continues to diminish in direct proportion to the cultivation of his symbolic potential.

When Richard finally appears, significantly '*aloft*', as if raised on a dais, the language of Buckingham and Catesby becomes emphatically indicative (III.vii.97, 202), suggesting that pointing and gesticulating accompany the would-be monarch's arrival. Like Quartfield and Salewit, the rogues who extol a 'monstrous' fish in Jasper Mayne's play, *The City-Match* (1637–8?), to win over incredulous spectators, Buckingham and Catesby collaborate to highlight Richard's uniqueness.[35] The Duke has also supplied Richard with two 'churchmen' (III.vii.47) and a 'prayer-book' (III.vii.46), enhancing the impact of the performance with demonstrative 'props' (III.vii.95), a term that in fact features in Buckingham's opening peroration. In its parodic piety, then, the longed-for disclosure does not disappoint. What is most striking, however, is less the 'monster' as saint as the temporary transference of 'monstrous' significance from the body of Richard to the body of the nation-state. The spectacle of Richard's 'monstrosity' is extended to include the vision of a feminized England 'monsterized' through dissipation and debauchery. Not only does such an overtly sexualized construction take energy from contemporary succession materials which communicate their preoccupations via metaphors of bodily fragmentation and abuse; it also confirms the play's anxious relation to the perceived decline of the Tudor line:

Know then, it is your fault that you resign . . .
The lineal glory of your royal House,
To the corruption of a blemish'd stock;
Whiles in the mildness of your sleepy thoughts –
Which here we waken to our country's good –
The noble isle doth want her proper limbs;
Her face defac'd with scars of infamy,
Her royal stock graft with ignoble plants,
And almost shoulder'd in the swallowing gulf
Of dark forgetfulness and deep oblivion . . .
                              (III.vii.116, 120–8)

Arresting in this concluding address is the idea of Richard remember-
ing England: the future sovereign must restore to the country a collective national memory at the same time as he refigures the state, for the
'isle' is seen as an amputated torso missing its defining appendages. It
is because Richard's 'lineal' descent has already been established, and
because his own 'blemishes' have been relocated in rival claimants, that
he is able to assume such a responsibility. Assisting Richard's claims is
the horticultural metaphor of an adulterated, contaminated plant, and
here the speech avails itself of a familiar political commonplace. In
1606, Edward Forset described the 'institution of a State politique' as a

> body with the out-growing parts . . . to receiue nourishment,
> strength, flourishing, and fruitfulness from that root of a rightful
> regiment. If the root thriue, sucking abundantly of his heauenlie
> nutriment, the plant must needes prosper . . . but if the root be des-
> titute of grace, as depriued of his sapp, it induceth vpon the whole
> stocke of the State, a withering decay and pining barrennesse.[36]

Such rhetorical appropriation lends a certain legitimacy to an otherwise
specious argument, one that gains strength, too, from the exploitation
of two further tropes of 'monstrosity'. The image of a royal stock 'graft
with ignoble plants' suggests mixing, hybridization and a 'monstrous'
coming together of unequals. It is a conjunction that has plunged
England into a 'swallowing gulf / Of dark forgetfulness and deep
oblivion'. These lines recall the 'bottomles pit' and engulfing darkness
of Revelation.[37] The *coup de théâtre* of Buckingham's persuasion is
the implication that it is a Christ-like Richard, and none other, who
can claw England back from a 'monstrous' degeneration into the final
cataclysm.

Typically for *Richard III*, however, the surface meanings of Bucking-ham's speech are continually sliding. Viewed within its contextual parameters, the address opens out a more disturbing scenario of identi-fications. Most importantly, Buckingham's opportunist positioning of Richard as rightful owner of the 'monstrous' whore of England is polit-ically charged. Deformed, ravaged and hence vulnerable, England's body is open to rival claimants to the throne and to outsiders' corrup-tive influence. In this sense, the alterity of Richard's 'monstrosity' (he is a 'devil' [I.iii.118], a 'cacodemon' [I.iii.144], a 'black intelligencer' [IV.iv.71], a 'carnal cur' [IV.iv.56] and a 'valiant crook-back prodigy') allies him with the 'foreign prince', the 'stranger' who would take over from Elizabeth and whose identity vexed the imaginative energies of the succession writers.[38] Support for such a reading comes from some of the additional ways in which contemporaries figured the sovereign's replacement. In his 1598 treatise, Wentworth dwelled upon the dangers of the Queen unwittingly approving a non-English candidate 'so mon-strouslie brutish and voide of reason . . . he should be thought general-lie a monster amongst men'. This successor, the 'vilest monster which [nature] bringeth out, [and] the cruellest beast which shee nourisheth', would prove the bane of England, Wentworth argues, consuming and devouring the country, unleashing 'riuers of blood' and causing 'strong men [to] be slaine in the fielde [and] children and infants murthered in euerie towne'.[39] Judged against such anxieties, *Richard III* can be under-stood in part as a displaced enactment of, and an erotic speculation about, a sexually predatory ruler who enforces a 'foreign' yoke and imperils national destiny. The deaths of Clarence, Hastings and the princes are not too far away from Wentworth's late sixteenth-century narrative of civic breakdown. A mixed creation, Richard is the blank page onto which both the familiar image of Elizabeth and a fantasy of reconstitution can be projected. By the same token, he is a property that powerfully anticipates a less easily recognizable political configuration – 'the forms of things [still] unknown'.[40]

III

One of the anxieties around a 'stranger' ascending the English throne was the notion that local institutions would crumble beneath the weight of 'foreign' habits, separatism and power contests. To represent this possibility, sixteenth-century commentators had recourse to a striking metaphor. Writing in 1579 on the Queen's proposed marriage to the Duke of Alençon, and responding to contemporary fears about the monarchical implications of the match, John Stubbs compared her suitors to 'boars in a fat new-broken-up ground' who 'by sowing some seeds of dissensions to breed partialities in the country, do root out the ancient homegrowing nobility and turn under perpetual slavery . . . the country people . . . and . . . seize themself of the absolute kingdom'.[41] Its historical distance from the 1590s notwithstanding, the passage looks forward to Shakespeare's play by bringing together the idea of a divisive monarch who eradicates traces of indigenous 'blood' and the motif of the pig or the boar. Anne's derisory reference to Richard as a 'hedgehog' (I.ii.104) has, by the end of the play, been transformed into Richmond's characterization of the protagonist as 'The wretched, bloody, and usurping boar, / That . . . Swills your warm blood like wash, and makes his trough / In your embowell'd bosoms' (V.ii.7–10). This deployment of the metaphor signals a challenge to Richard's rhetorical ascendancy, for it replaces his supposed protectorship of the body politic with the suggestion that he gnaws 'cannibalistically' at his people's hearts: finally, then, it is his proximity to the pig, hog and boar that registers most forcefully.

Writing on sixteenth- and seventeenth-century varieties of carnival, Peter Stallybrass and Allon White note: 'Amongst the menagerie of fairground creatures, it was undoubtedly the pig which occupied a focal symbolic place at the fair.'[42] Fairs, of course, were key locations for the display of 'monsters' and, in discursive and material embodiments of 'monstrosity', pigs played a crucial part. The tense years of the 1560s, for instance, witnessed a plethora of ballads about the birth of 'monstrous' pigs, an indication, perhaps, of the anxieties aroused by the anomaly of an unmarried Queen ascending to the throne.[43] Pigs and 'monsters' consorted with each other, too, beyond the confines of the broadside. Themselves the objects of exhibition when a physical anomaly could be capitalized on, pigs and boars loomed large in reflections on human and animal couplings, functioning as charged instances of 'monstrous' transgressions of species boundaries.[44] An English translation of a narrative by the early sixteenth-century Swedish historiographer, Olaus Magnus, tells of a 'beautiful maid . . . who was taken by a Big Boar, & forced to his Den, & got w[i]th childe by him, & brought forth a man-boy, but all hair', while a 1573 account of the plague by William Bullein rehearses the births 'of many strange monsters . . . some a hogge with the hedde like a man'.[45] If the various meanings surrounding the pig and its relatives brand Richard, once again, as a fairground exhibit, a 'monstrous' anomaly and a 'foreign' body, they also establish him as a 'monstrous' progenitor, as a 1641 anti-Catholic pamphlet, commemorating England's deliverance from the Gunpowder Plot, demonstrates. Guy Fawkes' role as midwife to the birth of the plot is vilified:

> Out Monster-Tiger, a fell vipers brood,
> (That would'st suck with thy milk, thy mother's blood)
> Spawn'd with a *Richards* tush, not toothles borne,
> Drawing the fountaine-breast, thou wouldst have torne
> A passage to hir heart, gnawd that for food,
> And like *Prometheus* Vultur suckt on blood.[46]

The verse recasts numerous Shakespearean details – the comparison of the protagonist with the 'tiger' (II.iv.50), the suggestion that he is poisonous (I.ii.151), the claim that he was born with teeth and the idea, first broached in *Henry VI, Part III*, that Richard hacked out a 'bloody' route from his mother's womb to the 'open air'.[47] At the same time, it plays upon the sexual connotations of Richard's kinship with the boar, for his tusk is seen as the phallus with which a new order of traitors and villains can be disseminated. Such are the 'monstrous' capacities of the pig gene that Richard is permitted to recreate himself in the guise of Guy Fawkes, ensuring a direct 'line' between himself and his inheritors. Pigs, hogs and boars lead backwards to the 'monstrous' irresolution of the Elizabethan succession; they also push ahead to a Ricardian fantasy that, only in the play's after-life, is granted realization.

By inserting Richard into a pig/boar role, the play grants an additional fluidity to Richard's improvization of a range of identities. Certainly, over the course of the play, Richard revels in propagating varieties of a shifting self, as when he employs 'dissembling looks' (I.ii.241) to appear 'virtuous and . . . Christian-like' (I.iii.316) and makes public shows of grief for the departure of vanished friends and relatives (III.v.24). Such impersonatory strategies link Richard, as Jonas Barish has argued, to the mythical Proteus, whose fabled transformations attracted a lively early modern response.[48] Proteus, of course, was, like Richard, a 'Monster' who, in Philip Stubbes' 1583 assessment, 'could . . . chaunge him self into . . . many fourmes and shapes'.[49] Chief among the various animals that this 'monster' imitated was the pig, to the extent that several contemporary writers interpreted a Protean ability as no more than a kind of swinish self-indulgence: 'by Proteus', Stephen Bateman observed in 1577, is 'signified . . . a hoggish affection'.[50] Thus, when Richard, in *Henry VI, Part III*, describes himself as being able to 'Change shapes with Proteus for advantages', more than one level of meaning comes into play.[51] The connection with Proteus signals for Richard a dedication to the gratification of the baser instincts of the self as well as a confirmation of his 'monstrous' antecedents.[52] At a subsidiary level, it introduces a complicating classical element into the 'monstrous' composition that is Richard, an ingredient that undergirds his hybridity and stresses the ongoing process of his physical form. Because this form is constantly evolving, moreover, an additional political context emerges. As the temporal concerns of contemporary England are registered through Richard's incorporation of the traits of the 'monster' and the 'mola', so, too, does his Protean role-play speak loudly to the condition of the country in the 1590s, to a nation-state awaiting the imprint of its final form.

Adding a complicating element to the 'monstrous' designations that make up Richard's 'monstrosity', then, are contorting inflections. From the early seventeenth century onwards contortionists are recorded as exhibiting themselves as Bartholomew Fair.[53] The most elaborate record of this practitioner of physical changeability, however, comes only with the later seventeenth century. Known as the 'English Posture-Master', Joseph Clark, who served originally at the court of the Duke of Buckingham, went on to appear at Southwark Fair and died in the early 1690s, is celebrated in a list of 'Imposters, Heresiarchs *and* Heterodoxi' compiled by John Evelyn in 1697 (Figure 7). Placed in Evelyn's catalogue alongside more familiar 'monsters' such as Lazarus and John Baptist Colloredo, Mary Davis and Barbara Urselin, Clark is described as having 'so flexible and subtile a Texture, as [he could] contort his Members into several disfigurations, and . . . put out of joynt almost any Bone or *Vertebra* of his Body, and . . . re-place it again'.[54] Particular to this account is Clark's impersonation of 'monstrosity' – his ability to mime various 'disfigurations'. It was a skill returned to in a 1698 Royal Society report, in which Clark is credited with being able to 'appear in all the Deformities that can be imagin'd, as Hunch Back'd, Pot Belly'd, Sharp Breasted . . . he will appear as great an Object of Pity as any; and has often impos'd on the same Company, where he has been just before, to give him Money as a Cripple; he looking so much unlike himself, that they could not know him'. Anatomical flexibility is set off by Clark's physiognomical plasticity, for he also has expertise in turning 'His Face into all Shapes, so that by himself he acts all the uncouth, demure, odd faces of a Quaker's Meeting'. It is not to be wondered at, perhaps, that a famous surgeon, '*Mullens* . . . lookt on [Clark] in so miserable a Condition, that he would not undertake his Cure'.[55] To locate an early modern material manifestation for Richard's Protean theatricality, one might do no better than to focus on the body of the contortionist whom contemporaries labelled *'Proteus Clark'*.[56]

Clearly, between Clark and Richard are some intriguing points of contact. Like Richard, Clark provokes an emotional response as a 'Cripple' or a 'Hunch-back', fools spectators with dissimulated sanctification and possesses a preternatural predilection for moving between physical states (seeming, as it were, to be able to switch from 'monster' to 'mola' with ease). Popular parallels, however, are perhaps not as interesting as the ideological uses to which a willed 'monstrosity' is seen to be put. For Richard, 'monstrosity' forms part of a purposeful project. Physical difference is manipulated via trickery to empower the protagonist and hasten the spectator's downfall. With Anne, for example, he develops a process of reversal identification, visiting his own characteristics on his accuser and tactically annexing the visual imagination. Manipulating threads of invisible association, Richard transforms Anne into the basilisk with which he has just been compared:

> *Anne.* Never hung poison on a fouler toad.
>   Out of my sight! Thou dost infect mine eyes.
> *Richard.* Thine eyes, sweet lady, have infected mine.
> *Anne.* Would they were basilisks, to strike thee dead.
> *Richard.* I would they were, that I might die at once;
>   For now they kill me with a living death.

(I.ii.151–6)

Defined in a 1626 dictionary as a 'serpent' which 'destroyes . . . with [its] lookes', the basilisk is a peculiarly apposite 'monster' for Richard to invoke, since it allows him, via its links with visual contagion, first to damage and then to seize on Anne's spectacular powers.[57] Soon afterwards, Richard is able to announce that Anne will 'debase her eyes on [him]' (I.ii.251). As the term 'debase' makes clear, an essential instrument in Anne's arsenal, her gaze, will be diluted and hybridized: there is even, given the sexual charge of the exchange, the prospect of 'monsterization'. By interfering with the gaze, Richard is able to revise further early modern theorizations of the body, making 'monstrosity' a quality that is performed rather than inherently possessed: an important development in his fortunes comes when he argues that Elizabeth and Jane Shore's 'monstrosity' belongs with their staging of a secret intrigue. Such an engineered challenge to the mechanisms of understanding has a political edge. It points up a situation in which, because concepts of identity and mimesis have been sapped of their expected significance and adulterated by new associations, there is no longer a fit between how the monarch acts and how the state functions. To reinstall a body politic in which analogies and elements all reside in their proper places requires a reinforcement of traditional 'monstrous' constructions. It is in answer to this need that Richmond makes his appearance.

IV

As *Richard III* approaches the close, its motifs of 'monstrosity' come together in conclusive conjunctions. In particular, the final stages concatenate ideas about 'natural' succeeding and apocalyptical ending, about animals and contortionists, about reproduction and inheritance, and about 'monsters' and 'molas' that have preoccupied the play as a whole. By far the most striking feature of the last scenes is the waning command of Richard himself. When Buckingham, for instance, announces that 'Hastings, and Edward's children, Grey and Rivers, / Holy King Henry . . . Edward [and] Vaughan' have 'miscarried' (V.i.3–5), he uses a metaphor that evokes a miscarried birth. In alluding to parturient incompletion, Buckingham raises both the spectre of the 'mola', the shapeless prematurity with which Richard is linked, and the possibility of an aborted succession. In his decline, it is as a 'mola', indeed, that Richard is increasingly discovered. The passage of the ghosts takes Richard back in history to his earliest infractions: it is as if the belated 'monster' has run its course and the untimely 'mola' is taking its place. Types of 'monster' themselves (they were described in a 1581 account of Bosworth as 'deformed Images'), the ghosts are dismissed by Ratcliffe as 'shadows' (V.iii.216), a term that points up the ways in which Richard, too, is becoming a shadowy version of his former self – in Graham Holderness' words, a 'disintegrating personality'.[58] He is returning to the generational 'chaos' of *Henry VI, Part III* from which he originally emerged.[59]

The failing powers of Richard are further communicated though his increasingly desperate use of 'monstrous' discourses. To his troops he describes Richmond's forces as 'A scum of Bretons and base lackey peasants, / Whom their o'er-cloyed country vomits forth' (V.iii.318–19). The idea of vomiting up a 'skum' that is 'base' in nature places this metaphor of over-indulgence in the territory of the 'monstrous' delivery – this is a 'venting' that is also a 'birthing'. These rival forces, Richard claims, are 'rats' (V.iii.332) and 'bastard Bretons, whom our fathers . . . left . . . the heirs of shame' (V.iii.334, 336). Once again, Richard invokes a theory of clean lines, paternal connections and rightful succession to de-'monstrify' his own anomalies. By associating the 'Bretons' with rats, moreover, Richard places them lower than the 'monstrous' progeny of

pigs on the hierarchical scale. Nor does the enemy pose a genuine military threat, Richard asserts. Because the general is a 'milksop' (V.iii.326),
the argument runs, the might of his army is weakened. Here Richard
brands Richmond a nursing child and an effeminate. Women and reproduction, in different ways, have already been characterized as 'monstrous' elsewhere in the play, and Richard gives implicit approval to
those identifications to vilify his opponent. But ultimately Richard
cannot contort himself to engineer another rhetorical victory. Numerous apocalyptical references suggest that Richard will soon be judged:
the sun 'disdains to shine' (V.iii.279), it is a 'black day' (V.iii.281) and
'The sky doth frown and lour' (V.iii.284). In the 1658 English translation of Levinus Lemnius with which this chapter opened, the apocalypse is interpreted as the time at which 'monsters' are restored to bodily
wholeness: 'by rising again they shall lay aside all deformities of their
bodies that were ill favoured to behold, and be well formed . . . and all
lame crooked and imperfect limbs shall be made perfect'.[60] No such
transformation can be said to await Richard, for he has already relocated
the differences of his form and emptied out 'monstrosity' of its usual
meanings. Instead, the 'monster' that will be cured is the body of
England, and it is to achieve that end that Richmond's rescue mission
is orchestrated.

As the saviour of England, Richmond has numerous qualities in his
favour. He is, primarily, a reconstitutive phenomenon. The 'remem-
brance' of his 'fair dream' (V.iii.234) is enlivening, suggesting that he
has been inspired in sleep to re-member the mutilated 'monstrosity' of
his country. Part of Richmond's energy resides in his ability to divide
himself over all parts of the battle. Where Richard by this point seems,
to adopt Ian Frederick Moulton's formulation, 'aggressively singular',
doomed to the sterile fate of a single 'monster' that, in the play, has
found it impossible to reproduce, Richmond appears vigorously multiple: 'I think there be six Richmonds in the field' (V.iv.11), the protagonist complains.[61] More importantly, perhaps, Richmond has a discursive
facility of 'monstrosity', which he both manipulates and reinstates.
Techniques of bodily demonstration come easily to Richmond – 'the
ransom of my bold attempt / Shall be this cold corpse upon the earth's
cold face' (V.iii.266–7), he exclaims – as does the exploitation of a variety
of 'monstrous' associations. When Richmond declares his victory, for
instance, he states that Richard, a 'bloody dog', is 'dead' (V.v.2). Here
several levels of 'monstrous' significance are at work. Along with the
pig, the dog was one of the final animal forms that, in Renaissance constructions, Proteus chose to inhabit.[62] In its allocation of a canine iden-

tity to Richard, therefore, Richmond's line suggests that the Protean 'monster' has reached the end-point of a transformative cycle. Now the essential, bestial essence of Richard has been realized. But the dog, like the hog, was also tied in the contemporary mind to other 'monstrous' relatives. 'Monsters' with dog-like faces were thought to inhabit the world's furthest reaches; infants resembling dogs were popularized as 'monstrous births'; and children delivered attached to dogs were seen as signs of political malfeasance (Figure 8).[63] Performing mongrels and children covered with canine fur, moreover, established dogs as a central symbolic utility in early modern fairground entertainments.[64] Clearly, not all of these constructions are summoned in Richmond's statement. Given the various permutations of 'monstrosity' that have circulated in the play, however, it might be suggested that Richmond labels Richard a dog to condemn the baseness of his 'monstrous' behaviour. In so doing, he exiles his enemy from the political arena and returns him to the fairground, to the impersonations and practices that once gave Richard a rhetorical advantage.

With Richard vanquished, Richmond is free to announce his plan for the reformation of England. His concluding address both reiterates the tropes of 'monstrosity' that have informed the play in its entirety and pushes them in some new directions:

> Inter their bodies as become their births . . .
> And then, as we have ta'en the sacrament,
> We will unite the white rose and the red.
> Smile, heaven, upon this fair conjunction,
> That long have frown'd upon their enmity . . .
> England hath long been mad, and scarr'd herself . . .
> O now let Richmond and Elizabeth,
> The true succeeders of each royal House,
> By God's fair ordinance conjoin together,
> And let their heirs, God, if Thy will be so,
> Enrich the time to come with smooth-fac'd peace,
> With smiling plenty, and fair prosperous days.
> Abate the edge of traitors, gracious Lord,
> That would reduce these bloody days again,
> And make poor England weep in streams of blood.
> Let them not live to taste this land's increase,
> That would with treason wound this fair land's peace.
> Now civil wounds are stopp'd; peace lives again.
>   (V.v.15, 18–21, 23, 29–40)

For a play keenly invested in body politics, this is a fitting conclusion. Bodies, first, will be suitably buried and not accorded the maimed rites of the start. No longer, therefore, are bodies able to speak acts of 'monstrous' significance: the reference to stopping 'civil wounds' is a reminder of the corpse of Henry VI, which, unstopped, communicated Richard's crimes. To these obsequies a sacramental dimension is attached. Earlier, the body of England had been desecrated, ravished and made 'monstrous' by Richard, a type of false Christ; now, however, the country's repair will be enabled by the idealized sexual union of Richmond and Elizabeth of York, which follows hard on the taking of communion and a celebration of an authentic deity's anatomy. Physical reparation is glimpsed, too, in the references to 'succeeders'. Because a true 'line' is restored in the 'lineaments' of Richmond and Elizabeth of York, two possibilities are avoided – the 'monsterization' of the nation and the ascension to the throne of a 'monstrous' interloper.

It is difficult to agree, therefore, with Robert C. Jones, who argues that 'Richmond offers the nation a new start, but not much sense of renewal'.[65] For what is enacted in Richmond is the process whereby England frees itself of the contortions that, visited upon its frame, have played havoc with temporal sequences. To pursue the metaphor, the body of the contortionist is finally assuming a more familiar outline. Some of this is registered in the use of the word 'fair', which occurs no less than seven times in the play's closing moments. Elsewhere in Shakespeare, 'fair' signifies physical 'perfection', and this is certainly the sense in which the term is being deployed here.[66] A more 'perfect' physical body is taking over from one 'monsterized' either through political vicissitude or through theatrical performance. Bodily wholeness restored, reproduction can be contemplated. As much as Richmond's speech institutes reintegration, so does it also anticipate fructification. At an immediate level, the process is political. In 1606, Edward Forset remarked that a 'Commonwealth . . . may (by the losse or want of her true subiects) become stark lame, or by some foule disorders made deformed and mishapen'. To 'redresse such . . . impotencies', Forset adds, 'she is driuen to . . . take vnto her new lymbs'.[67] Encoded in the word 'impotencies' is the suggestion that 'monstrosity' has robbed the commonwealth of its sexual vitality: only fresh appendages can restore a crucial reproductive power. In the middle stages of the play, such political commonplaces were misused (even 'monsterized') in Buckingham's persuasion to London's mayor and citizens. But with these final moments, thanks to Richmond's material and symbolic provision of 'increase', political theorization can be unproblematically reintroduced.

At another level, Richmond is stamped a reproductive figure because of his marriage. Elizabeth of York, it is contemplated, will be generative – the mother of 'heirs'. Given the location of *Richard III* in the 1590s, it is tempting to see in this prediction a wish-fulfilment scenario, a projection of miraculous fertility onto another Elizabeth, the ruling sovereign.[68] Because Richmond, as Henry VII, founded the Tudor dynasty, moreover, the play moves close to contemplating an incorporative solution to the succession problem – an inter-familial union between a representative of the Queen (Elizabeth of York) and the reigning monarch's grandfather. Within the context of the play, however, these incestuous implications are suppressed. Instead, the image of a fruitful Elizabeth of York becomes the means whereby the combat between women and Richard is simultaneously resurrected and resolved. For much of Act V, women have been conspicuously absent, a sharp contrast with their rhetorical prominence in Acts I, II and III. Now, in the parturient abilities of Elizabeth of York, we find a reformulation of the 'monstrous' rhetorical abilities of her female relatives. As an inheritrix, she metaphorically enjoys the qualities of her predecessors and infuses Richmond's words with their collective memories. Thus it is a colouring by a kind of femininity that makes the play's ending distinctive. Yet that femininity is also dependent on Richmond's masculinity, upon the 'plenty' through which he, too, is discovered. In this connection, the myth of Proteus is neatly inverted. As A. Bartlett Giamatti argues, Proteus was a double-sided 'monster' in the English Renaissance, both a conduit for animalistic negativity and an index of civility, concord, law-making, virtue and the 'writer's plenitude'.[69] It is not difficult to find in Richmond's 'plenty', and in his institution of 'peace', a recreation of this figure and the banishment of Richard's more destructive Protean tendencies. If Richard as Proteus is dismissed here, so are the 'monster' and the 'mola' to which the protagonist is also tied. To return to the opening anecdote about a woman's 'plenitude', we are left with the 'Man-child . . . that soon as it was christened . . . had very little life remaining in it'. Although Lemnius and Shakespeare are working at many removes, and offer very different conclusions to their respective narratives, it is tempting to see in the dramatist's Richmond a working through of the physician's 'Man-child' – a 'Christened' masculinity gives 'life' to a country in which 'monsters' and 'molas' have 'deformed' bodies 'natural' and 'politic'.

V

Richard III is a play rife with questions about future political develop-ment. It addresses such considerations as the perpetuation and repro-duction of the state, the instruments whereby the country's destiny can be predicted and the forms that the configuration of England will adopt. Embedded in the drama's fabric are reflections on the qualities required of a royal successor and on the ways in which the growth of the kingdom can be ensured. Put briefly, the drama looks backwards to con-template the treatment England might receive at the hands of history. In the same moment as it ventilates these preoccupations, *Richard III* speculates about the authority of those qualified to pronounce upon a nation's destiny – whether this be women or men – and sees in bodies both separate and whole convenient vehicles through which to communicate.

The immediate context for the play's political focus, this chapter has suggested, was the uncertainty attendant on the Elizabethan suc-cession. It is within such a framework, and alongside a sequence of prophecies about the succession that circulated throughout the 1590s, that we can begin to understand *Richard III*'s fascination with connec-tive 'lines', with degenerative animals, with 'monsters' that take time forwards and with 'molas' that time time back – the 'shapes' women create.[70] For a play informed by the declining presence of Elizabeth and the end of her 'line', it is perhaps not to be wondered at that women should feature as productive – generating spectacular images of them-selves, speaking with rhetorical copia, delivering predictions of apoca-lyptical confusion. Nor might it appear surprising that there should be an obsessive return to matters of material parturition. And, as we have seen, birth and 'monstrosity' in *Richard III* are frequently regarded as inseparable.

In the staging of its concerns, the play looks to 'monsters' for a pow-erful grammar of signification. 'Descanting' on 'deformity', *Richard III* exploits the strategies of both the fairground and the 'monster' pam-phlet. From the fairground 'monster'-booth it draws its use of language, spatial choreography, barriers to vision and scenes of revelation. In 'monster' literature it finds moral and physical equations, the provision of testimony and attempts to sort through questions of historical causal-ity. In these senses, *Richard III* would seem to imitate the representational trajectory of a play such as *Tamburlaine the Great* (1587–88). Unlike Marlowe's epic narrative, however, Shakespeare's drama pushes further its investment in the culture of the 'monster', conjuring the image of the 'monster'-booth to enable the audience to gaze at the spectacle of its country's political anomalies. Through types of 'monstrosity', it is suggested, spectators may be empowered to appreciate national as well as physical inner mysteries. 'Monsters' furnish expressive vocabularies for speculation about the unfolding of political organizations, since the very existence of the 'monster' necessitates an investigation into origins and influences. Similarly, while *Richard III*, in common with *Tamburlaine the Great*, explores the discursive possibilities of Revelation, that oft-cited location for 'monsters', it does so not to postpone the final end but to confirm its inevitability. Both a 'black intelligencer' (IV.iv.71) and a 'bloody dog' (V.v.2), Richard is cousin to the black dog described in a 1577 account of a disruption to a Norwich church service. The appearance of the dog, to the accompaniment of thunder, lightning and a tempest, causes the churchgoers to imagine that 'doomes day was already come'.[71] When Richard is visited with a canine identity in the play's concluding moments, therefore, it is in anticipation of the apocalyptical deliverance of a country he has ravaged and almost annihilated.

Richard III, then, does not rest on a straightforward rendering of 'monstrous' tropes or *topoi*. The play reworks the rhetorical appurtenances of 'monstrosity', testing and stretching terms and concepts that, only at the close, are conventionally reinstated. 'Monstrosity' is invoked in numerous senses, and Richard himself constitutes a confusing amalgam of single and multiple 'monstrous' features. Nor is Richard ever described as a 'monster': he is simply a composite of 'monstrous' markers and behaviours. This is an index, perhaps, of what happens to a discourse when politics appropriates it to meet a representational imperative. The particular conjunction of politics and 'monsters' in *Richard III* 'monsterizes' an already 'monstrous' language and institution, a reflection of the level of anxiety generated by the succession crisis in the 1590s. To judge from the end of the play, the solution to such processes of 'monsterization' is the installation of Richmond's unambiguous physical form: the 'monsterized' afflictions of England are cured through the ministrations of a perfecting anatomy. With Joseph Clark, too, one encounters the assumption that the non-normative body can be corrected, although, in this case, the famous surgeon '*Mullens*' refuses to 'undertake' a 'Cure'. In contemplating the possibility that the 'monster' can be returned to the fold of visual familiarity, *Richard III* looks forward to a later cultural obsession with correcting corporeal infraction. In the present historical juncture, physical difference is not so much an object of wonder as an experimental space in which medicine might practise its transformative and increasingly marvellous art. The futures inscribed in *Richard III*'s 'monsters' and 'molas' are Protean in the extreme.

4
'As it is credibly thought': Conceiving 'Monsters' in *Othello*

On 11 June 1569, a visitor with a memorable exhibition held court over the Durham citizenry:

> A certaine Italian brought into the Cittie . . . a very greate strange & monstrous serpent in length sixxteene feete in quantitie & dimensions greater than a greate horse which was taken & killed by special pollicie in Aethiopia within the Turke's dominions. But before it was killed, it had devoured (as it is credibly thought) more than 1000 persons And Allso destroyed a Whole Countrey.[1]

At once here it is the confused state of national boundaries that receives attention. An Italian has access to a region of the sub-Saharan continent, which itself is under Turkish control. Adding to the uncertainty is the vagueness surrounding 'a Whole Countrey', a fourth geographical entity which lacks a precise anchorage. Overshadowing territorial conjurations, however, is the emphasis on the preternaturally destructive capacities of the 'serpent'. From the point of view of a theatrical performance, an elaboration of the powers and provenance of the 'serpent' was no doubt the centrepiece of the presenter's 'spiel'. A relative of the travelling mountebank, the Italian, the passage suggests, framed his description within the parameters of sixteenth- and seventeenth-century travellers' tales, mapping a history of deliverance and conquest to extol the winning virtues of a 'monstrous' attraction.[2] In fact, in its representation of the 'extraordinary body' of the 'serpent', the report stands as a quasi-colonial narrative, a drama in which militaristic stratagems and annihilatory appetites loom large as the distinguishing features. Given that the account of the Italian's 'monstrous serpent' forms part of a local government parish register, which is otherwise preoccupied with the humdrum business of births and deaths, it seems that this non-domestic spectacle made a telling impact on its English audience. The 'serpent' is 'credible', I think, because its construction answers to prevalent assumptions about 'foreign' environments, and to anxieties about national fragility and dissolution, circulating in early modern culture. As such, this singular location of 'monstrosity' is acutely responsive to 'habits of thought', and to conceptual mechanisms, at work in the contemporary psyche.

Via a similar method of cultural mediation, *Othello* (1601–2) makes available a 'monstrous' construction of Africa which is accommodated within specifically English modes of interpretation and mentalities. Arguably, the play is able to execute this process so successfully because of exploiting the stereotypical associations of its Italianate affiliation. In particular, what *Othello* draws on is a range of 'monstrous' conceptions: these are represented in part as the 'action of conceiving, or fact of being conceived, in the womb'.[3] But they also appear variously as the mutually reinforcing attitudes of a social mindset, as twinned arrangements, as tokens of endearment and as failures of judgement. Together, the 'monstrous' conceptions of *Othello* call into question prescribed markers of national differentiation and highlight the pressured operations of early modern credulity. One of the animating impulses of the play – and here a further kinship with the spirit of the Durham description is afforded – is the endeavour to separate out, on the one hand, prevailing myths and errors about 'monsters' and, on the other, convictions based on authenticated report and 'ocular proof'.[4] In this respect, Shakespeare's drama reveals itself to be intriguingly situated at the inauguration of empirical philosophy.

Crucial to this dynamic, I will argue here, are those conceptions of Africa on which *Othello* trades. From Iago's perspective, Othello is an 'erring Barbarian' (I.iii.356), one 'defective' (II.i.228) in 'loveliness . . . sympathy . . . manners and beauties' (II.i.226–8). As the loaded terms of the speech suggest, Iago rehearses well-established views about the peoples of sub-Saharan regions. From at least the early sixteenth century onwards, links between Africa and 'barbarisme' were being promulgated in the popular imaginary.[5] So, too, were realizations which saw Africa as the repository of 'monstrous' indigenous inhabitants, of a population 'defective' in European standards of physical attractiveness. 'There be in [Africa] dyuers . . . of sondry physonomy and shape, monstrous . . . of . . . shewe', commented Joannes Boemus in 1555, anticipating Caius Julius Solinus' 1587 opinion on Ethiopia: 'in the furthest part . . . are nations of Monstrous . . . visages'.[6] Iago's racial 'othering' of

Othello both participates in and is in tension with such a configuration of Africa, for, as the expansion of European territories gathered pace over the course of the sixteenth and seventeenth centuries, and as the slave trade took on an increasingly institutional character, older, classical commonplaces were reworked to meet the demands for representation and description. Of course, many of these aspects of *Othello* have been touched on before. Numerous critics have focused on the play's absorption in issues of race, with Janet Adelman, Emily C. Bartels, Dympna Callaghan, John Gillies, Andrew Hadfield and Ian Smith claiming respectively that race functions as a mode of projection, as a free-floating signifier, as a constitutive element of theatrical impersonation, as a component of transgression, as a metaphor for Ireland and as a figure for the failure to perform a hegemonic rhetoric.[7] As part of an interest in teasing out *Othello*'s racial investments, a smaller group of critics has attended to questions of 'monstrosity': for instance, James R. Aubrey argues for the 'spectacular charge' of the play's 'monstrous' preoccupations; Karen Newman addresses gendered relations between 'monsters' and miscegenation; and Patricia Parker unravels 'monstrous' wordplay.[8] This chapter builds on both sets of critical work, contending that the multiple operations of race in *Othello* depend on a comparably broad and even diffuse spectrum of manifestations of 'monster'. *Othello* is distinctive for establishing converging and conflicting sites for 'monstrosity', upsetting, in the process, expectations about its conventional homes and alerting an audience to the dangers of mistaken identification. The result of the play's figurative refusals is not only to destabilize contemporary systems of classification; it is also to insist on the necessity for a type of reasoned response, one structured around codified modalities of 'thought' and belief. As this chapter argues, it is within the context of the play's insistence on rationality that we need to read its dialogue both with the philosophy of Francis Bacon and with the pursuits of the Royal Society. For, like the early scientific institutions of the seventeenth century, *Othello* rests finally as a dramatic library of rarities, a theatrical laboratory in which 'monsters' past and present, literal and material, vie for the investigative limelight.

I

Involvement in the multiplicity of *Othello*'s 'monstrous' conceptions is initially encouraged via Iago's animalistic account of the elopement. 'Even now . . . an old black ram / Is tupping your white ewe!' (I.i.87–8), he shouts to Brabantio, continuing, 'Arise, arise . . . Or else the devil will make a grandsire of you' (I.i.88, 90). At once, the sheepish substitution defamiliarizes Othello and Desdemona, the human players. Simultaneously, because of its mocking play with stolen possessions and nightime arousal ('ewe' puns upon 'you', and 'arise' hints at phallic tumescence), the speech identifies an illicit sexuality as motivating the couple's disappearance. Complicating the construction of sexual relations is the suggestion of a coming together of different groupings. Quickly, for instance, the genetically congruous 'ram' and 'ewe' are replaced by a more radically opposed species conjunction: a goat, commonly believed in the period to be one of the devil's many guises, will physically engage a sheep, blackening the purity of Brabantio's white status and debasing the nature of his paternal inheritance. Interestingly, by the time of *Othello*'s composition in 1601–2, inter-species sexual congress was invariably regarded as a transgression with a specifically African flavour. Thus Helkiah Crooke remarked in a 1631 medical treatise that 'in *Africa* where Beasts of diuers kinds meet . . . and mis-match themselves, there are often many Monsters generated'.[9] Such theories of reproductive hybridity and Iago's subsequent exclamations to Brabantio are mutually reinforcing. '[Y]ou'll have your daughter covered with a Barbary horse; you'll have your nephews neigh to you, you'll have coursers for cousins and jennets for germans!' (I.i.109–12), the ancient cries, his speech hinting at additional layerings of adulteration through the introduction to the Venetian's family of a 'barbaric' element (the 'Barbary horse'). Most worrying about this new arrival is its dismantling effect on national boundaries, for now north African blood (from 'Barbary') intermingles with an Iberian ingredient ('jennets' were small Spanish horses) in an imagined eradication of Brabantio's Italian ascendancy.

By conjuring Africa, Iago, in a dramatic anticipation of the 1631 medical treatise, is empowered to articulate the 'monstrous' resonances of Othello and Desdemona's union. If the continent informs the reference to the 'Barbary horse', so, too, does it animate Iago's claim to Brabantio that 'your daughter and the Moor are now making the beast with two backs' (I.i.114–15). Familiar from contemporary iconography as the 'beast with two backs' was the centaur, a 'monster' commonly located in, and associated with, Ethiopian regions.[10] Since the centaur was seen, in Eric C. Brown's words, as a miraculously 'single beast', Iago's centaurian implication is that Desdemona will be incorporated within, and distinguished by, Othello's African ancestry.[11] The 'beast with two backs' also recalls both Renaissance images of conjoined twins, which were popularized as locked in a dual-backed embrace in ballads and medical works, and the Ovidian emblem of the hermaphrodite.[12] Once again, in the play's symbolic economy, these implied 'monsters' work to Othello and Desdemona's detriment, underlining ideas of gendered confusion and quasi-incestuous physical intimacy. Emerging from the 'monstrous' appearance of Othello and Desdemona's love-making is its 'monstrous' potential. 'Making' is ambiguous, suggesting, as it does, both 'forming an image of' and 'materially creating'. 'Blackness', writes Arthur L. Little, 'figures as the ocular sign of a cultural need to create and destroy monsters: create them so that they may not create themselves; destroy them so that they may not procreate or multiply.'[13] In *Othello*, likewise, the 'monstrous' significance of a cross-racial encounter is imagined in its 'monstrous' progeny, in offspring that bears the hybridized, sinful traces of a metaphorically bestial origin.[14] Even the black progenitors of Iago's aside – 'Hell and night / Must bring this monstrous birth to the world's light' (I.iii.402–3) – replicate precisely such an engendering of 'monstrous' issue. Blackness will present Desdemona, the 'world's light', with a 'monsterized' Othello, a creation that will both sterilize the threat of the general's marriage and hasten his individual downfall.

In that Iago in this scene anticipates the eventual revelation of a 'monster', he in some senses discharges the responsibilities of the fairground 'Monster-Master'. Indeed, throughout the opening stages, the ancient aspires to this capacity, hanging out a metaphorical 'flag and sign' (I.i.154), deploying 'shows' (I.i.51) to elicit excitement and finally offering to lead the way to the site (or booth) where the 'monster' is accommodated – the 'Sagittary' (I.i.156). Signifying, as its does, the centaur, the tavern's name executes a number of tasks, reawakening memories of the 'Barbary horse', redirecting attention to the 'monstrous' sexual business of which Othello and Desdemona stand accused, and recalling the prospect of a degenerative transformation. Iago's demonstrative role has its place in, and exploits the preoccupations of, a culture in which blackness was frequently exhibited as a source of wonder and entertainment. At the marriage of James VI of Scotland to Anne of Denmark in 1589 in Oslo, the King arranged for a group of 'young Negroes' to dance 'naked in the snow in front of the royal carriage': although the record is brief, it would seem that the performance's aesthetic uniqueness was its mobilization of black forms against a white backdrop.[15] A comparable instance of display comes from a 1600 account of a public holiday in London during which 'a speciale place was builded onely for' the ambassador of the King of Barbary and his embassy 'neere to the Parke doore, to beholde that dayes triumph'.[16] 'From what we know of Elizabethan pageants and triumphs,' Jack

D'Amico states, 'these visitors must have been as much on view as viewing, a part of the exhibition and show'.[17] As in *Othello*, moreover, blackness becomes doubly intriguing to western eyes if it can be spectated upon as a sexualized curiosity. Thus, when an English woman married to a native Guinean gave birth, the father and child were soon constituted as visual attractions. Wrote George Best in 1578, possibly in the wake of a visit: 'I my selfe have seene an Ethiopian as blacke as a cole . . . who taking a faire English woman to wife, begat a sonne in all respects as blacke as the father was'.[18] The fascination of the pair, it would seem, lies in the intermingled racial/sexual history that their bodies enshrine: what is hinted at in Iago's reference to the 'Sagittary' is, in Best's description, played out for scopophilic potential.

Iago's demonstrative role is additionally notable for the ways in which its rhetorical characteristics are mimicked in Brabantio's paternal outrage. Hence, the presumed seducer of his daughter is immediately branded by Brabantio as 'Damned' (I.ii.63), a spiritual condition that chimes with Iago's earlier description of Othello as a 'devil' (I.i.90). A fresh charge is that Othello has 'corrupted' (I.iii.61) Desdemona through 'spells and medicines bought of mountebanks' (I.iii.62). Since fairground mountebanks were themselves visited with 'monstrous' designations in the contemporary consciousness, Brabantio's speech moves towards an elaboration of the 'monstrous' content of Iago's opening slurs.[19] In this sense, Iago seems not, as is traditionally thought, to enjoy an overarching agency; rather, his contribution accesses a shared culture of racism, patriarchy and visual discrimination, opening up an ideology of which he is only a partial representative.

Nowhere is this better illustrated than in the scene where Brabantio seeks to explain Desdemona's departure. Commenting on his daughter, he remarks: 'It is a judgement maimed and most imperfect / That will confess perfection so could err' (I.iii.100–1). As Ian Smith states, 'err' refers to 'geographic wandering . . . out of the proper limits'.[20] The verb-form, however, a relative of the noun, 'error', also connotes a 'mistake in the making of a thing, [a] miscarriage . . . [a] flaw [or a] malformation'.[21] In Brabantio's conception of events, therefore, Desdemona is becoming 'monstrous', unfixed (like the travelling mountebank) and (because 'gypsies' were traditionally the practitioners of fairground magic) even adversely racialized.[22] This, of course, is a paradoxical formulation, since Brabantio's convictions rest on a construction of Desdemona as 'perfection' and Othello, by implication, as 'imperfection', a term typical of pamphlets investigating 'monstrous births' and their causes.[23] Familiar, too, is Brabantio's reasoning that 'For nature so preposterously to err / Being not deficient, blind, or lame of sense, / Sans witchcraft could not' (I.iii.63–5). 'Erring' is being used richly here, I think, both in the sense of 'Error', the 'monster vile' and 'foule' in Book One of Spenser's *The Faerie Queene*, first published in 1590, and as an illustration of an 'error' of 'nature' – a 'monster' or *lusus naturae*.[24] As John Jonston wrote in a 1657 account of 'monstrous births': 'Nature in working intends her own businesse, but because divers obstacles may happen . . . it is no wonder if she erre sometimes.'[25] For Brabantio adequately to conceive of Desdemona's 'erring', Othello must be stigmatized as just such an 'obstacle', as a 'monster' who displaces 'nature' from an accustomed course.

By the time Othello makes his appearance on stage, therefore, an audience has been alerted to understanding him through various 'monstrous' registers. The protagonist's entrance confirms the implications of the opening excursus, but it also begins the process of uprooting conceptions of 'monsters' from their usual emplacements. Both a presenter who locates 'monstrosity' outside himself and a self-consciously fashioned exhibit boasting a wondrous lineage, Othello accords with the requirements of his culture and exceeds them in equal measure. He states:

> Her father loved me, oft invited me,
> Still questioned me the story of my life . . .
> I ran it through, even from my boyish days
> To th' very moment that he bade me tell it,
> Wherein I spake of most disastrous chances . . .
> Of being taken by the insolent foe
> And sold to slavery; of my redemption thence
> And portance in my travailous history . . .
> And of the cannibals that each other eat,
> The Anthropophagi, and men whose heads
> Do grow beneath their shoulders.
>   (I.iii.129–30, 133–5, 138–40, 144–6)

Like the Italian mountebank who, it seems, engaged the Durham populace by sketching the narrative odyssey of his 'monstrous serpent', Othello here offers a biography of himself similar to those accompanying contemporary exhibitions. To the rehearsal of his career, moreover, there is attached an emphatically stated theatrical aspect, with Othello performing to his on-stage audience. Unlike those sixteenth-century blacks on display in England, however, whose bodies could be read as statements of their enslaved condition, Othello commands attention because he has resisted a history of captivity. Othello in Venice is doubly 'extraordinary' – a 'barbarian' who has effected the classic early modern escape from 'Barbary' and gained deliverance.[26]

Othello's story also has a peculiarly gendered reception. This is indicated when he states that Desdemona 'gave me for my pains a world of sighs' (I.iii.160). As is the case so often in *Othello*, the formulation is ambivalent, both confirming the protagonist's association with popular commercial entertainment (Desdemona pays to hear a 'spiel' that smacks of the fairground) and distinguishing him from its debasing effects. By recalling her reception of his 'pilgrimage' (I.iii.154), for instance, Othello is able implicitly to challenge the claim that Desdemona orally swallowed 'some mixtures powerful' (I.iii.105); rather, he asserts, she aurally 'and with a greedy ear / Devour[ed] up [his] discourse' (I.iii.150–1). Specifically, the 'discourse' Othello offers Desdemona is a typical narrative of 'monstrosity', even if it is one that, in the early modern period, would have not always been deemed credible. While the existence of 'cannibals' was rarely in doubt, contemporary writers were more chary about the authenticity of the *anthropophagi* or 'men whose heads' grow 'beneath their shoulders'.[27] Of African '*others without heades*', William Cuningham commented in 1559, '*I suppose* [them] *fables rather then any truth*', while Samuel Purchas in 1613 was more categorical. These 'monsters', he writes, 'I neither believe nor report'.[28] In short, Othello mounts a version of sub-Saharan 'monstrosity' that sits uneasily with the emergent scepticism of the play's historical juncture. J. Hillis Miller has argued that 'each story and each repetition of it . . . leaves some uncertainty or contains some loose end unravelling its effect, according to an implacable law that is not so much psychological or social as linguistic'.[29] This, I suggest, is part of what an audience is encouraged to recognize in Othello's storytelling: the very familiarity of his elaborations of Africa sows doubts; the clichés he rehearses invite disbelief. For Othello, then, conceiving of himself involves not only demonstration and applause; it simultaneously necessitates the purposeful application of an outmoded 'monstrous' exoticism.

In particular, it would seem, Othello's self-dramatizations are directed towards Desdemona, who is seen as susceptible to them and appetitive for more. There is a mutually reinforcing link, for instance, between Othello's reflection upon his wife's 'greedy ear' and Iago's pronouncement that 'when she is sated with his body she will find the error of her choice' (I.iii.351–2). Several critics have attended to the points of intersection distinguishing the play's representation of appetite and sexuality, with Karen Newman commenting on the 'masculine fear of a cultural femininity envisioned as . . . always seeking increase', and Patricia Parker concentrating on the synecdochal link between the 'figures of the "Cannibals"' and Desdemona's 'form of domestic consumption'.[30] The connections pursued in this work are illuminating, but they neglect, I think, two further aspects of the oral/aural Desdemona, which are crucial for *Othello*'s subsequent development. First, because 'cannibals' were often conflated with more the obviously 'monstrous' *anthropophagi* in early modern travelogues, it might be argued that Othello's 'round unvarnished tale' (I.iii.91) witnesses the inception of his own construction of Desdemona as 'monstrous' other. Second, building on the representation of a Desdemona who is unwilling to discriminate between Othello's fictions, the play highlights the perils of female error. Making a choice on the basis of desire, Desdemona is inserted into an anti-rational space, into feminine modalities of 'thought' marked by vulnerability and credulity. Both dazzled female and sexually transgressive agent, Desdemona incarnates the attractions of the 'monster' while remaining central to its institution and future operations.

II

If particular manifestations of 'monstrosity' are forcefully linked to femininity, other incarnations attach themselves with a singular power to male figures. Notably, jealousy, famously personified as the 'green-eyed monster' (III.iii.168), is seen to have an instrinsically masculine habitation. As the allusion to 'green' implies, Othello is seen as 'monstrous' because overtaken by the bilious imbalance of his inner constitution; 'monstrosity' is additionally implied in, and racial categories further complicated by, the unexpected imposition of green eyes onto a black face. In a discussion of heterosexual relations, Emilia extends the figure of jealousy introduced by her husband to characterize a peculiarly gendered condition. 'They are not ever jealous for the cause, / But jealous for they're jealous' (III.iv.160–1), she states, figuring jealousy as an inherent part of the male psyche. Her conclusion – jealousy 'is a monster / Begot upon itself, born on itself' (III.iv.161–2) – assumes for the emotion a parthenogenetic independence: self-perpetuating, it has the capacity newly to create itself without recourse to outside assistance. For Desdemona, such a generative act is cerebrally based. 'Heaven keep that monster from Othello's mind' (III.iv.163), she states. Implying that jealousy will attack and colonize the conceptual mechanism itself, Desdemona focuses attention on the mobility of the emotion and on the ways in which the play's 'monstrosities' assume a variety of internal purchases.

The suggestion that 'monstrosity' finds its most convenient habitation in the brain is articulated by Othello himself. 'By heaven, [Iago] echo'st me' (III.iii.109), he cries, continuing:

> As if there were some monster in thy thought
> Too hideous to be shown. Thou dost mean something . . .
> And when I told thee [Cassio] was of my counsel
> In my whole course of wooing, thou criedst 'Indeed?'
> And didst contract and purse thy brow together
> As if thou then hadst shut up in thy brain
> Some horrible conceit.
>
> (III.iii.110–11, 114–18)

Commenting on Othello's conviction that his 'ancient' is metaphorically pregnant with a 'monster' of 'hideous' implications, Patricia Parker observes that these lines 'explicitly' recall 'the play's opening figure of a "purse" which can be opened and closed at will'.[31] Since a purse was a common Renaissance figure for the 'matrix' or the womb, one can assume that, again following Parker, the 'monstrous birth' will also reveal (and judge) the 'woman's secret place'.[32] While sensitive to the play's stylistic density, this reading bypasses, I think, the more important fact of Othello and Iago's doubled relations. Earlier, Othello had recourse to a fantasy of being 'twinned . . . at . . . birth' (II.iii.208). At this critical stage, a version of that dual delivery is realized, as Iago chimes with Othello ('thou echo'st me') in an antiphonal dialogue, repeating his replies, duplicating his questions and refusing to assume an individuated stance.

Not only does the 'monster' caged in Iago's head echo the condition of Othello himself; it is also strictly defended, accessible solely through a revelation that carries with it the possibility of greater intimacy.[33] The final lines of Othello's speech – 'If thou dost love me / Show me thy thought' (III.iii.118–19) – link disclosure with affirmation of amatory entanglement. Thus, the imagined birth betrays the 'secret' not so much of the 'woman's . . . place' as of the process whereby Othello releases his own 'monsters', a sequence of events that is essentially homoerotic rather than hetereosexual in orientation. Noting the 'symmetrical and exponential sexuality' of twins, Hillel Schwartz argues that 'the more pressing the ambiguities of our re-creations, the more we have looked toward binary pairs to determine how, one by one, each of us might make a stand'. The 'vanished twin', he goes on, 'the Control, stands proxy to our paradoxical sense of . . . incompletion', discovering 'our longing for a consummate companionship even as we exalt a unique personhood'.[34] In his quasi-sexualized connection to Othello, Iago, I suggest, represents just such a twin, a measure of the general's unfinished sense of himself, of his uncertain narrative repetitions, of his failure to secure Venetian integration. At the level of metaphor, the ancient will form another centaur or conjoined partnership, a twinned 'monstrosity' that the play has not yet properly envisaged.

The spectres of twinning and homoeroticism haunt, too, Iago's account of Cassio's dream:

> In sleep I heard him say 'Sweet Desdemona,
> Let us be wary, let us hide our loves,'
> And then, sir, would he gripe and wring my hand,
> Cry 'O sweet creature!' and then kiss me hard
> As if he plucked up kisses by the roots
> That grew upon my lips, lay his leg o'er my thigh,
> And sigh, and kiss, and then cry 'Cursed fate
> That gave thee to the Moor!'
>
> (III.iii.421–8)

Demonstrated by the ancient is the horror already in the general's mind – the prospect of an unchaste marital bed. Through the alliance with Othello, Iago thus puts a graphic gloss on a scenario which has so far lacked a fully realized visualization. The protagonist's exclamation – 'O monstrous! monstrous!' (III.iii.428) – suggests an internalizing of the 'monstrous' associations of his union with Desdemona, but, as a doubled response, it simultaneously points up his increasing twinship with Iago. Worryingly, this is a twinned combination imagined as rape: the allusions to picking flowers ('he plucked up kisses by the roots') imply defloration and thus disempowerment, the growing ascendancy of a dominant twin over his weaker and more credulous sibling. The critics Arthur L. Little and Ian Smith have detected homosexual dimensions to the relation of Cassio's dream and, certainly, in the dreamy substitution of Iago for Desdemona, there is an implicitly sodomitical element.[35] This is reinforced in the punning references to 'hand' (masturbation), 'hard' (tumescence), 'pluck' (coitus) and 'root' (the phallus).[36] But the passage's homoeroticism extends beyond the merely stylistic. Invariably labelled 'monsters' in early modern thought, 'sodomites' were additionally charged with themselves delivering 'monstrous' progeny; an early seventeenth-century medical authority wrote that 'vpon Sodomie . . . horrible Monsters haue been brought into the World'.[37] Iago's vision is 'monstrous' because it evokes a twinning that, transcending other relationships, carries 'monstrous' issue in its train.

Terms such as 'hide' and 'wary' establish Iago's speech as a representation of dissimulation and illegitimacy, opening up the possibility of another 'monstrous' identification. 'I have a pain upon my forehead, here' (III.iii.288), Othello states, attempting to excuse his infirmity but also anticipating the arrival of the cuckold's characteristic horned markers. This is elaborated on when, several scenes later, Othello announces: 'A horned man's a monster, and a beast' (IV.i.62). The line rehearses a conventional equation between cuckoldry and 'monstrosity'; at the same time, however, it reconnects Othello to the 'monstrous' and 'barbaric' races, to peoples from which, elsewhere in the play, he seeks to be distanced. For horned 'monsters' made up the so-called *cornuti*, popularly found in Ethiopia; as Donald Lupton noted in 1636: in 'some parts of this *Countrey* it is thought that there bee men with hornes . . . and . . . people that feede upon mans flesh, and devoure their own parents'.[38] The link developed here between the 'monstrous' races and the 'cannibals', whose practices, Lupton suggests, exhibit quasi-incestuous features, has a direct bearing on *Othello*'s construction of the protagonist's vacillating 'monstrosity'. Thus, condemning Desdemona, he is driven, in a radical racial readjustment, to exclaim: 'I will chop her into messes!' (IV.i.197). Both 'cannibals' and racialized 'others' lurk behind this statement, particularly in view of its similarity to Lear's comment on 'The barbarous Scythian, / Or he that makes his generation messes / To gorge his appetite'.[39] Despite earlier attempts to differentiate himself, Othello, it is implied, is re-racialized by the 'monstrosity' of his fictitious cuckoldry, prompted to revert to typical discourses of Africa and tempted even to imagine consuming his own kind.

The identification of a 'monstrous' cuckoldry is elaborated in *Othello*'s deployment of the associations of more familiar creatures. In this respect, Othello's parting shot to the Venetian representatives – 'Goats and monkeys!' (IV.i.263) – is peculiarly suggestive. Goats, of course, share kinship with cuckolds and devils, both of which, through the course of *Othello*, are visited with racially 'monstrous' characteristics. Monkeys, along with 'monsters', formed integral parts of contemporary fairground entertainments and represented, in addition, material and symbolic commodities.[40] As Kim F. Hall argues, 'exotic' apes constituted 'domesticated amusements . . . that emphasized the luxury and wealth of the owners'.[41] As well as signifying the loot of the imperial impera- tive, monkeys could be prominent players in the colonial discourses of the period: Sir Thomas Herbert's 1634 opinion, for instance, was that the animals were sexually used by African peoples.[42] Othello's simian identification, then, is illuminating at several levels, concatenating reflections upon possession and taming as well as miscegenation, parturition and display.

Both animals are evoked in the satyr, a mythical creature that com- bined the distinguishing features of the goat and the monkey and that was located in the global margins. 'Vnder the *Equinoctiall* toward the East & south,' writes Edward Topsell in a 1607 discussion of 'monsters', is found the 'Satyre', which 'in his head, face, horns, legs and from the loynes downwarde resembleth a Goat, but in his belly, breast, and armes, an Ape.'[43] Like the centaur, the satyr impresses as a twinned phenomenon, a confection of different parts that, nevertheless, func- tions as a coherent whole. 'Such a one,' Topsell continues, 'was sent by the king of *Indians* to Constantine . . . & when it was dead and bowelled, they poudred it with spices, and carried it to be seene at Constantinople.'[44] Not only is the satyr delineated here as a gift; it is also discovered as the typical target of a curious gaze. In the same way, Othello, in the scene leading up to his explosive invocation of goats and monkeys, is looked at as a 'monstrosity' fascinating in its hybrid- ity. Spectated upon by Iago and Lodovico, he is represented as an in- compatibly doubled personality, simultaneously a wife-batterer and the 'noble Moor whom . . . passion could not shake' (IV.i.264, 266). From a 'horned . . . monster', the play suggests, Othello is graduating to a less singular and assimilable type of 'monstrosity', an index of the conflicted density of his social behaviour.

Even those not traditionally tied to such a pejorative classifica- tion find themselves identified by a 'monstrous' label. Most obviously, the drama stages a revision to the conventional characteristics of its national constituencies, displacing 'monstrosity' from Turks to Christians even as it also gestures to the 'monstrosity' of Othello's African alterity. Thus, during the Cyprian brawl, the 'Christians', as Jack D'Amico states, 'like *anthropophagi*, attack one another' in a 'civil tempest'.[45] Not surprisingly, Othello is drawn to describe the generically blurred, and nationally shameful, riot as a 'monstrous' (II.iii.213) occur- rence. Chief among the disordered celebrants is Cassio who, implicitly twinned with the Turk, is made a 'monster', as the lieutenant's own negatively ethnicized reflections indicate. Only the 'bestial' (II.iii.260) part of himself remains, Cassio cries, now he has been 'transformed' (II.iii.288) by the 'devil' of 'drunkenness' (II.iii.291). Cultivation of the devil as a deity was everywhere apparent in Africa and the New World, sixteenth- and seventeenth-century travel narratives argued; 'wild beasts' were endemic; and the indigenous peoples betrayed an essentially 'bestial' nature.[46] Abetted by Iago, then, Cassio is driven to racialize himself, to see his loss of control as a lapse into a non-human condition. In reply, Iago deploys assurances of known, domestic species categorizations ('wine is a good familiar creature' [II.iii.304]), exacerbating the lieutenant's conviction of a 'monstrous' divagation from duty and virtue. And, once he has dismantled the subjectivity of his central affiliations, Cassio is suitably relocated, spending much of the rest of the play in its spatial perimeters.

If Cassio is earmarked with the stigma of Africa and Turkey, he is simultaneously, in a neat replication of the Othello/Iago equation, twinned with Desdemona, who is herself not unaffected by the play's unsettling distribution of its 'monstrous' conceptions. There is, in short, as Othello understands it, a 'monstrosity' attached to, and inhering in, Desdemona ('demona', interestingly, is etymologically linked to both 'monster' and 'demonstrate'). In the drama's central scenes, Othello gives vent to a belief in a 'monsterizing' nature, ventriloquizing Venetian culture's dominant interpretive paradigms: 'And yet how nature', he states, 'erring from itself' (III.iii.231). Meditating upon women's 'appetites' (III.iii.274) and labelling his wife a 'young and sweating devil' (III.iv.42), Othello thus imbues Desdemona with demonic and quasi-'cannibalistic' qualities. Matching the 'monster' sensed by Othello is, as Joseph A. Porter comments, a 'subliminal demon' which 'works mischief with Desdemona's name'.[47] Indeed, on three occasions, Othello calls his wife 'Desdemon' (III.iii.55, IV.ii.42 and V.ii.279): at once a term of endearment, the abbreviation also conveys reduction and belittlement. Such a demonic diminution of Desdemona belongs with that process of racializing 'monstrosity' which the play pursues elsewhere. It depends, too, upon the gendered lead set in contemporary colonial narratives, in which indigenous women, in particular, were viewed as 'monstrous', devilish, appetitive and sexually indiscriminate.[48] A 1597 comment of Jan Huygen van Linschoten's on Angola is typical: 'the women [are] much giuen to lust and vncleanenesse, specially with straungers, which among them is no shame'.[49] For Othello, then, Desdemona becomes the metaphorical analogue to his own 'monstrous' blackness, a woman whose 'monstrous' lapse from 'nature' can only be registered in racial rhetoric. 'Her name, that was as fresh / As Dian's visage,' Othello states, 'is now begrimed and black / As mine own face' (III.iii.389–91). According to the logic entertained by Othello, chastity inevitably degenerates into immodesty, fairness into blackness and 'perfection' into 'monstrosity', with Desdemona manifesting the whole spectrum of these antithetical binaries. At the level of nationality, moreover, despite their innocence, both Desdemona and Cassio are key to the play's endeavour to resituate 'monsters' geographically, for *Othello* forces 'monstrosity' into a peculiarly Italianate mould, privileging not so much its barbarism as the imagined multiplicity of its 'civil' (IV.i.64) and local disguises.

III

Throughout *Othello*, the claims and accusations that complicate its fabric are subjected to scrutiny. Even at the start, the vulgarized, 'superstitious' charges laid at Othello's door are thrown into relief by the will of the Venetian senate to judge their valued general more favourably, and this pattern of testing allegations is extended when Brabantio's narrative of forced abduction is challenged by Desdemona's elaboration of her willing submission 'to the Moor my lord' (I.iii.189). By recasting the same stories in several forms, the play continually displays an urge to question the evolution of its own assumptions. At the same time, *Othello* highlights the need for additional information, stressing the inherent partiality of the representational imperative.

Part and parcel of such an interrogative procedure is the play's attitude towards the interpretive utility of 'proof'. On the level of rhetoric, *Othello* privileges tangibly apprehended varieties of 'proof', part of its emphasis on, in Virginia Mason Vaughan's phrase, investigative modes of 'rational deliberation'.[50] 'Proof', in these cases, is elaborated as a type of demonstration, an agent for exposing 'error', and its production is invariably associated with exhibition. Thus, with the Venetian senate, verbal argument only achieves validity via the promise of material evidence ('To vouch this is no proof, / Without more certain and more overt test' [I.iii.107–8]), while, in Othello's case, apparently irrefutable 'facts' demand the display of a corresponding 'ocular proof' (III.iii.363) as support. However, as Katharine Eisaman Maus has noted, juries in early modern England 'made . . . no qualitative distinction among kinds of proof until well into the seventeenth century'.[51] Hence, Iago's claim that the recollection of his night with Cassio 'may help to thicken other proofs / That do demonstrate thinly' (III.iii.432–3) indicates both the accumulations of 'proof' experienced by contemporary courts and the ways in which such an emphasis on accreted materiality can fall prey to fraudulent impersonation.

Vital to any accumulation of 'proof' in this play, fraudulent or otherwise, is visual testimony. Clearly, the implied ideal is that the efficacity of the eye is paramount: 'I'll see before I doubt' (III.iii.193), states Othello, positing the primacy of experiential perception over and above the spectre of intellectual cogitation. But, all too frequently, a complicating scenario is in evidence, with the optical instrument being represented as overruled by mental processes. Iago's account of the origins of his malcontented sensibility is pertinent here. 'His Moorship' (I.i.32) ignored 'what his eyes had seen', Iago claims, 'the proof' (I.i.27) of the ancient's military pre-eminence. Galling for Iago, then, is that the power of vision has been compromised, replaced by non-visual mechanisms of judgement. The idea that the eye can be misled is returned to when the First Senator describes the Turkish fleet bound for Rhodes as 'a pageant / To keep us in false gaze' (I.iii.19–20). A persuasive fiction, the pageant points up optical trickery as a weapon of war in a rehearsal of *Othello*'s larger visual dynamic.

Attending to repeated invocations of 'proof' and the eye in *Othello* enables us to think differently about the 'monstrous' conceptions it mobilizes. Indications that vision can be deceived function as a warning that 'monstrosity' itself might constitute an 'error' of ocular experience. Indeed, such a possibility is enacted when Othello identifies a 'monstrosity' in Iago's visually charged fantasies. Everywhere in the play, furthermore, the responses elicited from the eye are juxtaposed with the reactions stimulated by a 'monster', never more obviously than when the sight of Desdemona produces a 'wonder' in Othello as 'great as' his 'content' (II.i.181): as in the 'monster' pamphlet, the protagonist reads visual pleasure in terms of an ability to marvel. Peter G. Platt reminds us that 'wonder and inquiry frequently are linked and are not oppositional concepts in early modern thought'.[52] We should not be surprised, therefore, that the eye in *Othello* is simultaneously registered as a mechanism for furthering curiosity and facilitating disclosure. On one occasion, Iago likens Othello's persistent questioning to a species of 'scanning' (III.iii.249): with its in-built pun on attempting to establish metrical correctness, this visually freighted term suggests minute examination. If Othello at this point resembles a poetic commentator, he also begins to take on some of the properties of a quasi-scientific researcher aiming to unveil 'truths' through visual investigation.

In fact, by privileging the eye semantically, the play provides a place for the protagonist as a pioneer in the arts of discovery, a demythologizing detective who aims to engineer enlightenment. Via the gathering of 'proof', Othello plans not only to expose women's inner mysteries – unlocking the 'closet' of their 'secrets' (IV.ii.22), in his words – but also to delve into and unravel the causes of more general conundrums. His lamenting refrain in the closing scene – 'It is the cause, it is the cause, my soul!' (V.ii.1) – reveals him simultaneously as a man with an evangelical mission to eradicate immorality and as a seeker after all-embracing explanations. As such, he can appear as one means whereby the various 'monstrous' conceptions that have circulated in the play world as a whole will finally be sorted and elucidated. The trend, notably in the work of Patricia Parker, has been to tie such tendencies in *Othello* to broad European developments in 'science and anatomy'.[53] However, the individualized concentration on Othello's manifesto suggests the utility of a complementary but narrower and more local interpretive template. By teasing out the particularities of the natural philosophy of Francis Bacon, an alternative perspective on the play's preoccupations is afforded, one that locates the virtues of 'proof' and vision in a specific, circumscribed and peculiarly English intellectual *œuvre*.

Although Bacon held the expanding scientific establishment at a dismissive distance, ignoring the work of William Harvey on the circulation of the blood and branding as an occultist fantasy William Gilbert's theories of magnetism, he did represent perhaps the most powerful voice in a related move to reform existing knowledge, to organize those species of plants, minerals and animals coming to European attention, to compile a register of natural history via rational criteria, and to agree on a nomenclature for collecting, describing and laying bare 'wonders' of the universe.[54] To this end, Bacon, particularly in *The Advancement of Learning*, composed in 1603–4, sets himself against the influence of 'superstitious narrations of sorceries, witchcrafts, dreams, divinations, and the like', judging them antithetical to the pursuit of 'truth' and a damaging inspiration to 'high and vaporous imaginations' that 'beget hopes and beliefs of strange and impossible shapes'.[55] As a means of offsetting such dangers, Bacon approves the virtues of his own conceptual tools, underscoring in *The Advancement of Learning* the need for 'Proofs and Demonstrations' and elaborating in *The Great Instauration* (1620) the advantages of visual evidence, of, in Denise Albanese's words, a 'scopic regime' of 'ocular assignment': 'I admit nothing but on the faith of the eyes, or at least of careful and severe examination; so that nothing is exaggerated for wonder's sake, but what I state is sound and without mixture of fables or vanity.'[56] These are the methods, Bacon suggests in *Novum Organum* (1620), whereby 'secrets' housed in the 'womb of nature' may be put to 'excellent use'.[57] Clearly, there are echoes here of *Othello*, which suggests that the protagonist's predilection for 'demonstration', and attachment to ocular testimony, have their places in a larger cultural network. Viewed in Baconian terms, the play stands both as a contributor to a shift in sensibility, itself a participant in an epistemological process, and as a product of a move towards empiricism. In addition, because Bacon genders the confrontation with 'nature', imaging 'secrets' as properties that have practical applications and favouring, in Evelyn Fox Keller's formulation, 'male imagery' of 'sovereignty, dominion and mastery', Othello's own role is complicated.[58] If the behaviour of Shakespeare's protagonist is energized by its associations with 'scientific' analysis, it is equally invigorated by its kinship with practices of dissection and the accumulation of bodily knowledge; as Bacon aspires to dominion over a hidden, female and 'natural' interior, so does Othello strive for a similar control over his wife's mysterious interstices.

But it is through 'monsters' that Bacon's philosophical project most eloquently articulates its themes, reinforcing Paulo L. Rossi's view that the inclusion of 'monstrous' forms in contemporary 'encyclopaedic works' registered a drive to 'achieve insight into universal principles by creating a harmonic, microcosmic synthesis'.[59] 'Monsters', for Bacon, as his *Novum Organum* indicates, do indeed appear inseparable from larger accumulative imperatives: 'We have to make a collection or particular natural history of all prodigies and monstrous births of nature,' he states, 'of everything in short that is in nature new, rare, and unusual. This must be done however with the strictest scrutiny, that fidelity may be ensured.'[60] Central to the enterprise is the valorization of 'scrutiny', a means of sifting the genuine from the counterfeit. Bacon, in fact, rationalizes a procedure for distinguishing a generative falsehood that finds its most eloquent manifestation in artificially created types of 'monstrosity': in *New Atlantis* (1624), the fictional 'Father' of Salomon's House describes 'means to make commixtures and copulations of different kinds; which have produced many new kinds, and them not barren, as the general opinion is'.[61] What is 'monstrous', then, may well be erroneous and, certainly, across Bacon's prose works, error is tied to trickery, and misapprehension is regarded as a species of 'monster' ripe for eradication: there are numerous references to 'defects', 'deficiency', 'errors' and 'wandering', which, as *Othello* shows, carry charged 'monstrous' meanings in their wake.[62] Judged against a Baconian paradigm, the play's construction of Desdemona's 'erring', and Brabantio's belief that her integrity must be examined, appear not so much as a summation of patriarchal anxieties as a dramatic rehearsal of emergent philosophical precepts. If Shakespeare's play can be seen as staging a theatrical recreation of a theoretical model, then Bacon's testimonies of 'proof' and the 'eye' come close to being granted a psychological enactment.

In that *Othello* represents a type of philosophical realization, the play gestures towards the Royal Society, which, in the later seventeenth century, sought through experiment and publication to put Bacon's ideals into practice. Despite the contrasting positions entertained by the earliest learned societies – neo-Aristotelians consorted with utilitarians and neo-Platonists – its members were united in a co-operative endeavour to improve knowledge, to exchange information and, in particular, to pursue all matters 'monstrous'.[63] The correspondence, reports and transactions of the institution disclose the investigative lure of cross-species animal productions, conjoined twins, hairy children, hermaphrodites and 'monstrous' calves, some examples of which were preserved in 'cabinet' form at Gresham College.[64] Perhaps of greater interest, however, are the means whereby debate and experiment were conducted. As Lorraine Daston and Katharine Park observe, 'high social standing and good will were not enough: specialist knowledge was also required . . . natural philosophers repeatedly cautioned one another on the dangers of credulity and on the need to sift the evidence of witnesses with great care'.[65] By prioritizing an interrogative treatment of representation, *Othello* captures the spirit of a developing discipline, one that finds its final form in a codified method for assessing the ontological status of 'belief'. In a similar vein, when the play puts on trial the claims of its witnesses, it does so through recourse to its highest represented authority: as an aristocratic voice of presumed impartiality, the Venetian senate works, like the Royal Society, as a final port of call, the yardstick with which 'monstrosities' of 'nature' and behaviour can be measured and judged.

More generally, the dialectic obtaining between the play and the institution is strengthened by the ways in which the activities of the Royal Society were envisaged in the social imaginary. When contemporaries extolled the virtues of the *cognoscenti*'s newly-founded 'scientific' seat, they did so in terms that replicated and focused the associations of *Othello*'s 'monstrous' languages. In a 1663 poem to the Royal Society, Abraham Cowley writes of the philosopher drawing the populace from 'errors of the way' and exposing the vacuity of 'painted Scenes, and Pageants of the Brain' (popular modes of theatrical representation are here seen as barriers to authentic discovery).[66] The idea is refined by Robert Hooke in a 1665 preface about the microscope; juxtaposing descriptions of a deceptively '*visible World*' and the superiority of a tested ocularity, he comments that, '*not having a full sensation of the Object, we must be very lame and imperfect in our conceptions about it*'.[67] Similarly admonitory was Thomas Sprat who, in a 1667 manifesto for the Society, concluded that its members must 'cleavest themselves of many vain conceptions . . . which lye like Monsters in their way'.[68] To this end, he advises, 'the knowledge of *Nature*' has to be separated from 'the devices of *Fancy*, or the delightful deceit of *Fables*'.[69]

The point – that the mind, distracted by cultural myth, is capable of bodying forth 'monstrous' inventions – lies, of course, at the epicentre of *Othello*. Through the destructive cooperation of Iago, Othello collapses back into the 'devices of *Fancy*' and the 'deceit of *Fables*'. Of course, such devices in this play have an adversely racial cast; the black imagination is delineated as inherently impressionable. For Othello, whose rhetorical methods, following Bacon, exaggerate 'for wonder's sake', is allowed to become the victim of 'high and vaporous imaginations' and, in particular, of the 'dreams' his ancient manufactures; even as he agitates for empiricist readings, it is suggested, the protagonist displays the impossibility of his ever securing them completely. No less catastrophically, Othello falls prey to Bacon's brand of 'divinations' (Iago's portentous predictions) and 'superstitious narrations' (unsubstantiated rumour-mongering). In so doing, he begins to tread the route Bacon so stridently advises against, begetting beliefs of 'strange and impossible shapes' and moving ever closer to Brabantio's universe of legerdemain and magic. It is telling that, to cite Bacon once more, Othello's final location bypasses the corridors of academe for cultural memories of 'sorceries and witchcraft'. It may be, of course, that these examples of a lack of behavioural rigour merely refract the racial ingredients of the play's ideological underpinnings. Contemporary 'scientific' developments were intricately bound up with colonial expansion and, since both are formative influences on Shakespeare's drama, Othello's own role splits unexpectedly. For the 'empiricist' scientist, who levelled his gaze at women, 'monsters' and racial others, even, on some occasions, placing dried or flayed bodies of Africans in 'cabinets of curiosities', was invariably white; as the play's only black representative,

Othello, by contrast, is theoretically anomalous as a investigative force.[70] As such, Othello not only implicitly usurps the prerogatives of the Venetian senate but also has the effect of destabilizing some of the rational assumptions on which its operations depend. One of the most arresting aspects of *Othello* is that its protagonist emerges not so much as a product of imperialism as its most unlikely practitioner.

At the same time, *Othello*'s recuperation of a 'superstitious' *mentalité* illuminates the porous boundaries of the 'new science' itself. A range of arcane and esoteric influences impacted on Bacon's thought.[71] As Charles Webster states, despite 'rhetoric to the contrary', Bacon 'was not able to disentangle himself from the metaphysical suppositions of many of the natural magicians and alchemists falling under his censure'.[72] He adds, significantly, that 'we find circumstantial evidence suggesting the waning of interest' in witchcraft and sorcery among the élite, 'but very little explicit defence of the sceptical position'.[73] Thus it is difficult to pinpoint a clear pattern of growing 'naturalization' or 'rationalization' over the course of the period; on the contrary, the so-called 'scientific' seventeenth century was marked by a discursive plurality and polysemy.[74] It is into such a matrix that the culminating moments of *Othello* can be most usefully inserted. In particular, it is through the Baconian notion of 'vanity' or 'vain conceptions' that the play best registers its responsiveness to the 'natural philosophies' of its historical moment. Crucially, 'vanity' finds a material equivalent in *Othello* in the handkerchief, a 'trifle' (V.ii.226) that accrues to itself a range of metaphysical and 'monstrous' signifiers. In so doing, the handkerchief crystallizes debate about types of 'proof' and brings to a critical head the play's 'conceiving' processes.

Huston Diehl has written that the handkerchief in *Othello* is used to advance 'fundamental questions about seeing, knowing, and believing, questions that are at the heart of sixteenth-century religious reforms'.[75] While the thrust of this argument is persuasive, it is also important to note that the theatrical property is not always invested with theological associations and takes on contrasting meanings according to its particular representational circumstances. In one of the first allusions to the handkerchief, for example, Desdemona states: 'I had rather have lost my purse / Full of crusadoes' (III.iv.25–6). At once these lines, punning on the purse and the womb, equate the disappearance of the handkerchief with the assumed ruin of Desdemona's virtuous sexual reputation. But there is also a deeper level of suggestion that furthers Desdemona's movement back into the 'superstitious' niches of Othello's consciousness. In contemporary popular literature, the fairground was represented as a dangerously eroticized and often peculiarly feminized space. A 1641 pamphlet describes an environment where 'many a handsome wench exchanges her maidenhead for a small favour, as a moiety of bone-lace . . . or the like toye' while issuing a saucy warning against cut-purses who conspire to 'make a motion into [a woman's] pocket, which is the . . . way to move you to impatience'.[76] *Othello* brings together these pieces of popular lore, constructing Desdemona as having had stolen from her a 'trifle' (her handkerchief) that imperils her chastity. Both play and pamphlet figure loss as an invasive action carrying with it potentially disastrous consequences, and both imply an equation between female negligence and a lack of bodily restraint.

By association, then, the play's leading characters are reconnected with an anti-rational sphere through the handkerchief, even with anxieties about damaging liaisons, impressionability, persuasion, exchange and the laxity of sexual discipline. Some of these constellations of implication are at work in Othello's description of the hand-kerchief's genealogy, which, interestingly, dwells not on hard-and-fast visual specificities but on looser, oral forms of testimony:

> That handkerchief
> Did an Egyptian to my mother give,
> She was a charmer and could almost read
> The thoughts of people. She told her, while she kept it
> 'Twould make her amiable and subdue my father
> Entirely to her love; but if she lost it
> Or made a gift of it, my father's eye
> Should hold her loathed . . .
> 'Tis true, there's magic in the web of it.
> A sibyl that had numbered in the world
> The sun to course two hundred compasses,
> In her prophetic fury sewed the work . . .
>
> (III.iv.57–64, 71–4)

Immediately obvious is the stress upon national mixtures and vernacu-lar influences. If an earlier 'gypsy'-mountebank provided Othello with character-altering potions, here, another 'gypsy', an Egyptian fortune-teller, furnishes the mother of 'the Moor' with an equally transforma-tive handkerchief. The effect of the recapitulation is to identify Othello increasingly with the taint of the fairground, with discursive modes that, over the course of the play, have taken on a pejorative connota-tion. By the same token, the ways in which the handkerchief is realized cut Othello off from Bacon's ideal investigative paradigm. Because he reads the handkerchief according to divination rather than 'scientific' logic, Othello is relocated to a narrative realm of 'sorceries'; and because he sees in his mother's inheritance magical powers, he is returned to a familiar landscape of 'witchcraft'. In this connection, it is perhaps not surprising that the 'eye', the seat of Baconian wisdom, is corrupted (what it perceives is 'loathed'), while 'fancy', that erring element of the imaginative faculty, is allowed to roam freely. For a brief moment, the play offers another bridge both to Robert Hooke's conception of *'lame and imperfect'* sensory apprehensions and to Thomas Sprat's 'false Images' that, 'like Monsters', interfere with authenticating analysis.

That the handkerchief represents a species of 'monster' is, indeed, not difficult to argue. First, the handkerchief shares a hybridized and adulterated history, having a simultaneously African and Egyptian lineage: the play has already demonstrated how 'monstrosity' is thought to reside in such cross-fertilizing conjunctions. Second, Othello advertises the properties of the handkerchief as if he were boasting of the virtues of a 'monster', his litany of the prized item's fabulous effects bearing more than a passing resemblance to the 'spiel' of the 'Monster-Master'. Thus it is that Desdemona is discovered as being moved to describe the handkerchief as a 'wonder' (III.iv.102). The term, enlisted so often as a synonym for the 'monster', both clarifies and places a heightened interest on the multiplicity of the handkerchief's 'monstrous' qualifications.

But it is perhaps in the handkerchief's broader dramatic effects that its deepest 'monstrosities' dwell. As the sight of the basilisk was rumoured to afflict the beholder's vision, so does the handerkerchief poison Othello's eye. Hence, he immediately requests 'poison' (IV.i.201) to dispatch his wife. The charismatic object, we might also note, is 'Spotted with strawberries' (III.iii.438), a fruit that, as James R. Aubrey states, is 'most commonly associated with maternal cravings'.[77] In the same way that the 'monster' was believed, via the eye of the mother-to-be, to be capable of distorting the shape of the unborn child, so does the handerkerchief inflame Othello's internalized burdens, the barbarism and jealousy that, only in the final scenes, gain release. Judged within the context of contemporary theories about the 'monsterizing' effect of maternal impressions, it might be suggested, then, that the handkerchief stands finally as a white page onto which is projected the 'monstrous' blemish of Desdemona's presumed guilt and infamy. In this process, Othello is figured as himself a type of mother, giving birth, because of a psychological imprint, to the handkerchief's symbolic potential. Of course, in his endeavour, Othello cannot practise a masculine version of 'scientific' objectivity; rather, he finds in the handkerchief an opportunity to pursue the traditional 'fancies' of the female imagination.

Contemporaries fascinated by maternal impressions were equally interested in the extent to which colour as well as form could, through the pregnant mother's invention, play itself out on foetal material. Dramatists and medical authorities took delight in listing occasions on which, because of an arresting hue that had caught the female eye, speckled lambs had been born to white sheep, piebald colts to white mares and black children to white parents.[78] Thus, in *Othello*, the dappled appearance of the handkerchief alerts an audience once again to the infinitely inconsistent nature of the ocular experience and, in particular, to the role of gender in the operation of vision. No less powerfully, the handkerchief's visual characteristics assume a racial dimension. It is as if the white and red combination inscribed on the handkerchief recalls the white and black conjunction of Othello and Desdemona at the same time as it registers the marginal position of the black protagonist in white Venetian society. Moreover, because red was typically falsified as a cosmetic that, in Annette Drew-Bear's phrase, covered 'white . . . modesty and virtue', and because 'blackness', according to Dympna Callaghan, was defined as an 'ornament, as an overlay of whiteness', one might also argue that these colours ultimately aspire to essentializing a white 'nature'.[79] Via an association with imitation, representation and concealment, the play's dominant colours seem to work towards a view of the world founded upon familiarly western hegemonic distinctions.

The background of the handkerchief is thus the blank canvas on which is played out a narrative intersection of 'monstrosity', race, gender and generation. Part of that narrative involves Desdemona's death at her husband's hands and, in this regard, it is suggestive that the drama establishes a link between the handkerchief and the bed-sheets, which, 'lust-stained' in Othello's mind, will 'with lust's blood be spotted' (V.i.36). The 'spotted' bedclothes recall a birthmark, which, as Oberon's benediction in *A Midsummer Night's Dream* (1595–96) makes clear, could sometimes be confused with more 'Despisèd' and 'prodigious' 'blots' dealt by 'nature's hand'.[80] At the same time, the bedsheets indicate the divided state in which Othello finally finds himself. On the one hand, since Desdemona dies by strangulation and no blood is spilled, the plan to soil the linen of the marital chamber remains a 'fancy' only, even an 'error' or a 'monster': Othello is now wholly encased within an imaginative sphere characterized by false impressions. We are left sensitized to the flaws inherent in a system of knowledge that systematizes sight as an answer to interpretive difficulty. On the other hand, even if the 'spotted' bedding remains illusory, the bed itself is a potently material presence, a signal reminder on stage of the abusing fictions that have fuelled Othello's gullibility. The bed, in fact, represents an ultimate form of 'proof': the 'sight' (V.ii.205) it contains eventually brings Othello to his senses, while the history inscribed upon it provides the Venetian delegation with incontrovertible evidence of their general's decline.

IV

Continual references to the bed in the last act tantalize with suggestions of expectancy and encourage speculation about a momentous exposure. 'Alas, what does this gentleman conceive?' (IV.ii.97), asks Emilia, clarifying the construction of Othello as a worryingly unknowable reproductive source. Practical business, such as when Othello closes and opens the curtains around the bed, adds weight to the sense of an imminent discovery: it is as if the protagonist, who has already assumed for himself some of the rhetoric of the 'Monster-Master', is preparing to produce his masterpiece.[81] Indeed, the increasingly theatrical tenor of these scenes confirms them as a variation on a 'monster' exhibition, suggesting an institutional tension between 'scientific' modalities of representation and those drawn from popular entertainment practices.

Hand-in-hand with the crescendo movement goes the play's increasing dependence on a grammar of 'unnatural' delivery. 'What's the matter?' (V.ii.105), asks Othello, bringing a run of references to 'matter' to a climax.[82] Edward Pechter writes that Othello's question epitomizes the 'anguished perplexity of the characters in the face of an often threatening action whose contours need to be defined'.[83] I would suggest, instead, that 'matter' is more obviously pertinent as a teasing variant on the 'mother' (or *mater*): through its evocation of such linkages, the drama invites an audience to meditate on the causes or origins of the event about to take place. It is significant, moreover, that 'matter' is returned to as a salient term precisely at those moments when questions of culpability and responsibility are in the air. As Anny Crunelle-Vanrigh observes in a discussion of *The Tempest* (1611), however, both 'matter' and 'mother' also share an etymological kinship with the 'monster', which suggests that, in *Othello*, the 'matter' on the point of emergence is 'monstrous' in proportion and implication.[84] What Act V discloses to us is a 'monster', a 'mangled matter' (I.iii.173) nurtured by, and about to be born to, the feminized imaginative faculty of Othello himself.

An additional indication of an approaching catastrophe is registered in the play's thematic concatenation of all of its synonyms for the 'extraordinary body'. By invoking variously the 'abortive' (V.ii.55–6), the 'error' (V.ii.108) and the 'fault' (V.ii.334) in its dénouement, *Othello* both wraps up into one 'monstrous act' (V.ii.186) the multiple conceptions with which it has been concerned and recalls the fact that, over the course of the drama, 'monstrosity' has been a shifting phenomenon, an unstable signifier and a locus of competing investigation and theoretical projection.[85] In a move that bespeaks a Baconian impulse to map each variety of 'monstrosity', the play also frames its culminating conflicts in apocalyptical terms. Not only does Othello read Desdemona's terrified expressions as 'portents' (V.ii.45) of her end; he simultaneously predicts that a 'huge eclipse / Of sun and moon' (V.ii.98–9) and a trembling of the 'affrighted globe' (V.ii.99) will accompany the 'alteration' (V.ii.100) of her extinction. David Robson notes that 'although apocalyptic discourse aims to define, contain, and domesticate otherness, it also serves to *reveal* the other'.[86] Through apocalyptic conjurations, Othello is constructed as aiming to reveal Desdemona's otherness, the 'monstrosity' to which she has been allied in his invention. And, in the demonstration, there will also be definition, conclusive 'proof' of her presumed fall from grace. These suggestions coalesce in Othello's statement that he will 'Put out the light!' (V.ii.7). Earlier, Iago imagined Desdemona as a 'light' besmirched by a 'monsterized' Othello; now, developing that metaphor, Othello determines to snuff out his wife's radiance because of the 'monstrosity' with which he thinks she is tainted. As this promise of a universal end gathers force, Othello, a type of black God, threatens to visit upon the world the colour of an ineluctable darkness.

It would seem, at once, as if such dramatic sequences push to their fullest extent both assumptions about, and expectations attached to, 'monsters'. Certainly, there is abundant evidence to suggest that the 'monster' exhibition is granted an ultimate consummation. Barbarity is enacted in the twinned deaths of Othello and Desdemona; a 'monster' is catastrophically released from his civil confines. In this sense, as Michael Neill observes, the ending 'enacts a violent re-absorption into the domain of the Other', part of the play's 'progressive racialization of the protagonist'.[87] The fulfilled horrors of Act V notwithstanding, *Othello*'s dénouement has been traditionally seen as resisting the delivery of its promises, particularly in the case of Iago. From the start, Iago

1. Margaret Vergh Griffith.

2. Mary Davis.

3. Barbara Urselin.

4. Tannakin Skinker.

5. Lazarus and John Baptist Colloredo.

6. A seventeenth-century 'cabinet of curiosities'.

7. Joseph Clark.

8. A boy conjoined to a dog.

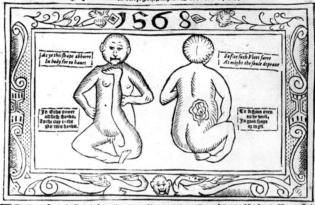

¶ The forme and shape of a Monstrous Child / borne
at Maydstone in Kent, the xxiiij. of October. 1568.

At Maydstone in Kent there was one Marget Mere, Daughter to Richard Mere of the sayd Towne of Maydstone, who being unmaryed, played the naughty packe, and was gotten with childe, being deliuered of the same childe the xxiiij. daye of October last past, in the yeare of our Lord. 1568. at vij. of the clocke in the after noone of the same day being Sonday, which child being a man child, had first the mouth slitted on the right side like a Libardes mouth, terrible to beholde, the left arme lying upon the brest, fast therto ioyned, hauing as it were stumps on the handes, the left leg growing upward toward the head, and the ryght leg bending toward the left leg, the foote therof growing into the buttocke of the sayd left leg. In the middest of the backe there was a broade lump of flesh in fashion lyke a Rose, in the myddest wherof was a hole, which voyded lyke an Issue. Thys sayd Childe was borne alyue, and lyued xxiiij. houres, and then departed this lyfe. Which may be a terrour aswell to all such workers of filthynes & iniquity, as to those ungodly liuers. Who (if in them any feare of God be) may mooue them to repentance and amendement of lyfe. Which God for Christes sake graunt both to them and us. Amen. Witnesses hereof were these, William Plomer, John Squier Glasier, John Sadler Goldsmith, besides diuers other credible persons both men and women.

✤ A warnyng to England.

THis monstrous shape to thee England
Playn shewes thy monstrous vice.
If thou ech part wylt understand,
And take thereby aduice.

For wearing first the gasping mouth,
It doth full well declare:
What rauine and oppression both
Is vsed wyth greedy care.

For, for the backe. and gorging paunch,
To lyue in wealth and ease:
Such toylmen take that none may staunch
Their greedy maide, nor please.

For in such sort. their mouthes they infect,
With lying othes, and slaightes:
Blaspheming God, and Prince reiect,
As they were brutish beastes.

Their filthy talke, and poysoned speech,
Disfigures so the mouth):
That som wold think ther stood þ breech
Such filth it breatheth forth.

The hands which haue no fingers right
But stumps sit for no vse:
Doth well set forth the idle plight,
Which we in these daies chuse.

For rich and poore, for age and youth,
Eche one would labour flye:
Few seekes to do the deedes of truth,
To helpe others thereby.

The leg so clyming to the head,
What meaneth it but this:
That some do seeke not to be lead,
But for to leade amis.

And as this makes it most monstrous,
For foote to clyme to head:
So those Subiects be most vicious,
That refuse to be lead.

The hinder part doth shew us playne,
Our close and hidden vice,
Which both behind us run amayne,
In vyle and shamefull wyse.

Wherefore so run in England now,
Let this Monster them teach:
To mend the monstrous life they show,
Least endles death them reach.

¶ Imprinted at London by John Awdeley, dwelling in little Britain streete without Aldersgate. The xxiiij. of December.

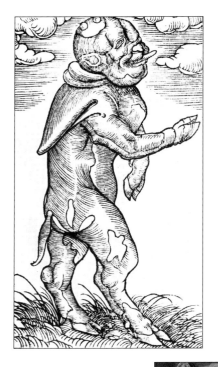

10. The monkcalf.

11. The 'Trusty Servant'.

The laſt terrible Tempeſti-
ous windes and weather.
Truely Relating many Lamentable Ship-wracks, with drowning
of many people, on the Coaſts of England, Scotland, France and
Ireland : with the Iles of Wight, Garſey & Iarſey.

Shewing alſo, many great miſ-fortunes, that haue lately hapned on Land, by
reaſon of the windes and rayne, in diuers places of this Kingdome.

Imprinted at London for *Ioſ: Hunt* and are to be ſold by *Iohn Wright*, 1613.

12. *The last terrible tempestious windes and weather* (London, 1613; S.T.C. 25840).

has enticed with the possibility of an exposure of the 'inner man', a showing of, in Elizabeth Hanson's words, his 'utter unintelligibility', a demonstration of 'The native act and figure of [his] heart' (I.i.61).[88] Clearly, here, a discovery of 'monsters' within is anticipated; over the course of the play, however, it is not so much a 'monster' that Iago threatens to unveil as a vaguer and more inchoate 'thing'. Gordon Williams observes that 'thing' was a vulgar synonym for the female pudenda in the period, and this is borne out by the ways in which Iago continually surrounds the term with a web of insinuation: to see the 'thing', the ancient suggests, is to acknowledge a woman's 'common' (III.iii.306) – or open – sexuality.[89] But, in the moment of his own un-covering, neither the mysteries of Iago's motivation nor the 'mon-strosities' of female lust are made available. As Iago states, in an expression that puns upon the 'thing' that remains repressed, 'Demand me nothing ... From this time forth I never will speak word' (V.ii.300–1). To adopt the terminology of the contemporary fairground, this is a demonstration that stops short of a 'monstrous' finale.

In the concluding stages, therefore, revelation and concealment are at odds; inscrutability is twinned with illumination; and the action hesitates in the face of opposed narrative options. As critics have recognized, the latter is particularly evident in Othello's final address in which he simultaneously pledges allegiance to the 'Venetian ... state' (V.ii.352) and identifies with the 'base Indian' who 'threw a pearl away / Richer than all his tribe' (V.ii.345–6). However, crucial in the expressed kinship is the fact that the 'Indian' is, like Othello, constructed through ocular misapprehension: his discarding of the 'pearl' is represented as an 'error' of his 'subdued eyes' (V.ii.346), as an inability to recognize the 'rarities' of his natural environment. The speech implicitly binds ratio-nal, empirical principles to consumerism, even as it recognizes the suc-cessful utilization of these principles as a privilege of western authority. Reading himself through the 'Indian' means that Othello bows out of the drama having located his Baconian shortcomings in his non-white status.

Into the void vacated by Othello several potential showpersons are inserted, their very variety indicating a bifurcation of impresario-'monster' relations. Both Emilia and Lodovico are involved, with Desdemona's attendant acting as curtain-drawer and the Venetian gentleman taking responsibility for the instructive commentary of the 'Monster-Master'. Because Lodovico is represented as a 'proper man' (IV.iii.34), however, the additional implication is that he incarnates Baconian qualities of accuracy and exactitude.[90] The interpretive tradi-tions splintered in Othello are in Lodovico merged. In his twinned capacity, Lodovico advises Iago to 'Look on the tragic loading of this bed: / This is thy work. The object poisons sight, / Let it be hid' (V.ii.361–3). The bed is hidden not so much, as Michael Neill comments, because it is 'hideous', but because, at a metaphorical level, at least, it accommodates a 'monstrous' conception hatched and on display to all.[91] And, in a move that highlights these significances, Lodovico commands Iago to 'Look': as he had persuaded others to look, now is the ancient required to gaze himself in an injunction that executes yet another realignment of the play's visual directorship.

But Iago is not only required to 'Look'. He is also looked at, as Lodovico's gestural labelling of him as a 'Spartan dog' (V.ii.359) indicates. As such, Iago becomes a material, on-stage embodiment of the 'circumcised dog' (V.ii.353) evoked by Othello as he writes his own obituary. At the start, Othello was stamped with devilish imputations; at this point, however, it is Iago, the 'inhuman dog' (V.i.62), who is judged a 'demi-devil' (V.ii.298). More is conveyed in these floating terms than Othello and Iago's uncanny twinship. First, in keeping with the Iberian resonances of Iago's name, 'inhuman dog' recalls the Spanish noun for black dogs and horses, *moro*: in a typical *volte-face*, the play thus begins here a process of racial displacement.[92] Second, given that both dogs and devils were thought either to be types of 'monster' or to share characteristics with them, one might argue that the play continues to tutor the audience in matters of 'monstrous' identification.[93] *Othello* aims to suggest, in fact, that the 'monster' that has been produced is not Desdemona's death, still less the 'monstrous' behaviour of Othello, but the 'monstrous' mystery of Iago's inner compulsions. Such a reading finds support in the ways in which Iago is put on show in Lodovico's speech: because the bed is 'hid', the ancient becomes the focus of visual attention. Paradoxically, Othello's erroneous conceiving has generated Iago's 'monstrosity', not his own. Judged in this light, we might not be surprised by the sole reference to a 'monster' in an early seventeeth-century ballad entitled 'The Tragedie of Othello the Moore': 'Iago was the monster's name,' it asserts.[94] True to its Baconian inspiration, *Othello* finally declares that a viewer can be easily deceived in the detection of 'monstrosity' and that its ultimate locations are never self-evident.

V

Deliveries and demonstrations, fairgrounds and handkerchiefs, 'unnatural' couplings and exotic progeny – *Othello* detects 'monsters' in all of these locations. But the play also reveals that 'monstrosity' enjoys a loose and even indeterminate habitation: it is not represented as generated by biology alone; it is not only apprehended aesthetically; and it does not limit itself to accepted national groupings. Even as it rehearses many of the familiar 'monstrous' *topoi* of the period, therefore, *Othello* countenances a less easily defined set of constructions – that 'monsters' belong to myth, that they reside in names, that they are inseparable from gendered types of credulity, that they are essentially cerebral in nature. In particular, *Othello* is distinctive for reflecting on the 'monstrous' as a process of fabrication: either 'monsters' gather in the interstices of actions and stories, the drama suggests, or they exist as the invented effects of cultural transgression and breakdown. By alerting us to these counterfeit forms of 'monstrosity', *Othello* pushes 'monsters' to the forefront of an audience's consciousness, to the extent that positions of superior vantage are queried, questions of responsibility are stimulated and 'monstrous' conceptions become, in some senses, our own.

The variety of 'monsters' in *Othello* notwithstanding, a common denominator is 'monstrosity' as a space where discussions of 'proof' and ocular power can be pursued. At this ideological meeting-point congregate rationality and scepticism, which, playing themselves out through *Othello*, work towards an additional unhingeing of unitary emplacements of the 'monstrous'. Thus, while the drama can deploy narrative intersections of blackness and classical 'monstrosity', and while it represents a white value system eventually triumphing over black 'otherness', it simultaneously resists an unambiguous endorsement of conventional racial paradigms and subjects mythologies of 'monstrosity' to dismantling treatment. The suggestion is that 'monstrosity' does not depend only on colour and that 'race' is an illusive conceptual criterion. By the same token, western empirical philosophies are themselves not free from censure since their very workings betray 'monstrous' and 'unnatural' tendencies. Alongside its racial destabilizations, *Othello* upsets familial binaries. Its twinned pairings, for instance, constitute conjunctions that are just as antagonistic as more obviously oppositional arrangements. In this respect, it is striking that Iago, in what amounts to a racial reversal, is delineated as the archetypally 'dark' and 'sinister twin' who, in Hillel Schwartz's words, represents 'the worse but seductive half' of a subjectivity 'struggling to mature in the present'.[95] A comparably arresting exploded binary is found in the play's gendered identifications, for its conclusion implies that women and unknowability are not inevitably partners; rather, it is men, and their unfathomable 'monstrous' interiorities, that defy explication. In juxta-posing its 'monstrous' conceptions against a rationalist perspective, then, *Othello* not only undoes contemporary technologies of classifica-tion; it also rebukes a subject position that would 'other' women to shore up a masculinist hegemony.

Pushing at the parameters of the 'monstrous', and evicting 'mon-strosity' from traditional niches, *Othello* occupies a uniquely pivotal place in early modern cultural practice. Poised at a seminal moment in the history of natural philosophy, *Othello* steers a balanced course between 'superstitous' and 'scientific' modalities, recalling fictions and anticipating discoveries in such a way that 'science' takes on the appearance of play and drama is identified as a type of experiment. A Baconian reification of material visual evidence is the feature that most obviously gives *Othello* a significance beyond an early seventeenth-century historical juncture, allowing it to transcend constructions of 'proof' subscribed to by the courts and to contemplate more hard-and-fast methods for distinguishing between what is 'monstrous' and what is not. *Othello* joins forces with the 'new science' to offer a challenge to the legal bodies of its time and to meditate upon other forms of insti-tutional idealism. However, the play fails to locate in 'science' a wholly adequate instrument of understanding. For, although it entertains rationality and is unwilling to abandon it completely, *Othello* is forced to recognize that a scrutinizing approach to the world is insufficient, that the eye can make mistakes, that the West cannot congratulate itself on being able accurately to define either the 'monstrous' or the differ-ent. Structures of belief and credulity neither smoothly insert them-selves into, nor are entirely banished by, any one interpretive model, even if the play, itself yet another conceptual tool for comprehension, still yearns for that overarching possibility.

5

'Were I in England now': Localizing 'Monsters' in *The Tempest*

'It is an axiom of contemporary criticism,' notes Barbara Fuchs, 'that *The Tempest* [1611] is a play about the European colonial experience in America.'[1] Certainly, colonialist readings of Shakespeare's drama have had a dominant impact over the last two decades. Opinion has maintained that *The Tempest* investigates a politically oppressive system in which Prospero is figured as an imperial overlord and in which Caliban, whose linguistic conversion, slavery and territorial dispossession precipitate his rebellion, has appeared as a native American subject. Prospero's relation to his island, critics have argued, is profoundly implicated in early modern plantation policies, and this is reinforced both by references to the Caribbean and by the evocation of New World stereotypes: Caliban's name, in a now familiar commonplace, is said to be anagrammatic of 'cannibal'. Clarifying the New World associations is Shakespeare's apparent debt to the pamphlets of the Virginia Company, one of which details the experiences of Sir Thomas Gates and his men who, shipwrecked, were forced to winter on Bermuda.[2] More recent assessments of the play, however, have pointed to the limitations of such an interpretive template. The extent to which *The Tempest* evades colonialist paradigms is an area of increasing concern. It has been pointed out, for instance, that Bermuda is explicitly referred to but once ('the still-vexed Bermudas') in a phrase that indicates the distance of Shakespeare's island from an American or a Caribbean context.[3] In addition, the Mediterranean provenances of the play, a vocal lobby is asserting, dictate that Prospero must be seen more as a refugee than an explorer, that Caliban can only partly be identified as 'cannibalistic', and that Sycorax, whose origins reside in Algiers, is assessed in terms of her own enslavement of indigenous inhabitants.[4]

Implicit in such a critical reconfiguration is a tendency to grant the play's ideological investments an alternative geographical location. Thus critics such as David J. Baker, Jerry Brotton, David Scott Kastan and Richard Wilson have sought to prise the play away from a New World anchorage, situating it instead in vacillating placements of Ireland and in European dynastic, political and piratical struggles.[5] This shifting of *The Tempest*'s ground is part and parcel of a gradual domestication of the play, a reorientation of its preoccupations that bypasses colonial themes in favour of more local concerns. Perhaps the most obvious manfestation of the development is seen in newer studies which follow the critical/geographical trajectory of *The Tempest* to its furthest point and insist upon the crucial contribution of England, and English forms of mind, to the play's effect. Typical here are Crystal Bartolovich, Douglas Bruster and Frances E. Dolan, who argue respectively that *The Tempest* has as its major consideration the uncertain 'locatability' of London, the 'authority and work' of 'early modern playhouses', and household politics of insubordination and petty treason.[6]

In its approach to *The Tempest*, this chapter builds upon the lead established by these recent discussions, arguing that the play, in its engagement with 'monsters' and 'monstrosity', answers primarily to the determinants of English habits and institutions. In a more persistent manner than *Othello*, *The Tempest* continually reflects 'monstrosity' back upon its audience, articulating it not so much in terms of the New World encounter as through the lens of local constructions of 'monstrous births', the fairground's spatial choreography, the contemporary accumulative impulse and marvellous aesthetic transformations, all of which are seen to have a peculiarly English purchase. Crucially, *The Tempest*'s favoured manoeuvre is to sideline a colonially identified exoticism and to pose its questions within the frame of a domestic theatrical culture, whether this takes the form of Prospero's magical demonstrations, Ariel's athletic spectacles, quasi-ethnographic performances or conceptual interrelations between the display practices of 'museums' and playhouses.[7] By reading 'monsters' via theatrical mechanisms, *The Tempest* is stimulated to related reflections upon generation and causation: the tempest that opens and closes the dramatic proceedings can be traced, I suggest, to a specifically English imaginative context, while Caliban, whose 'monstrosity' has all too often been seen as inseparable from his colonial imprint, is characterized by a fluctuating role that owes more to familiarly class-bound attitudes towards procreation and physical difference.[8] Caliban, in fact, is hardly a unitary colonialist projection; rather, he is a creature of becoming who is

notable eventually for failing to accord with any one 'monstrous' designation. Nor do *The Tempest*'s generative cogitations end with the play's
most obvious 'monster'. They extend outwards to include Prospero's
part both as the producer of wonders and as an instrument of the
apocalypse; performing in this capacity, the magician functions to articulate concerns about religious division and national unification that
were, at a critical historical juncture, particularly pertinent to Shakespeare's patron, James I.

I

Critical tradition has often debated *The Tempest* inside the genre of the
court masque, a form that the play certainly utilizes. Approaching
the drama by way of the distinguishing features of popular culture,
however, suggests that, as an institution, the fairground is more deeply
engrained in *The Tempest*'s theatrical fabric. The play's allusions are
rooted in this occasional form of entertainment; the diversity of the fairground's attractions is implicit in the narrative; and the wonder associated with its spectacles is a crucial ingredient of the dramatic effect. In
particular, *The Tempest* is closely allied to, and capitalizes upon, such
performative acts and 'monstrous' representatives as those observed at
the fair by Henry Farley in 1621: 'a strange out-landish Fowle / A quaint
Baboon . . . a Gyants bone . . . a Puppit play . . . A Woman dancing on a
Rope . . . a Iuglers cheats, / A Tumbler shewing cunning feats'.[9] Hence,
apes are implied in the identification of Trinculo as a 'jesting monkey'
(III.ii.44), a formulation that brings to mind fairground humour, imitation and the collapse of animal and human boundaries; and puppets
are evoked in allusions to the 'quick motion' of the 'rabble' (IV.i.37, 39),
the 'living drollery' (III.iii.21) of the spirits and the 'demi-puppets'
(V.i.36) Prospero commands. On the one hand, these references analogize a sense of Prospero's manipulation of the denizens of his island
world; on the other, they point to 'monstrous' forces requiring control,
since, as Scott Cutler Shershow states, the 'puppet show' was characterized by the 'physical deformity of its artificial players'.[10] The play's
most clearly constructed 'monster', Caliban, who might also be seen as
a type of puppet, is no less ensnared in the fairground environment.
Abandoning Prospero and pledging loyalty to Stephano and Trinculo,
Caliban sings: ''Ban, 'Ban, Ca-Caliban / Has a new master – get a new
man! / Freedom, high-day!' (II.ii.179–81). Gestured at here, I think, is
the early modern hiring fair. Taking place on holidays (high-days or
hire-days), this annual gathering, at which 'monsters' were exhibited,

permitted domestic servants either to renew their contracts or to seek out fresh masters for more favourable terms of employment. The occasion was marked, as Michael Roberts observes, by 'carnivalesque boisterousness', 'inversionary motifs' and a stress on 'food and drink, songs and dances'.[11] Caliban's musical refrain is illuminating at several levels: it suggests that his drunken behaviour is identifiable as a form of servant empowerment, that his economic utility can be bargained for in a fairground of his own devising, and that 'monstrosity' and social mobility are equally important constituents of his anomalousness.

Barbara Mowat has argued that Prospero 'belongs more to the mundane world of the streetcorner "art-magician" or "jugler" . . . than to the arcane, terrifying Hermetic or demonic spheres'.[12] Certainly, Prospero can be profitably tied in part to such a role, nowhere more obviously than in his predilection for promising exposure and mobilizing demonstration. 'Approach, my Ariel. Come' (I.ii.188), Prospero intones, dictating his spirit's entrances in a quasi-magical manner and also revealing Caliban with a comparable command: 'Come forth, I say' (I.ii.315). These summonings into being of his servants offer spectacular corroboration of Prospero's demotic conjurations. Since Caliban, the 'monster', is instructed to issue from a 'rock' (I.ii.343), however, a more persuasive identification for Prospero would seem to be that of the contemporary 'Monster-Master'. Figuratively the master of a 'monster', Prospero discovers Caliban from inside a 'rock'/booth with all the flourishes of his fairground impresario counterparts.

The fascination of the travelling 'Monster-Master' in the early modern period did not inhere only in his display of a single exhibit's extraordinary qualities; an equally significant dimension of the performance was the assembly of unfamiliar artifacts, or 'strange and woonderfull syghts', that he would make available to an excited audience: the 'Monster-Master' was also the collector.[13] In many respects, Prospero, too, is balanced between a range of performative categories that cut across class-determined demarcations. While still Duke of Milan, Prospero betrays a collective urge, amassing 'volumes' (I.ii.166), coveting his 'own library' (I.ii.167) and pursuing, to the exclusion of matters of state, 'study' of the 'liberal arts' (I.ii.73–4). Prospero, in short, becomes a bibliophile 'rapt in secret studies' (I.ii.77). As such, he represents a dramatic realization of the English virtuoso, an aristocrat or gentleman who compiled books as adjuncts to 'collections of curiosities' and who, in Marjorie Swann's words, acquired studies of '"conceits" and "secrets"' that catered for a contemporary 'interest in "curious" information'.[14]

Once ousted from his political seat, Prospero continues in a collective vein, assembling and categorizing memories, courtiers, spirits and celestial forces. 'Be collected' (I.ii.13), he instructs Miranda, recuperating the shards of her subjectivity and endeavouring to sort the disparate elements of his own experience into a coherent whole. The magician's pursuit of the 'curious' in Milan functions as a prelude to his cultivation of the 'monstrous' in exile. For, thanks to Caliban, he accedes to ownership of the valuable properties 'o' th' isle' (I.ii.337), *rariora naturae* such as 'pig nuts' (II.ii.162), a 'jay's nest' (II.ii.163), the 'nimble marmoset' (II.ii.164) 'clust'ring filberts' (II.ii.165) and 'Young scamels' (II.ii.166). This catalogue of 'qualities' (I.ii.337), interestingly non-English in orientation, points to the proximity of the *wunderkammern* in which, in an anticipation of the 'museums' of the eighteenth and nineteenth centuries, natural singularities and 'monstrous' abberations alike vied for prominence.[15] The points of contact between contemporary 'cabinets' and Prospero's absorption in natural history are illustrated, in particular, in the reference to 'Young scamels'. Because the 'scamel' could connote both an unfledged Irish bird and a Guianan godwit, it represents a species of 'strange out-landish Fowle' that has not yet been fully integrated into the hierarchies of English classification.[16] Prospero's island thus presents itself as a kind of enactment of the 'cabinet', a theatricalization of the diversity of its contents. By conceiving the world through its objects, the Milanese magus brings it, in Denise Albanese's words, into an 'equivalent knowability [and] . . . domestication in the . . . space of the *theatrum mundi'*.[17] He deploys demonstration and accumulation to manage the 'strangeness' (V.i.247) of his island world, finding in these practices both opportunities for his psychological repair and the establishment of a magisterial authority.

Upon Ariel, in particular, in an inculcation of his dominion, Prospero is compelled to exercise his will. In common with Caliban, some aspects of Ariel have a colonial underpinning, as when the spirit recounts exacerbating the terrifying effects of the tempest:

> I boarded the King's ship; now on the beak,
> Now in the waist, the deck, in every cabin,
> I flamed amazement. Sometime I'd divide
> And burn in many places; on the topmast,
> The yards and bowsprit would I flame distinctly,
> Then meet and join.
>
> (I.ii.196–201)

In this simulation of impressions in the firmament, Ariel's fiery display can be seen as species of Saint Elmo's fire, hinted at in the pamphlet about the wreck of Sir Thomas Gates' ship, but elaborated in Thomas Churchyard's *The Wonders of the Ayre*, which was printed in 1602.[18] The key passage runs:

> Marriners . . . haue seene . . . lights hanging on the mast, which . . . are a very euill signe . . . if there be but one of them seene . . . that presageth shipwracke . . . if two lights be seene, they bring goodnesse and hope of happy fortune, and presageth that the ship shall haue a good voyage . . . many euils fall immediatly in those partes where those strange and prodigious sights and signes are to be seene.[19]

As in Churchyard's account, Ariel's actions before the Neapolitans are invested with a prophetic significance. Shipwreck is forewarned in the single fire, while eventual deliverance, reconciliation and a safe return to Italy are anticipated in the divided flames. The 'euils' that accompany the spirit's appearance, similarly, might be tied to the tribulations undergone by the shipwrecked party once Prospero's island is reached.

Even if Ariel's significance as a pyrotechnic guide to future events can be traced to an assumed debt to the Virginia pamphlets, however, this fails to account either for the local meanings of his transformations or for the English associations of his activities. In fact, the 'tricksy' (V.i.226) Ariel shares a greater affinity with the fairground dancer 'on a Rope' or even the 'tumbler shewing cunning feats'. A forerunner of the circus acrobat or trapeze artist, Ariel is most obviously marked by an extraordinary dexterity, since he revels in skills that allow him 'to fly, / To swim, to dive into the fire' and 'to ride / On the curled clouds' (I.ii.190–2). In so doing, the spirit generates 'amazement' in much the same way that contemporary tightrope walkers elicited marvelling responses. In Salop in 1590, for instance, upon 'a gable roape tighted and drawen strayte', a visiting 'hongarian did assende and goe . . . with his bare feete . . . and wold fall stridlenges vppon the . . . roap and mowntinge vp againe . . . very myraculous to the beholders . . . he went to & fro . . . in daunsinge and turninge hym sellff . . . in . . . woonderfull maner'.[20] Like Ariel, the Hungarian is notable for an assumed capacity to inhabit several places at the same time; like Prospero's airy spirit, too, he appears to confound expectations about a body's physical abilities. Captivating his audience in this manner, the rope-dancer ensures the wondrous reaction that sets the seal on his performance's success.

Wonder, indeed, is perhaps *The Tempest*'s most salient conceptual referent for the simultaneously entrancing and disquieting peculiarities of the island experience: it comes to serve as a catch-all category that encapsulates the variety of inexplicable circumstances in which the characters find themselves. When Ferdinand meets Miranda (the very etymology of her name suggesting that she is to be 'wondered at'), both mobilize a language of wonder to approximate the nature of the encounter, suggesting the pervasive utility of the term as a descriptor of cultural estrangement. Wonder, however, is not only the marker of the unaccountable and the different; it is simultaneously a tool wielded by Prospero in his efforts to reclaim political ascendancy. On Ariel, for instance, Prospero places prodigious responsibilities, deploying his 'chick' (V.i.316) to engineer in the courtiers a wonder that will lead to repentance. The central stages map Prospero's attempts to produce in his enemies a spiritual transformation as miraculous and awe-inspiring as the displays in which his spirits participate. The scheme is least successful with the play's unregenerates. Thus, when Antonio's plot is foiled by the musical intervention of the invisible Ariel, he explains away his behaviour with the ruse of a noise; ''twas a din to fright a monster's ear, / To make an earthquake' (II.i.312–13), he states, in a formulation that implies a lack of wonder, merely a secular and sensual apprehension. But with the rest of the company Prospero's strategy reaps greater rewards. Confronted by '*several strange shapes bringing in a banquet*' (III.iii.19.1), Gonzalo states that 'these . . . people of the island . . . though they are of monstrous shape, yet . . . are more gentle-kind than . . . Our human generation' (III.iii.30–3); the observation stages a wonderful manoeuvre, since it traces a route back from the spectacle to the realization that 'monsters' are of local, Italianate extraction. Similarly, appalled by Ariel's verbal *monstrum* or warning (the spirit is disguised as a harpy, a mythical creature described in a 1626 dictionary as a 'monstrous devouring bird'), Alonso is driven to lament both the death of his son and the usurpation of Prospero: 'O, it is monstrous, monstrous! / Methought the billows spoke and told me of it, / The winds did sing it to me; and the thunder' (III.iii.95–7).[21] In the light of Ariel's impersonation, it is suggested, Alonso begins to read into his wonderful landscape the signs of his moral bankruptcy. By the same token, the episode sets the scene for a miraculous reformation. Douglas Biow has argued that wonder, as well as triggering 'speculative inquiry' into 'the causes of things', calls attention 'to the transgression of boundaries defining a cultural system', to the rupture of 'discernible normative . . . constraints'.[22] This is precisely the register within which

Prospero's brand of wonder operates: his theatrical artistry sparks off reflections upon the origins of criminality, permits transgressors to return to the fold, and reinstitutes a political order that is reassuringly familiar in its essential outlines.

Wonder, then, stimulates a desire for knowledge and might even be seen as the precondition for self-discovery. In this respect, Prospero's entertainment before Ferdinand and Miranda serves a vital purpose. Iris, Ceres and Juno join to present a masque in which 'foison' (IV.i.110), 'Honour' and 'riches' (IV.i.106) are blessed in an anticipation of the imminent betrothal. What seems to have escaped notice in discussions of the celebration is the fact that Iris, the rainbow, is the daughter of Thaumas, the god identified as the etymological origin of *thaumalein* or wonders. Philip Fisher states:

> To understand philosophy we must go to its *arche*, wonder, but to think out wonder, we must descend genetically (father to daughter) to the rainbow. Philosophy and the rainbow appear across the fulcrum of wonder, by which they are both to be known, and are understood to be related, in the most fundamental way: the way of *arche* and *genealogein*.[23]

According to this explanation, to be open to wonder is to become aware of the generational connections between the primary stage of things and subsequent developments, between gods and their creations, and between parents and children. Prospero also, I would suggest, is concerned in the masque to instil in his onlookers a sense of vital interrelations – of the bonds uniting the sources of magic and their chief practitioner, the lovers and their 'oaths' (IV.i.52), and the father, the daughter and the prospective son-in-law. Insisting upon 'abstemious' (IV.i.53) virtues, Prospero aims through the 'majestic vision' (IV.i.118) of the masque to lead Ferdinand and Miranda to a recognition of spiritual hierarchies and a deeper knowledge of themselves. The fact that Ferdinand acknowledges the entertainment as a 'rare' and 'wondered' (IV.i.123) phenomenon points to the success of the scheme: redeploying the wonder that defines the fairground, Prospero avoids its commercial orientation in the interests of a quasi-philosophical education.

II

Overshadowing the natural wonders Prospero accumulates, and the wondrous effects he generates, is another wonder, the 'monster',

Caliban. Once again, critical discussion of Caliban, which includes readings of his 'monstrosity', has tended to concentrate on colonial influences. Hence, in that he is 'puppy-headed' (II.ii.148), Caliban can be seen to resemble the *cynocephali*, the dog-headed people of Ethiopia and India, and in that his 'eyes' are not 'set in [his] head' (III.ii.8), he brings to mind the African and American *anthropophagi*, whose heads grew beneath their shoulders.[24] Caliban's unassimilable alterity has been understandable only through the tried and trusted tropes of contemporary travellers' tales. Over the course of *The Tempest* as a whole, however, interpretive systems closer to home are brought into play to situate Shakespeare's 'savage and deformed slave'. One of Prospero's primary explanations for the 'monster', for instance, is that his mother, Sycorax, a 'damned witch' (I.ii.263), enjoyed congress with a demon: 'got by the devil himself / Upon [his] wicked dam' (I.ii.319–20), Caliban is thereby himself stamped as a 'devil, a born devil' (IV.i.188). In the spirit of Marlowe's *Tamburlaine the Great* (1587–88), Prospero here rehearses common questions about the capability of demons to produce issue; in so doing, he places his faith in a historically grounded and theologically established debate about supernatural sexuality. Prospero's distance from colonial models is more stridently articulated when he reprimands Caliban for having attempted to rape Miranda; 'filth as thou art' (I.ii.346), he states, 'I have used thee . . . with humane care, and lodged thee / In mine own cell' (I.ii.345–7). With this accusation, Prospero gravitates to the contemporary notion that, as King Lear states, the ultimate 'monster' is 'ingratitude'.[25] 'As a violation of moralized, often naturalized, bonds of family, country, or religion', writes Barbara M. Benedict, 'the original monstrous trait of ingratitude symbolizes the rejection of human identity itself. Satan exemplifies this kind of violation of nature by betraying his father, God, and his own character when he rejects his angelic status.'[26] For Prospero, then, Caliban is 'monster' because he fails to respect the gift of an accommodating paternal protection: it is a modality of interpretation both familial and domestic in its ideological investments.

As these interlaced constructions of Caliban suggest, *The Tempest* discovers 'monstrosity' by depending on a variety of theoretical paradigms. Caliban, furthermore, is regarded inconsistently according to the dynamics of the competing cultural encounters to which he is exposed, which suggests that 'monstrosity' constitutes a site where class-inflected readings congregate. One instance will suffice to illustrate this: although Stephano and Trinculo frequently label Caliban a 'monster', 'monster' as a descriptive approximation is never deployed by Prospero. Rather, the magician relies on a conceptual apparatus of the 'monster' without the application of the specific term. The implication, at least in the play, is that classification of the 'monstrous' takes on different inflections in the light of its precise interpretive circumstances. The scenes in which Caliban mainly appears also suggest that the characters' efforts to visualise the 'monster' will of necessity fail, for throughout the figure is a blank page – a kind of 'picture of Nobody' (III.ii.124–5) – onto which are projected conflicting anxieties and ambitions. Each character moulds Caliban in a different image, and the sum total of those imagined representations can never cohere: a 'tortoise' (I.ii.316) is not a 'fish' (II.ii.24), and a fish does not possess 'long nails' (II.ii.162). It is only in theatrical production, where a directorial perspective is privileged, that visual anomalies are resolved, uncertainty is clarified, the social determinants of perception are subordinated and 'monstrosity' moves out of the realm of the individual beholder. In that Caliban resists settling into an agreed form, he becomes, as Julia Reinhard Lupton argues, a '*creature* . . . of continued or potential process, action, or emergence . . . a thing always . . . undergoing creation'.[27] As such, Caliban stands as a test case for the possibilities and limitations of representation, for the self-conscious acknowledgement by the theatre of the flaws and feasibilities of its 'monstrous' enterprise.

This process of providing an audience with a series of Calibans, not all of which have immediately obvious colonial counterparts, is best exemplified in the scenes of comic business. When Trinculo espies the 'monster', for instance, a constellation of birth metaphors alerts us to Caliban's provisional condition, to a physical body characterized by its inchoate aspects. The indeterminate status of the cloud (an explosive delivery is suggested in the 'foul bombard that would shed his liquor' [II.ii.21]) is mirrored in the undecided appearance of Caliban, who seems to Trinculo to be neither 'man' nor 'fish' (II.ii.24):

A strange fish! Were I in England now, as once I was, and had but this fish painted, not a holiday-fool there but would give a piece of silver. There would this monster make a man – any strange beast there makes a man. When they will not give a doit to relieve a lame beggar, they will lay out ten to see a dead Indian. Legged like a man, and his fins like arms! Warm, o' my troth! I do now let loose my opinion, hold it no longer: this is no fish, but an islander, that hath lately suffered by a thunderbolt. (II.ii.26–35)

On immediate impressions, the jester's speech seems to point to a colonial context. Not only does Trinculo play the role of a comic ethno-
grapher itemizing departures from a physical norm in order to set
Caliban in a rhetorical framework; he also aligns himself with the contemporary practice of displaying New World 'monsters' for profit. The
closest analogue for Trinculo's 'dead Indian' is Epinew, a living native
American who, captured at Martha's Vineyard in 1611, was brought to
England by Captain Edward Harlow at the Earl of Southampton's
expense. In England until 1614, when he returned home, Epinew,
according to contemporary accounts, was an immediate sensation. Of
'so great a stature, he was shewed vp and downe *London* for money as
a wonder', Epinew, in addition, 'learned so much *English* as to bid those
that wondred at him, welcome, welcome'.[28] Like Southampton, who
recognized that the wonder encoded in the reception of Epinew was
marketable, Trinculo is imagined as just such an entrepreneurial aristocrat, fashioning himself as a gentleman through an imitative 'monstrous' exhibition and agitating to ascend to the status of his social
superiors. In other respects, the Trinculo/Caliban encounter seems only
tangentially a colonial intervention. For Caliban is marked more by his
local colourings; in particular, he is assessed within the conventions of
English ballads, many of which were devoted to describing either a
'strange fish' or a 'monstrous birth' (Figure 9).[29] Just as Trinculo runs
through a titular description of Caliban, an image and a commentary,
so was the contemporary ballad, in David Cressy's words, composed of
a 'banner headline, a gruesome picture, and some sensational moraliz-
ing verse'.[30] His colonially driven aspirations notwithstanding, Trinculo
is compelled to situate 'monstrosity' in a vernacular idiom: his theatricalization provides ample testimony of his chosen form's interpretive
utility, since one of the chief characteristics of the 'monster' ballad was
the ideological congruity of the visual representation and the textual
explication. The domesticating tendencies in evidence here are
expressed more forcefully in the stage action of Trinculo creeping under
Caliban's gabardine. At once, of course, the gesture highlights the geographical proximity of a 'monster' that shares the same accommodation as a 'man': the implication is that the two may soon become
indistinguishable. But there is also the suggestion that, as a consequence
of the scene's coupling, a new 'monstrous' form with two sets of
members is in the making: in the space of only a few lines, Caliban has
shifted alarmingly in the physical particularities through which he is
constituted.

In common with Trinculo, Stephano initially places on Caliban's 'monstrosity' a colonial focus. His immediate points of reference are 'savages and men of Ind' (II.ii.57). In Stephano's simultaneous reference to 'tricks' (II.ii.57), however, there is an echo of Prospero and his 'Iuglers cheats', suggesting that the butler's imperial identifications take second place to his role as an ironic showman. Thus, in assuming that the form beneath the gabardine has 'four legs' (II.ii.58–9) but only one head, Stephano regards Caliban not so much as a New World 'monster' as a conjoined twin – a type of *eusomphalien pygopage* or *syncephalus ectopagus*.[31] In his doubled condition, Caliban is judged to have a particularly high stake in the commodity market, to the extent that, rather than occupying a paltry booth at an English fair, he will be transported to 'Naples [as] . . . a present for any emperor' (II.ii.67–8). Elsewhere in the play, Prospero takes considerable pains to engineer the conjunction of Ferdinand and Miranda for political profit; here, in a witty anticipation of that project, Stephano imagines himself exploiting the 'monstrous' convergence that is Caliban and Trinculo to facilitate his own fraternization with the European élite.

In his essays, first published in English in 1603 and then again in 1613, Montaigne describes a '*monstrous Childe*' who was 'Vnder his paps . . . joyned to an other childe, [which] had no head, and . . . the conduite of his body stopped, the rest whole'.[32] It may have been that Shakespeare, who certainly consulted Montaigne in his composition of *The Tempest*, found in this passage a prompt both for the 'monstrous' multiplication of Caliban and for the uncertainty surrounding his physical extremities. The representation of the creature beneath the gabardine chimes, most revealingly, however, with English discussions of conjoined twins, as Stephano's increasingly frustrated attempts at definition indicate. Once Caliban–Trinculo has spoken with both voices, Stephano is obliged to modify his terms of identification: 'Four legs and two voices; a most delicate monster! His forward voice now is to speak well of his friend, his backward voice is to utter foul speeches and to detract' (II.ii.85–7). This assessment depends, first, on the argument, familiar from contemporary ballads, books of 'secrets' and popular pamphlets, that one 'monstrous' body could accommodate two separate sensibilities – hence the confusion of some writers as to whether conjoined twins possessed two souls or merely one.[33] It repeats, at a deeper level, the frequently rehearsed construction of conjoined twins as active-passive in their behavioural traits: a stronger sibling, it was maintained, invariably dominated a weaker.[34]

Holinshed's chronicles, first published in 1577 and then in an enlarged edition in 1587, describes a 'monster' (born in Northumberland during the reign of King Constantine of Scotland) answering precisely to this typology. With 'one whole bellie from the nauill downe . . . and from the nauill vpwards . . . diuided into two bodies', Holinshed states, so were there:

> two contrarie wils or desires in the same, euer lusting contrarilie, as when the one did sleepe, the other would wake; when the one required to haue meat, the other passed for none at all. Oftentimes would they chide and brall togither, insomuch that at length they fell so far at variance, that they did beat and rent either other verie pitifullie with their nailes.[35]

Animating the account is the idea of a physical intimacy that has a concomitant psychological inimicality. The suggestion of a self-destructive personality, moreover, continues even into death:

> At length the one with long sickenesse wearing away and finallie deceassing, the other was not able to abide the greeuous smell of the dead carcase, but immediatlie after died also.[36]

If the chronicle wraps up its description with the inevitability of extinction, *The Tempest*, by contrast, concludes its narrative of a two-headed 'monster', now recognized by Stephano as a type of *spondylodymus*, *ischiopagus* or *dicephalus dipus dibrachius*, with a conjuring into existence.[37] The efforts of the jester and the butler to position Caliban within familiar frames of reference have as their climax Stephano's playing midwife to a grotesque delivery, one which is also linked to an evacuation of waste: 'I'll pull thee by the lesser legs – if any be Trinculo's legs, these are they . . . Thou art very Trinculo indeed! How cam'st thou to be the siege of this mooncalf? Can he vent Trinculos?' (II.ii.98–102). The tumbling out of the gabardine into theatrical clarification is symbolically freighted at multiple levels. Most obviously, of course, the scene is devoted to possibly the only 'monstrous birth' in early modern drama, even if that moment of nativity is parodic in kind. No less parodic is the implied imitation of Prospero, since Stephano drunkenly replicates the magus' earlier acts of demonstration and predilection for calling up life from a 'rock' or 'monstrous' impressions from the incorporeal air. Crucially, Stephano discovers Trinculo, casting Caliban as a 'monster' and a mother that gives birth to 'matter' (II.ii.56);

in this respect, one might argue that birth distinguishes itself from the exhibition of a 'monster' in being the ultimate, and most domestic, form of revelation. Complicating the 'monstrous birth' still further is the suggestion that it is accompanied by a quasi-surgical separation: although Caliban and Trinculo stand again as autonomous, the desta-bilizing properties of the original 'monster' remain undiminished. For Caliban has both changed and reverted, been created and uncreated, in a process of becoming confined to a single scene.

Even if delivery has stripped Caliban of one layer of ambiguity, the cultural need to tie him to recognizable early modern contexts still asserts itself. A space into which can be poured antithetical interpreta-tions, Caliban is constantly represented (or reborn) as the play proceeds. In the remaining scenes with Stephano and Trinculo, Caliban's 'mon-strosity' is increasingly the target of domesticating, belittling impulses, although, interestingly, these moves towards subordination rarely assume self-evident colonial dimensions. Most frequently deployed as an descriptor for Caliban is 'mooncalf'. Enlisted on three occasions (II.ii.102, 106, 129), the term has in its immediate range of meaning a 'false conception' and a 'congenital idiot'.[38] The designation suggests that Caliban's potential development has been forestalled or cut short: briefly, the 'monster' is imagined as an arrested, rather than an ongoing, process. But 'mooncalf' circulated no less expressively in the period as a synonym for the 'monkcalf', the 'monstrous' animal born in 1523 in Freiburg with a mantle resembling a cowl and seized upon by Martin Luther as an emblem of a degenerate papacy (Figure 10). According to German broadsheet propaganda that soon appeared in English translations, the 'monkcalf' signified the benighted, brutal and idolatrous condition of the Roman Church; by implication, therefore, Stephano and Trinculo figure Caliban as a similarly unenlightened creature who can be dominated because he has strayed in his divine allegiances.[39] The potency of a popular discourse continues to filter into these scenes, although here it is the scriptural polemic of the Reformation, rather than the structural versatility of the English ballad, that is put to work.

Efforts towards the establishment of ascendancy notwithstanding, Caliban does not sit comfortably within the niches that his new masters devise. Once his eloquence has shown itself (in being reborn the 'monster' acquires a voice), Caliban has once again to be accommo-dated, since a speaking, poetic subjectivity is at odds with both a construction of mental deficiency and with theories of frustrated devel-opment. We might not be surprised, therefore, that the process of finding a local model for the 'monster' finds its logical outcome in his material domestication: Caliban is obliged to become a domestic, a 'servant-monster' (III.ii.4), and to be restricted to that part. The placing of Caliban in service reflects ironically back upon the trades of his employers, pointing up the comic reduplication of Stephano and Trinculo's own class modalities. At the same time, the confinement of Caliban within this role invites a comparison with the 'Trusty Servant', a Winchester College wall-painting from the early 1580s, which represents a domestic as a *hircocervus*, a 'monstrous' but idealized union of man, hog, deer and ass (Figure 11). The painting is accompanied by allegorical verses that explain the individual virtues of the servant's various animal parts, and was clearly used to encourage in the pupils a like-minded consciousness of social responsibility.[40] The messy physical assembly that is Caliban's 'monstrous' body is ideologically implicated in the hybridized appearance of the 'Trusty Servant', but it also needs to be borne in mind that Shakespeare's 'monster' is seen to fall far short of the perfect dependant. The combination of Caliban's service and physical anomalousness leads Stephano and Trinculo to stigmatize him as a 'very shallow monster' (II.ii.138), a 'very weak monster' (II.ii.139), a 'credulous monster' (II.ii.140), a 'most perfidious and drunken monster' (II.ii.144–5), an 'abominable monster' (II.ii.153) and a 'howling monster' (II.ii.174) – in short, a perceived distance from standards of employee excellence becomes the means whereby the 'monster' is abused at the level of of linguistic ability and intellectual integrity. From the perspective of the fairground, the fiction entertained by Stephano and Trinculo is that the servant they have hired is a 'poor' (II.ii.140) substitute for his 'trusty' college equivalent.

But the process of Caliban's transformation into other 'monstrous' identities is double-edged and does not only work to his detriment. Thanks to the intervention of Ariel in the comic scenes, dramatized locations of the 'monstrous' shift into new quarters. In a variation of the episode devoted to Caliban's birth, Ariel fills the conjoined twin role vacated by Trinculo, the spirit enacting the aggressive voice which comes into conflict with the 'monster' and his initially more passive temperament. Part and parcel of the invisible ventriloquized performance is the dispersal of the 'monstrosity' that, for much of *The Tempest*, centres on Caliban alone. Even in the first stages of their encounter, Caliban had regarded Stephano as a 'wonder' (II.ii.159) in a reversal of the visual premises of the fairground 'monster'-booth's theatricality. Now, in the light of Ariel's participation, the displacement is hastened, for Caliban describes Trinculo as a 'pied ninny' (III.ii.62) or parti-coloured simpleton. Crucially, the phrase constitutes a reworking of Caliban's own characteristics as a 'freckled' (I.ii.283) mooncalf ('idiot'), implying that the 'monster' is beginning to shed himself of the weight of 'monstrous' designations imputed against him. Caliban, it might be suggested, is constructed as coming to entertain Gonzalo's argument that 'monstrosity' is rarely removed, always local and adjacent. Not only does the turning by the 'monster' upon his former twin indicate the arbitrary transparency of non-normative classifications; it simultaneously announces the onset of Caliban's humanity.

III

As the trajectory of the comic business suggests, 'monsters' in *The Tempest* are not limited simply to extraordinary generic differences or to a single dramatic sequence. The 'monstrosities' on display in the sub-plot, in fact, mime larger 'monstrous' fluctuations animating the play as a whole. In some senses, *The Tempest* is primarily concerned with 'disability' and 'imperfection' in all of their manifestations. Time and time again the drama's metaphors return to playing variations on physical ailments, flaws and compromises. Miranda affirms that Prospero's 'tale' would 'cure deafness' (I.ii.106); Ariel claims that the shipwrecked party has arrived without a 'blemish' (I.ii.218); Ferdinand, stained with a 'canker' (I.ii.416) of grief, refused earlier offers of marriage because of 'some defect' (III.i.44) in the 'women' (III.i.43) to whom he was introduced; and Prospero regrets his 'infirmity' (IV.i.160). Throughout, it would appear as if the material body is an inherently unstable property in danger of becoming a 'monsterized' version of its potentially more perfect self.

Concern about the physical body is only a short step away from anxiety about the reproductive body and, in this connection, it is striking that birth can never be represented or alluded to in *The Tempest* without the entertainment of accompanying complications. That is, heterosexual intercourse is hedged about with qualifications because of an apprehension about the uncertainty of its consequences. Thus, no 'worse' than a princess 'issued' (I.ii.59) from Prospero's marriage with his wife; 'trust' can only 'beget ... falsehood' (I.ii.93–5); and 'Good wombs', the usually guileless Miranda notes, 'have borne bad sons' (I.ii.120). Prominent in these formulations is the suggestion of offspring that, in terms of class and morality, are the precise antitheses of their parentage. The fullest elaboration of the idea is provided by Prospero, who broods obsessively on 'that which breeds' (III.i.76) between the lovers. His warning to Ferdinand runs:

> If thou dost break her virgin-knot before
> All sanctimonious ceremonies may
> With full and holy rite be ministered,
> No sweet aspersion shall the heavens let fall
> To make this contract grow; but barren hate,
> Sour-eyed disdain, and discord shall bestrew
> The union of your bed with weeds . . .
>
> (IV.i.15–21)

On the one hand, the speech appears to contend that a premarital sexual engagement would only be unproductive ('barren hate'). On the other, it implies that such a coupling might indeed be fruitful; the 'union', however, would be covered with 'weeds', suggesting a birth so shameful that concealment is required. The horror, lurking among the parasitic vegetation choking the paradisial garden, is that of the 'monstrous birth', one consequence of incontinence. Yet another Caliban is the preoccupation here, a 'monster' who has already articulated a wish to people the island with his own kind. In his reply to Prospero, Ferdinand states that he hopes for 'fair issue' (IV.i.24). Kim F. Hall has argued that the 'language of fairness', because of its participation in a culture that distinguished between types of 'skin colour', was a 'key factor in the . . . development of racial distinctions in the period'.[41] I would suggest, rather, that 'fair', as it is deployed by Ferdinand, builds on the 'monstrous' threats put into play by Prospero, for the term, as well as referring to physical beauty, could connote an appearance free from 'blemish or disfigurement'.[42] The desire for perfect progeny is shared by potential grandfather and son-in-law alike. By pointing up these parallel reproductive projections, *The Tempest* not only seeks to banish the 'foul' (IV.i.139) precedent of Caliban's assault on Miranda; it also strives to establish the political need for a purity of lineage unaffected by adulterating influences.

The desire to supervise the reproductive process voiced in this exchange is, in fact, endemic in *The Tempest* as a whole. It initially announces itself, paradoxically, by way of formulations that stress Prospero's reliance on events seemingly outside his control. Hence the magician is able to avoid shipwreck and assemble exiled courtiers only because of particular conjunctions of planets; similarly, he arrived at the island by 'providence divine' (I.ii.159). As critics have noted, however, Prospero simultaneously strives against a dependent status and is ambitious for self-sufficiency. In this endeavour, gendered anxieties, which manifest themselves in constructions of the maternal function and the contaminating powers women are thought to exercise, are not surprisingly to the fore. Stephen Orgel writes that Prospero's wife 'is missing as a character, but [he], several times explicitly, presents himself as incorporating the wife, acting as both father and mother'.[43] ' "Farewell, my wife and children!" ' (I.i.60–1) cry the mariners, and it is precisely a situation in which women are absent, repressed or appropriated that the play goes on to anatomize.

What has not received notice is the extent to which the play, as a consequence of the banishment of maternal properties, favours acts of parthenogenesis. In *The Tempest*, men are envisaged as agitating to give birth without the agency or intervention of female influence. Worryingly, it is with the unregenerate that the aspiration most clearly expresses itself. The parthenogenetic abilities of Antonio, for instance, are hinted at when Sebastian observes to the usurping Duke that 'the setting of thine eye and cheek proclaim / A matter from thee, and a birth, indeed, / Which throes thee much to yield' (II.i.227–9). Both the momentous theme in the offing and the imminent birth are blurred in the remark; rising above them, however, is the suggestion that Antonio has internally conceived his burden in a self-generating capacity. It should come as no surprise, then, that Prospero, in particular, chafes at Antonio's part in having 'new created / The creatures that were mine, I say: or changed 'em, / Or else new formed 'em' (I.ii.81–3). Richard Strier usefully notes that Antonio here resembles 'the Christian God, creating out of nothing'.[44] One might also want to add that Prospero is discovered as reacting enviously to his brother's parthenogenetic powers, since the series of verb substitutions littering the speech (the magus hesitates between 'created' and 'changed' before settling on the more adjudicative 'formed') points to an unwillingness to acknowledge a superior shaping force. Such a mastery over reproductive actions is even taken up, in order to be parodically translated, at lower levels of the social scale, as when Caliban improvises upon his name in playful fashion: "Ban, 'Ban, Ca-Caliban / Has a new master – get a new man!' (II.ii.179–80). Although there is no suggestion of metaphorical pregnancy in Caliban's song, there is the comparably insistent registration of a sensibility recreating itself, speculating of its own accord upon new emergent identities.

Interestingly, in attempting to outdo his rivals and subjects, Prospero does not simply pursue the imitative option; instead, he is constructed as bringing together in an overwhelmingly empowering combination parthenogenesis, 'monstrous births' and artistic agency. In this sense, Prospero is dramatized in line with contemporary definitions of the author, whose work, commentators argued, bore more than a passing relation to a 'monstrous' delivery. Sir Philip Sidney states in *Arcadia*, first completed in 1580, that if his 'idle work . . . though in itself it have deformities . . . had not been in some way delivered, [it] would have grown a monster', the which perception informs a similar remark in his *An Apology for Poetry* (1580–1); the poet, he writes, 'lifted up with the vigour of his own invention, [delights] . . . in making things either better than Nature bringeth forth, or, quite anew, forms such as never were in Nature'.[45] The capacity of the artist individually to fashion 'monsters' and, in so doing, to change the course of 'nature', lies at the heart of *The Tempest*'s theatrical aesthetic. First, by electing to transform his spirits into portents, Prospero becomes a displaced originator of prodigious or 'monstrous' offspring. Second, by asserting a unique authority over the mechanisms of birth – he delivers Ariel from his sylvan hysteria (I.ii.292–3) and, significantly, has to remind the spirit of his confinement on a monthly basis (I.ii.262) – Prospero is enabled both to reorient 'nature' and to practise a redemptive 'art' (I.ii.291). Part of his reformatory programme, for instance, involves the production out of the heavens of the 'wondered' (IV.i.123) masque. Prospero's parturition of wonders is more sharply observed still. As a 'father and a wife' (IV.i.123), Prospero *'discovers'* (V.i.171.1) Ferdinand and Miranda at chess by pulling aside a curtain, adding, 'I will requite you with as good a thing, / At least bring forth a wonder to content ye' (V.i.169–70). To adapt the fairground metaphor, Prospero, ever the showman, invites his courtier-clients to enter the 'monster'-booth ('Pray you look in' [V.i.167]), only to change his mind and promise that the 'wonder' within will be brought outside. That 'wonder', in a telling duplication of the doubled 'monster' that was Caliban and Trinculo, is a con-joined phenomenon; in addition, like the quarreling twins of before, Miranda–Ferdinand represents a 'miracle' (V.i.177) that is at variance with itself. But the dispute of the lovers, I would suggest, takes second place to the power being consolidated in their presenter. For, having been implicitly usurped by Stephano as the discoverer of a 'monster' that is one and not one, Prospero here reasserts himself. Crucially, he delivers a legitimized conjunction of a man and a woman as opposed to an illegitimate meeting between a 'man' and a 'monster'. Enacting this role, Prospero confirms his place as the island's only author, its only marvellously productive artist.

IV

Perhaps the most spectacular wonder produced by Prospero is that of the tempest itself. Critical tradition has tended to approach the play's tempest either by way of its Virgilian precursor or its colonial correlative (the storms off Bermuda that wrecked Sir Thomas Gates' ship). In attempting to pinpoint the ways in which *The Tempest* was delivered from its own cultural circumstances, however, we might do better to attend to a local model. In 1607, Wales and the West Country were besieged by extreme floods, and the pamphlets that lamented them in the same year provide a telling preview of the watery inundations and violent precipitations that frame *The Tempest*, an early version of which was presented at Whitehall in 1611. 'You haue all this while been Spectators of sad and tragicall euents, which now . . . haue been presented on the *Theater* of the world,' declared one writer, adding, 'The true shape of such monstrous & prodigious birthes as these are, cannot at first be perfectly discouered . . . till the earth be fully deliuered of this burden of Waters, the true & lively portraiture of this mishapen Creature is not to be beheld.'[46] The passage concatenates some of the major motifs of *The Tempest*, emphasizing, as it does, an encounter between a viewer and a wonder, a 'monstrous birth' whose final form is still in process, and natural forces that can be twisted into disproportion: that Shakespeare adapted these constructions sensitizes us to a culture that habitually mediated tempests in terms of the theatricality of 'monstrosity'. Memories of the 1607 floods were reawakened in 1613 when another round of climatic disturbances ravaged the country. Winds and tempests resulted in widespread devastation, and the inevitable accompanying pamphlets, some of which plagiarized the language of the 1607 publications, again enlisted tropes of 'monstrosity' in a material commentary on shipwrecks and miraculous marine 'deliverances' (Figure 12).[47] One 1613 pamphlet went a stage further, arguing that meterological chaos had caused the '*Ayre* . . . in sulphurous flakes [to] drop downe all on fire' and that the 'monstrous birth of Winds and Waters [had] brought forth' a 'number of most strange shapes'.[48] Clearly, here, there is a further node of connection with Shakespeare's play, particularly in view of the fact that *The Tempest*, too, privileges the actions of a magician-protagonist who, in rescuing the Neapolitans from shipwreck, will 'deliver all' (V.i.313). One might also want to add that, apart from the attention to the 'monstrous' generation of 'strange . . . shapes' (V.i.289, I.ii.479), the drama figures its central turmoil in terms of a sky that, threatening to 'pour down stinking pitch' (I.ii.3), appears to be on 'fire' (I.ii.5). It was in 1613, of course, that *The Tempest* received its revival both at Blackfriars and the Globe and, in a celebration of the marriage of James I's daughter Elizabeth to the Elector Palatine, at court. Given the mutually constitutive languages of the 1613 tempest publications and performances of the play at this time, it is tempting to argue not only for reciprocal relationship but also for the possibilities of revision: Shakespeare, one might speculate, modified or updated the earlier version of *The Tempest* to meet the requirements of a new climatic environment.

The performative occasions of the play have attracted considerable comment in recent years. Because *The Tempest* was twice staged before a royal assembly, critics have been driven to pursue thematic clusters that seem to illuminate the formative involvement of Shakespeare's patron, James I. In particular, the marriage between Ferdinand and Miranda has been seen as complimenting James' role as a mediator between warring Protestant and Catholic European principalities, while the drama's politics have been judged a warning to the King about the dangers of absolutist government.[49] Other discussions have found in Sycorax a reference to James' condemnations of magic, and in Prospero a hint of the monarch's elevation both of Orphic models of authority and of a creative influence over his subjects.[50] A further constellation of Jamesian interests – one that offers a clarifying contextual milieu for the play's local 'monsters' – has, however, so far escaped notice. From an early stage, James cultivated the study of 'monsters'; this revealed itself, first, in an academic curiosity about non-normative material bodies and, second, in a rhetorical fondness for tropes of a 'monstrous' turn.[51] Thus, in *Daemonology* (1597), James contemplates the reproductive implications of sexual unions between women and devils; in *Basilikon Doran* (1599), flatters himself that his work is '*rightlie proportioned . . . without any monstrous deformitie*'; and, in his speech to parliament in 1603, rejects the notion that, as 'Head' of and 'Husband' to an 'Isle' that is his 'Wife', he possesses a 'diuided and monstrous Body'.[52] Clearly, a play that debated processes of extraordinary reproduction would have struck a chord with a King who was himself driven to contemplate the prospect as part of his ongoing supernatural enquiries. At the same time, the suggestion, voiced by James, that the author is capable of 'monstrous' work is not too far removed from the mobilization in *The Tempest* of Prospero and his wondrously generative art. Nor, given the play's preoccupation with doubled progeny, does James' rejection of the 'diuided and monstrous Body' identification fail to resonate: his metaphor is further marked by its manipulation of marital roles and elaboration of the island as a nation-state. Once again, these are characteristic manoeuvres in *The Tempest*, suggesting that the local inflection of the play's 'monsters' is implicated in its local theatrical circumstances. With a studied appropriateness, the play engages one of the sources of its imaginative possibility by rehearsing the sovereign's 'monstrous' philosophizing; in so doing, it allows itself to reflect not so much upon English institutions as upon the emergent construction of Great Britain. For, in the same way that Prospero aims at a marital con-junction that will consolidate his ducal power, so did James, through occupying the thrones of England and Scotland, endeavour to bring about a similarly cohesive national polity. From one vantage-point, such union is 'monstrous'; from another, it entails the felicitous scenario of the absorption of differences into an integrated political entity.

Further implicating James in *The Tempest* and its 'monsters' is his alacrity at invoking as an interpretive template the grammar attached to, and the assumed imminence of, the apocalypse. For James, the 'mon-strous' denizens of Revelation could be summoned to situate all manner of momentous natural and political events. A 1585 celebration of the Battle of Lepanto, for instance, quickly abandons the theme of the Turkish threat to dwell upon the greater danger of the 'Antichrist' and the 'whoore' of Babylon, ciphers for the Catholic Church.[53] A 1609 warning to European monarchs about the eradication of Christian lib-erties develops the theme by attacking the apocalypse's 'monstrous Beast, with seuen heads and ten hornes', while a 1618 sonnet about a blazing star advises the populace 'to remember' that 'Doomsday is not past'.[54] In 1613, when *The Tempest* was revived, apocalyptical expecta-tions were finding an outlet in a wide range of cultural productions. They were articulated first in the flood and storm pamphlets, which explained contemporary calamities and consummations as signs of dire judgements to come.[55] But they found a ready niche, too, in Shakespeare's play, both in the tempest that inaugurates the action and in Prospero's renunciation of his preternatural practices:

> I have bedimmed
> The noontide sun, called forth the mutinous winds,
> And 'twixt the green sea and the azured vault
> Set roaring war; to the dread rattling thunder
> Have I given fire, and rifted Jove's stout oak
> With his own bolt; the strong-based promontory
> Have I made shake, and by the spurs plucked up
> The pine and cedar. Graves at my command
> Have waked their sleepers, oped, and let 'em forth
> By my so potent art.
>
> (V.i.41–50)

In discussions of the speech's rhetorical showiness, critics have been quick to point out a close rehearsal of Medea's incantation in Arthur Golding's 1567 translation of Ovid's *Metamorphoses*.[56] Coloured, as it is, by Ovidian example, Prospero's abjuration, in fact, strives to outdo rather than merely duplicate its classical predecessor. Most obviously, Prospero's address represents a collection or even 'cabinet' of rare abilities that, to adapt Barbara M. Benedict's reading of early modern curiosity, enacts a 'psychological desire for containment and self-possession': the magician gathers about him the achievements of his trade at precisely the moment when he is in need of centring and defining his power.[57] Illustrating the consolidation of control, the summary of magical activity also stands as an utterance of apocalyptical proportions. The eclipses, thunder, lightning, earthquakes and openings of graves alluded to here form integral parts of the Revelation narrative, to the extent that both 'Monster-Master' and virtuoso appear compromised by Prospero's recollection of his performances as embattled deity.[58] At the level of the dramatic action, the speech thus displays Prospero occupying a quasi-divine role, looking back at his skill in revivifying in order to anticipate the planned resurrection of his abusers' consciences. Deeper into its political interstices, however, this culminating peroration is itself animated by the spectral influence of James. By invoking the apocalypse, *The Tempest* casts a skewed glance towards the sovereign, reflecting, through Prospero's godly machinations, upon James as the guardian of spiritual values and defender of the establishment. The capability of the magician to 'set' and resolve apocalyptical 'war' becomes the means whereby *The Tempest* mediates the King's construction of himself as a balm for religious conflict. Apocalypse, in short, is the conduit of communication between a dramatist and a patron implicitly represented as the organizing authority behind the avoidance of potentially 'monstrous' historical developments.

As the 'revels' (IV.i.148) end and Prospero's 'pageant' (IV.i.155) dissolves, we are reminded of the jointly reinforcing connections between apocalyptical awakenings and fairground entertainment, theatrical demonstration and divine revelation. To 'reveal' is etymologically related to the old French, *révéler* (to revolt, make a din and make merry), from which are derived the verb, to 'revel', and the noun, 'revel', a parish fair.[59] There may also be a link between *révéler* and *réveiller* (to wake up or revive) that pushes to the forefront of an audience's consciousness the psychological resurrections in train at the end of the play. Certainly, the suggestion of the shedding of one identity and the rebirth of another is forcibly made: Prospero leaves behind his recent role as Master of the Revels, the official who approves what is and is not 'monstrous', to discover himself as Duke of Milan. Even in this political part, the magician is loath to relinquish theatrical dominion completely, and it is striking that Prospero prevaricates over telling 'the story of my life' (V.i.304), as if clinging to some mystifying vestiges of wonder. But Prospero's authority is fallible, and his elusive excuse for Caliban – 'this thing of darkness I / Acknowledge mine' (V.i.275–6) – expresses an equally enigmatic range of tendencies. The remark's immediate effect is to complete the process of Caliban's domestication: Prospero, owning (and authoring) the 'monster', accepts his proximity. As such, Prospero's comment displays a residual attraction to the 'monstrous', which entails a twin-like dependency. Shakespeare, himself the father of twins, constructs Prospero as reclaiming the logic of the comic scenes, in which a kinship with the 'monstrous' is indicated via the business beneath the gabardine. Zakiya Hanafi writes that the 'transformational techniques' of technology 'function by enhancing or manifesting the latent bestiality or monstrousness that now is represented as lying dormant inside us all', and his assessment is more than relevant to *The Tempest*'s ultimate alliance between Prospero and Caliban.[60] Through the technology of magical demonstration, it is implied, Prospero comes to identify his own 'monstrosity' and, through conjuring Caliban, begins to appreciate the impossibility of ever adequately separating out 'monster' and 'man'. In this sense, Prospero has Caliban to thank for 'learning' (I.ii.364) him humanity.

The notion that Caliban enjoys access to humanity is not as implausible as it might appear and is, in fact, prepared for in two interrelated ways. In a number of respects, the final stages of *The Tempest*, confirming the 'monster' as local, enact Caliban's departure from 'monstrosity'. On the point of breaching Prospero's 'cell', Caliban and the drunken company are briefly distracted by *'glistering apparel'* (IV.i.193.1) suspended on a 'line' (IV.i.193) at the entrance. Heather James argues that what the 'confederates' (IV.i.140) 'stumble upon is no illusory temptation but the wardrobe of a theatre's tiring-house'.[61] Without doubt, metatheatrical elements are implied in the scene; from another perspective, however, the spectacle has more obvious affinities with the fairground 'monster'-booth, whose colourful advertisements, hanging at the threshold, beckoned the way to the 'monstrous' interior. In a move that clarifies the association, Stephano and Trinculo don the splendid finery, ignoring Caliban's sound advice that the 'luggage' (IV.i.231) is 'trash' (IV.i.223). By refusing to acknowledge the 'monster',

Stephano and Trinculo, I suggest, turn 'monsters' themselves. Not only do the butler and jester, in aping their betters, begin to resemble fairground 'apes' (IV.i.249); because of their impatience to wear the new clothes, they are inserted into a contemporary praxis that saw socially transgressive dress and 'monstrosity' as synonymous. Outrageous clothes, for instance, could be displayed like any 'monster', as a 1565 case involving a London apprentice suggests; his 'monsterous hose' was 'treshured . . . in the nether hall [the Guildhall] where [it] may . . . be . . . seen . . . as an example of extreme folye'.[62] More generally, the potential of clothes to assume 'monstrous' dimensions was a frequently deployed rhetorical commonplace. Hence, writing of the 'Monstrousnesse of Apparell' in 1623, Francis Rous observed that contemporary 'fashionists' were 'monstrous' because 'excessiue in measure . . . extraordinarie in shape' and 'great and little' in 'deformitie'.[63] 'Monstrous' in that they, too, are deformed by their garments, Stephano and Trinculo are irrevocably marked as 'monsters' when set on by spirits in the form of hunting dogs. Not surprisingly, therefore, in the final scene, the two form with Caliban a comically indistinguishable triumvirate. They have been made into 'strange stuff' (IV.i.234) and are grouped together with the 'monster' as unclassifiable 'things' (V.i.264). Crucially, in that he has resisted the lure of the '*glistering apparel*', Caliban, it is implied, has continued to divest himself of the 'monstrosity' through which he has been identified. His 'monstrosity', the conclusion contends, is gravitating, instead, to his parody masters, who, in yet another ironic inversion, are now themselves viewed as marketable.

By declining to follow the path of 'monsterization', Caliban draws ever closer to a human model, and this is reinforced in his closing determination, 'I'll be wise hereafter, / And seek for grace' (V.i.294–5). William M. Hamlin writes that 'grace' is being used here to connote 'virtue'; Caliban, he states, aims at 'an independent project of self-betterment'.[64] I would suggest, rather, that 'grace' is deployed in the parallel senses of the 'divine influence which operates . . . to regenerate' and the 'attractiveness . . . belonging to elegance of proportions'.[65] That is, Caliban agitates to be resurrected out of his 'monstrosity' into a normative aesthetic appearance. Via 'grace', Caliban is represented as striving after the achievement of a 'human shape' (I.ii.284), an aspiration which is also registered in Prospero's final characterization of him as a 'demi-devil' (V.i.272): the 'monster' is only half way to 'monstrosity'. Caliban's approach to humanity is additionally hinted at in his fate. Because he is not referred to in the preparations for the return to Milan, the implication is that the 'monster' plays no part in the island exodus.

If only metaphorically, the island is turned over to him, and he is no longer 'cheated' (III.ii.41) of his inheritance. Such a development, however, flies in the face of contemporary legal theory, for, as Sir Edward Coke stated in 1628, a 'monster which hath not the shape of man kinde, cannot be heire or inherit any land'.[66] Prospero, then, discovered in line with a number of influential court cases, is constructed as overturning the inheritance laws of his age.[67] The dismantling of Caliban's 'monstrosity' takes place at the level of an implied visual reorientation; it is also realized in a new property dispensation that reverses the bases of the island's economic arrangements.

At once it would seem as if Prospero is unaffected by this 'sea-change' (I.ii.401). His epilogue reveals him still the virtuoso and impresario who looks forward, not to the exportation of 'med of Ind' (II.ii.57) but to the political wonder that is his daughter, and who continues in accumulative vein, even if the catalogue elaborated is of possessions lost:

> I must be here confined by you,
> Or sent to Naples. Let me not,
> Since I have my dukedom got,
> And pardoned the deceiver, dwell
> In this bare island by your spell,
> But release me from my bands
> With the help of your good hands.
> Gentle breath of yours my sails
> Must fill, or else my project fails,
> Which was to please. Now I want
> Spirits to enforce, art to enchant;
> And my ending is despair
> Unless I be relieved by prayer,
> Which pierces so that it assaults
> Mercy itself, and frees all faults.
> As you from crimes would pardoned be,
> Let your indulgence set me free.
>
> (V.i.322–38)

Yet closer scrutiny suggests that the speech is less confident in its identifications. If the man cannot be master, having relinquished authority to the 'monster', he can continue only as powerless exhibit, the other side of the same dialectical coin. 'Monstrosity' having transferred itself to the clowns, it also drifts towards Prospero; indeed, in many respects,

Prospero speaks as Caliban in the final scene, both in terms of rhetorical formulations and cultural aspirations. The 'thrice double ass' (V.i.295) expression deployed by Caliban, for instance, finds an echo in Prospero's 'every third thought' (V.i.311), and like Caliban, always his metaphorical twin, Prospero sues for grace. The conclusion towards which *The Tempest* pushes is that Prospero is in part made 'monstrous' by Caliban or, at least, rare, singular and extraordinary. It should come as no surprise, therefore, that Prospero is envisaged here as simultaneously 'confined' (these are the circumstances in which Caliban labours at the start) and disabled (in that he is incapable of using his own 'hands', the magician brings to mind the exhibitions of contemporary limbless or physically challenged performers).[68] As a 'monster' in search of 'mercy', Prospero refers to the audience, on whom he depends not only for release and relief but also for deliverance. Through being 'monstrously' reborn, with the theatre's spectators as a parthenogenetic parent, the magus-'monster' can become the actor and abandon the part, can clarify the blurring perimeters of a dissolving playworld. And, by soliciting a liberating 'indulgence', Prospero stages a by now familiar manoeuvre and centres attention on the local manifestations of the audience's theatrical experience.

V

In arguing for *The Tempest* as less centrally implicated in the discourses and practices of the New World, one might stand accused of enacting another form of colonialism on the play, banishing one interpretive model in order to impose a new critical hegemony. By positing the crucial contribution of local constructions of 'monstrosity', however, the aim of this chapter has not been to minimize *The Tempest*'s ideological extraneousness or to exorcize its differences; rather, it has been to suggest that the exotic is always rooted in the familiar, and to underline how structures of domination are filtered through domestic modalities. In particular, an emphasis on the local reveals that discovery is less of a material and geographical aspiration than it is an index of the theatrical imperative.

In *The Tempest*, 'monstrosity' and theatricality make singularly cosy bedfellows. Compared to other dramatic productions in the early modern repertory, *The Tempest* is perhaps the only work that thematizes the process whereby contemporary 'monstrous' entertainment was licensed and staged, for Prospero, among his many other parts, stands *par excellence* as a Master of the Revels – the presiding genius of the fairground, the supervisor of celebration, the controller of revelation, the authorizer of resurrection. *The Tempest* thus makes visible the institutional bases of the theatricalization of 'monstrosity' and, in so doing, alerts us to the fact that 'monsters' are inevitably socially and culturally determined. Certainly, a social freight is attached to *The Tempest*'s 'monsters': Caliban is experienced by (indeed, is constituted through) both 'high' and 'low' representatives of the contemporary order, in such a way as to suggest that he accedes to humanity only when taken out of circulation as the object of a class-dictated gaze. Pointing up such a construction of Caliban, *The Tempest* not only illustrates the social porousness of 'monsters' as metaphors; it also highlights the interpenetration of, and cross-fertilization between, types of demonstrative entertainment. From a rarefied, royal form of masque, *The Tempest* can move to a demotic, vernacular species of show, with the play's 'monsters' a crucial element in its theatrical versatility and latitude.

If *The Tempest* has as one its subjects the institutional praxis of 'monstrosity', it also draws attention to the economic ingredients of 'monstrous' representation. Once again, a comparison with the fairground would seem to be operative here: in asking for applause at the end of the play, Prospero, a 'monster' still bearing residual traces of the showman, advertises the marketability of a production in which he has been at centre-stage. And, by responding in kind, spectators, types of consumers in the 'monster'-booth, display their approval of the economic transaction in which they have participated. To adopt the metaphor, an audience is placed in a position of mastery and is invited to judge a play that, in being hired for a performance, has been its 'monstrous' servant. Lending our 'hands' to Prospero entails, of course, giving our assent to Shakespeare and, in this connection, it is tempting to suggest that *The Tempest* ultimately figures the dramatist's farewell to the sorts of 'monstrous' theatre that, over the course of his career, had provided him with material sustenance. *The Tempest* has traditionally been seen as Shakespeare's imaginative valediction to the playhouse; it might also stand as an economic paean to aesthetic opportunities provided by a fairground artistry.

To reflect on Shakespeare as dramatist is to speculate about Shakespeare as author. Throughout *The Tempest*, the virtues of a single authorial undertaking, as we have seen, are privileged. However, as earlier parts of this chapter have also argued, unitary forms of authorship (and even, by implication, of subjectivity) are seen to have a slim purchase. Creativity resides, instead, in the activity of twinship or the practice of collaboration. Twinning in *The Tempest* is rarely expected (the 'dainty'

Ariel and the 'delicate' Caliban appear together but once) and more often extraordinary or 'monstrous'. Thus, in the epilogue, when Prospero requests his audience's appreciation, the play enacts its final 'monstrous' combination, that of the playwright and the wider imaginative community. Each is coloured by the other, to the extent that, as Peter G. Platt states, the 'spectator . . . becomes the thaumaturge – complete with the power and responsibility of the profession'.[69] In this play, which Shakespeare may have given birth to on several occasions (making it, like Caliban, a work in process), the dramatist, then, acknowledges as his own 'darkness' the increasing difficulty of the individual authorial enterprise. Notably, after *The Tempest*, Shakespeare worked only in partnership; this is indicated, as Jeffrey Masten states, in '*The Two Noble Kinsmen* [1613], the lost *Cardenio* [1613], and (perhaps) *Henry VIII* [1613]'.[70] Conjoined with John Fletcher, Shakespeare, the doyen of writerly primacy, never regained the authorial preeminence which, in *The Tempest*, is so abundantly on display; instead, in line with his creations, he was to become adulterated and dependent, made 'monstrous' by his art.

6

'If there be never a servant-monster': Translating 'Monsters' in *Bartholomew Fair*

The lure of its title notwithstanding, *Bartholomew Fair* (1614) surprisingly boasts but five brief references to 'monsters'. The only play in the early modern canon explicitly to figure the fair, the commonest haunt of all things 'monstrous', *Bartholomew Fair* is conspicuous for refusing to deliver on the 'monsters' that its subject would seem to necessitate. Contrary to the expectations of a contemporary audience, Jonson's drama declines the opportunity to represent either the 'monster' or the 'man with the monsters' (III.i.11–12); in short, an anticipated execution of Trinculo's fairground fantasy, the exhibition of Caliban, is frustratingly absent from the play's theatrical proceedings.[1]

The framing device of *Bartholomew Fair*, of course, directly confronts this absence. In the Induction, the scrivener poses a particular question. 'If there be never a servant-monster i' the Fair' or 'a nest of antics', he asks, 'who can help it?' (Induction, 128–30). Taking on the role of a Jonsonian mouthpiece, the scrivener takes up a carelessly superior tone in relation to contemporary stage entertainment, explaining the play's seeming lack of 'monstrous' material in terms of the author's aesthetic sensibility: 'He is loth to make Nature afraid in his plays, like those that beget *Tales*, *Tempests*, and such like drolleries, to mix his head with other men's heels' (Induction, 130–2). As critics have recognized, these lines communicate a critical construction of Shakespeare's so-called 'late plays', the romances.[2] '*Tales*' evokes *The Winter's Tale* (1611), with its 'antic' dance of the twelve satyrs, while '*Tempests*' points to *The Tempest* (1611) and to some of its most singular features – Caliban, the 'servant-monster', and Prospero's masque-like entertainments (or 'living drollery').[3] In the opening disclaimers, then, Shakespeare is positioned in a negative light as an artist who, answering to the pressure of demotic tastes, has mortgaged himself to a populist and spectacular brand of dramaturgy. By contrast, Jonson, the Induction implies, will restore to the theatre a superior brand of verisimilitude, one which has no patience with distorting and 'monstrous' modalities of representation. The scrivener's substitution of the 'Justice of Peace' (Induction, 125) for a 'juggler' (Induction, 125–6) is pertinent in this respect, for an institutional embodiment of 'truth' is elevated over and above an archetype of visual dissimulation and trickery. Elaborating the link between 'monstrosity' and representation is the socially freighted allusion to mixing the head with the heels. At a metaphorical level, Jonson, the passage implies, will refuse to be made 'monstrous' by adulterating himself with Shakespeare: he will not run the risk of doubling his physical form, or inverting his bodily anatomy, through association with a playwright in the grasp of the class-marked demands of an undiscriminating audience.

The Induction's rejection of the 'servant-monster' chimes interestingly with a more general Jonsonian strategy: throughout his career, the dramatist had recourse to tropes of 'monstrosity' in an endeavour to distinguish the self-constructed sublimity of his own enterprise. As author, Jonson regarded himself as standing apart both from his literary contemporaries and from his potential consumers. '*Neque, me vt miretur turba, laboro: Contentus paucis lectoribus*' ('Content with a few readers, I do not labour that the crowd may admire me') runs the Horatian motto emblazoned on the title-page of the First Folio, an apt sentiment for a writer who modelled his artistic life on its appeal to a cultured élite and its distance from a plebeian audience. Lending an additional force to the adage is the implication that Jonson will not be gazed at, 'monster-like', by the illiterate multitude.[4] The suggested equation between Jonson and the 'monster' is picked up in John Taylor's elegy on the writer, published in 1637: 'You that are men of worth', he states, 'I speake to you, / Not to the partial and prejudicate: / Nor to the ribble rabble sencelesse crue, / The *Hydra* monster inconsiderate'.[5] Once again, a 'monstrous' trope is appropriated for a writerly purpose, with Taylor's exhortatory formulation here distinguishing between a non-'monstrous', gentle modality of understanding and a 'monstrous', non-gentle state of ignorance.

But Jonson did not only deploy 'monsters' to castigate those who failed to appreciate his *œuvre*; he also enlisted the metaphorical resource to censure poets and playwrights who failed, in his eyes, properly to conform to his aesthetic programme. Thus, Asper, in *Every Man out of His Humour* (1599), condemns 'the monstrousness of time, / Where every servile imitating spirit . . . strives to fling / His ulcerous body in the Thespian spring, / And straight leaps forth a poet'.[6] That these are

Jonsonian convictions is confirmed by the epistle to *Volpone* (1606), which argues, in an unmediated voice, that 'the too-much licence of *Poetasters*, in this time, hath much deformed their mistress'.[7] An indulgence in sexual profligacy, the rupturing of structures of decorum and the ruination of the female muse – these and other examples of a corruptive operation are implicit in Jonson's pronouncement. To combat such a state of affairs, Jonson devises a two-part solution. Confident in his elevated office and exalted role, he proposes in *Volpone*, first, that he will 'raise the despised head of *Poetry* again, and stripping her out of those rotten and base rags, wherewith the Times have adulterated her form, restore her to her primitive habit, feature and majesty' (Epistle, 127–30). This elaboration of the 'monstrous' motif reveals the author agitating to reverse the spoiling process; casting himself in the role of a royal dresser, Jonson imagines a delivery of poetry from sexual shame and moral opprobrium, and a class promotion that reaffirms the literary status quo. The second part of Jonson's reformatory programme concentrates on activities of reception. When Probee, in *The Magnetic Lady* (1632), speaks of 'the solemn vice of interpretation, that deforms the figure of many a fair scene, by drawing it awry', for instance, a Jonsonian imperative is abundantly apparent.[8] For Jonson sought continually to police the potentially 'monstrous' business of interpretation, either through extra-dramatic meditations or through the intricate prosaic paraphernalia that surrounded his work. In Jonson's mind, it seems, to allow an audience freedom of judgement was to propel them into the dangerous 'monstrosities' of delusion and error.

To reflect on Jonson's aesthetic principles is therefore to acknowledge an authorial anxiety about the ease with which the traditional arts could become 'monsterized' versions of themselves. In this connection, it may not be accidental that Jonson apparently admired Shakespeare for his ability to resist the temptations of just such a process. 'It [is] an honour to *Shakespeare*,' claimed Jonson, 'that in his writing, (whatsoever he penn'd) hee never blotted out line' or disfigured his scripts with corrections and revisions.[9] Such veneration of Shakespeare (and it does not seem to have been an isolated instance) is more often than not, however, overshadowed by pejorative comment.[10] Indeed, the evasion of the 'monster' in *Bartholomew Fair*, and the play's unflattering references to *The Tempest*, assume a greater import in the light of the notorious rivalry that marked the writers' relations. The notion of a conflict between Jonson and Shakespeare's career paths is fairly easy to substantiate.[11] Evidence suggests that, with Shakespeare, public and court theatrical forms were comfortably merged, unlike Jonson, who was uncertainly involved in these two areas of entertainment. Whereas Shakespeare seems rarely to have offended his patrons or establishment ideology, Jonson was frequently at odds with the authorities and was imprisoned on several occasions. A commercially successful actor-shareholder, Shakespeare can be read as having experienced few financial difficulties, retiring to become a gentleman; the opposite applied to Jonson who, aspiring to the status of a classical poet and committed only inconsistently to the drama, was often dogged by his creditors. Different priorities between the writers no doubt also resulted in a historically particularized open friction, at least from Jonson's perspective. As Richard Dutton notes, 'Both *The Winter's Tale* and *The Tempest* were performed at court in November 1611 and both were among the five or six plays of Shakespeare chosen to celebrate the marriage of Princess Elizabeth to the Elector Palatine in February 1613; only one of Jonson's, *The Alchemist*, was chosen.'[12] The implication would seem to be that Jonson's drama was judged less appropriate than that of his Stratford counterpart, to the extent that, for whatever reason, he endured the humiliation of being passed over for coveted royal attention.

As one means of confronting the vexatious successes of his writerly *alter ego*, this chapter argues, Jonson stages in *Bartholomew Fair* a 'translation' of Shakespeare's 'monstrous' preoccupations – languages and situations explored in *Othello* (1601–2) but more fully focalized in *The Tempest*. Parallels animating *Bartholomew Fair* and *The Tempest* have been spotted before, of course, with critics Thomas Cartelli, Alvin Kernan and Scott Cutler Shershow arguing respectively for Jonson's reinvention of quintessentially Shakespearean pastoral patterns, for his urban relocation of the 'regenerative insights' of a 'strange enchanting place', and for his redeployment of the 'paradigm . . . of performance'.[13] But these discussions fall short, I suggest, of adequately assessing the extent to which Jonson mediates his rivalry, for 'monsters' and 'monstrosity' in *Bartholomew Fair* are represented always at several removes and frank conversation is played down in favour of bifurcated recastings and ghostly re-enactions. Jonson, I argue, takes up an evasive strategy in relation to the 'monstrous': confining 'monstrosity' to a muted and parodic register is one way of diminishing its theatrical significance. Crucially, by 'translating' *The Tempest*, Jonson is empowered both to explicate Shakespeare (Stephen Mailloux has stated that any translation constitutes an act of interpretation) and to 'other' his rival, locating him within an inferior representational modality.[14] As Walter Benjamin argues, 'translation is . . . a somewhat provisional way of coming to terms with . . . foreignness . . . [it] signifies a more exalted language [that] . . . transplants the original'.[15]

For Jonson, 'translating' Shakespeare initially entails a de-'monstering' or un-wondering of *The Tempest*. Either 'monsters' are bypassed in favour of varieties of spectacular human folly, for instance, or the morphology of 'monstrosity' is subjected to a demystifying critique. Likewise, conventions of 'monstrosity' and spectacle, and interpretive applications of the 'monster', are granted only a comically understated treatment. Such are the means on which Jonson depends to institute an anti-sensational form of theatre. Concomitant with Jonson's strategic 'translation' practice goes a recasting of *The Tempest*. Hence, traces of Prospero inhere in the representation of both Overdo and Ursula, the 'pig-woman' (Induction, 123) who, placed at the 'heart o' the Fair' (I.v.152), commands a booth that in early performances would have occupied a prominent 'upstage centre' position.[16] At an immediate level, this chapter argues, Ursula functions to recuperate and privilege a typically Shakespearean theme, a maternal function that, in *The Tempest*, is notably sidelined. However, Ursula also signifies a 'rude' and 'vulgar' culture of 'monstrous' sights, and metropolitan 'trifles', that Jonson sought to distance himself from, and was drawn to, at one and the same time.[17] The chapter concentrates on Ursula because, in this sense, she sits uneasily alongside the 'translatory' imperative, the 'pig-woman' revealing a species of 'monstrosity' that goes beyond the figurative constraints of dramatic emulation. A figure of excess, Ursula bursts the dyke of her extra-theatrical function and reveals less the triumph of Jonson's authorial sovereignty than the playwright's submission to vernacular 'monstrosities' that, elsewhere, he endeavoured to resist. In the puppet show, too, 'monstrosity' is unwittingly reinstated. Here, the impulse to dislodge the wonder characteristic of the Shakespearean masque, and the effort to correct an anti-theatrical polemic that branded playhouses as seats of 'monstrosity', are compromised by a demonstration that is paradoxically all the more 'monstrous' for operating outside of traditional markers of gendered identification. More generally, the representation of puppets that, in answering back and disrupting the proceedings, almost usurp their controller stands as an apt correlative for an author who, despite his better attempts, finds his narrative continually beset by 'monstrous' eruptions. At a fundamental level, then, *Bartholomew Fair* fails to negate its 'monstrous' contexts, providing an exemplary instance of Jeffrey Jerome Cohen's theory that the 'monstrous' is 'too large to be encapsulated'.

The 'monster's very existence', he observes, 'is a rebuke to boundary and enclosure'.[18]

By directing attention to a 'translation' that strives to avoid the 'monstrous', this chapter builds on the work of critics such as Jonathan Haynes and W. David Kay who have detailed Jonson's frustrated bids to fashion for himself a 'distinctive voice' out of the 'popular' theatrical 'tradition'.[19] It extends these arguments not only in attending to moments of interruption in *Bartholomew Fair* but also in charting the play's publication history. Turning once again to Jonson's theories of his craft, the final parts of the chapter suggest that the exclusion of *Bartholomew Fair* from the 1616 edition of the *Workes* represents a move to exorcize a play that has been 'monstrously' but unwittingly contaminated. Judged in this manner, *Bartholomew Fair* affords insights into the particular social inflections of the 'monster' show in the same moment as it illuminates the labour of defining and deflecting the author's artistic progeny. Material performances, stage dramas and actions directed towards securing authorial posterity may appear distinctive, but the 'monster' is the infiltrating and socially motile force that ties them together and exposes the impossibility of unadulterated cultural production.

I

Jonson's 'translation' of Shakespeare is perhaps most immediately obvious in the ways in which *Bartholomew Fair* offers enticing prospects of 'monsters', only to grant an audience stylistic or parodic versions of the 'original'. Repeatedly, the play summons familiar formulae of 'monstrosity', even if the promises embedded in such rhetorical invocations are rarely matched by the action that ensues. Thus Littlewit's opening remark – 'I ha' such luck to spin . . . like a silk-worm, out of myself' (I.i.1–3) – introduces the idea of a 'monstrous' transformation; as the play later demonstrates, however, the proctor rests essentially unchanged in the impercipience and self-conceit of his behaviour. Littlewit's statement prepares the way for comparable utterances in which 'monsters' appear never too far from the surface, the play hinting at a typology of non-normative bodies, and blurred or split identities, central to the early modern construction of the 'monstrous'. When the guardian, Wasp, for example, says of Cokes that 'If a leg or an arm on him did not grow on, he would lose it i' the press' (I.v.111–13), the assertion gains its impact from the suggestion of a 'monstrous' development – a destabilizing dwindling into limblessness. Evocations of corporeal difference combine with references to physiological or psychological deviations that are no less suggestively coloured with 'monstrous' hues. 'Ale for Arthur, and beer for Bradley' (II.ii.142) announces Overdo, his request flirting with a 'monstrous' severing of his adopted name into its component parts and a disintegration of a coherent selfhood. Alternatively, the play can entertain the opposite scenario, a combining or merging of personalities into a disindividuated whole. Edgworth and Nightingale, the 'secretary' (II.iv.27) and the 'ballad-man' (II.iv.28), are, according to Mooncalf, 'never asunder' (II.iv.28). Admittedly, the comment is couched metaphorically; nevertheless, it conveys intriguingly a quasi-emblematic representation of a conjoined form, the accommodation of two subject-positions within a single physical entity. Throughout *Bartholomew Fair*, it seems, the accepted characteristics of the human frame and of a centred subjectivity have an uncertain purchase; they run the risk of diminishing or blurring, of falling prey to ontological confusion.

If the flagging of the parodic potential of 'monsters' is initiated through rhetorical 'translation', it is continued via interventions in the contemporary philosophical endeavour to subject 'monsters' to a divinely-sanctioned explanatory mechanism. In keeping with Shakespearean drama, *Othello* and *The Tempest* included, *Bartholomew Fair* avails itself of the language and symbolic properties of Revelation. Yet *Bartholomew Fair* does so not in the spirit of discovering an ultimate 'monstrosity' but with the effect of reinforcing pre-existent transgressions and venalities, all of which are paltry and minor in orientation. Hence, although 'judgement' is constantly threatened, such as in Nightingale's ballad (III.v.102–3), and although allusions to 'the claw of the Beast' (I.ii.71), the 'tail of Antichrist' (I.ii.76), the 'purple strumpet' (III.vi.89) and 'Babylon' (III.vi.87) freely circulate, no *deus ex machina* is foregrounded in a meting out of reward and punishment. Similarly, the mutedly uneventful ending of the play suggests only the comic incongruity between a New Testament register and ordinary material realities. Such a 'translation' of the biblical book illuminates an interrogative stance towards Revelation as an interpretive instrument and an emptying of the affective influence of its constitutive elements. Predictions, for instance, so important a part of revelatory 'monstrous' lore, are frequently countenanced, but, more often than not, their mystificatory authority is degraded, as when Dame Purecraft has her 'nativity-water cast' to find out her 'fortune' (I.ii.43, 45). 'Marks' and 'signs' enter the narrative to take on comparably ironic inflections. 'Monstrous' tokens of godly indignation are rarely the focus; instead, 'marks' and 'signs' are understood in secular guise as an absent magistrate's handwriting or as the banners before the booths. Complementing these mocking theatrical properties are the numerous 'sights' with which the fair teems. Occasionally, such 'sights', familiar from Revelation as prodigies, are, as in *Othello*, lent a 'monstrous' dimension. Thus, Littlewit's comment that the expectant Win 'may long' (III.vi.9), among other 'sights i' the Fair' (III.vi.4), to see the 'bull with the five legs' (III.vi.7) functions as a reworking of the early modern belief that, as Audrey Eccles states, a 'child could be born with the marks of some of the things' its mother 'had so earnestly desired' while pregnant.[20] But these more self-evident conjurations of a 'monster' are, in fact, avoidances: the play tantalizes by evoking both the idea of maternal impressions and the theatrical possibility of a 'monstrous' bull. Promises are contracted in such a manner as to be broken, with *Bartholomew Fair* electing never to extend its 'sights' to a typically apocalyptic climax. On the contrary, the opposite is the case in that the play's 'sights' have as a common point of reference either a faked marriage licence or Overdo's imaginary warrant. In this way, *Bartholomew Fair* once again gestures towards the 'monster' only to enact a withdrawal, frustrating a mindset tutored in 'monstrosity' through misleading invitations that lead not so much to the 'monster'-booth as to travestied, disaffiliated and far-flung familial relations.

Implicit in the play's formulations and implications is the avoidance of the 'monster' as a descriptor and the distance of 'monsters' from statements centred upon inherently 'monstrous' questions. The 'monster', one might argue, is present at no more than the level of unfulfilled implication and is apprehensible only through association. But the elusiveness of the 'monster' in *Bartholomew Fair* is precisely the point, suggesting that Jonson marks out his dramatic territory via a thematic vacuum, through a move that pushes to the periphery both Shakespeare and the fictions and extravagances his work is purported to incarnate. More specifically, simultaneously dangling and denying 'monstrosity', *Bartholomew Fair* moves attention towards alternative concentrations of the 'monstrous'. For, if no 'servant-monster i' the Fair' is available, there is certainly in its place no shortage of 'monstrous' derelictions and 'antic' actions among the event's clientele. Writing on early modern popular institutions, Peter Stallybrass and Allon White state that 'plebeian fair-goers were themselves part of the spectacle for the bourgeois observer'.[21] The gendered dimensions and class reverberations of *Bartholomew Fair*'s logic of the spectacle, however, suggest a more complex picture. Women, for instance, are the initial objects of the fairground gaze, as when Littlewit says of his fantastically hatted wife: 'I challenge all Cheapside to show such another' (I.ii.5–6). A para-doxical imperative is held in play here, since the boast suggests both the bourgeois order's narcissistic self-inspection and a reifying belittle-ment (Win is revealed as a disembodied marvel characterized by extra-ordinary attire). Likewise, elsewhere in the play, a spectacular economy is detectable in the ways in which the upper echelons of the fair's con-sumers – and not just its plebeian representatives – are put on display. Both Busy and Overdo have to endure the indignity of the stocks (they are so humiliated, significantly, in order to be 'wonder'd at' [IV.vi.120–1]), while Cokes is discovered as an even more ridiculous exhibition. Such is the visibility of his captivation by the fair, Cokes is in danger of 'set[ting] up a booth' (II.vi.86) himself; later in the play, stripped of his accoutrements and robbed, like Desdemona, of his hand-kerchief, the Harrovian gentleman is described as a 'spectacle' (III.ii.3) and even seen as a displaced 'monster'. Because Wasp looks for him at the booth showing 'the Bull with the Five Legs and Two Pizzles' (V.iv.81–2) – typically, the venue is not seen – the suggestion is that Cokes is made 'monstrous' by the connection or, at least, regarded as an equally appealing rival attraction. The limblessness that earlier threatened Cokes is here extended in the idea of a commercially profitable denudation. In the visual system of *Bartholomew Fair*, then, spectators become spectacles the moment they cease to observe. In the process, conventional social assumptions about the ownership of the gaze are upset, and a range of classes is uncovered as 'monstrously' affected.

Emerging from these scenes is the implication that manifestations of human folly are more than a match for 'monsters' in the exhibitionary practices of early modern culture. Gullibility and the desire to gaze at absurdity are such that, in *Bartholomew Fair*, 'monsters' even take second place in the hierarchical gradation of the different. This perspective on the fair and its denizens may sit alongside Jonson's dismissal of Shake-speare's cultivation of the 'monstrous'; it certainly makes up an integral part of the author's own conception of a humanity that, in thrall to humoral affectations, is itself fit for demonstration. The idea is fully realized when Wasp regards Cokes as carrying versions of 'monstrosity' about with him as a concomitant part of his essential condition: 'the Fair and . . . drums and rattles . . . are already i' your brain: he that had the means to travel your head . . . should meet finer sights than any are i' the Fair and make a finer voyage on't, to see it all hung with cockle-shells, pebbles, fine wheat-straws . . . a chicken's feather, and a cob-web'

(I.v.88–94). The emphasis falls on Cokes' mind as a concatenation of the fairground, as a repository of trifles from the natural world. In this sense, Cokes is envisaged not only as a miniaturized fairground but also as a microcosmic *wunderkammer.* Having established the connection, the passage goes on to demolish the wonder evoked by the prospect of an exposure of the cabinet contents. For only the prosaic, and not the strange, is present in Cokes' collection, as is suggested in the bathetic litany of familiar artifacts. The human body may be internally displayed, but what is shown is nothing less than an unreflecting intellect: the voyage, on which the encounter with wonder depends, leads back to little more than already discovered commonplaces. Even here, therefore, an acknowledgement of the 'monstrous' that represents a flight from the 'monstrous' is still abundantly apparent. Running against the grain of the assumed meanings of the environment it figures, *Bartholomew Fair* performs a 'translation' that, drawing upon language and spectacle, ideally functions to escape 'monsters' rather than engaging with them in direct confrontation.

II

Although a critical engagement with *Othello* and *The Tempest* is suggested in *Bartholomew Fair*'s 'translation' of the 'monstrous', it is more explicitly elaborated when Overdo and Ursula take centre-stage. Revised expressions of dominant Shakespearean preoccupations, Overdo and Ursula are key to the effort to rise above Shakespeare by finding in his theatre opportunities for ironic diversion. In his emphasis on 'enormity' – the term has 'abnormality' and 'irregularity' as its equivalents – Overdo, for instance, invites comparison with two Shakespearean predecessors.[22] Initially, his pursuit of deviation in civic spaces, and his admission that he might err in his judgement (II.i.34–6), point to *Othello* and to his equally ill-fated attempts to seek out 'monstrosity' where it is least expected. As *Bartholomew Fair* proceeds, however, it is Prospero who emerges as Overdo's more obvious analogue.[23] Like Prospero, Overdo functions as showman, and the 'discovery' (II.ii.115) of 'wonders' (II.ii.118) is his first priority. As part of that magisterial imperative, Overdo will 'beget a project' (III.v.1) aimed at the correction of 'monstrosity': his attempt to 'rescue' (II.iv.61) Moooncalf from Ursula, the 'strange woman' (II.iv.62), is a case in point. To bring these and other plans to fruition, Overdo is driven to 'break out in rain and hail, lightning and thunder' (V.ii.5–6) and to 'discover [himself], before [his] time' (V.iv.20–1); echoes of *The Tempest* sound loudly here, particularly in the light of that play's immersion in parthenogenetic births and tempestuous occurrences. But Overdo rests eventually as no more than a minor metropolitan magus in a shrunken setting; rather than unveiling 'monstrosities', he is powerless before them and able to iden- tify only adulterated 'gingerbread-progeny' (II.ii.3–4) as his crowning achievement. Clearly, there is a reductive logic at work here, with Overdo's inefficiency standing in humiliating counterpoint to Pros- pero's arguably more authoritative hold on 'monstrous' matters. The accomplishments of Shakespeare's magician are robbed of some of their wonder through the parallel. Too, the representation of Overdo's failure to master 'monsters' is indicative of the fact that, in *Bartholomew Fair*, there are no 'monsters' to be found; with 'monstrosity' relegated, altered or simply removed, there can be no place for the magistrate's incon- gruous scheme for reforming 'enormity'.

If Overdo constitutes one re-enactment of Prospero, Ursula embodies another. A burlesque restaging of Prospero's summoning into being of the 'monster', Caliban, accompanies her first appearance. First, the 'pig- woman' orders Mooncalf, who is '*within*' (II.ii.46), to enter and be active about his business; then, she reflects anxiously upon her servant's learn- ing difficulties: 'How can I hope that he'll discharge his place of trust . . . that remembers nothing I say to him?' (II.ii.87–9). A number of 'translations' are set in motion at this point: Mooncalf's name replicates the term applied to Caliban in the more populist, comic scenes of *The Tempest*, while Ursula's frustration chimes with Prospero's lament at the lack of progress shown by his 'monster', suggesting a satirical treat- ment of plebeian registrations of physical difference, an impatience with aristocratic constructions of 'monstrosity' and education, and a quotidian grounding of the 'nature' and 'nurture' dichotomy. Jonson does not only imitate the social dynamic of *The Tempest*; he also regen- ders its equations of power, since Ursula's brand of female influence is presented as an earthy substitute for Prospero's masculine hegemony. In this sense, Ursula might stand simultaneously for Sycorax, the witch who, 'with child' (I.ii.269), haunts the margins and memories of Pros- pero's island. The mother of a 'monster', Sycorax, I suggest, provides the imaginative conditions for Ursula, whose own maternal properties are conveyed in Overdo's realization of her as 'the very womb and bed of enormity' (II.ii.107). Prospero rules *The Tempest* as a supernaturally 'wondered father' (IV.i.123), but Ursula holds sway over *Bartholomew Fair* as a naturally 'enormous' matrix. More generally, Ursula is envis- aged as an infernal development of one of the narratives that, in *The*

Tempest, is touched on only briefly, and this is clarified in *Bartholomew Fair*'s metaphorical deployments. If the 'damned' (I.ii.263) Sycorax, argues Prospero, 'got' Caliban through sexual congress 'with the devil himself' (I.ii.319), Ursula, 'having the marks upon her of . . . the devil' (III.vi.33–5), can claim Mooncalf as her demonic 'incubee' (II.ii.84) and can preside over a booth 'positioned onstage', as Julie Sanders states, 'to resemble the old hell-mouth of medieval mystery plays'.[24] In the light of the maternal associations that cluster about Ursula, moreover, one might argue that Jonson explores a further repressed trajectory – the mother's ownership of Caliban and a genealogy of 'monstrosity' that *The Tempest* elects only imperfectly to communicate. And, where Sycorax enslaves spirits and dominates 'potent ministers' (I.ii.275) through 'sorceries terrible' (I.ii.264), Ursula enchants via her control of tobacco and ale; she subdues at the level of food and drink, and all the fair's customers are her servants. Pork and alcohol, *Bartholomew Fair* implies, are the stimulants of the masses, and there is no need for magic if these transformative agents can be possessed and manipulated.

Critics have traditionally understood Ursula's 'enormity' and her control of food and drink inside Mikhail Bakhtin's theory of the the 'grotesque', a category defined as 'a mobile, split, multiple self [and] a subject of pleasure in processes of exchange . . . [which] is never closed off from either its social or ecosystemic context'.[25] Partly in view of her maternal overlap with Sycorax, but also because of her association with excess, I would like to argue that Ursula can be just as profitably tied not so much to a 'grotesque' as to a 'monstrous' designation. Elizabeth Grosz explains that the 'major terata recognized throughout history are largely monsters of excess', and her formulation has been developed by Margrit Shildrick in a discussion of maternal power and the reproductive woman's changing body shape: 'It is not just that the mother is always capable of producing monstrosity,' she states, 'but that she is monstrous in herself. It is above all the very fecundity of the female, the capacity to confound definition *all on her own*, that elicits normative anxiety.'[26] Over the course of the play, Ursula emerges as 'monstrous' in precisely these respects, since *Bartholomew Fair* makes an unconscious virtue of the shifting boundaries of her physical form and the generative energies with which she is endowed. Further, Ursula might be judged 'monstrous' in that she prefigures an alternative cultural configuration, a later historical moment at which 'fatness' and 'monstrosity' were to become synonymous.[27] In a sense, then, there is a 'monster' in the 'heart o' the Fair' (I.v.152). The 'monster' we see, however, is not so much a Shakespearean 'servant-monster' as a Jonsonian 'monstrous' mistress.

III

The 'monstrosity' of Ursula is initially communicated via a process of spectacular discandying that suggests primal transgression and bodily metamorphosis. 'I am all fire, and fat . . . I shall e'en melt away to the first woman, a rib, again . . . I do water the ground in knots as I go . . . you may follow me by the S's I make' (II.ii.49–53), she states. Beyond her associations with a narrative of original sin, Ursula is, as with the 'monster', on display in this scene and characterized by the demonstration of a physical aberration. Like Desdemona, Ursula is also here tied to a conception of woman as inherently 'monstrous' in her tendency to stray from the path of normative standards in a wandering and erroneous movement. Yet rather than bolstering a contestation of Shakespeare, such a typological construction cements Ursula more closely to a plebeian and populist discursive framework. For not only is Ursula stamped with the stigma of the fair; she also figures as one of its chief participants and as a conductor for its 'monsterizing' activities. In particular, Ursula is drawn as authorizing a process of abusive sophistication. The ale and tobacco that she markets will, under her aegis, be radically affected: 'threepence a pipeful', she instructs, 'and a quarter of a pound of coltsfoot mix'd with it too, to eke it out . . . Froth your cans well i' the filling . . . and jog the bottles o' the buttock . . . skink out the first glass . . . and mis-take away the bottles . . . before they be half drunk off' (II.ii.90–3, 97–9, 102–4). Douglas Bruster intriguingly argues that the play's discovery of a deceitful business initiative underscores a 'fear of women's innate corruption'.[28] Certainly, the revelation of Ursula's methods illuminates continuing gendered anxieties; however, it might also be pointed out that the practice of the 'pig-woman' operates at the level of 'monstrous' imitation. With the aid of Mooncalf, whose name connotes a 'false conception' or 'mola', Ursula will falsify the measures of her wares; in so doing, she puts into circulation imperfect versions of the actual article, 'translations' of the 'true' product. Paradoxically, Ursula, the incarnation of excess, will short-change her customers: both in terms of her own 'enormities', and the diminishments that she supervises, the 'pig-woman' regulates a prostituted economy that is 'monstrous' in outline. In this sense, Ursula is 'monstrous' in that she is the producer of 'monstered' goods and the chief agent of their commodification at one at the same time.

The 'monstrous' contribution of Ursula to the economy of
Bartholomew Fair is seen at once as destructive, engulfing and eradicating in equal measure. Crucially, the play manages to cast Ursula in such
a pejorative role by forging links between pigs and appetite. Here,
Bartholomew Fair looks forward to Tannakin Skinker, the Dutch 'hog-
faced gentlewoman', and to narratives circulating in the late 1630s that
mocked her for eating 'as a Swine doth in [the] swilling Tub' and for
being fitted with a 'silver trough' to aid the process.[29] In *Bartholomew
Fair*, a comparable thematic trajectory is pursued first in the depiction
of Ursula herself as a type of 'monstrous' pig. Both a 'sow of enormity'
(V.vi.58) and 'pig-woman', she is inseparable from, and conflated with,
the animals that she cooks and cultivates. Second, Ursula is constructed
as running her booth in such a way as to appeal to and satisfy the
hunger of the the fair's entire population: as she says, she is able to 'stop
[the] mouth, and stay [the] stomach, at all times' (II.iii.50–1). (The
implication is that Ursula is also capable of controlling the ownership
of speech.) But Ursula's involvement in a praxis of appetite is not simply
an index of her empowerment. A damaging aspect is simultaneously
entertained, as when Ursula is charged with eating 'cow's udders'
(II.iii.16): the accusation is particularly unsettling, suggesting, as it does,
the ingestion of a maternal conduit for nurture and sustenance. A variation on the premiss occurs at those moments where Ursula is described
as a 'mother' (II.v.70) to a 'litter of pigs' (II.iii.2). Celia R. Daileader
points out that such references make Ursula 'an animal that eats its
own'.[30] This trenchant observation can be developed if we pursue its
logical outcome: feasting on her own kind, Ursula becomes 'monstrous'
in being credited, as is Othello, with 'cannibalistic' predilections.
Nowhere is this 'monsterized' Ursula more fully realized than in her
threatening behaviour towards Mooncalf; 'In, you rogue,' she exclaims,
'and wipe the pigs, and mend the fire, that they fall not, or I'll both
baste and roast you, till your eyes drop out, like 'em' (II.v.65–8). The
overriding impression is that the mother makes her own child available
for public consumption. Ursula is envisaged as turning her progeny into
merchandise, deconstructing kin to perpetuate the fair's feeding culture.
There is also the hint that Ursula will elect herself to eat the pig-like
product that has been so carefully prepared: she will return Mooncalf,
her metaphorical offspring, to her stomach (or womb) in a process of
reverse creation, of 'monstrous' execution.

Ursula's annihilatory underside is indicated again in the abusive
rhetoric laid at her door. Among other accusations, for example,
Quarlous states that Ursula is 'able to give a man the sweating sickness

with looking on her' (II.v.103–4). A woman capable of harming men through her appearance is a type of gorgon, the classical 'monster' possessed of the power to turn men to stone.[31] Of the gorgons, perhaps the most celebrated was Medusa, who, because figured as a 'frightening assemblage of exaggerated parts', represented, according to David Hillman and Carla Mazzio, a 'warning against ... the loss of bodily coherence'.[32] *Bartholomew Fair* dramatizes a reworking of these symbolic significations, for Ursula, rather than turning men into stone, is staged as equipped with the gift of contaminating her onlookers with the markers of her own physically unstable condition: the perennial fear of the effects of the 'monster'-booth is here wittily played out. Elsewhere, Ursula speaks of dropping and dwindling (II.ii.78, 80); in precipitating 'sweating sickness', the 'pig-woman' will thus relocate her dissolution and cause men, as well, to melt and pine. Not only does this constitute a reflection upon a woman's efficacy in disrupting through ocular influence; it also points to an ability to reorganize at the level of gender, since Quarlous, Ursula's masculine detractor, is assigned the characteristics of the 'sow of enormity', his female adversary.

If Ursula incarnates the 'monstrous' threat of a loss of coherence, then she also communicates the dangers of the potential disappearance of differentiation. This finds its most complete articulation in the statement that the 'pig-woman' resembles a 'bog' (II.v.85) or a 'quagmire' (II.v.84): he 'that would venture for 't', the argument runs, 'might sink into her, and be drown'd a week, ere any friend he had could find where he were' (II.v.88–90). Playing again on the theme of a movement inwards to engulfment, Jonson's dramaturgy is energized at this point by its anticipation of Barbara Creed's concept of the 'monstrous-feminine'. According to Creed, the 'monstrous-feminine' manifests itself both as the *vagina dentata* or toothed vagina, 'symbolic of the all-devouring woman', and also as 'the archaic mother', with her 'incorporating ... power ... to obliterate the subject'.[33] Bodies and appetites, integration and individuation, birth and death – all intersect in the excess that is Ursula, to the extent that she comes to figure as an abyss in which the limits of the body are robbed of effective meaning, in which physical resistance is emasculated, in which geographical awareness is thrown into disarray, and in which the only knowledge is of a coming to consciousness of the dematerialization of a distinctive identity.

The threatening properties of Ursula are reflected in the ways in which she operates in *Bartholomew Fair* as the focus for masculine anxiety. Frequently the object of vituperation, Ursula is, on one occasion, rounded upon so violently by the gentlemen that Knockem fears that 'they'll kill the poor whale, and make oil of her' (II.v.121–2). The comment seals Ursula within a 'monstrous' frame of reference: whales in the early modern period were proverbially described as 'monsters' or 'monstrous fish', and their appearance was greeted with wonder and awe. Yet a deeper 'monstrosity' is at work in the suggestion that Ursula is to be converted into oil, since the burning of whale-oil was a contemporary commonplace; if only in fantasy, the 'pig-woman' winds up as a fiery substance that clarifies her 'monstrously' diabolical associations.[34] In this way, Ursula is viewed as the object of a process of backward 'translation'; if she will not droop away herself (through the sweaty loss of water), she will be made to resolve by others (via the extraction of her oil). And, because whale-oil was also used in the period as an ingredient in cosmetics, soaps and manufacturing lubricants, Ursula, it is implied, has as her final destination a metamorphosis into an economic product. Ironically, her fate is that of a unit of commodification, a liquid part of a larger 'monstrous' whole.

Counterbalancing her destabilizing and destabilized traits, Ursula is imaged as 'monstrously' creative. Like Sycorax, who is 'grown into a hoop' (I.ii.258) in her pregnancy, Ursula appears as enjoying an inordinately generative power. The fluids which she sheds may connote the expectant woman's 'breaking of the waters', while the reference to Eve invites us to read her through the lens of the biblical genesis. Even Ursula's physical movement is formulated as a signal reminder of her fertility, since her very 'Motion' is said to 'breed vapours' (II.iii.44). Typically, Ursula as fructifier is also Ursula as 'monstrous' mother; hence, she plans, states Knockem in a resonant registration of the 'pig-woman' as the producer of an annual institution, to 'grunt out another Bartholomew Fair' (II.iii.2–3). It is within the context of Ursula as 'monstrously' creative, I suggest, that we can begin to understand the play's association of her with bears. Of course, it is entirely possible that the ursine Ursula operates as a meditation upon contemporary 'monstrous' children born, according to one account, 'with the gestures, grins and very grumblings of a bear' or as a dramatic prototype for Barbara Urselin, another 'monster' characterized as a muddle of human and animal traits.[35] But it is more helpful to look at Ursula in the company of early modern medical treatises, one of which, written by Helkiah Crooke in 1631, contends that the 'Beare . . . bringeth foorth her young . . . and perfecteth them by licking . . . [they] appeare deformed or vnformed but are not so indeed . . . because they . . . are couered with a slimy . . . moysture which the Dam licking off makes their proportion appeare'.[36]

Leah S. Marcus suggests that Ursula is bear-like because 'she is forever being baited by the other characters'.[37] I would argue, instead, that Ursula is developed as an ironic recasting of the arguments Crooke rehearses. Both 'she-bear' (II.iii.1) and 'Ursa major' (II.v.178–9) or 'Great Bear', Ursula brings customers and clients, prostitutes and cut-purses, to her booth; all of them are, in some senses, licked out of proportion into disproportion under her protectorship or, at least, encouraged to 'monstrosity' through her promptings. Ursula, in short, disfigures her 'young' – her vendibles, wares, children and pigs. Her broods are 'monsterized' via contact with her, and she is the origin of their 'monstrously' fashioned material possibility.

By metaphorically licking her customers into 'monstrosity', Ursula permits her clientele to indulge their baser instincts. Crucially, Ursula licenses the carnal appetites of women, never more obviously than when Win is pushed to indulge her longing 'to eat of a pig' (I.v.151) and Mistress Overdo is allowed freely to drink. But *Bartholomew Fair* does not only address the satisfaction of female desire; it also uncovers the physical consequences, as is implied in those scenes where Win and Mistress Overdo avail themselves of Ursula's booth in order to defecate and urinate. For example, Win – 'I have very great what sha' call 'um' (III.vi.120–1), she states – seeks out a 'dripping pan' (III.vi.123–4) for relief, while Mistress Overdo, who is similarly 'distemper'd with these enormities' (IV.iv.184), is also driven to use the receptacle: 'I cannot with modesty speak of it out' (IV.iv.188). Gail Kern Paster writes that 'this discourse inscribes women as leaky vessels by isolating . . . [the] production of fluids . . . as excessive' in an argument that has been developed by Shannon Miller; the 'incontinence of women', this commentator maintains, 'links them to sexual openness'. Both critics, then, read Win and Mistress Overdo's submission to bodily processes as instances of a peculiarly gendered moral transgression.[38] Moral derelictions, however, are invariably entangled with 'monstrous' delinquencies, and *Bartholomew Fair* is quick to exploit the confusion. In the play, pigs, pregnancy, appetite and babies come together in a particularly suggestive thematic concatenation. It is one that, because mobilized around Ursula's booth, acquires a 'monstrous' flavour. Thus, the expulsion of waste-products from the body can express, as in *The Tempest*, types of 'monstrous birth', ventings that are also deliveries: in being purged of 'enormities', women are released from the 'monsters' that have dictated the course of their behavioural deviation. Ursula's 'monstrous' creativity, in other words, has spread beyond herself to encompass a range of related 'monstrous' multiplications. In parodying a 'monstrous' delivery that, in *The Tempest*, is already stamped with comic meanings, Jonson may well be attempting to go beyond the demotic tendencies of his rival, to neutralize the 'monstrous' by subjecting it to an even more exaggerated 'translation'. Yet one might want to argue, too, that the 'monstrous births' that hover at the edges of *Bartholomew Fair* are no less relevant as indications of the play's own engulfment by a 'monstrous' maternity, of confines breached and of an increasingly tenuous hold on an imitative dramatic economy.

IV

As Ursula is ideally imagined as an adaptation of a Shakespearean maternal theme, so does the puppet show function, at least in part, in a 'translatory' capacity. One might argue, for instance, that the puppet show stages a de-'monsterizing' of contemporary constructions of popular performance. By inviting the audience to look for '*sin within yourselves*' (V.v.88), the puppet Dionysius is able to reject Busy's polemical accusation, familiar from early modern anti-theatrical discussions, that the playhouse is a seat of 'monstrous' contamination. In common with the rest of *Bartholomew Fair*, the puppet show strives to move a typology of 'monstrous' playing to a different venue. But the de-'monstering' qualities of the puppet show are also compromised by residual 'monstrosities' that mark it out as a more stubbornly populist cultural property. Here, the eruptive 'monstrosity' of Ursula once again offers a salutary comparison. Hence, the puppet show simultaneously registers as an inherently 'monstrous' type of entertainment: occupying the same site as Ursula's establishment, it even carries over, and rematerializes, her booth's 'monstrous' subtexts.[39] Throughout, the show is labelled by Busy as an 'abomination' and, to a degree, the descriptor is appropriate, since 'abominable' has its origins in the Latin phrase, *ab homine*, meaning 'away from man, inhuman' or 'monstrous'.[40] 'Monstrosity' is reinforced in the role of Leatherhead, who is identified by Captain Whit, the Irish bawd, as a 'mashter o' de monshtersh' (V.iv.28) or 'master of the monsters': if only in a brief incarnation, then, and with puppets substituting for 'extraordinary bodies', a 'man with the monsters' (III.i.11–12) is permitted to come to the fore. Confirming the extent to which the puppet show is immersed in 'monstrosity' is the reference to one of the 'motions' (V.i.6) on offer: this, significantly, is '*Sodom and Gomorrah*' (V.i.9–10), the biblical story of God's punishment of sinful excess via an apocalyptical tempest.

In seeking to understand the overall place of the puppet show among the 'translatory' instruments of *Bartholomew Fair*, it is helpful, first, to remind ourselves of Jonson's notorious dislike of this species of popular pastime. Writing in *Discoveries* (*c.* 1623–5), Jonson commented that the 'Puppets are seene now in despight of the Players'; as Frances Teague suggests, the statement conveys an anxiety about a 'spectrum of popular entertainment' gravitating 'from the fairground to the playhouse'.[41] The 'monstrosity' of the puppet show in *Bartholomew Fair* thus emerges from Jonson's conception of artistic hierarchies and from his own conflicted vacillation between fairground forms and theatrical practices. Branded with a 'monstrous' signature, and carrying the weight of the author's critique, the puppet show, in addition, provides a further purchase on Jonson's rivalry with Shakespeare: this time, however, it is not so much a 'low' modality of representation that is parodied as an élite variety of performative pursuit. Scott Cutler Shershow has argued that 'puppet' carries with it connotations of infantilization: the word, he states, derives from *pupa*, 'which in classical Latin meant either "little girl" or "doll"'. Through the semantic senses of 'doll', he continues, 'puppet' could also be extended into a 'psychosexual' arena and 'be commonly used . . . as [a] term of reproach and contempt for women'.[42] Discussing the theatrics of sexuality from a different perspective, Clare McManus writes of the court masque that it, too, involves 'an admission of sexuality', not least, she suggests, in the 'bare limbs' of the female performers and the 'sexual indecorum' of royal women on stage.[43] In view of the overlap between puppets and masques at the level of the gendered physical body, and in the light of the central place occupied by the puppet show in *Bartholomew Fair*, I would like to suggest that Jonson looks to manipulated dramatic action as a 'translation', as a device for the comic relocation of a equally climactic moment in *The Tempest*, which is Prospero's summoning of the masque. Deploying a performance model that he disparagingly regarded in an ironic relation to the spirit-goddesses of *The Tempest* represents, it might be argued, Jonson's crowning strategy for defining and claiming aesthetic ascendancy. Furthermore, because puppets are inexorably entangled with childishness and the demotic as well as with 'monstrosity', Shakespeare's masque can lose some of its aristocratic pretension and take on an additionally vulgarized note. In this connection, it is not surprising that the puppet-show appears as a sorry 'modern' (V.iii.114) diminution of a lofty platonic and romantic ideal, as an indication of the lowest common denominator of audience response and as a type of 'spectacle' (V.iv.2) entirely lacking in wonder and cultural sophistication. All that is elicited by the show, *Bartholomew Fair* suggests, are unreconstituted expressions of ignorance and folly.

As the performance unfolds, the points of contact weaving between the puppet and the masque are more stridently articulated. In particular, it is via a rehearsal of gendered assumptions that the two forms of theatrical activity are seen to dovetail. The show concludes when, in a wholly unexpected gesture, the puppet *'takes up his garment'* (V.v.99.1) to reveal not the 'monstrosity' of a 'male' who 'putteth on the apparel of the female' (V.v.92–3), or even a 'female' who dons the attire of the 'of the male' (V.v.93), but a neutral (and neutered) 'nothing' (a concept of which the play is particularly fond). This is, then, a startling moment in theatrical terms, since, as Laura Levine states, the puppet signifies 'not the loss or collapse of gender . . . but its radical and given absence'.[44] On the one hand, one might argue that the puppet's revelation of a non-existent gender illuminates another de-'monstering' manoeuvre on Jonson's part: Revelation is mocked in that 'nothing' is uncovered, and the 'monstrosity' of impersonation is betrayed as an insubstantial fiction. On the other, the climactic non-exposure of the puppet could be seen as a further instance of 'monstrosity' breaking free of its confines, particularly since it is accompanied by Leatherhead's loss of control over his string-drawn charges. In that the puppets appear to take on an independent agency, Leatherhead becomes a 'master' who notably fails to manipulate his 'monsters'. Nor is the 'nothing' presented for inspection devoid of anomalousness; it is described as a 'demonstration' (V.v.101) or 'monstrosity', and there is arguably 'something' 'monstrous' in the display of an eradication of gender. A ballad about a 'monst[r]ous child' born in Southampton in 1602 clarifies the point: the child is a 'monster', it is claimed, because 'not of a male or a female kinde'.[45] In the same way that Ursula exceeds her temporal boundaries, moreover, so does the puppet show function proleptically to anticipate a later model of 'monstrous' entertainment. By the late nineteenth and early twentieth centuries, when the 'monster' exhibition had gravitated into the 'freak show', the marketing of 'extraordinary bodies', building upon the eroticism of some early modern displays and responding to a developing sub-culture of film and photography, had taken on distinctively pornographic dimensions.[46] The 'demonstration' of a gendered 'abomination' in *Bartholomew Fair* does seems to resonate with the more fully-fledged pornographic tendencies of the modern fairground institution, even if Jonson's play, produced, as Ian Frederick Moulton reminds us, at a juncture when ' "pornography" [was] an anachronism', deals only in substitutes and simultaneously frustrates and delivers upon an audience's sexual curiosity.[47] *Bartholomew Fair* is pre-pornographic in disallowing the physical unveiling of a human performer; at the same time, it aspires to pornography in offering a historically unique glimpse of a 'monsterized' divestiture.

On initial appearances, it could be argued that the ending of *Bartholomew Fair* accommodates itself constructively to that state of affairs in which 'monstrosity' has spilled beyond its dramatic bulwarks. The parting offer of Overdo – 'I invite you home with me to my house, to supper' (V.vi.113) – is exemplary here, pointing, as it does, toward healing integration and away from branding and separation. A motif of *communitas* is similarly evident in Cokes' request that the 'actors' (or puppets) be invited, too: 'we'll ha' the rest o' the play at home' (V.vi.117–18), he states. Here, *Bartholomew Fair* invests in a purposeful blurring between male and female, puppet and player, 'real' and imaginary, without, it seems, expressing anxiety about the morphological loosening attendant upon such a coming together of opposites. But living with 'monstrosity', it seems, is a costly and personally destabilizing business. Overdo, for instance, is described as 'but Adam, flesh and blood' (V.vi.100) in an evocative phrase which suggests a carnal connection to Ursula, the 'pig-woman'; like her, the magistrate is being remade in reverting to a biblical prototype. In common with the 'sow of enormity', who has been infectious, Overdo is dwindling and dissolving, confronting and owning 'original' frailties and temptations. Because of Overdo's capitulation to the impossibility of reforming 'enormity', the conclusion is notably lacking in any attempt to effect regeneration; instead, 'nothing' emerges as distinctive or different; 'enormity' persists in the image of an escalating celebration; and 'monstrosity' is acknowledged as a common but incommutable condition. Of course, one might read the closing scene as Jonson's impertinent 'translation' of Prospero's summation of his relation to the 'monster', Caliban: 'this thing of darkness I / Acknowledge mine' (V.i.275–6). Overshadowing the possible connection with *The Tempest*, however, is *Bartholomew Fair's* gloomy realization that neither Shakespeare nor a populist convention of 'monstrosity' can be superseded; only resigned acculturation and agreement, these final stages indicate, are feasible. The 'monstrous being', writes Elizabeth Grosz, 'is at the heart of' the viewer's 'own identity, for it is all that must be ejected or abjected from self-image to make the bounded, category-obeying self possible'.[48] Not only in the ending, but also in the boundary crossings of Ursula, and the anarchic continuations of the puppet show, *Bartholomew Fair* is pressed to recognize that the attempt to eject the 'monstrous' can frustratingly result in its dramatic reinstatement. Despite a reliance upon 'translation', Jonson is obliged to confront in *Bartholomew Fair* not only the unassimilable force of the 'monstrous' but also its fondness for flouting circumscription and making a travesty of the delimiting artistic enterprise.

V

Inspired by plays such as *Othello* and *The Tempest*, *Bartholomew Fair* is conceived of as a counterblast to its Shakespearean predecessors. The sidelining of Shakespeare is the motivating force behind the development of peculiarly gendered narratives, and a mockery of the dramatist is implicit in the ways in which the fair's denizens are constructed as displacing conventional centres of 'monstrous' entertainment. But *Bartholomew Fair* emerges, ultimately, as an imperfect Shakespearean retaliation: Jonson finds that the head and the heels are entangled, that the narrative assumes an independent direction, and that the play depends on 'monstrous' contexts even without 'monsters' being conjured explicitly. Jonson's play tussles, it seems, with the misconception that the 'monstrous' belongs to a separable category; it also strives to confront the populist energies released when an engagement with the 'monstrous', however oblique, is pursued.

In this sense, *Bartholomew Fair* constitutes a 'translation' whose effect is only to recall to an audience the power of the primary Shakespearean stimulus. The play, in fact, rehearses a central trait of the 'translating' imperative. Walter Benjamin has written that 'any translation contains the life of the originals', and his formulation provides the basis for Jacques Derrida's argument that, in philosophy, 'another language comes to disturb the first one. It doesn't inhabit it, but haunts it. Another text, the text of the other, arrives in silence with a more or less regular cadence, without ever appearing in its original language, to dislodge the language of translation . . . It disassimilates it.'[49] *Bartholomew Fair* is disassimilated in precisely these respects. Not only is the play haunted by Shakespearean ghosts; it is also finds its dominant strategic register overpowered by 'monstrous' forces beyond itself, even if these are never clearly dressed in their 'original' form. However much he agitates to rise above Shakespeare, then, Jonson is still moulded by the 'text of the other', the 'cadence' of his own and his rival's shared 'monstrous' environment.

Discussing the literary rivalry between Jonson and Shakesepare, Don E. Wayne writes that 'what the Jonsonian subject describes as *its* other, as the mode of being from which it struggles to distinguish itself, is a condition not of alienation but of fragmentation'.[50] Such a splitting is not difficult to identify in the contrarily opposed operations of *Bartholomew Fair*, since the play makes an unwitting demonstration of an attraction to ludic energies and anarchic impulses in the same moment as it endeavours to accommodate those tendencies within a grander authorial design. The dramatist, one might argue, was never to succeed in withdrawing from the 'monstrosities' of the demotic sphere because fragmented by a dependence on their sustaining representational opportunities. A writerly subjectivity divided is seen, too, in the occasion of the play's first performance: *Bartholomew Fair* was staged at the Hope Theatre on 31 October 1614 and at court the following day. In itself this is not necessarily unusual. However, the fact that Jonson wrote individual prologues and epilogues to match these varying circumstances of production suggests that, perhaps erroneously, he imagined 'monsters' to work only in a discrete and particularized fashion and not in overlapping concert with a range of social constituencies.

A further instance of the attempt to separate out the effects of the 'monstrous' is seen in *Bartholomew Fair*'s publication record. Omitted from the First Folio of 1616, the play was printed (but not distributed) in 1631, only being actually published in 1640. Following in the footsteps of Jonson, who in his *Conversations with Drummond* of c. 1619 mentions a now lost 'apologie of a Play of his St Bartholomees faire', critics have propounded numerous theories for the expulsion of the play from the magisterial *Workes*.[51] It has been suggested, for instance, that *Bartholomew Fair* was too collaborative in orientation, too experimental in dramaturgical technique, too 'sprawling' in its 'licence' and too unfinished in appearance to be released, in 1616, as a product worthy of the permanency of print.[52] Such speculation is attractive, but is complicated, I suggest, by taking into account this chapter's broader discussions about the persistence with which the 'monstrous' resists a restricting impulse. Clearly, set alongside the unadulterated aesthetic ideals which Jonson promoted, *Bartholomew Fair* represents an anomaly, a 'monstrous' blot on an unspotted palette. At an immediate level, the play, because compromised by its vernacular connections, is incompatible with an authorial desire for independence from the wider public. For this is a work in which, despite protestation, Jonson is both placed before the masses as a spectacle and shaped by a 'monsterizing' consumer culture. *Bartholomew Fair* makes it difficult for Jonson absolutely to command the interpretive transaction; rather, it permits him only a kinship with the sullied poetasters he elsewhere condemns. In short, between the author's proposed reformation of poetry, and the eruptions of 'monstrosity' that define *Bartholomew Fair*, there appears an unbridge-able divide.

Within this context, the rejection of the play from the 1616 *Workes* takes on a greater transparency; the fate of *Bartholomew Fair* is further illuminated, moreover, when we consider the underlying logic to which the First Folio subscribes. Commenting on the *Workes*, Martin Butler writes that

> texts are revised and ordered so as to suggest the gradual coming to maturity of a single, controlling consciousness; their standardized presentation expresses Jonson's ownership of his works, and the already classic status of his achievement; the dedicatory epistles chart his serenely developing career and display his accumulated social capital; [and] generic organization helps to de-emphasize his texts' dependence on the world of ordinary contingency.[53]

The First Folio, then, refracts an artfully contrived attempt to establish uniformity, and this is clarified in Jonson's decision to drop from it various collaborative undertakings, such as plays of hybridized parent-age. Everything is directed, as Timothy Murray states, towards firmly determining 'the picture of [Jonson's] own textual sovereignty', towards carving out for himself, as Shakespeare had never done, an immortal authorial niche.[54] Impossible to accommodate within the non-'monstrous' template of the First Folio, the play reveals only an imper-fect Jonson – a writer trapped between being both like and unlike Shake-speare, a dramatist striving for social separateness from his rival in the same moment as he unconsciously pays him parodic homage. Tellingly, 'monsters' and 'monstrous' subtexts even penetrate Jonson's immersion in issues of posterity and futurity. For *Bartholomew Fair* is a play in which 'monsters', as well as Jonson, exceed their temporal parameters. It is a work in which the development of the display of the 'monster' as a material practice is forcefully, if sketchily, anticipated. And in that he foresaw the simultaneous progress and adulteration of the 'monster' exhibition, Jonson was unique among his contemporaries in being able implicitly to contemplate the institution's eventual demise.

Epilogue

Although Jonson excluded *Bartholomew Fair* (1614) from the First Folio, when suffering from ill-health and the threat of financial ruin later in life, he did attempt to have the play published. While a folio containing *Bartholomew Fair* was planned, however, Jonson was forced in 1631 to abandon the project. This hinged partly on the disastrous contribution of John Beale, a 'Lewd Printer', who refused to 'perfect' his work to Jonson's satisfaction and who was happy for sheets of the play to go forward with, in E. A. Horsman's words, 'oddities of spacing, changes of type, mispunctuation and textual errors'.[1] The play, it seems, had become a more 'monsterized' version of its already 'monstrous' self. If Jonson was defeated in his endeavour to produce *Bartholomew Fair* in 'perfect' form, those involved in the dissemination of Marlowe and Shakespeare might have applauded themselves for having been more successful. In his 1590 address to the readers, Richard Jones, the printer of *Tamburlaine the Great* (1587–88), states:

> I have (purposely) omitted and left out some fond and frivolous jestures, digressing and (in my poor opinion) far unmeet for the matter, which I thought might seem more tedious unto the wise than any way else to be regarded – though, haply, they have been of some vain conceited fondlings greatly gaped at, what times they were showed upon the stage in their graced deformities.[2]

The suggestion that the play functioned as a type of 'monster' to be viewed by the multitude carries in its wake a class-sensitive criticism, even a hint of the ethics of 'decency' that were, eventually, to bring about the disappearance of the 'monster' exhibition as popular entertainment. But more striking, arguably, is the implication that Jones, as printer, can work in a de-'monstering' capacity. Not only will his textual amputations paradoxically give the play a greater aesthetic value; so will his decision to remove *Tamburlaine the Great* from the demeaning and therefore 'monstrous' show of the public stage. The idea is developed, with the author being granted a slightly higher imaginative profile, in John Heminge and Henry Condell's preface to the 1623 edition of Shakespeare's complete works:

> It had bene a thing . . . worthie to haue bene wished, that the Author himselfe had liu'd to haue set forth, and ouerseen his owne writings . . . as where (before) you were abus'd with diuerse stolne, and surreptitious copies, maimed, and deformed by the frauds and stealthes of iniurious imposters, that expos'd them: euen those, are now offer'd to your view cur'd, and perfect of their limbes; and all the rest, absolute in their numbers, as he conceiued them.[3]

In contrast to Jones, who reduces the 'monstrous' excrescences of the Marlovian text to shape it into a more amenable utterance, Heminge and Condell increase the Shakespearean corpus or, at least, bring together the previously disconnected shards of the dramatist's work. Until the First Folio, it is implied, Shakespeare's plays were exhibited as 'monstrous' imitations of far finer originals; now, in a reversal of that practice, Heminge and Condell will recover those adulterated fragments and make them whole via the agency of textual rebirth. By virtue of their unspoken intercourse with the conceiving artist, the editors are licensed once again to place Shakespeare on display. These Shakespearean ministers deputize themselves to execute what the author, 'by death departed', is unable personally to perform; in so doing, they make their creation available for inspection, for ultimate approval or 'censure' (sig. A3[r]). Ever since, one might suggest, the academic industry has preoccupied itself with attempting to generate, like Heminge, Condell and their ilk, either 'perfect' copies (even two-text editions bear witness to the urge accurately to reproduce the entirety of Shakespeare's sixteenth- and seventeenth-century cultural manifestations) or 'perfect' readings of early modern theatre. Each of these intellectual contributions is, at some level, a refiguring of the critical landscape that corrects the disfigurements of an earlier interpretive mode.

    I first started to think about this book in Chicago when I attended the annual meeting of the Modern Language Association of America. Half way into the conference, I visited the Field Museum of Natural History on Lake Shore Drive. There, the latest natural history spectacle

– 'D.N.A. to Dinosaurs' – quickly made itself apparent. With cabinets boasting skeletal remains, animatronic wizardry and computer-generated simulacra, the event was advertised as a 'freak show', complete with banners, a proscenium arch, curtains and invitations to enter inside. Two banners, 'The Missing Link?', which pictured reptilian creatures of the Devonian period of evolution, and 'Men or Monsters?', which drew attention to the model of a Neanderthal boy, stood out from the rest. For those images adorning the brightly-lit corridors of the Field Museum were, in some senses, the inheritors of the 'monstrous' practices of the early modern playhouse, albeit filtered through a spectrum of other historical developments – the Enlightenment of the eighteenth century, the heyday of the 'freak show' during the Victorian period, the decline of the institution and its transformation into other media, forms and venues in modernity. Despite the technological virtuosity of 'D.N.A. to Dinosaurs' and its seeming distance from the drama, then, a window onto a Shakespearean past was afforded. 'The Missing Link?' took us back to Caliban and to his indeterminate piscine, amphibian, animal and human connections, while 'Men or Monsters?' alerted an audience to multiple later realizations of Shakespeare's 'monster' – in particular, to his reincarnation on the stage as a simian construction or a colonial subject. A culminative registration of random moments of 'monstrous' visibility, 'D.N.A. to Dinosaurs' illuminated the importance of early modern discourses of 'monstrosity' to the interwoven fates of the *wunderkammern* and the fairground booth. In the populist underpinnings of metropolitan corporate culture, and in the global interests that now dictate the absorption of knowledge, can be glimpsed the infinitely adaptable properties of the early modern 'monster'.

Back at the conference, a further manifestation of the 'monster' exhibition's journey into modernity announced itself. At the Modern Language Association of America, which is aptly billed as a fair, members pay their dues to attend the annual gathering, to inspect the contents of the publishers' booths and to marvel at the wonders of intellectual discovery. Apart from its importance as a forum for employment, the conference depends for its effect upon the scholar-speakers, who, types of Prospero, are involved in exhibiting the progeny of their labours, establishing original species of understanding and entrancing with critical magic. The theatre of Shakespeare's time is put on show in these readings in the same moment as we place ourselves before the public gaze to receive judgement, leading to the suspicion that the academic has replaced the 'Monster-Master' as the impresario of the present.

Such an identification struck me with a renewed force when, towards the completion of this book, I participated in a Channel Four documentary in London entitled 'Born Freak'. Presented by Mat Fraser, a disabled actor, 'Born Freak' plots the attempt to find a place for the non-normative performer in a culture dominated by, and in thrall to, an all-encompassing ideology of the 'body beautiful'. As part of its performative itinerary, the programme visits many of the institutions and locations historically associated with 'monster'-booths, such as a mock Victorian 'freak show', the annual fair in St Giles, Oxford, Coney Island in New York and the Edinburgh Festival. Crucially, Mat Fraser is the key player is this rehearsal of the fortunes of the 'freak', to the extent that he impersonates 'Sealo', a famous performer with shortened arms from the 1940s and 1950s, before a specially invited audience, participates in a fringe event entitled 'The Happy Sideshow' and chats with Riba Schappell who, in spite of the physical conjunction to her sister, Lori Schappell, works as a country-and-western musician. 'Born Freak' articulates many of the concerns central to an experience of the 'extraordinary body': the persistence with which an older language of physical alterity filters into more recent constructions is touched upon, for instance, as is the dialogue between British and American modalities of discovering anomalous anatomies, the conflicted reception by spectators of a disabled performance and, perhaps most significantly, the role of the viewer in the perception of the 'freak'. As for my role, I was involved in 'Born Freak' to talk with Mat Fraser about the performative dimensions of early modern 'monsters'. To facilitate discussion, I displayed images of Lazarus Colloredo and Barbara Urselin, some of which appear as illustrative matter in this book. On the one hand, such a procedure was unsettling: now fully confirmed as a 'Monster-Master', I was being filmed partly in order to advise a disabled actor on how he would have been treated in the past. Thanks to the Modern Language Association and other, similar meetings, I had been authorized to pronounce upon the history of disability in the wider public sphere. On the other hand, the conversational exchange had an emancipatory effect, allowing additional insights into the 'monsters' of the early modern theatre and their subsequent narratives. Hence, it became apparent that, although the 'freak show' has long been abandoned, the theatricalization of the alternatively furnished body continues as a recognizable discipline. Similarly, the self-made 'freaks' ('bearded ladies' and tattooed men and women) that Mat Fraser encounters, and asks about, during his travels can trace their inception to the exhibiting culture of the

sixteenth- and seventeenth-century stage: their emergence is even anticipated in a play such as *Bartholomew Fair*. 'Monstrous' discourses put
into circulation in the early modern period, then, do not dissolve;
rather, they reverberate well into the twentieth and twenty-first centuries. Shakespearean drama is testimony to the beginnings of a fascination for, and a curiosity about, the 'monstrous', to a cultural dynamic
that is still felt, even if it is now reconstructed and replayed in a range
of very different theatrical arenas.

Notes

Introduction

1. *The Tempest*, ed. Stephen Orgel (Oxford and New York: Oxford University Press, 1987), II.i.24–32.
2. [William Shakespeare and William Rowley], *The Birth of Merlin*, ed. R. J. Stewart and Denise Coffey (Longmead: Element, 1989), III.iv.pp. 106–7.
3. *Anthony and Cleoptra*, ed. Michael Neill (Oxford and New York: Oxford University Press, 1994), IV.xiii.33–7.
4. J. Barry Webb, *Shakespeare's Animals: A Guide to the Literal and Figurative Usage* (Hastings: Cornwallis Press, 1996), p. 119.
5. I draw here on Rosemarie Garland Thomson's *Extraordinary Bodies: Figuring Physical Disability in American Culture and Literature* (New York: Columbia University Press, 1997).
6. P. G. W. Glare, *Oxford Latin Dictionary*, 2 vols (Oxford: Clarendon, 1983), II, p. 1131.
7. Alden T. Vaughan, 'Trinculo's Indian: American Natives in Shakespeare's England', in Peter Hulme and William H. Sherman, eds, *'The Tempest' and Its Travels* (London: Reaktion, 2000), pp. 49–59.
8. For non-dramatic examples of the pervasive presence of 'monsters' in the period, see Lady Margaret Hoby, *Diary of Lady Margaret Hoby, 1599–1605*, ed. Dorothy M. Meads (London: Routledge, 1930), p. 171; Ralph Josselin, *The Diary, 1616–1683*, ed. Alan Macfarlane (Oxford: Oxford University Press, 1976), p. 60; North Yorkshire County Record Office, PR/MIT 1/1, MIC 2676, 13 September 1650; Oxfordshire Archives, PAR 236/1/R1/3, 14 January 1619; Richard Polwhele, *The History of Cornwall*, 7 vols (Dorking: Kohler & Coombes, 1978), VII, p. 28.
9. John Marston, *The Poems*, ed. Arnold Davenport (Liverpool: Liverpool University Press, 1961), p. 179. See also *Mistris Parliament brought to bed* (London, 1648; Wing M2281), p. 1; H[enry] P[eacham], *The worth of a penny* (London, 1641; Wing P949A), p. 19; *The terrible, horrible, monster of the West* (London, 1649; Wing T765), sig. A3ʳ.
   Tessa Watt observes that labourers' wages in the 1580–1626 period were 8 pence a day, and that, from 1626 to 1639, they had risen to a daily sum of 10 pence. See her *Cheap Print and Popular Piety 1550–1640* (Cambridge: Cambridge University Press, 1991), p. 12.
10. See Thomas Heywood, *The Silver Age* (1610–12), in *The Dramatic Works*, ed. R. H. Shepherd, 6 vols (London: Shepherd, 1874), III, I, p. 89, III, pp. 126–7, 129; John Lyly, *Gallathea* (1583–5), in *'Gallathea' and 'Midas'*, ed. Anne Begor Lancashire (London: Arnold, 1969), IV.i.1–20, IV.iii.1–9, V.ii.1–6, 57–61; *The Marriage of Wit and Science* (1567–8), ed. Arthur Brown, Malone Society (1960 [1961]), III.i.889–910; Salvianus, *A second and third blast of retrait from plaies and theaters* (London, 1580; S.T.C. 21677), p. 105.

11. Michael Baird Saenger, 'The Costumes of Caliban and Ariel Qua Sea-Nymph', *Notes and Queries*, 42 (1995), pp. 335–6. See also John G. Demaray, *Shakespeare and the Spectacles of Strangeness: 'The Tempest' and the Transformation of Renaissance Theatrical Forms* (Pittsburgh: Duquesne University Press, 1998), p. 71.

12. Clearly, there was never a clean, quick split between 'rationalism' and 'superstition', for these interpretive modes continued to intersect even as they became increasingly distinct.

13. See Allen G. Debus, *Man and Nature in the Renaissance* (Cambridge: Cambridge University Press, 1978), pp. 8, 9, 52, 67–70.

Chapter 1

1. *Bartholomew Fair*, ed. E. A. Horsman (Manchester: Manchester University Press, 1979), III.i.10–12.

2. Stephen Gosson, *The schoole of abuse* (London, 1579; S.T.C. 12097), sig. B3^r.

3. William Prynne, *Histrio-mastix* (London, 1633; S.T.C. 20464), pp. 39, 90.

4. William Rankins, *A mirrour of monsters* (London, 1587; S.T.C. 20699), fo. 2^r; Prynne, *Histrio-mastix*, pp. 172, 892.

5. Corporation of London Records Office, Repertory 15, fo. 414^v; Elizabeth Joceline, *The Mother's Legacy to her Unborn Child* (1622), ed. Randall T. Roffen (London: Macmillan, 1894), pp. 31–2; Francis Rous, *Oile of scorpions* (London, 1623; S.T.C. 21344), pp. 166–8, 173–5.

6. C. G., *The minte of deformities* (London, 1600; S.T.C. 11491), sig. Bii^r.

7. Jeffrey D. Mason, 'Street Fairs: Social Space, Social Performance', *Theatre Journal*, 48 (1996), p. 318.

8. Thomas Crosfield, *The Diary*, ed. Frederick S. Boas (London: Milford, 1935), p. 79.

9. Henry Chettle and John Day, *The Blind Beggar of Bednall Green* (1600), ed. W. Bang (Louvain: Uystpruyst, 1902), IV, ll. 1639–41; Thomas Frost, *The Old Showmen and the Old London Fairs* (London: Tinsley, 1874), p. 151; Henry Morley, *Memoirs of Bartholomew Fair* (London: Warne, 1892), pp. 194, 280.

10. N. W. Bawcutt, ed., *The Control and Censorship of Caroline Drama: The Records of Sir Henry Herbert, Master of the Revels, 1623–73* (Oxford: Clarendon, 1996), pp. 212–13.

11. S. P. Cerasano, 'The Master of the Bears in Art and Enterprise', *Medieval and Renaissance Drama in England*, 5 (1991), p. 196.

12. Matthew Bliss, 'Property or Performer?: Animals on the Elizabethan Stage', *Theatre Studies*, 39 (1994), p. 47.

13. Rosemarie Garland Thomson, *Extraordinary Bodies: Figuring Physical Disability in American Culture and Literature* (New York: Columbia University Press, 1997).

14. Francis Beaumont, *The Knight of the Burning Pestle*, ed. Sheldon P. Zitner (Manchester: Manchester University Press, 1984), III, 278–9.

15. Jasper Mayne, *The City-Match*, in W. C. Hazlitt, ed., *A Select Collection of Old English Plays*, 4th edn, 15 vols (London: Reeves and Turner, 1874–6), XIII, III.i.p. 249.

16. R. W. Ingram, ed., *Coventry*, Records of Early English Drama (Toronto, Buffalo and London: University of Toronto Press, 1981), p. 440; J. Alan B. Somerset, ed., *Shropshire*, Records of Early English Drama, 2 vols (Toronto, Buffalo and London: University of Toronto Press, 1994), I, p. 226.
17. John Evelyn, *Numismata* (London, 1697; Wing E3505), p. 277; Samuel Jeake, *An Astrological Diary of the Seventeenth Century: Samuel Jeake of Rye, 1652–1699*, ed. Michael Hunter and Annabel Gregory (Oxford: Clarendon, 1988), p. 100; Robert Plot, *The natural history of Stafford-shire* (London, 1686; Wing P2588), pp. 294–5.
18. [Richard Flecknoe], *The diarium, or journall* (London, 1656; Wing F1212), pp. 44–5; *The true effigies of the German giant* (London, 1660; Wing T2692).
19. Ben Jonson, *Three Comedies*, ed. Michael Jamieson (Harmondsworth: Penguin, 1966), V.i.6–9.
20. Bawcutt, ed., *Control and Censorship*, p. 142; Ingram, ed., *Coventry*, p. 443; I. P., *A meruaylous straunge deformed swyne* (London, 1570?; S.T.C. 19071).
21. Bawcutt, ed., *Control and Censorship*, pp. 83, 152, 175, 189, 204; George Chapman, *Sir Gyles Goosecappe* (1601–3), in *The Tragedies*, ed. Allan Holaday (Cambridge: Brewer, 1987), I.i.11–12; Crosfield, *Diary*, p. 79; David Galloway, ed., *Norwich, 1540–1642*, Records of Early English Drama (Toronto, Buffalo and London: University of Toronto Press, 1984), pp. 115, 126, 142, 150, 215; Mayne, *The City-Match*, p. 248; Thomas Randolph, *Hey for Honesty* (1626–28?/1648–49?), in *The Poetical and Dramatic Works*, ed. W. Carew Hazlitt, 2 vols (London: Reeves and Turner, 1875), II, I.i.p. 393.
22. Bawcutt, *Control and Censorship*, p. 204; Galloway, ed., *Norwich*, p. 115.
23. Thomas Nabbes, *The Works*, ed. A. H. Bullen, 2 vols (London: Wyman, 1887), I, II.ii.p. 27.
24. Zakiya Hanafi, *The Monster in the Machine: Magic, Medicine, and the Marvellous in the Time of the Scientific Revolution* (Durham, NC and London: Duke University Press, 2000), pp. 36, 47; Stephen Pender, 'In the Bodyshop: Human Exhibition in Early Modern England', in Helen Deutsch and Felicity Nussbaum, eds, *'Defects': Engendering the Modern Body* (Ann Arbor: University of Michigan Press, 2000), p. 108; *The terrible, horrible, monster of the West* (London, 1649; Wing T765), sig. A1ʳ.
25. See Sir William Davenant, 'The Long Vacation in London' (mid-1630s), in *The Shorter Poems*, ed. A. M. Gibbs (Oxford: Clarendon, 1972), p. 129; '*An Ancient* SONG *of* Bartholomew-Fair' (1655), in Thomas D'Urfey, *Wit and Mirth: or Pills to Purge Melancholy*, 6 vols (London: Tonson, 1719–20), IV, pp. 169–70; James Shirley, 'A Fairing' (1646), in *The Dramatic Works*, ed. William Gifford and Alexander Dyce, 6 vols (London: Murray, 1833), VI, pp. 412–13.
26. Bawcutt, ed., *Control and Censorship*, pp. 79, 80, 190, 192, 212. See also Galloway, ed., *Norwich*, p. 96; Somerset, ed., *Shropshire*, I, pp. 19, 247.
27. William Cartwright, *The Plays and Poems*, ed. G. Blakemore Evans (Madison: University of Wisconsin Press, 1951), p. 455.
28. See *At the . . . this present day shall be showne rare dancing on the ropes* (London, 1630; S.T.C. 21315.8); Henry Parrot, *The mastive, or young-whelpe of the olde-dogge* (London, 1615; S.T.C. 19333), sig. A4ᵛ; Hyder E. Rollins,

'The Black-Letter Broadside Ballad', *Publications of the Modern Language Association of America*, 34 (1919), p. 295.

Bills, of course, were also used to advertise forthcoming dramatic events. See Jonathan Bate, 'Introduction', in Jonathan Bate and Russell Jackson, eds, *Shakespeare: An Illustrated Stage History* (Oxford: Oxford University Press, 1996), p. 3; Andrew Gurr, *The Shakespearean Stage 1574–1642* (Cambridge: Cambridge University Press, 1985), p. 11.

29. *Bartholomew faire or a variety of fancies* (London, 1641; Wing P980), p. 4; Galloway, ed., *Norwich*, pp. 146–7; Shirley, 'A Prologue', in *Works*, VI, p. 494.
30. Ben Jonson, *Every Man in His Humour*, ed. Martin Seymour-Smith (London: Benn, 1966), I.ii.111–13.
31. *The terrible, horrible, monster*, sig. A1ʳ.
32. The speaker is set up in opposition to the trickery of displays such as those staged by Floram Marchand, the French 'Water-drinker' who confounded audiences with the illusion of turning water into wine. See Thomas Peedle, *The falacie of the great water-drinker discovered* (London, 1650; Wing P1052); Henry Wilson and James Caulfield, *The Book of Wonderful Characters* (London: Hotten, 1869), pp. 126–30.
33. See Galloway, ed., *Norwich*, p. 146; John Spalding, *Memorialls of the Trubles in Scotland and in England, 1624–1625*, 2 vols (Aberdeen: Spalding Club, 1850–51), II, p. 125.
34. *Macbeth*, ed. Nicholas Brooke (Oxford and New York: Oxford University Press, 1994), V.vii.55–7.
35. The bodies of 'tyrants' such as Cromwell were known to have been exhibited for profit in the period. See John Frederick Varley, *Oliver Cromwell's Latter End* (London: Chapman and Hall, [1939]), pp. 50–1.
36. George Chapman, *Bussy d'Ambois*, ed. N. S. Brooke (Manchester: Manchester University Press, 1979), III.i.25, 27–8.
37. Albert Feuillerat, ed., *Documents Relating to the Office of the Revels in the Time of Queen Elizabeth* (Louvain: Uystpruyst, 1908), pp. 175, 208.
38. The use of the curtain is borne out by details in contemporary dramas and engravings. See Thomas Heywood, *The three wonders of this age* (London, 1636; S.T.C. 13365.5); *Historia aenigmatica, de gemellis Genoae connatis* (London, 1637; S.T.C. 11728.6); *The kingdomes monster vncloaked from Heaven* (London, 1643; Wing K587); Mayne, *The City-Match*, pp. 251, 258.

Further music and 'spiel' on the part of the 'Monster-Master' may have been utilized to intensify the climactic *frisson* and bring fresh drama to the moment of contact between the everyday and the unfamiliar. See Mayne, *The City-Match*, p. 255; *The terrible . . . monster*, sigs A3ʳ–A4ᵛ.
39. *The Winter's Tale*, ed. J. H. P. Pafford (London and New York: Methuen, 1981), V.iii.22, V.ii.23–5. The second gentleman's speech may well be alluding back to the ballads peddled by Autolycus, which concern, among other subjects, 'monstrous births' and strange fish (IV.iv.263–6, 276–82).
40. John Stow, *The annales of England* (London, 1592; S.T.C. 23334), p. 1181.
41. Bawcutt, ed., *Control and Censorship*, p. 181; David Underdown, *Fire from Heaven: Life in an English Town in the Seventeenth Century* (London: Harper-Collins, 1992), p. 105; William Whiteway, *William Whiteway of Dorchester: His Diary 1618–1635*, Dorset Record Society, 12 (1991), p. 154.

42. I borrow here from Jeffrey Jerome Cohen, 'Monster Culture (Seven Theses)', in Jeffrey Jerome Cohen, ed., *Monster Theory: Reading Culture* (Minneapolis and London: University of Minnesota Press, 1996), p. 6.

43. T. I., *A world of wonders* (London, 1595; S.T.C. 14068.5), sig. E1ᵛ.

44. *A myraculous, and monstrous, but yet most true, discourse* (London, 1588; S.T.C. 6910.7), sig. A1ᵛ. See also Thomas Dekker, *Old Fortunatus* (1599), in Thomas Dekker, *The Dramatic Works*, cd. Fredson Bowers, 4 vols (Cambridge: Cambridge University Press, 1953–61), I, V.ii.16–18; T. I., *A world of wonders*, sigs E1ᵛ–2ʳ; John Marston, *The Malcontent* (1603), ed. George K. Hunter (Manchester: Manchester University Press, 1975), I.viii.18–20.

45. *A brief narrative of a strange and wonderful old woman that hath a pair of horns* (London, 1670; Wing B4610), p. 6.

46. Frost, *The Old Showmen*, p. 34; Wilson and Caulfield, *Wonderful Characters*, p. 386.

47. John Evelyn, *The Diary*, ed. E. S. de Beer, 6 vols (Oxford: Clarendon, 1955), III, p. 198; Hyder E. Rollins, ed., *An Analytical Index to the Ballad-Entries (1557–1709) in the Registers of the Company of Stationers of London* (Chapel Hill: University of North Carolina Press, 1924), p. 259.

48. Wilson and Caulfield, *Wonderful Characters*, p. 386.

49. *Ad populum: or, a low-country lecture* (London, 1653; Wing A468), sig. A2ᵛ; R. C(hamberlain), *Jocabella, or a cabinet of conceits* (London, 1640; S.T.C. 4943), no. 417; Henry Glapthone, *Wit in a Constable* (1639), in *The Plays and Poems*, [ed. R. H. Shepherd], 2 vols (London: Pearson, 1874), I, V.i.p. 232; Rollins, ed., *An Analytical*, pp. 142, 220, 222, 257, 259; Hyder E. Rollins, ed., *A Pepysian Garland: Black-Letter Broadside Ballads of the Years 1595–1639* (Cambridge, MA: Harvard University Press, 1971), pp. 449–54; Tannakin Skinker, *A certaine relation of a hogfaced gentlewoman* (London, 1640; S.T.C. 22627).

50. *The strange wonder of the world, or the great gyant described* (London, 1653; Wing S5922), p. 8.

51. Rollins, ed., *Pepysian Garland*, pp. 449, 451.

52. Spalding, *Memorialls of the Trubles*, II, pp. 125–6.

53. Hyder E. Rollins, ed., *The Pack of Autolycus* (Cambridge, MA: Harvard University Press, 1927), p. 11; Spalding, *Memorialls of the Trubles*, II, p. 125; William Winstanley, *The New Help to Discourse* (London: B.H., 1716), p. 72.

54. Rollins, ed., *Pepysian Garland*, pp. 449; Skinker, *A certaine relation*, sigs A3ᵛ–A4ʳ.

55. Thomas Bedford, *A true and certaine relation of a strange-birth* (London, 1635; S.T.C. 1791), p. 13; Edward Burrough, *Many strong reasons confounded* (London, 1657; Wing B6011A), sig. A1ʳ; William Elderton, *The true fourme and shape of a monsterous chyld* (London, 1565; S.T.C. 7565); Anthony Munday, *A view of sundry examples* (London, 1580; S.T.C. 18281), sig. Ciiiᵛ; *The true effigies of the German giant.*

56. T. I., *A world of wonders*, sig. E2ʳ.

57. Bawcutt, ed., *Control and Censorship*, p. 178; William Cartwright, *The Ordinary* (1635), in *Plays and Poems*, II.iii.805–7; Crosfield, *Diary*, p. 54; Mayne, *The City-Match*, p. 248; Archibald E. Trout, 'Some Associations of Hull Fair', manuscript in Central Library, Kingston-upon-Hull, pp. 5–6.

58. Bawcutt, ed., *Control and Censorship*, p. 201; Galloway, ed., *Norwich*, pp. 227, 233; Rollins, ed., *Pack of Autolycus*, pp. 7–14; Spalding, *Memorialls of the Trubles*, II, pp. 125–6.
59. Spalding, *Memorialls of the Trubles*, II, p. 126.
60. H. B., *The true discripcion of a childe with ruffes* (London, 1566; S.T.C. 1033); C. R., *The true discripcion of this marueilous straunge fishe* (London, 1569; S.T.C. 20570); *The strange wonder*, p. 7.
61. The grieving parents of a 'monstrous' child were not infrequently given money, but only on compassionate grounds. See *Gods handy-worke in wonders* (London, 1615; S.T.C. 11926), sig. A4ᵛ; 'Nature's Wonder?' (1664), in John Holloway, ed., *The Euing Collection of English Broadside Ballads in the Library of the University of Glasgow* (Glasgow: University of Glasgow Press, 1971), p. 387; John Vicars, *Prodigies and apparitions* (London, 1642–3; Wing V323), p. 23.
62. Bedford, *A true and certaine relation*, p. 4; Guildhall Library, MS 9234/3, fo. 53ʳ; William Leigh, *Strange newes of a prodigious monster* (London, 1613; S.T.C. 15428), sig. B1ʳ; *Two most remarkable and true histories* (London, 1620; S.T.C. 13525), pp. 9–10.
63. J. A. Twemlow, ed., *Liverpool Town Books, 1550–1603*, 2 vols (Liverpool: Liverpool University Press, 1918–35), II, p. 16.
64. Galloway, ed., *Norwich*, p. 173; Trout, 'Some Associations of Hull Fair', p. 6.
65. Henri Lefebvre, *The Production of Space*, tr. Donald Nicholson-Smith (Oxford: Blackwell, 1991), p. 86.
66. John D., *A discription of a monstrous chylde* (London, 1562; S.T.C. 6177); Norman Jones, *The Birth of the Elizabethan Age: England in the 1560s* (Oxford: Blackwell, 1993), p. 42; Henry Machyn, *The Diary, 1550–1563*, Camden Society, 1st ser., 42 (1848), p. 284.
67. David Harris Willson, *King James VI and I* (London: Cape, 1966), pp. 26, 65, 182–3.
68. Vicars, *Prodigies and apparitions*, p. 21.
69. *A myraculous, and monstrous, but yet most true, discourse*, sig. A2ᵛ; Rollins, ed., *Pack of Autolycus*, p. 13.
70. Marcel Mauss, *The Gift: Forms and Functions of Exchange in Archaic Societies*, tr. Ian Cunnison (London: Cohen & West, 1970).
71. Heywood, *The three wonders*; David Wiles, *Shakespeare's Clown: Actor and text in the Elizabethan playhouse* (Cambridge: Cambridge University Press, 1987), p. 150; Edward J. Wood, *Giants and Dwarfs* (London: Bentley, 1868), p. 273.
72. Ashmolean Museum, Hope Collection, Jeffrey Hudson file; *The Lives and Portraits of Remarkable Characters*, 2 vols (London: Arnett, 1820), I, pp. 11–14; Thomas A. Shepherd, *London and Its Environs in the Nineteenth Century* (London: Jones, 1829), pp. 64–5; *Master* Slater, *The new-yeeres gift* (London, 1636; S.T.C. 22631).
73. John Tradescant, *Musaeum Tradescantianum* (London, 1656; Wing T2005), p. 44.
74. Anthony Alan Shelton, 'Cabinets of Transgression: Renaissance Collections and the Incorporation of the New World', in John Elsner and Roger Cardinal, eds, *The Cultures of Collecting* (London: Reaktion, 1994), p. 185.

75. Tradescant, *Musaeum Tradescantianum*, p. 48.
76. Paula Findlen, 'Jokes of Nature and Jokes of Knowledge: The Playfulness of Scientific Discourse in Early Modern Europe', *Renaissance Quarterly*, 43 (1990), p. 309; Rosamond Wolff Purcell and Stephen Jay Gould, *Finders, Keepers: Eight Collectors* (London: Pimlico, 1993), p. 20.
77. Paula Findlen, *Possessing Nature: Museums, Collecting, and Scientific Culture in Early Modern Italy* (Berkeley, Los Angeles and London: University of California Press, 1994), pp. 48–9.
78. Martin Welch, 'The Foundation of the Ashmolean Museum', in Arthur MacGregor, ed., *Tradescant's Rarities: Essays on the Foundation of the Ashmolean Museum* (Oxford: Clarendon, 1983), p. 52; Southampton City Archives, D/M 1/3, letter-book of Samuel Molyneux, fo. 127.
79. Thomas Platter, *Thomas Platter's Travels in England 1599*, tr. Clare Williams (London: Cape, 1937), p. 172.
80. Henry Farley, *S*[t]. *Paules-Church her bill for the parliament* (London, 1621; S.T.C. 10690), sigs E4[r–v].
81. Barbara J. Balsiger, 'The *Kunst- und Wunderkammern*: A Catalogue Raisonné of Collecting in Germany, France and England 1565–1750', unpublished PhD thesis, University of Pittsburgh, 1970, p. 185; John Morton, *The Natural History of Northampton-shire* (London: Knaplock & Wilkin, 1712), p. 435.
82. Robert Basset, *Curiosities: or the cabinet of nature* (London, 1637; S.T.C. 1557), fo. A5[v].
83. Lewes Lavater, *Of Ghostes and Spirites Walking by Nyght*, ed. J. Dover Wilson and Mary Yardley (Oxford: Oxford University Press, 1929), p. 8; Ambroise Paré, *The workes of that famous chirugion* (London, 1634; S.T.C. 19189), p. 961. I cite from the English translation of Paré's work, which was first published in French in 1573.
84. Thomas Cooper, *Thesaurus linguae Romanae & Britannicae* (London, 1565; S.T.C. 5686), sig. HHhh2[v]; Helkiah Crooke, *A description of the body of man* (London, 1631; S.T.C. 6063), p. 299; John Sadler, *The sicke womans private looking-glasse* (London, 1636; S.T.C. 21544), p. 133.
85. G. A., *No post from heaven* (London, 1643; Wing A8), sig. A2[v]; *Against Whoredom, and Adultery* (1547), in Ronald B. Bond., ed., *'Certain Sermons or Homilies' (1547) and 'A Homily against Disobedience and Wilful Rebellion' (1570)* (Toronto, Buffalo and London: University of Toronto Press, 1987), p. 179; Robert Anton, *The philosophers satyrs* (London, 1616; S.T.C. 686), p. 41; William Averell, *A meruailous combat of contrarieties* (London, 1588; S.T.C. 981), sig. B1[v]; Edmund Calamy, *The monster of sinful self-seeking* (London, 1655; Wing C259), sig. A3[r], pp. 13, 15; Thomas Dekker, *Lanthorne and candle-light* (London, 1609; S.T.C. 6485), sigs A3[v], C1[r], L2[r]; John Derricke, *The Image of Irelande* (1581), ed. John Small (Edinburgh: Black, 1883), sigs Diii[r], Div[v], Eiv[r]; Henry Goodcole, *Natures cruell step-dames* (London, 1637; S.T.C. 12012), p. 17; Robert Hitchcock, *A pollitique platt for the honour of the prince* (London, 1580; S.T.C. 13531), sig. ai[r]; Henry Miller, *God the protector of Israel* (London, 1641; Wing M2060A), pp. 2, 18; Sir Cahir O' Dogherty, *News from Lough-Foyle* (London, 1608; S.T.C. 18784), sigs A3[v], A4[r]; Richard Rawlidge, *A monster late found out and discovered* (London, 1628; S.T.C. 20766), p. 5; Rous, *Oile*, p. 88.

86. Pierre Boaistuau, *Certaine secrete wonders of nature* (London, 1569; S.T.C. 3164.5), fo. 12ᵛ.

87. See Samuel Clarke, *A mirrovr or looking-glasse* (London, 1657; Wing C4551), pp. 249–50; Nicholas Culpeper, *A directory for midwives* (London, 1651; Wing C7488), p. 140; Thomas Edwards, *Gangraena* (London, 1646; Wing G229), pp. 4–5; William Gouge, *Of domesticall duties* (London, 1634; S.T.C. 12121), p. 185; Thomas Heywood, *The hierarchie of the blessed angells* (London, 1635; S.T.C. 13327), pp. 541–42; Giambattista della Porta, *Natural magick* (London, 1658; Wing P2982), pp. 42–3; *Strange newes out of Kent* (London, 1609; S.T.C. 14934), sig. Biᵛ; I. R., *A most straunge, and true discourse, of the wonderfull judgement of God* (London, 1600; S.T.C. 20575); Skinker, *A certaine relation*, sig. A4ᵛ; Henry Smith, *A preparatiue to mariage* (London, 1591; S.T.C. 22685), p. 51; Andrew Willet, *Hexapla in Leviticum* (London, 1631; S.T.C. 25688), p. 434.

88. Paré, *The workes*, pp. 962–63.

89. Bedford, *A true and certaine relation*, p. 12.

90. Basset, *Curiosities*, p. 10.

91. Nicolaas Fonteyn, *The womans doctour* (London, 1652; Wing F1418A), p. 146.

92. Thomas Lupton, *A thousand notable things, of sundry sortes* (London, *c.* 1590, S.T.C. 16957.5), p. 20.

93. Cartwright, *The Ordinary*, II.iii.805–7. See also Crooke, *A description of the body of man*, p. 300; Antonio de Torquemada, *The Spanish Mandevile of miracles* (London, 1600; S.T.C. 24135), fo. 10ʳ; Sir Kenelm Digby, *Two discourses* (London, 1644; Wing D1448), p. 329.

   That narratives involving miraculous gestations or prodigious nativities circulated with no less frequency than those devoted to the origins of birth 'defects' suggests a wide readership and eager audiences. Assuming various forms in the discourses of the period was the proverbial account of the white or black woman who, through the force of imagination, delivered an infant of the opposite race. 'The Queen of *Ethiop* dreampt upon a night / Her black womb should bring forth a virgin white', announces the Induction to Brome's play, *The English Moor* (1636–37), continuing, ''tis no better than a Prodegy / To have white children in a black country' (Richard Brome, *The English Moor*, in *The Dramatic Works*, ed. John Pearson, 3 vols [London: Pearson, 1873], II, IV.v.pp. 65–6. See also William Bullein, *A dialogue bothe pleasaunte and pietifull, against the feuer pestilence* [London, 1573; S.T.C. 4037], pp. 110–11; [Sir Kenelm Digby], *A late discourse made in a solemne assembly* [London, 1658; Wing D1435], p. 104).

94. Andreas Gerardus, *The regiment of the pouertie* (London, 1572; S.T.C. 11759), sig. Diiiʳ; Levinus Lemnius, *The secret miracles of nature* (London, 1658; Wing L1044), p. 15.

95. Torquemada, *The Spanish Mandevile*, fos 10ʳ⁻ᵛ.

96. Chapman, *Bussy d'Ambois*, I.ii.156–160.

97. *Historia aenigmatica*. See also John Cleveland, *Poems* (London, 1653; Wing C4689), pp. 34–5; Nathaniel Highmore, *The history of generation* (London, 1651; Wing H1969), p. 95.

98. Skinker, *A certaine relation*, sig. A4ʳ. See also Evelyn, *Numismata*, p. 277; J. Greene, 'Account of a Man with a Child growing out of his Breast', *The*

Gentleman's Magazine, 47, December (1777), pp. 482–3; Stephen Pender, '"No Monsters at the Resurrection": Inside some Conjoined Twins', in Cohen, ed., *Monster Theory*, p. 156.

99. *A brief narrative*, p. 6.
100. Houghton Library, Harvard University, fMS Eng 1015, fo. 8ᵛ; Munday, *A view of sundry examples*, sig. Civᵛ; *Strange neᐸwᐳes* (London, [1606]; S.T.C. 4658), sig. B3ʳ.
101. Andrew Clark, ed., *The Shirburn Ballads 1585–1616* (Oxford: Clarendon, 1907), pp. 133–9.
102. Thomas Churchyard, *A warning for the wise* (London, 1580; S.T.C. 5259), sig. C1ʳ; John Hilliard, *Fire from heaven* (London, 1613; S.T.C. 13507), sig. B4ᵛ.
103. Cooper, *Thesaurus*, sig. HHhh2ᵛ; Lavater, *Ghostes and Spirites*, p. 8.
104. Bullein, *A dialogue bothe pleasaunte and pietifull*, p. 110.
105. Cohen, 'Monster Culture (Seven Theses)', p. 6.
106. Slater, *The new-yeeres gift*, pp. 103–5.
107. Vicars, *Prodigies and apparitions*, p. 22.
108. See Lloyd E. Berry, ed., *The Geneva Bible: A facsimile of the 1560 edition* (Madison, Milwaukee and London: University of Wisconsin Press, 1969), New Testament, fos 114ᵛ–122ʳ.
109. *Gods handy-worke*, sigs A4ᵛ, B2ʳ.
110. Edward Topsell, *The historie of serpents* (London, 1608; S.T.C. 24124), p. 190.
111. Samuel Purchas, *Purchas his pilgrim* (London, 1619; S.T.C. 20503), pp. 324, 326, 495.
112. *Rump: Or an Exact Collection of the Choycest Poems and Songs Relating to the Late Times*, 2 vols (London: Privately published, [1874]), I, pp. 124–5.

Chapter 2

1. *Tamburlaine the Great*, in Christopher Marlowe, *The Complete Plays*, ed. Mark Thornton Burnett (London: Everyman, 1999), I: Prologue, 1–8. All further references appear in the text.
2. Joy Kenseth, '"A World of Wonders in One Closet Shut"', in Joy Kenseth, ed., *The Age of the Marvellous* (Hanover: Hood Museum of Art, 1991), p. 94; J. Alan B. Somerset, ed., *Shropshire*, Records of Early English Drama, 2 vols (Toronto, Buffalo and London: University of Toronto Press, 1994), I, p. 237.
3. I am here, of course, seeking to refine recent arguments that Marlowe's use of the mirror convention is distinctly unconventional. See Johannes H. Birringer, 'Marlowe's Violent Stage: "Mirrors" of Honour in *Tamburlaine*', *ELH*, 51 (1984), p. 224; Janet Clare, 'Marlowe's "theatre of cruelty"', in J. A. Downie and J. T. Parnell, eds, *Constructing Christopher Marlowe* (Cambridge: Cambridge University Press, 2000), p. 84; Troni Y. Grande, *Marlovian Tragedy: The Play of Dilation* (Lewisburg: Bucknell University Press, 1999), pp. 44, 45, 56, 58, 69.
4. Anthony Alan Shelton, 'Cabinets of Transgression: Renaissance Collections and the Incorporation of the New World', in John Elsner and Roger

192 Constructing 'Monsters' in Shakespearean Drama and Early Modern Culture

Cardinal, eds, *The Cultures of Collecting* (London: Reaktion, 1994), p. 179. Nor may it be accidental that prodigy- and wonder-books also advertised themselves as mirrors: see William Averell, *A wonderfull and straunge newes* (London, 1583; S.T.C. 982.5), sig. Avi^r; J[ohn] B[ulwer], *Anthropometamorphosis* (London, 1653; Wing B5461), sig. ***2^v.

5. Roy W. Battenhouse, *Marlowe's 'Tamburlaine': A Study in Renaissance Moral Philosophy* (Nashville, TN: Vanderbilt University Press, 1964); Eugene M. Waith, *The Herculean Hero in Marlowe, Chapman, Shakespeare and Dryden* (London: Chatto and Windus, 1962), pp. 60–87.

6. See, for instance, Emily C. Bartels, *Spectacles of Strangeness: Imperialism, Alienation, Marlowe* (Philadelphia: University of Pennsylvania Press, 1993), p. 60; Thomas Cartelli, *Marlowe, Shakespeare, and the Economy of Theatrical Experience* (Philadelphia: University of Pennsylvania Press, 1991), pp. 67, 72; Stephen Greenblatt, *Renaissance Self-Fashioning: From More to Shakespeare* (Chicago: Chicago University Press, 1980), pp. 193–221; Roger Sales, *Christopher Marlowe* (Basingstoke: Macmillan – now Palgrave Macmillan, 1991), pp. 54–9. As will become clear, my stress on 'manufacture' owes much to Greenblatt's discussion of 'self-fashioning'.

7. Bartels, *Spectacles of Strangeness*, p. 67. Although Bartels refers to the 'monstrous' imputations of Tamburlaine's enemies at several points in her fine discussion (pp. 69, 70, 81), 'monstrosity' is not her central focus.

8. David H. Thurn, 'Sights of Power in *Tamburlaine*', *English Literary Renaissance*, 19 (1989), pp. 3–4.

9. J. A. Simpson and E. S. C. Weiner, eds, *The Oxford English Dictionary*, 20 vols (Oxford: Clarendon, 1989), I, p. 166.

10. James Biester, *Lyric Wonder: Rhetoric and Wit in Renaissance English Poetry* (Ithaca, NY and London: Cornell University Press, 1997), p. 10; Peter G. Platt, *Reason Diminished: Shakespeare and the Marvellous* (Lincoln, NB and London: University of Nebraska Press, 1997), p. 63.

11. Katie Whitaker, 'The culture of curiosity', in N. Jardine, J. A. Secord and E. C. Sparry, eds, *Cultures of Natural History* (Cambridge: Cambridge University Press, 1996), p. 76.

12. David Williams, *Deformed Discourse: The Function of the Monster in Mediaeval Thought and Literature* (Exeter: University of Exeter Press, 1996), p. 117. Criticism has generally passed over the 'gigantic' implications of Tamburlaine, although passing references draw attention to the theme. See, for instance, Raphael Falco's comment that Tamburlaine is 'A human giant with the strength of a god, a Scythian Achilles' (*Charismatic Authority in Early Modern English Tragedy* [Baltimore and London: The Johns Hopkins University Press, 2000], p. 30).

13. Elizabeth Cropper, 'On Beautiful Women, Parmigianino, *Petrarchismo*, and the Vernacular Style', *Art Bulletin*, 58 (1976), p. 376. The argument in this paragraph has also been stimulated by Nancy Vickers, '"The blazon of sweet beauty's best": Shakespeare's *Lucrece*', in Patricia Parker and Geoffrey Hartman, eds, *Shakespeare and the Question of Theory* (New York and London: Methuen, 1995), pp. 95–115.

14. Somerset, ed., *Shropshire*, I, p. 235; John Stow, *The annales of England* (London, 1592; S.T.C. 23334), p. 1181; *The true effigies of the German giant* (London, 1660; Wing T2692). See also Thomas Heywood, *The three wonders of this age* (London, 1636; S.T.C. 13365.5).

15. Edward J. Wood, *Giants and Dwarfs* (London: Bentley, 1868), p. 94. See also Folger Shakespeare Library, MS V.a.510, fos 52^v, 68^v; Simon Goulart, *Admirable and memorable histories containing the wonders of our time* (London, 1607; S.T.C. 12135), p. 287.

16. Henry Crowther, 'Anthony Payne, the Cornish Giant', *Journal of the Royal Institution of Cornwall*, 10 (1890), pp. 3–7.

17. Jonathan Crewe, 'The Theatre of the Idols: Marlowe, Rankins, and Theatrical Images', *Theatre Journal*, 36 (1984), pp. 327–8.

18. Folger Shakespeare Library, MS M.b.7, fo. 153; I. G., *The wonder of our times: being a true and exact relation of the body of a mighty giant* (London, 1651; Wing G29), pp. 1, 3, 5; Goulart, *Admirable and memorable histories*, pp. 286–9.

19. Caius Julius Solinus, *The worthie worke* (London, 1587; S.T.C. 22895a.5), sig. Diiii^r. For the exhibition of 'giants' bones', see Antonio de Torquemada, *The Spanish Mandevile of miracles* (London, 1600; S.T.C. 24135), fos 21^v–2^v; Henry Farley, *S^t. Paules-Church her bill for the parliament* (London, 1621; S.T.C. 10690), sig. E4^r; Krzysztof Pomian, *Collectors and Curiosities: Paris and Venice, 1500–1800*, tr. Elizabeth Wiles-Portier (Cambridge: Polity, 1990), p. 46.

20. Pierre Grimal, *The Dictionary of Classical Mythology* (Oxford: Blackwell, 1986), pp. 119, 433, 457.

21. Laurence Coupe, *Myth* (London and New York: Routledge, 1997), p. 18.

22. Coupe, *Myth*, pp. 8–9.

23. Richard Levin, 'The Contemporary Perception of Marlowe's Tamburlaine', *Medieval and Renaissance Drama in England*, 1 (1984), pp. 53, 55. See also Cartelli, *Marlowe, Shakespeare, and the Economy of Theatrical Experience*, who expertly argues that contemporary 'citizens' may have been 'pleasurably aroused' by 'The Tamburlaine Phenomenon' (p. 71).

24. Rosemarie Garland Thomson, *Extraordinary Bodies: Figuring Physical Disability in American Culture and Literature* (New York: Columbia University Press, 1997), p. 29.

25. Sales, *Christopher Marlowe*, pp. 54–9; Richard Wilson, 'Visible Bullets: Tamburlaine the Great and Ivan the Terrible', *ELH*, 62 (1995), p. 51.

26. Stephen Bateman, *The doome warning all men to the judgemente* (London, 1581; S.T.C. 1582), p. 7; Pomponius Mela, *The worke* (London, 1590; S.T.C. 17785), sig. Gii^v; de Torquemada, *Spanish Mandevile*, fo. 11^r.

27. Bateman, *The doome warning*, p. 387; Donald Lupton, *Emblems of rarities* (London, 1636; S.T.C. 16942), p. 239.

28. Bateman, *The doome*, p. 7; Joannes Boemus, *The fardle of facions* (London, 1555; S.T.C. 3197), sigs Niiii^v–Nv^r; John Block Friedman, *The Monstrous Races in Medieval Art and Thought* (Cambridge, MA and London: Harvard University Press, 1981), p. 10; Frank Lestringant, *Cannibals: The Discovery and Representation of the Cannibal from Columbus to Jules Verne* (Berkeley and Los Angeles: University of California Press, 1997), p. 49; Mela, *The worke*, sigs Giv^r, Ni^r; Solinus, *The worthie worke*, sig. Tii^v.

29. William Shakespeare, *King Lear*, ed. R. A. Foakes (London: Thomson, 2000), I.i.117–19. For related views, see James William Johnson, 'The Scythian: His Rise and Fall', *Journal of the History of Ideas*, 20 (1959), p. 251; Caius Plinus Secundus, *The historie of the world* (London, 1601; S.T.C. 20029), pp. 124, 147, 154; Sebastian Munster, *Cosmographiae universalis lib. VI* (Basileae: Henrichum Petri, 1554), p. 1058.

30. Fred B. Tromly, *Playing with Desire: Christopher Marlowe and the Art of Tantalization* (Toronto, Buffalo and London: University of Toronto Press, 1998), p. 77.
31. Further 'cannibal' references inform these scenes: Tamburlaine encourages Bajazeth to eat himself (I:IV.iv.36–8, 45–7) and then Zabina (I:IV.iv.48–50). See also Tromly, *Playing with Desire*, pp. 77–9, 191.
32. On orality, see Ann Lake Prescott, 'Rabelaisian (Non) Wonders and Renaissance Polemics', in Peter G. Platt, ed., *Wonders, Marvels, and Monsters in Early Modern Culture* (Newark: University of Delaware Press, 1999), p. 135. For 'giants' as 'cannibals', see Folger Shakespeare Library, MS J.a.1, booklet 15, fo. 187ʳ; R. I., *The History of Tom Thumb* (1621), ed. Curt F. Buhler (Evanston, IL: Northwestern University Press, 1965), p. 15. On the appetites of 'giants', see Robert Crowley, *Philargyrie of greate Britayne* (London, 1551; S.T.C. 6089.5), sig. Aiiiʳ; de Torquemada, *Spanish Mandevile*, fo. 23ʳ; Folger Shakespeare Library, MS V.a.510, fo. 54ʳ.
33. For a list of some of these 'monstrous' features, see George Hakewill, *An apologie or declaration of the power* (Oxford, 1635; S.T.C. 12613), p. 206.
34. Alison Findlay, *Illegitimate Power: Bastards in English Renaissance Drama* (Manchester and New York: Manchester University Press, 1994), p. 107; Grimal, *Dictionary*, pp. 461–2, 552; S. K. Heninger, *A Handbook of Renaissance Meterology* (Durham, NC: Duke University Press, 1960), pp. 126–7.
35. Ginevra Bompiani, 'The Chimera Herself', in Michael Feher, Ramona Naddaff and Nadia Tazi, eds, *Fragments for a History of the Human Body*, 3 vols (New York: Zone, 1989), I, p. 370.
36. Elizabeth Grosz, 'Intolerable Ambiguity: Freaks as/at the Limit', in Rosemarie Garland Thomson, ed., *Freakery: Cultural Spectacles of the Extraordinary Body* (New York and London: New York University Press, 1996), p. 65.
37. Anthony Munday, *The triumphes of re-united Britania* (London, 1605; S.T.C. 18279), sig. B1ᵛ.
38. See Jeffrey Jerome Cohen, *Of Giants: Sex, Monsters, and the Middle Ages* (Minneapolis: University of Minnesota Press, 1999), pp. 29–61; Raphael Holinshed, *Holinshed's Chronicles of England, Scotland and Ireland*, 6 vols (London: Johnson, 1807–8), I, p. 22; Ann Lake Prescott, *Imagining Rabelais in Renaissance England* (New Haven and London: Yale University Press, 1998), pp. 18–19.
39. Jeffrey Jerome Cohen, 'Monster Culture (Seven Theses)', in Jeffrey Jerome Cohen, ed., *Monster Theory: Reading Culture* (Minneapolis and London: University of Minnesota Press, 1996), p. 7.
40. Waith, *The Herculean Hero*, p. 77.
41. G. A., *No post from heaven* (London, 1643; Wing A8), sig. A2ᵛ; Robert Anton, *The philosophers satyrs* (London, 1616; S.T.C. 686), pp. 41, 70; Edmund Calamy, *The monster of sinful self-seeking* (London, 1655; Wing C259), sig. A3ʳ, pp. 13, 15; Grimal, *Dictionary*, p. 219; Heninger, *A Handbook*, p. 126; T. I., *A world of wonders* (London, 1595; S.T.C. 14068.5), sigs D3ʳ⁻ᵛ. For the exhibition of the stuffed hydra, see Edward Topsell, *The historie of serpents* (London, 1608; S.T.C. 24124), p. 202.
42. Mark Thornton Burnett, 'Tamburlaine: An Elizabethan Vagabond', *Studies in Philology*, 84 (1987), pp. 308–23; William C. Carroll, *Fat King, Lean Beggar:*

Representations of Poverty in the Age of Shakespeare (Ithaca, NY and London: Cornell University Press, 1996), pp. 73, 80.

43. Laurence Humphrey, *A view of the Romish hydra confuted in seven sermons* (London, 1588; S.T.C. 13966), sig. *2ᵛ; Sir Cahir O'Dogherty, *News from Lough-Foyle* (London, 1608; S.T.C. 18784), sig. B2ᵛ; E. C. S., *The government of Ireland under sir John Perrot* (London, 1626; S.T.C. 21490), p. 71.

44. Walter Stephens, *Giants in Those Days: Folklore, Ancient History, and Nationalism* (Lincoln, NB and London: University of Nebraska Press, 1989), p. 66. See also Debra Higgs Strickland's view that 'a monster . . . clarified by negative example what it meant to be a good Christian' ('Monsters and Christian Enemies', *History Today*, 50.2 [2000], p. 51).

45. Cohen, *Of Giants*, pp. 19, 25, 53, 68; Ruth Waterhouse, '*Beowulf* as Palimpsest', in Cohen, ed., *Monster Theory*, p. 33; Williams, *Deformed Discourse*, p. 117. Coupling across species and even classes and types was also held a reason for the generation of 'monsters': see Sir John Ferne, *The blazon of gentrie* (London, 1586; S.T.C. 10824), p. 10; Daniel Rogers, *Matrimoniall honovr* (London, 1642; Wing R1797), p. 61; Andrew Willet, *Hexapla in Exodum* (London, 1608; S.T.C. 25686), p. 505.

46. Pierre Boaistuau, *Certaine secrete wonders of nature* (London, 1569; S.T.C. 3164.5), fo. 16ᵛ.

47. Thomas Heywood, *The hierarchie of the blessed angells* (London, 1635; S.T.C. 13327), p. 541. See also T[homas] B[romhall], *A treatise of specters* (London, 1658; Wing B4886), p. 40; *A courtlie controuersie of Cupids cautels* (London, 1578; S.T.C. 5647), p. 99. Medical authorities Ambroise Paré and John Sadler, however, claimed that evil spirits lacked semen and were therefore incapable of producing issue: see Ambroise Paré, *The workes of that famous chirurgion* (London, 1634; S.T.C. 19189), pp. 988–9; John Sadler, *The sicke womans private looking-glasse* (London, 1636; S.T.C. 21544), pp. 140–2.

48. See William Leigh, *Strange newes of a prodigious monster* (London, 1613; S.T.C. 15428), sig. A3ᵛ; Levinus Lemnius, *The secret miracles of nature* (London, 1658; Wing L1044), p. 24; Thomas Lupton, *A thousand notable things, of sundry sortes* (London, *c.* 1590; S.T.C. 16957.5), pp. 151–2.

49. M. J. Power, 'London and the Control of the "Crisis" of the 1590s', *History*, 70 (1985), p. 380.

50. Meredith Anne Skura, *Shakespeare the Actor and the Purposes of Playing* (Chicago and London: University of Chicago Press, 1993), p. 155.

51. Walter W. Greg, ed., *Henslowe Papers* (London: A. H. Bullen, 1907), pp. 144, 148; *Anthony and Cleopatra*, ed. Michael Neill (Oxford and New York: Oxford University Press, 1994), IV.xiii.36–7.

52. François Citois, *A true and admirable historie* (London, 1603; S.T.C. 5326), fo. 8ᵛ.

53. Alexander Gurth, *Most true and more admirable newes* (London, 1597; S.T.C. 12531.5), sig. B1ᵛ. For examples, see Catherine Cooper, *A most notable and prodigious historie* (London, 1589; S.T.C. 5678), pp. 3, 4, 6, 12; Eva Fliegen, *The pourtrayture* (London, *c.* 1620?; S.T.C. 11088.3); Folger Shakespeare Library, MS V.a.510, fos 116ʳ–17ᵛ; *The strange newes* (London, 1561; S.T.C. 18507), sig. Diiᵛ.

54. Robert Hobson, *The arraignement of the whole creature* (London, 1631; S.T.C. 13538.5), pp. 240, 314. See also Louis Le Roy, *Of the interchangeable course,*

or variety of things in the whole world (London, 1594; S.T.C. 15489), p. 108.
Hobson's comment, of course, also draws upon the proverbial wisdom that
Africa was home to all manner of 'monsters': see Henry Miller, *God the pro-
tector of Israel* (London, 1641; Wing M2060A), p. 18; William Prynne, *The
unlovelinesse of love-lockes* (London, 1628; S.T.C. 20477), sig. B1ʳ; Griffith
Williams, *Vindiciae regvm; or, the Grand Rebellion* (Oxford, 1643; Wing
W2675), pp. 1–2.

55. Peter Burke, *Popular Culture in Early Modern Europe* (London: Temple Smith,
1978), p. 112.

56. Somerset, ed., *Shropshire*, I, p. 276. For Marocco's feats, see Sidney H. Atkins,
'Mr Banks and his Horse', *Notes and Queries*, 167, 21 July (1934), pp. 38–44;
N. W. Bawcutt, ed., *The Control and Censorship of Caroline Drama: The
Records of Sir Henry Herbert, Master of the Revels, 1623–73* (Oxford: Claren-
don, 1996), p. 82; Sir William Davenant, 'The Long Vacation in London'
(1630s), in *The Shorter Poems*, ed. A. M. Gibbs (Oxford: Clarendon, 1972),
p. 129; Sir Kenelm Digby, *Two discourses* (London, 1644; Wing D1448), p.
321; Emma Phipson, *The Animal-Lore of Shakspeare's Time* (London: Kegan
Paul and Trench, 1883), pp. 109–11; N. Zwager, *Glimpses of Ben Jonson's
London* (Amsterdam: Swets and Zeitlinger, 1926), pp. 46–50.

57. Thomas Dekker and George Wilkins, *Iests to Make You Merrie* (1607), in
Thomas Dekker, *The Non-Dramatic Works*, ed. Alexander B. Grosart, 5 vols
(London: Hazel, Watson and Viney, 1884–6), II, p. 317; Ben Jonson, *Every
Man Out of His Humour* (1599), in *The Complete Plays*, ed. G. A. Wilkes, 4
vols (Oxford: Clarendon, 1981–2), I, IV.vi.53–5.

58. Simpson and Weiner, eds, *Oxford English Dictionary*, VIII, p. 176.

59. The phrase 'woonderfull and strange' is taken from a 1591 account of a
performance by Marocco: see Somerset, ed., *Shropshire*, I, p. 276.

60. Johannes H. Birringer, *Marlowe's 'Dr Faustus' and 'Tamburlaine': Theological
and Theatrical Perspectives* (Frankfurt-am-Main, Bern and New York: Lang,
1984), p. 147.

61. Sara Munson Deats, *Sex, Gender, and Desire in the Plays of Christopher Marlowe*
(Newark: University of Delaware Press, 1997), p. 138; Simon Shepherd,
Marlowe and the Politics of Elizabethan Theatre (Brighton: Harvester, 1986),
pp. 186–7; Lisa S. Starks, ' "Won with thy words and conquered with thy
looks": Sadism, Masochism, and the Masochistic Gaze in *1 Tamburlaine*', in
Paul Whitfield White, ed., *Marlowe, History, and Sexuality: New Critical Essays
on Christopher Marlowe* (New York: AMS, 1998), p. 184.

62. Francis Beaumont and John Fletcher, *The Dramatic Works*, ed. Fredson
Bowers, 10 vols (Cambridge: Cambridge University Press, 1966–96), II,
V.iii.55–7. Extra-dramatic narratives suggest that displays of mummified
state enemies were common European practice. See John Leo, *A geograph-
ical historie of Africa* (London, 1600; S.T.C. 15481), p. 316; *An oration
militarie to all naturall Englishmen* (London, 1588; S.T.C. 18836.5), sig. B1ʳ;
John Polemon, *The second part of the booke of battailes* (London, 1587;
S.T.C. 20090), fo. 82ʳ.

63. [William Shakespeare and William Rowley], *The Birth of Merlin*, ed. R. J.
Stewart and Denise Coffey (Longmead: Element, 1989), V.ii.p. 137. See also
Jonson, *Every Man Out of His Humour*, V.vi.37–40.

64. Elisabeth Bronfen, *Over Her Dead Body: Death, Femininity and the Aesthetic*
(Manchester: Manchester University Press, 1992), p. 103.

65. Ben Jonson, *The New Inn* (1628–29), ed. Michael Hattaway (Manchester: Manchester University Press, 1984), V.iv.91–8; Thomas Middleton and William Rowley, *The Spanish Gipsy* (1623), in Thomas Middleton, *The Works*, ed. A. H. Bullen, 8 vols (London: Nimmo, 1885–86), VI, IV.i.pp. 187–8; Edward Webbe, *The rare and most wonderfull things* (London, 1590; S.T.C. 25151.5), sig. D2ʳ.

66. Edward L. Schwarzschild, 'Death-Defying/Defining Spectacles: Charles Willson Peale as Early American Freak Showman', in Thomson, ed., *Freakery*, p. 83.

67. See Susan Stewart, 'Death and Life, in that Order, in the Works of Charles Willson Peale', in Lynne Cooke and Peter Wollen, eds, *Visual Display: Culture Beyond Appearances* (Seattle: Bay Press, 1995), pp. 30–53.

68. John Sanderson, *The Travels of John Sanderson in the Levant, 1584–1602*, ed. Sir William Foster, Hakluyt Society, 2nd ser., 67 (1930 [1931]), p. 45.

69. Thomas Platter, *Thomas Platter's Travels in England 1599*, tr. Clare Williams (London: Cape, 1937), p. 172; Arthur MacGregor, 'The Tradescants as Collectors of Rarities', in Arthur MacGregor, ed., *Tradescant's Rarities: Essays on the Foundation of the Ashmolean Museum* (Oxford: Clarendon, 1983), p. 21.

70. Certainly, this was the theatrical decision favoured by the RSC in its 1992 production of the play: Tamburlaine's injunction was answered by the appearance in the gallery of the decayed corpse of his consort.

71. C. L. Barber, *Creating Elizabethan Tragedy: The Theatre of Marlowe and Kyd* (Chicago and London: University of Chicago Press, 1988), p. 71; Ian McAdam, *The Irony of Identity: Self and Imagination in the Drama of Christopher Marlowe* (Newark: University of Delaware Press, 1999), p. 96; Thurn, 'Sights of Power', p. 20.

72. John Vicars, *Prodigies and apparitions* (London, 1642–43; Wing V323), p. 3.

73. John Stow, *The annales of England* (London, 1631; S.T.C. 23340), p. 743.

74. See Margaret Aston, 'The Fiery Trigon Conjunction: An Elizabethan Astrological Prediction', *Isis*, 61 (1970), pp. 166, 177; Bernard Capp, *Astrology and the Popular Press: English Almanacs 1500–1800* (London and Boston: Faber, 1979), pp. 166, 168; Howard Dobin, *Merlin's Disciples: Prophecy, Poetry, and Power in Renaissance England* (Stanford: Stanford University Press, 1990), pp. 107–8; John Doleta, *Straunge newes out of Calabria* (London, 1586; S.T.C. 6992), sigs Aiiiʳ, Avʳ, Aviʳ; Thomas Tomkis, *Albumazar: A Comedy [1615]*, ed. Hugh G. Dick (Berkeley and Los Angeles: University of California Press, 1944), pp. 37, 39.

75. Abraham Fleming, *A bright burning beacon* (London, 1580; S.T.C 11037), sigs C1ᵛ, C3ʳ⁻ᵛ; E1ᵛ; Folger Shakespeare Library, MS V.a.339, fo. 171ᵛ; *Gods handyworke in wonders* (London, 1615; S.T.C. 11926), sig. B3ᵛ; Thomas Twyne, *A shorte and pithie discourse, concerning earthquakes* (London, 1580; S.T.C. 24413), sig. Biiiᵛ. For natural theories that earthquakes were caused by the release of trapped winds and vapours, see Robert Basset, *Curiosities: or the cabinet of nature* (London, 1637; S.T.C. 1557), pp. 101–3; Sir Thomas Browne, *Pseudoxia epidemica* (London, 1650; Wing B5160), p. 69; William Fulke, *A most pleasant prospect* (London, 1602; S.T.C. 11438), fo. 19ᵛ; David Person, *Varieties: or, a surveigh of rare and excellent matters* (London, 1635; S.T.C. 19781), Book III, p. 79.

76. Anthony Munday, *A view of sundry examples* (London, 1580; S.T.C. 18281), sig. Divʳ.

77. Fleming, *A bright burning beacon*, sigs G2ᵛ, G4ʳ. On eclipses in general, see Thomas Blundeville, *The theoriques of the seven planets* (London, 1602; S.T.C. 3160), p. 174; Adam Foulweather, *A wonderfull, strange and miraculous, prognostication for this yeer 1591* (London, 1591; S.T.C. 11209), sig. B2ʳ; Goulart, *Admirable and memorable histories*, p. 58.
78. For heavenly apparitions accompanying the sieges of cities during European wars, see L. Brinckmair, *The warnings of Germany* (London, 1638; S.T.C. 3758), p. 10; Fulke, *A most pleasant prospect*, fo. 9ʳ; Goulart, *Admirable and memorable histories*, p. 52.
79. Fulke, *A most pleasant prospect*, fo. 46ʳ. On the prodigious significance of 'armies in the clouds', see Bateman, *The doome*, p. 84; Brinckmair, *The warnings*, pp. 31, 44; Thomas Hill, *A contemplation of mysteries: contayning the rare effectes of certayne comets* (London, 1574?; S.T.C. 13484), fo. 10ʳ; Huntington Library, California, Ellesmere MS. 6174.
80. Averell, *A wonderfull and straunge newes*, sigs Biiʳ, Bviᵛ; Brinckmair, *The warnings*, p. 10; Fulke, *A most pleasant prospect*, fo. 51ʳ. See also Hill, *A contemplation*, fo. 8ᵛ; Holinshed, *Chronicles*, II, p. 174.
81. Aston, 'The Fiery Trigon Conjunction', p. 177; Dobin, *Merlin's Disciples*, pp. 107–8.
82. Richard Harvey, *An astrological discourse vpon the great and notable coniunction* (London, 1583; S.T.C. 12911), p. 44.
83. Giovanni Cipriano, *A most strange and wonderfull prophesie vpon this troublesome world* (London, 1595; S.T.C. 5324), sigs Aiiiʳ, Aivᵛ; Thomas Tymme, *A silver watch-bell* (London, 1610; S.T.C. 24424), pp. 48, 51, 54, 56. For scriptural antecedents, see Lloyd E. Berry, ed., *The Geneva Bible: A facsimile of the 1560 edition* (Madison, Milwaukee and London: University of Wisconsin Press, 1969), New Testament, Revelation (VI.12–14), fos 116ᵛ (VIII.5, 7, 10, 12), 117ʳ (XVI.21), 120ʳ.
84. Battenhouse, *Marlowe's 'Tamburlaine'*, p. 216; R. M. Cornelius, *Christopher Marlowe's Use of the Bible* (New York, Berne and Frankfurt-am-Main: Peter Lang, 1984), p. 71; Henry W. Wells, *Elizabethan and Jacobean Playwrights* (New York: Columbia University Press, 1939), pp. 80–1.
85. Coupe, *Myth*, p. 85.
86. Eugene Hill, 'Marlowe's "more Exellent and Admirable methode" of Parody in *Tamburlaine I*', *Renaissance Papers* (1995), p. 38.
87. Hill, 'Marlowe's "more Exellent and Admirable methode"', p. 38.
88. See Cornelius, *Christopher Marlowe's Use of the Bible*, pp. 145, 154, 159, 169, 181, 188; John P. Cutts, 'The Ultimate Source of Tamburlaine's White, Red, Black and Death?', *Notes and Queries*, 203 (1958), pp. 146–7; Lynette and Evelyn Feasey, 'Marlowe and the Prophetic Dooms', *Notes and Queries*, 195 (1950), pp. 356–9, 404–7, 419–21; Malcolm Kelsall, *Christopher Marlowe* (Leiden: E. J. Brill, 1981), p. 87. The exception is Hill, 'Marlowe's "more Exellent and Admirable methode"', who argues that Tamburlaine represents a 'parody of the Good shepherd' (p. 39).
89. Berry, ed., *The Geneva Bible*, New Testament, *Revelation* (XIIII.8), fo. 119ʳ.
90. For a similar argument, see Thurn, 'Sights of Power', p. 21.
91. Coupe, *Myth*, pp. 74–5.
92. Lorraine Daston and Katharine Park, *Wonders and the Order of Nature, 1150–1750* (New York: Zone Books, 1998), p. 209.

93. Arthur Freeman, *Thomas Kyd: Facts and Problems* (Oxford: Clarendon Press, 1967), p. 182.
94. Millar Maclure, ed., *Marlowe: The Critical Heritage, 1588–1896* (London, Boston and Henley: Routledge & Kegan Paul, 1979), pp. 39–40.

Chapter 3

1. Levinus Lemnius, *The secret miracles of nature* (London, 1658; Wing L1044), p. 24. The episode is also narrated, with slight variations, in Thomas Lupton, *A thousand notable things, of sundry sortes* (London, *c.* 1590; S.T.C. 16957.5), p. 151.
2. Most contemporary medical authorities described the 'mola' merely as a shapeless substance. See, for instance, Philip Barrough, *The methode of physicke* (London, 1583; S.T.C. 1508), p. 153; Nicolaas Fonteyn, *The womans doctour* (London, 1652; S.T.C. F1418A), p. 146; Jacob Rueff, *The expert midwife* (London, 1637; S.T.C. 21442), p. 137. Physicians, dramatists and travel writers alike, however, saw as synonymous 'molas' and 'mooncalves', also understood in the period as 'monsters'. See Helkiah Crooke, *A description of the body of man* (London, 1631; S.T.C. 6063), pp. 297–8; Ben Jonson, *News from the New World* (1620), in *Ben Jonson*, ed. C. H. Herford and Percy and Evelyn Simpson, 11 vols (Oxford: Clarendon, 1925–52), VII, p. 520; Samuel Purchas, *Purchas his pilgrim* (London, 1619; S.T.C. 20503), p. 491. An alternative term for 'monsters', moreover, was 'abortives' (also known as 'molas'). See L. Brinckmair, *The warnings of Germany* (London, 1638; S.T.C. 3758), p. 50; William Shakespeare, *King John* (1595–96), ed. A. R. Braunmuller (Oxford and New York: Oxford University Press, 1994), III.iv.153–9; *A true relation of the French kinge his goode successe* (London, 1592; S.T.C. 13147), sig. B4ᵛ.
3. *Richard III*, ed. Antony Hammond (London and New York: Routledge, 1990), I.i.27. All further references appear in the text.
4. William Clowes, *A briefe and necessarie treatise* (London, 1585; S.T.C. 5448), fo. 59ᵛ; John Arthur, *Deeds against nature, and monsters by kinde* (London, 1614; S.T.C. 809), sig. B1ʳ. For similar views, see *The Compost of Ptholomeus* (London, [1540?]; S.T.C. 20480a), sig. Riiʳ; Michael Torrey, '"The plain devil and dissembling looks": Ambivalent Physiognomy and Shakespeare's *Richard III*', *English Literary Renaissance*, 30 (2000), pp. 129, 142.
5. Lemnius, *The secret miracles*, pp. 24–5.
6. *Henry VI, Part II*, ed. Ronald Knowles (Walton-on-Thames: Nelson, 1999), V.i.157; *Henry VI, Part III*, ed. Andrew S. Cairncross (London and New York, Routledge, 1989), III.ii.161–2, V.vi.51.
7. *Henry VI, Part III*, V.vi.53.
8. See, for instance, [*Ballad describing natural portents*] (London, 1580?; S.T.C. 1325); T[homas] B[romhall], *A treatise of specters* (London, 1658; Wing B4886), p. 196; William Bullein, *A dialogue bothe pleasaunte and pietifull, against the feuer pestilence* (London, 1573; S.T.C. 4037), p. 111; Caius Julius Solinus, *The worthie worke* (London, 1587; S.T.C. 22895a.5), sig. Diᵛ.

9. Linda Charnes, *Notorious Identity: Materializing the Subject in Shakespeare* (Cambridge, MA: Harvard University Press, 1993), p. 30. Richard Marien-stras, 'Of a Monstrous Body', in Jean-Marie Maguin and Michèle Willems, eds, *French Essays on Shakespeare and His Contemporaries: 'What would France with Us?'* (Newark: University of Delaware Press, 1995), p. 160; Torrey, ' "The plain devil" ', p. 123.
10. Susan Frye, *Elizabeth I: The Competition for Representation* (New York and Oxford: Oxford University Press, 1993), p. 99.
11. John Guy, 'The 1590s: The second reign of Elizabeth I?', in John Guy, ed., *The Reign of Elizabeth I: Court and Culture in the Last Decade* (Cambridge: Cambridge University Press, 1995), p. 17.
12. Christopher Haigh, *Elizabeth I* (London and New York: Longman, 1998), p. 21; J. Hurstfield, 'The Succession Struggle in Late Elizabethan England', in S. T. Bindoff, J. Hurstfield and C. H. Williams, eds, *Elizabethan Government and Society: Essays Presented to Sir John Neale* (London: Athlone, 1961), pp. 371–2.
13. Carole Levin, *'The Heart and Stomach of a King': Elizabeth I and the Politics of Sex and Power* (Philadelphia: University of Pennsylvania Press, 1994), pp. 166–7; J. E. Neale, *Elizabeth I and Her Parliaments, 1559–1601*, 2 vols (London: Cape, 1969), II, pp. 251–66.
14. T. E. Hartley, ed., *Proceedings in the Parliaments of Elizabeth I, 1558–1601*, 3 vols (Leicester: Leicester University Press, 1981–95), I, pp. 130–1; Robert Parsons, *A conference about the next succession to the crowne of Ingland* (London, 1594; S.T.C. 19398), I, p. 126.
15. Peter Wentworth, *A pithie exhortation* (London, 1598; S.T.C. 25245), pp. 8, 21.
16. Lloyd E. Berry, ed., *John Stubbs' 'Gaping Gulf' with Letters and Other Relevant Documents* (Charlottesville, VA: University Press of Virginia, 1968), p. 160.
17. Sir John Harington, *A Tract on the Succession to the Crown (A.D. 1602)* (London: Roxburghe Club, 1880), p. 77. See also Wentworth, *A pithie exhortation*, pp. 55, 81.
18. Robert N. Watson, *Shakespeare and the Hazards of Ambition* (Cambridge, MA: Harvard University Press, 1984), p. 22.
19. See IV.iv.194, IV.iv.237 and V.iii.166.
20. Wentworth, *A pithie exhortation*, pp. 7, 22. On Elizabeth as 'mother', see Helen Hackett, *Virgin Mother, Maiden Queen: Elizabeth I and the Cult of the Virgin Mary* (Basingstoke: Macmillan – now Palgrave Macmillan, 1995), pp. 77–8, 118–19; Levin, *'The Heart and Stomach of a King'*, pp. 87, 195.
21. Marjorie Garber, *Shakespeare's Ghost Writers: Literature as uncanny causality* (New York and London: Methuen, 1987), p. 39.
22. Jean E. Howard and Phyllis Rackin, *Engendering a Nation: A Feminist Account of Shakespeare's English histories* (London and New York: Routledge, 1997), p. 108.
23. Thomas Bedford's *A true and certaine relation of a strange-birth* (London, 1635; S.T.C. 1791), a pamphlet about the birth of conjoined twins in Plymouth, contains a clergyman's sermon (pp. 9–22); a 'monstrous birth' delivered by a sectarian woman in Colchester is described by a 'godly Minister' in Thomas Edwards, *Gangraena* (London, 1646; Wing G229), pp. 4–5; and *A myraculous, and monstrous, but yet most true, discourse* (London,

1588; S.T.C. 6910.7), which concerns the horned woman, Margaret Vergh Griffith, boasts a preface by a 'learned Preacher' (sig. A1ᵛ).

24. Torrey, ' "The plain devil and dissembling looks" ', p. 141.

25. Edmund Spenser, *The Faerie Queene*, ed. A. C. Hamilton (London and New York: Longman, 1977), p. 41.

26. *Henry VI, Part III*, V.vi.83.

27. Ian Frederick Moulton, ' "A Monster Great Deformed": The Unruly Masculinity of Richard III', *Shakespeare Quarterly*, 47 (1996), p. 265.

28. See Hackett, *Virgin Mother, Maiden Queen*, pp. 80–1; Frances A. Yates, *Astraea: The Imperial Theme in the Sixteenth Century* (London, Boston, Melbourne and Henley: Ark, 1975), pp. 58, 65–6.

29. Thomas Brightman, *A revelation of the Apocalyps* (Amsterdam, 1611; S.T.C. 3754), sig. C1ʳ; Cambridge University Library, MS Ee.5.36, fo. 8ᵛ; Folger Shakespeare Library, MS V.a.339, fo. 22ʳ; *A wonder woorth the reading, of a woman in Kent Street* (London, 1617; S.T.C. 14935), sig. A1ᵛ.

30. Garber, *Shakespeare's Ghost Writers*, p. 45.

31. See *Henry VI, Part II*, V.i.215; *Henry VI, Part III*, II.ii.136.

32. I am thinking here of the fate of the titular blasphemer in Anthony Painter, *Anthony Paint[er] the blaspheming caryar* (London, 1613; S.T.C. 19120), sigs A3ᵛ, B1ᵛ.

33. Diane Purkiss, 'Producing the voice, consuming the body: Women prophets of the seventeenth century', in Isobel Grundy and Sue Wiseman, eds, *Women, Writing, History, 1640–1740* (London: Batsford, 1992), pp. 140–1.

34. Charnes, *Notorious Identity*, p. 45.

35. See Jasper Mayne, *The City-Match*, in W. C. Hazlitt, ed., *A Select Collection of Old English Plays*, 4th edn, 15 vols (London: Reeves and Turner, 1874–6), XIII, III.i.pp. 252–9.

36. Edward Forset, *A comparative discourse of the bodies natural and politique* (London, 1606; S.T.C. 11188), pp. 26–7.

37. See Lloyd E. Berry, ed., *The Geneva Bible: A facsimile of the 1560 edition* (Madison, Milwaukee and London: University of Wisconsin Press, 1969), New Testament, fos 116ᵛ–17ʳ.

38. *Henry VI, Part III*, I.iv.75. On the 'foreign prince' see, for instance, William Camden, *The History of the Most Renowned and Victorious Elizabeth, Late Queen of England* (1608–15), ed. Wallace T. MacCaffrey (Chicago and London: University of Chicago Press, 1970), p. 136; Harington, *A Tract on the Succession*, p. 55; Hartley, ed., *Proceedings in the Parliament*, I, pp. 130–1; Parsons, *A conference*, II, pp. 112, 114, 223; Sir Thomas Wilson, *The State of England* (1600), ed. F. J. Fisher, Camden Society, 3rd ser., 16 (1936), pp. 2, 6.

39. These quotations are taken from Wentworth, *A pithie exhortation* (pp. 25–6 and 65) and from his *A treatise containing M. Wentworths ivdgement* (p. 75), which is appended to the same volume.

40. *A Midsummer Night's Dream* (1595–6), ed. Peter Holland (Oxford and New York: Oxford University Press, 1995), V.i.15.

41. Berry, ed., *John Stubbs' 'Gaping Gulf'*, p. 53.

42. Peter Stallybrass and Allon White, *The Politics and Poetics of Transgression* (London: Methuen, 1986), p. 44.

43. These ballads include *The description of a monstrous pig* (London, 1562; S.T.C. 6768), William Fulwood, *The shape of .ij. mo[n]sters* (London, 1562; S.T.C. 11485) and I. P., *A meruaylous straunge deformed swyne* (London, 1570?; S.T.C. 19071). The births are discussed, along with other anomalous animal deliveries of the decade, in Sir John Hayward, *Annals of the First Four Years of the Reign of Queen Elizabeth*, Camden Society, 1st ser., 7 (1840), p. 107; Raphael Holinshed, *Holinshed's Chronicles of England, Scotland and Ireland*, 6 vols (London: Johnson, 1807–8), IV, p. 204; T. I., *A world of wonders* (London, 1595; S.T.C. 14068.5), sig. D4ᵛ; John Jewel, *The Works*, ed. Rev. John Ayre, Parker Society, 26 (1850), p. 1253; Henry Machyn, *The Diary, 1550–1563*, Camden Society, 1st ser., 42 (1848), pp. 281–2.

44. See R. W. Ingram, ed., *Coventry*, Records of Early English Drama (Toronto, Buffalo and London: University of Toronto Press, 1981), p. 443; John Webster, John Ford and Philip Massinger, *The Fair Maid of the Inn* (1626), in John Webster, *The Complete Works*, ed. F. L. Lucas, 4 vols (London: Chatto and Windus, 1927), IV, IV.ii.165.

45. Folger Shakespeare Library, MS M.b.7, fo. 73ʳ; Bullein, *A dialogue*, p. 113. See also Antonio de Torquemada, *The Spanish Mandevile of miracles* (London, 1600; S.T.C. 24135), fo. 149ʳ; Thomas Heywood, *The hierarchie of the blessed angels* (London, 1635; S.T.C. 13327), p. 541.

46. A. B. C. D. E., *Novembris monstrum* (London, 1641; Wing E3), p. 33. Richard's association with the Gunpowder Plot became proverbial. See Francis Herring, *Mischeefes mysterie: or, treasons master-peece, the powder-plot* (London, 1617; S.T.C. 13247), p. 67.

47. *Henry VI, Part III*, III.ii.174–81. On the parturitional aspects of the speech, see Janet Adelman, *Suffocating Mothers: Fantasies of Maternal Origin in Shakespeare's Plays, 'Hamlet' to 'The Tempest'* (New York and London: Routledge, 1992), p. 3.

48. Jonas Barish, *The Antitheatrical Prejudice* (Berkeley, Los Angeles and London: University of California Press, 1981), p. 99.

49. Philip Stubbes, *The anatomie of abuses* (London, 1583; S.T.C. 23376), sig. Fvʳ.

50. Stephen Bateman, *The golden booke of the leaden goddes* (London, 1577; S.T.C. 1583), sig. E2ʳ. See also Immanuel Bourne, *The rainebow, or, a sermon preached at Pauls crosse* (London, 1617; S.T.C. 3418), p. 20.

51. *Henry VI, Part III*, III.ii.192.

52. For a pertinent illustration of the hog/'monster' connection, see the Lord's comment on Christopher Sly in *The Taming of the Shrew* (1592), ed. H. J. Oliver (Oxford and New York: Oxford University Press, 1984): 'O monstrous beast, how like a swine he lies' (Induction, 31).

53. Helen Augur, *The Book of Fairs* (New York: Harcourt, Brace and Company, 1939), p. 182; Sean Shesgreen, *The Criers and Hawkers of London: Engravings and Drawings by Marcellus Laroon* (Stanford: Stanford University Press, 1990), p. 210.

54. John Evelyn, *Numismata* (London, 1697; Wing E3505), p. 277. On Clark's career, see Shesgreen, *Criers and Hawkers*, p. 208; Cornelius Walford, *Fairs, Past and Present: A Chapter in the History of Commerce* (London: Elliot Stock, 1883), p. 215.

55. 'Of the Posture Master', *Philosophical Transactions*, 242, July (1698), p. 262.
56. Evelyn, *Numismata*, p. 277.
57. Henry Cockeram, *The English dictionarie* (London, 1626; S.T.C. 5462), sig. X8ᵛ.
58. Stephen Bateman, *The doome warning all men to the judgemente* (London, 1581; S.T.C. 1582), p. 281; Graham Holderness, *Shakespeare: The Histories* (Basingstoke: Macmillan – now Palgrave Macmillan, 2000), p. 106.
59. *Henry VI, Part III*, III.ii.161.
60. Lemnius, *The secret miracles*, p. 58.
61. Moulton, ' "A Monster Great Deformed" ', p. 262.
62. See Bourne, *The rainebow*, pp. 20–21; Robert Burton, *The Anatomy of Melancholy* (1621), ed. Thomas C. Faulkner, Nicolas K. Kiessling and Rhonda L. Blair, 3 vols (Oxford: Clarendon, 1989–94), I, p. 52.
63. John Barthlet, *The pedegrewe of heretiques* (London, 1566; S.T.C. 1534), fo. 12ʳ; Heywood, *The hierarchie*, p. 541; Pomponius Mela, *The worke* (London, 1590; S.T.C. 17785), sig. Qiiiᵛ; Caius Plinus Secundus, *The historie of the world* (London, 1601; S.T.C. 20029), p. 147; Solinus, *The worthie worke*, sigs Tiiᵛ–Tiiiʳ.
64. Joannes Caius, *Of Englishe dogges* (London, 1576; S.T.C. 4347), p. 35; Margaret Cavendish, *CCXI sociable letters* (London, 1664; Wing N872), p. 405.
65. Robert C. Jones, *Renewing the Past in Shakespeare's Histories* (Iowa City: University of Iowa Press, 1991), p. 43.
66. See *The Tempest*, ed. Stephen Orgel (Oxford and New York: Oxford University Press, 1987), IV.i.24.
67. Forset, *A comparative discourse*, p. 60.
68. Several critics have noted parallels between the two Elizabeths. See Barbara Hodgdon, *The End Crowns All: Closure and Contradiction in Shakespeare's History* (Princeton, NJ: Princeton University Press, 1991), p. 108; Howard and Rackin, *Engendering a Nation*, p. 117.
69. A. Bartlett Giamatti, 'Proteus Unbound: Some Versions of the Sea God in the Renaissance', in Peter Demetz, Thomas Greene and Lowry Nelson, eds, *The Disciplines of Criticism: Essays in Literary Theory, Interpretation, and History* (New Haven and London: Yale University Press, 1968), pp. 444, 448, 471.
70. On prophecies in the 1590s, see Howard Dobin, *Merlin's Disciples: Prophecy, Poetry, and Power in Renaissance England* (Stanford: Stanford University Press, 1990), pp. 110–11, 117.
71. Abraham Fleming, *A straunge, and terrible wunder* (London, 1577; S.T.C. 11050), sig. Avᵛ.

Chapter 4

1. Durham Record Office, EP/Du. SN 1/2, fo. 15ʳ.
2. For travellers' tales of 'monstrous' snakes inhabiting Africa and the New World, see H., 'A treatise of Brasil' (1601), in Samuel Purchas, ed., *Hakluytus Posthumus, or, Purchas His Pilgrimes*, 20 vols (Glasgow: J. MacLehose, 1905–7), XVI, p. 496; John Jonston, *An history of the wonderful things of*

nature (London, 1657; Wing J1017), p. 232; Sebastian Muenster, *A treatyse of the newe India* (London, 1553; S.T.C. 18244), sig. gvii^v.

3. See the definitions of 'conception' outlined in J. A. Simpson and E. S. C. Weiner, eds, *The Oxford English Dictionary*, 20 vols (Oxford: Clarendon, 1989), III, p. 654.

4. *Othello*, ed. E. A. J. Honigmann (Walton-on-Thames: Nelson, 1997), III. iii. 363. All further references appear in the text.

5. See Peter Heylyn, *Microcosmus* (London, 1621; S.T.C. 13276), p. 381; John Leo, *A geographical historie of Africa* (London, 1600; S.T.C. 15481), pp. 4, 10.

6. Joannes Boemus, *The fardle of facions* (London, 1555; S.T.C. 3197), sig. Cii^r; Caius Julius Solinus, *The worthie worke* (London, 1587; S.T.C. 22895a.5), sig. Tiii^r.

7. See Janet Adelman, 'Iago's Alter Ego: Race as Projection in *Othello*', *Shakespeare Quarterly*, 48 (1997), pp. 125–44; Emily C. Bartels, '*Othello* and Africa: Postcolonialism Reconsidered', *The William and Mary Quarterly*, 54 (1997), pp. 45–64; Dympna Callaghan, *Shakespeare without Women: Representing Gender and Race on the Renaissance Stage* (London and New York: Routledge, 2000), pp. 75–96; John Gillies, *Shakespeare and the Geography of Difference* (Cambridge: Cambridge University Press, 1994), p. 25; Andrew Hadfield, *Literature, Travel, and Colonial Writing in the English Renaissance, 1545–1625* (Oxford: Clarendon, 1998), pp. 226–32; Ian Smith, 'Barbarian Errors: Performing Race in Early Modern England', *Shakespeare Quarterly*, 49 (1998), pp. 168–86.

8. James R. Aubrey, 'Race and the Spectacle of the Monstrous in *Othello*', *Clio*, 22 (1993), p. 221; Karen Newman, *Fashioning Femininity and English Renaissance Drama* (Chicago and London: University of Chicago Press, 1991), pp. 71–93; Patricia Parker, *Shakespeare from the Margins: Language, Culture, Context* (Chicago and London: University of Chicago Press, 1996), pp. 229–72.

9. Helkiah Crooke, *A description of the body of man* (London, 1631; S.T.C. 6063), p. 300. The theory, originally deriving from Aristotle, is also explained in George Abbot, *A briefe description of the whole worlde* (London, 1599; S.T.C. 24), sigs Cviii^v–Di^r; Robert Basset, *Curiosities: or the cabinet of nature* (London, 1637; S.T.C. 1557), p. 11; André Thevet, *The new found worlde, or Antarctike* (London, 1568; S.T.C. 23950), fo. 5^r.

10. On the centaurs or *hippopedes*, see Donald Lupton, *Emblems of rarities* (London, 1636; S.T.C. 16942), p. 407; Conrad Lycosthenes, *Prodigiorum ac ostentorum chronicon* (Basilae: Henricum Petri, 1557), p. 8.

11. Eric C. Brown, ' "Many a Civil Monster": Shakespeare's Idea of the Centaur', *Shakespeare Survey*, 51 (1998), p. 187.

12. On two-backed conjoined twins, see John Evelyn, *The Diary*, ed. E. S. de Beer, 6 vols (Oxford: Clarendon, 1955), III, p. 255; Oxfordshire Archives, PAR 236/1/R1/3, burial entry of 14 January 1619; Ambroise Paré, *The workes of that famous chirugion* (London, 1634; S.T.C. 19189), pp. 966, 967, 979. On the Ovidian hermaphrodite, see William Collins Watterson, ' "O monstrous world": Shakespeare's Beast with Two Backs', *The Upstart Crow*, 13 (1993), pp. 79–93.

13. Arthur L. Little, *Shakespeare's Jungle Fever: National-Imperial Re-visions of Race, Rape, and Sacrifice* (Stanford: Stanford University Press, 2000), p. 86.
14. 'Bestiality', writes Arnold I. Davidson, 'the worst of the sins contrary to nature, exhibited its viciousness in the very structure of the human body itself, in the creatures produced by the willful violation of God's natural law'. See his 'The Horror of Monsters', in James J. Sheehan and Morton Sosna, eds, *The Boundaries of Humanity: Humans, Animals, Machines* (Berkeley, Los Angeles and Oxford: University of California Press, 1991), p. 57.
15. Ethel Carleton Williams, *Anne of Denmark* (Chatham: Mackay, 1970), p. 21.
16. John Nichols, ed., *The Progresses and Public Processions of Queen Elizabeth*, 3 vols (London: J. Nichols, 1823), III, p. 516.
17. Jack D'Amico, *The Moor in English Renaissance Drama* (Tampa: University of South Florida Press, 1991), p. 36.
18. George Best, 'Experiences and reasons of the Sphere' (1578), in Richard Hakluyt, ed., *The Principal Navigations, Voyages, Traffiques and Discoveries of the English Nation*, 12 vols (Glasgow: J. MacLehose, 1903–5), VII, p. 262. The 'Ethiopian' is apparently one of the native Guineans brought into England in the 1550s to help develop the slave trade. See John Lok, 'The second voyage to Guinea' (1554–55), in Hakluyt, ed., *The Principal Navigations*, VI, p. 176; William Towerson, 'The first voyage . . . to the coast of Guinea' (1555–56), in Hakluyt, ed., *The Principal Navigations*, VI, p. 200.
19. In Jonson's *Volpone* (1606), the central protagonist, himself the father of 'monsters', is condemned as 'monstrous' when he impersonates the mountebank, Scoto of Mantua. See Ben Jonson, *Volpone*, ed. Philip Brockbank (London: Benn, 1973), II.ii.17, 189.
20. Smith, 'Barbarian Errors', p. 168.
21. Simpson and Weiner, eds, *Oxford English Dictionary*, V, pp. 377–8.
22. For 'gypsies' at fairgrounds, see Thomas Dekker, *O per se O* (London, 1612; S.T.C. 6487), sig. L4^r; Wye Saltonstall, *Picturae Loquentes* (1631), ed. C. H. Wilkinson (Oxford: Blackwell, 1946), p. 50.
23. Basset, *Curiosities*, pp. 10, 171; Thomas Bedford, *A true and certaine relation of a strange-birth* (London, 1635; S.T.C. 1791), p. 12; John Sadler, *The sicke womans private looking-glasse* (London, 1636; S.T.C. 21544), p. 137.
24. Edmund Spenser, *The Faerie Queene*, ed. A. C. Hamilton (London and New York: Longman, 1977), Book I, canto i, stanza 13, p. 33; canto i, stanza 14, p. 34.
25. Jonston, *An history*, p. 333.
26. On the escape from Barbary, see Nabil Matar, 'English Accounts of Captivity in North Africa and the Middle East: 1577–1625', *Renaissance Quarterly*, 54 (2001), pp. 553–72; G. A. Starr, 'Escape from Barbary: A Seventeenth-Century Genre', *Huntington Library Quarterly*, 29 (1965), pp. 35–62.
27. On 'cannibals', see Andrew Battel, 'The strange adventures' (1589–1607), in Purchas, ed., *Hakluytus Posthumus*, VI, p. 378; Pieter de Marees, 'A description . . . of . . . Guinea' (1602), in Purchas, ed., *Hakluytus Posthumus*, VI, p. 306; Sir Thomas Herbert, *A relation of some yeares travaile* (London, 1634; S.T.C. 13,190), p. 14.

28. William Cuningham, *The cosmographical glasse* (London, 1559; S.T.C. 6119), p. 186; Samuel Purchas, *Purchas his pilgrimage* (London, 1613; S.T.C. 20505), p. 468. For a contemporary dramatic treatment dismissing the 'monstrous' races, see Thomas Dekker, Henry Chettle and William Haughton, *Patient Grissil* (1599), in Thomas Dekker, *The Dramatic Works*, ed. Fredson Bowers, 4 vols (Cambridge: Cambridge University Press, 1953–61), I, V.i.14–56.
29. J. Hillis Miller, 'Narrative', in Frank Lentricchia and Thomas McLaughlin, eds, *Critical Terms for Literary Study* (Chicago and London: University of Chicago Press, 1990), p. 72.
30. Newman, *Fashioning*, p. 86; Parker, *Shakespeare from the Margins*, p. 244.
31. Patricia Parker, *Literary Fat Ladies: Rhetoric, Gender, Property* (London: Methuen, 1987), p. 95.
32. Parker, *Shakespeare from the Margins*, p. 237. For the purse as 'matrix', see Thomas Vicary, *The Anatomie of the Bodie of Man* (1577), ed. F. J. Furnivall and Percy Furnivall (London: Oxford University Press, 1888), p. 77.
33. For the association of 'monsters' and cages, see John Day, *Humour out of Breath* (1607–8), in *The Works*, ed. Robin Jeffs (London: Holland, 1963), IV.iii.p. 462.
34. Hillel Schwartz, *The Culture of the Copy: Striking Likenesses, Unreasonable Facsimiles* (New York: Zone, 1996), pp. 27, 41, 47, 89.
35. Little, *Shakespeare Jungle Fever*, p. 85; Smith, 'Barbarian Errors', p. 182.
36. See Gordon Williams, *A Dictionary of Sexual Language and Imagery in Shakespearean and Stuart Literature*, 3 vols (London: Athlone, 1994), II, pp. 642–4, 1059–60; III, pp. 1168–9.
37. Crooke, *A description*, p. 300. See also Thomas Lodge, *Wits miserie* (London, 1596; S.T.C. 16677), pp. 52–3; Richard Rawlidge, *A monster late found out and discovered* (London, 1628; S.T.C. 20766), p. 5; Jacob Rueff, *The expert midwife* (London, 1637; S.T.C. 21442), pp. 157–8.
38. Lupton, *Emblems of rarities*, p. 406.
39. *King Lear* (1605–06), ed. R. A. Foakes (London: Thomson, 2000), I.i.117–19.
40. On fairground apes, see Margaret Cavendish, Duchess of Newcastle, *CCXI sociable letters* (London, 1664; Wing N872), p. 405; Henry Farley, *S^r. Paules-Church her bill for the parliament* (London, 1621; S.T.C. 10690), sigs E4^{r-v}; James Shirley, *Cupid and Death* (1651–3), in T. J. B. Spenser and Stanley Wells, eds, *A Book of Masques in Honour of Allardyce Nicoll* (Cambridge: Cambridge University Press, 1967), p. 394.
41. Kim F. Hall, ' "Troubling Doubles": Apes, Africans and Blackface in *Mr. Moore's Revels*', in Joyce Green MacDonald, ed., *Race, Ethnicity and Power in the Renaissance* (Teaneck: Fairleigh Dickinson University Press, 1997), p. 125.
42. Herbert, *A relation of some yeares travaile*, pp. 17, 18.
43. Edward Topsell, *The historie of foure-footed beastes* (London, 1607; S.T.C. 24123), p. 16.
44. Topsell, *The historie*, p. 16.
45. D'Amico, *The Moor in English Renaissance Drama*, p. 185.
46. Petrus Martyr Anglerius, *The decades of the newe worlde or west India* (London, 1555; S.T.C. 645), fos 16^r, 37^v, 125^v, 159^r, 181^r; Purchas,

Purchas his pilgrimage, pp. 513, 580, 629, 647, 703, 738; Jan Huygen van Linschoten, *John Huighen Van Linschoten* (London, 1597; S.T.C. 15691), p. 200.

47. Joseph A. Porter, 'Complement Extern: Iago's Speech Acts', in Virginia Mason Vaughan and Kent Cartwright, eds, *'Othello': New Perspectives* (Teaneck: Fairleigh Dickinson University Press, 1991), p. 88.

48. See Girolamo Benzoni, *History of the New World* (1572), ed. W. H. Smyth (London: Hakluyt Society, 1857), pp. 3–4; Muenster, *A treatyse of the newe India*, sigs lv^v–lvi^r; Dionyse Settle, *A true reporte of the laste voyage into the west and northwest regions* (London, 1577; S.T.C. 22265), sig. Ci^v. A fine critical discussion is Jennifer L. Morgan, '"Some Could Suckle over Their Shoulder": Male Travellers, Female Bodies, and the Gendering of Racial Ideology', *The William and Mary Quarterly*, 54 (1997), pp. 167–92.

49. Linschoten, *John Huighen*, p. 199.

50. Virginia Mason Vaughan, *'Othello': A Contextual History* (Cambridge: Cambridge University Press, 1994), p. 29.

51. Katharine Eisaman Maus, *Inwardness and Theatre in the English Renaissance* (Chicago and London: University of Chicago Press, 1995), pp. 104, 115.

52. Peter G. Platt, *Reason Diminished: Shakespeare and the Marvellous* (Lincoln, NB and London: University of Nebraska Press, 1997), p. 36. See also James Biester, *Lyric Wonder: Rhetoric and Wit in Renaissance English Poetry* (Ithaca, NY and London: Cornell University Press, 1997), p. 131.

53. See, for instance, Parker, *Shakespeare from the Margins*, p. 240.

54. See Anthony Quinton, *Francis Bacon* (New York: Hing and Wang, 1980), p. 79; Paulo L. Rossi, 'Science, culture and the dissemination of learning', in Stephen Pumfrey, Paolo L. Rossi and Maurice Slawinski, eds, *Science, Culture and Popular Belief in Renaissance Europe* (Manchester: Manchester University Press, 1991), pp. 162–4, 172; Steven Shapin, *The Scientific Revolution* (Chicago and London: University of Chicago Press, 1996), p. 85.

55. Francis Bacon, *The Advancement of Learning*, in *The Works*, ed. James Spedding, Robert Leslie Ellis and Douglas Denon Heath, 7 vols (London: Longman, 1857–9), III, pp. 331, 362.

56. Bacon, *The Advancement*, p. 392; Bacon, *The Great Instauration*, in *Works*, IV, p. 30; Denise Albanese, *New Science, New World* (Durham, NC and London: Duke University Press, 1996), p. 110.

57. Bacon, *Novum Organum*, in *Works*, IV, p. 100.

58. Evelyn Fox Keller, *Reflections on Gender and Science* (New Haven and London: Yale University Press, 1985), pp. 34, 38.

59. Rossi, 'Science, culture and the dissemination of learning', pp. 167, 172.

60. Bacon, *Novum Organum*, p. 169.

61. Bacon, *New Atlantis*, in *Works*, III, p. 159.

62. Bacon, *The Advancement*, pp. 282, 327, 328, 330, 331, 364; *Novum Organum*, pp. 168–9.

63. See K. Theodore Hoppen, 'The Early Royal Society', *The British Journal for the History of Science*, 9.3 (1976), p. 267.

64. Thomas Birch, *The History of the Royal Society of London*, 4 vols (London: Millar, 1756–7), I, p. 393, IV, p. 41; 'Extract of a Letter', *Philosophical Transactions*, 3 June, 26 (1667), pp. 479–80; John F. Fulton, *A Bibliography of the Honourable Robert Boyle* (Oxford: Clarendon, 1961), p. 139; Jacomo Grandi, 'An Extract of an Italian Letter', *Philosophical Transactions*, 25 April, 58 (1670), pp. 1188–9; Neremiah Grew, *Mvsaevm regalis societatis* (London, 1681; Wing G1952), p. 81; Henry Oldenburg, *The Correspondence*, ed. A. Rupert Hall and Marie Boas Hall, 9 vols (Madison and Milwaukee: University of Wisconsin Press, 1955–73), III, 491–97, IV, 78.

65. Lorraine Daston and Katharine Park, *Wonders and the Order of Nature, 1150–1750* (New York: Zone Books, 1998), p. 249.

66. Abraham Cowley, 'To the Royal Society', in *Poems*, ed. A. R. Waller (Cambridge: Cambridge University Press, 1905), pp. 448, 450.

67. Robert Hooke, *Micrographia* (London, 1665; Wing H2620), sigs a1^v, a2^v.

68. Thomas Sprat, *The history of the Royal Society* (London, 1667; Wing S5032), p. 35.

69. Sprat, *The history*, p. 62.

70. Samuel Pepys, *The Diary of Samuel Pepys*, ed. Robert Latham and William Matthews, 11 vols (Berkeley: University of California Press, 1970), VI, p. 215; Charles Richard Weld, *The History of the Royal Society*, 2 vols (London: Parker, 1858), I, p. 219.

71. Roy Porter, 'Introduction', in Pumfrey, Rossi and Slawinski, eds, *Science, Culture and Popular Belief*, p. 6; Jole Shackelford, 'Seeds with a Mechanical Purpose: Severinus, Semina and Seventeenth-Century Matter Theory', in Allen G. Debus and Michael T. Walton, eds, *Reading the Book of Nature: The Other Side of the Scientific Revolution* (Kirksville: Thomas Jefferson University Press, 1998), pp. 15–16; Perez Zagorin, *Francis Bacon* (Princeton, NJ: Princeton University Press, 1998), pp. 40–3.

72. Charles Webster, *From Paracelsus to Newton: Magic and the Making of Modern Science* (Cambridge: Cambridge University Press, 1982), p. 61.

73. Webster, *From Paracelsus*, p. 96.

74. See Daston and Park, *Wonders and the Order of Nature*, p. 187.

75. Huston Diehl, *Staging Reform, Reforming the Stage: Protestantism and Popular Theatre in Early Modern England* (Ithaca, NY and London: Cornell University Press, 1997), p. 136.

76. *Bartholomew faire or a variety of fancies* (London, 1641; Wing P980), p. 5. See also Dekker, *O per se O*, sig. L4^v; Saltonstall, *Picturae Loquentes*, p. 50.

77. Aubrey, 'Race and the Spectacle of the Monstrous', p. 237.

78. See, for instance, William Cartwright, *The Ordinary* (1635), in *The Plays and Poems*, ed. G. Blakemore Evans (Madison: University of Wisconsin Press, 1951), II.iii.802–18; John Cleveland, *Poems* (London, 1653; Wing C4689), p. 37; Antonio de Torquemada, *The Spanish Mandevile of miracles* (London, 1600; S.T.C. 24135), fo. 10^r; William Shakespeare, *The Merchant of Venice* (1596–7), ed. Jay L. Halio (Oxford and New York: Oxford University Press, 1994), I.iii.74–85.

79. Annette Drew-Bear, *Painted Faces on the Renaissance Stage: The Moral Significance of Face-Painting Conventions* (Lewisburg: Bucknell University Press, 1994), p. 23; Callaghan, *Shakespeare without Women*, p. 79.

80. Folger Shakespeare Library, MS V.b.15, p. 159; William Shakespeare, *A Midsummer Night's Dream*, ed. Peter Holland (Oxford and New York: Oxford University Press, 1995), V.i.400, 403–4.

81. On the 'discovery' elements of the scene, see David Carnegie, 'Stabbed through the Arras: The Dramaturgy of Elizabethan Stage Hangings', in Heather Kerr, Robin Eaden and Madge Mitton, eds, *Shakespeare: World Views* (Newark: University of Delaware Press, 1996), p. 190; Michael Neill, *Issues of Death: Mortality and Identity in English Renaissance Tragedy* (Oxford: Clarendon, 1997), p. 167.

82. For related instances of the term, see I.i.4, I.ii.38, I.iii.59, II.iii.236, 243, 248, IV.i.49, IV.ii.110, 116, V.i.74, V.ii.164, 167.

83. Edward Pechter, *'Othello' and Interpretive Traditions* (Iowa City: University of Iowa Press, 1999), p. 31.

84. Anny Crunelle-Vanrigh, ' "Unmixed with baser *'mater'*": Le Monstre et La Matrice dans *The Tempest*', in Claude Peltrault, ed., *Shakespeare 'La Tempête': Etudes Critiques* (Besançon: Université de Franche-Comté,1993), pp. 97–113.

85. For these terms as synonyms for 'monsters', see William Shakespeare, *The Complete Works*, ed. Stanley Wells and Gary Taylor (Oxford: Clarendon, 1991), p. 765; [William Shakespeare and William Rowley], *The Birth of Merlin* (*c.* 1620), ed. R. J. Stewart and Denise Coffey (Longmead: Element, 1989), III.iii.p. 104; Simpson and Weiner, eds, *Oxford English Dictionary*, V, p. 737; John Weever, *Epigrammes in the oldest cut, and newest fashion* (London, 1599; S.T.C. 25224), sig. D3ʳ.

86. David Robson, 'Frye, Derrida, Pynchon, and the Apocalyptic Space of Postmodern Fiction', in Richard Dellamora, ed., *Postmodern Apocalypse: Theory and Cultural Practice at the End* (Philadelphia: University of Pennsylvania Press, 1995), p. 63.

87. Michael Neill, ' "Mulattos", "Blacks", and "Indian Moors": *Othello* and Early Modern Constructions of Human Difference', *Shakespeare Quarterly*, 49 (1998), pp. 373–4.

88. Elizabeth Hanson, *Discovering the Subject in Renaissance England* (Cambridge: Cambridge University Press, 1998), p. 84.

89. Williams, *A Dictionary*, III, p. 1380.

90. See the definition of 'proper' in Simpson and Weiner, eds, *Oxford English Dictionary*, XII, p. 637.

91. Michael Neill, 'Unproper Beds: Race, Adultery and the Hideous in *Othello*', *Shakespeare Quarterly*, 40 (1989), p. 394.

92. On *el moro* and *morisco*, see Eric Griffin, 'Un-sainting James: Or, *Othello* and the "Spanish Spirits" of Shakespeare's Globe', *Representations*, 62 (1998), pp. 58–99.

93. Zakiya Hanafi discusses connections between 'monsters' and devils in *The Monster in the Machine: Magic, Medicine, and the Marvellous in the Time of the Scientific Revolution* (Durham, NC and London: Duke University Press, 2000), pp. 49, 51. For the association of 'inhumanity' and 'monstrosity' in the contemporary imagination, see Corporation of London Records Office, Repertory 29, fo. 5ᵛ.

94. William Shakespeare, *A New Variorum Edition of Shakespeare: 'Othello'*, ed. Horace Howard Furness (Philadelphia: J. B. Lippincott, 1886), p. 399.

95. Schwartz, *Culture of the Copy*, pp. 62, 65.

210   *Constructing 'Monsters' in Shakespearean Drama and Early Modern Culture*

Chapter 5

1. Barbara Fuchs, 'Conquering Islands: Contextualizing *The Tempest*', *Shakespeare Quarterly*, 48 (1997), p. 45.
2. Typical of such critical work are Francis Barker and Peter Hulme, 'Nymphs and reapers heavily vanish: The discursive con-texts of *The Tempest*', in John Drakakis, ed., *Alternative Shakespeares* (London and New York: Methuen, 1985), pp. 191–205; Paul Brown, ' "This thing of darkness I acknowledge mine": *The Tempest* and the Discourse of Colonialism', in Jonathan Dollimore and Alan Sinfield, eds, *Political Shakespeare: New essays in cultural materialism* (Manchester: Manchester University Press, 1985), pp. 48–71; John Gillies, *Shakespeare and the Geography of Difference* (Cambridge: Cambridge University Press, 1994), pp. 140–55; Stephen J. Greenblatt, *Learning to Curse: Essays in Early Modern Culture* (London: Routledge, 1990), pp. 16–39; Deborah Willis, 'Shakespeare's *Tempest* and the Discourse of Colonialism', *Studies in English Literature*, 29 (1989), pp. 277–89.
3. *The Tempest*, ed. Stephen Orgel (Oxford and New York: Oxford University Press, 1987), I.ii.229. All further references appear in the text.
4. For representative qualifications of the colonialist interpretation, see Paul Franssen, 'A Muddy Mirror', in Nadia Lee and Theo D'haen, eds, *Constellation Caliban: Figurations of a Character* (Amsterdam and Atlanta: Rodopi, 1997), p. 26; John S. Hunt, 'Prospero's Empty Grasp', *Shakespeare Studies*, 22 (1994), p. 281; Tristan Marshall, '*The Tempest* and the British Imperium in 1611', *The Historical Journal*, 41 (1998), pp. 376, 388; Meredith Anne Skura, 'Discourse and the Individual: The Case of Colonialism in *The Tempest*', *Shakespeare Quarterly*, 40 (1989), pp. 42–69.
5. See David J. Baker, 'Where is Ireland in *The Tempest*?', in Mark Thornton Burnett and Ramona Wray, eds, *Shakespeare and Ireland: History, Politics, Culture* (Basingstoke: Macmillan – now Palgrave Macmillan, 1997), pp. 68–88; Jerry Brotton, ' "This Tunis, sir, was Carthage": Contesting Colonialism in *The Tempest*', in Ania Loomba and Martin Orkin, eds, *Post-Colonial Shakespeares* (London and New York: Routledge, 1998), pp. 23–42; David Scott Kastan, *Shakespeare after Theory* (London and New York: Routledge, 1999), pp. 183–97; Richard Wilson, 'Voyage to Tunis: New History and the Old World of *The Tempest*', *ELH*, 64 (1997), pp. 333–57.
6. Crystal Bartolovich, ' "Baseless Fabric": London as a World City', in Peter Hulme and William H. Sherman, eds, *'The Tempest' and its Travels* (London: Reaktion, 2000), p. 19; Douglas Bruster, *Quoting Shakespeare: Form and Culture in Early Modern Drama* (Lincoln, NB and London: University of Nebraska Press, 2000), p. 117; Frances E. Dolan, *Dangerous Familiars: Representations of Domestic Crime in England, 1550–1700* (Ithaca, NY and London: Cornell University Press, 1994), pp. 60–71.
7. Clearly, the emergence of the 'museum' lies outside the early modern period. However, as Paula Findlen notes, the institution had its conceptual origins in the Italian *studio*, *galleria* and *theatro* (literally, the place where the muses live). See her 'The Museum: Its Classical Etymology and Renaissance Genealogy', *Journal of the History of Collections*, 1 (1989), p. 59.
8. For discussions that tie Caliban to 'monsters' encountered in the New World, see John Draper, 'Monster Caliban', *Revue de Littérature Comparée*,

40 (1966), pp. 603–4; John E. Hankins, 'Caliban the Bestial Man', *Publications of the Modern Language Association of America*, 62 (1947), pp. 794–5; Alden T. Vaughan and Virginia Mason Vaughan, *Shakespeare's Caliban: A Cultural History* (Cambridge: Cambridge University Press, 1993), pp. 75–8.

9. Henry Farley, *St. Paules-Church her bill for the parliament* (London, 1621; S.T.C. 10690), sigs E4^{r-v}.

10. Scott Cutler Shershow, *Puppets and 'Popular' Culture* (Ithaca, NY and London: Cornell University Press, 1995), p. 92.

11. Michael Roberts, '"Waiting upon Chance": English Hiring Fairs and their Meanings from the 14th to the 20th Century', *Journal of Historical Sociology*, 1 (1988), p. 136.

12. Barbara A. Mowat, 'Prospero, Agrippa, and Hocus Pocus', *English Literary Renaissance*, 11 (1981), p. 297.

13. Thus John Taylor, who visited Shrewsbury in 1583, 'brought . . . a deade childe . . . which had ij heades . . . a lyve sheep . . . which had . . . ij foondementes . . . ij pyssels and ij payre of codds . . . a pygge . . . which had ij lytyll hornes . . . And . . . a glasse artyfycially made . . . which wolld represent . . . to the sight of the beholders soondrye candells, chaynes fayces, Iuells and other thinges myraculously'. See J. Alan B. Somerset, ed., *Shropshire*, Records of Early English Drama, 2 vols (Toronto, Buffalo and London: University of Toronto Press, 1994), I, p. 237.

14. Marjorie Swann, *Curiosities and Texts: The Culture of Collecting in Early Modern England* (Philadelphia: University of Pennsylvania Press, 2001), pp. 3, 79.

15. See Lorraine Daston and Katharine Park, *Wonders and the Order of Nature, 1150–1750* (New York: Zone Books, 1998), pp. 135–72.

16. See Dympna Callaghan, *Shakespeare without Women: Representing Gender and Race on the Renaissance Stage* (London and New York: Routledge, 2000), pp. 116–17; Frank Kermode, ed., *The Tempest* (London: Methuen, 1979), p. 68.

17. Denise Albanese, *New Science, New World* (Durham, NC and London: Duke University Press, 1996), p. 46.

18. William Strachey's account of the 'apparition' of 'Saint Elmo' that appeared to Sir Thomas Gates and his men is extracted in Orgel, ed., *The Tempest*, Appendix B, pp. 211–12.

19. Franklin B. Williams, 'Thomas Churchyard's Thunder on the Right', *English Literary Renaissance*, 3 (1973), pp. 390–1. Williams' article prints an edition of this rare pamphlet.

20. Somerset, ed., *Shropshire*, I, p. 247.

21. Henry Cockeram, *The English dictionarie* (London, 1626; S.T.C. 5462), sig. T4^v.

22. Douglas Biow, *'Mirabile Dictu': Representations of the Marvellous in Medieval and Renaissance Epic* (Ann Arbor: University of Michigan Press, 1996), pp. 4, 5, 7.

23. Philip Fisher, *Wonder, the Rainbow, and the Aesthetics of Rare Experience* (Cambridge, MA: Harvard University Press, 1998), pp. 11–12.

24. Donald Lupton, *Emblems of rarities* (London, 1636; S.T.C. 16942), pp. 287–8; Sebastian Muenster, *A briefe collection and compendious extract of strau[n]ge and memorable thinges* (London, 1572; S.T.C. 18242), fo. 82^r;

Caius Julius Solinus, *The worthie worke* (London, 1587; S.T.C. 22895a.5), sig. Dd4^r. Some of these identifications are made in Robert Ralston Cawley, 'Shakespeare's Use of the Voyagers in *The Tempest*', *Publications of the Modern Language Association of America*, 41 (1926), pp. 723–4.

25. *King Lear* (1605–6), ed. R. A. Foakes (London: Thomson, 2000), I.v.37.

26. Barbara M. Benedict, *Curiosity: A Cultural History of Early Modern Inquiry* (Chicago and London: University of Chicago Press, 2001), p. 33.

27. Julia Reinhard Lupton, 'Creature Caliban', *Shakespeare Quarterly*, 51 (2000), p. 1.

28. Sir Ferdinando Gorges, *Sir Ferdinando Gorges and his Province of Maine*, ed. James P. Baxter, 3 vols (Boston: The Prince Society, 1890), II, p. 21; John Smith, *Travels and Works of Captain John Smith*, ed. Edward Arber and A. G. Bradley, 2 vols (Edinburgh: John Grant, 1910), II, p. 701.

29. See John Barker, *The true description of a monsterous chylde* (London, 1564; S.T.C. 1422); *The discription of a rare or rather most monstrous fishe* (London, 1566; S.T.C. 6769); C. R., *The true discripcion of this marueilous straunge fishe* (London, 1569; S.T.C. 20570).

30. David Cressy, *Travesties and Transgressions in Tudor and Stuart England* (Oxford: Oxford University Press, 2000), p. 32.

31. These terms are taken from Ambroise Paré, *On Monsters and Marvels*, ed. Janis L. Pallister (Chicago and London: University of Chicago Press, 1982), pp. 177–80.

32. Michel de Montaigne, *The essayes or morall, politike and millitarie discourses* (London, 1603; S.T.C. 18041), p. 409.

33. Stephen Bateman, *The doome warning all men to the judgemente* (London, 1581; S.T.C. 1582), p. 393; *The true discription of two monsterous chyldren* (London, 1565; S.T.C. 6774); Tannakin Skinker, *A certaine relation of a hog-faced gentlewoman* (London, 1640; S.T.C. 22627), sig. A4^r.

34. Pierre Boaistuau, *Certaine secrete wonders of nature* (London, 1569; S.T.C. 3164.5), fo. 36^r; Mrs John Kenner, *Thou shalt vnderstande* (London, 1553?; S.T.C. 14932.5), fo. 1^r.

35. Raphael Holinshed, *Holinshed's Chronicles of England, Scotland and Ireland*, 6 vols (London: Johnson, 1807–8), V, p. 228.

36. Holinshed, *Chronicles*, V, p. 228.

37. The terms are from Paré, *On Monsters and Marvels*, ed. Pallister, pp. 177–80.

38. See, for instance, Edward Sharpham, *The Fleire* (1605–6), in *The Works*, ed. Christopher Gordon Petter (New York and London: Garland, 1986), I.iii.66–9.

39. See Katharine Park and Lorraine J. Daston, 'Unnatural Conceptions: The Study of Monsters in Sixteenth- and Seventeenth-Century France and England', *Past and Present*, 92, August (1981), p. 26; Daston and Park, *Wonders and the Order of Nature*, p. 188. The fullest contemporary English account is Philipp Melanchthon, *Of two wonderful popish monsters* (London, 1579; S.T.C. 17797).

40. Mark Thornton Burnett, 'The "Trusty Servant": A Sixteenth-Century English Emblem', *Emblematica*, 6 (1992), pp. 237–53.

41. Kim F. Hall, *Things of Darkness: Economies of Race and Gender in Early Modern England* (Ithaca, NY and London: Cornell University Press, 1995), pp. 177, 264.

42. J. A. Simpson and E. S. C. Weiner, eds, *The Oxford English Dictionary*, 20 vols (Oxford: Clarendon, 1989), V, p. 671.
43. Stephen Orgel, 'Prospero's Wife', in Margaret W. Ferguson, Maureen Quilligan and Nancy J. Vickers, eds, *Rewriting the Renaissance: The Discourses of Sexual Difference in Early Modern Europe* (Chicago and London: University of Chicago Press, 1986), p. 54. See also Janet Adelman, *Suffocating Mothers: Fantasies of Maternal Origin in Shakespeare's Plays, 'Hamlet' to 'The Tempest'* (New York and London: Routledge, 1992), p. 237.
44. Richard Strier, ' "I am Power": Normal and Magical Politics in *The Tempest*', in Derek Hirst and Richard Strier, eds, *Writing and Political Engagement in Seventeenth-Century England* (Cambridge: Cambridge University Press, 1999), p. 12.
45. Sir Philip Sidney, *The Countess of Pembroke's Arcadia (The Old Arcadia)*, ed. Katherine Duncan-Jones (Oxford and New York: Oxford University Press, 1994), p. 3; Sir Philip Sidney, *An Apology for Poetry*, ed. Geoffrey Shepherd (Manchester: Manchester University Press, 1973), p. 100.
46. *More strange newes: of wonderfull accidents hapning by the late overflowings of waters* (London, 1607; S.T.C. 22916), sigs A3ᵛ, D1ᵛ. An identical use of the metaphors appears in *A true report of certaine wonderfull overflowings of waters* (London, 1607; S.T.C. 22915), sigs A3ʳ, B1ʳ.
47. Edmond Pet, *Lamentable newes, shewing the wonderfull deliverance of maister E. Pet* (London, 1613; S.T.C. 19792), *passim*; *The windie yeare* (London, 1613; S.T.C. 26092), sig. B2ʳ; *The wonders of this windie weather* (London, 1613; S.T.C. 25950), sig. A4ᵛ. *The windie yeare*, in particular, is plagiarized.
48. *The windie yeare*, sigs A4ᵛ, C1ʳ.
49. David Bevington, '*The Tempest* and the Jacobean Court Masque', in David Bevington and Peter Holbrook, eds, *The Politics of the Stuart Court Masque* (Cambridge: Cambridge University Press, 1998), pp. 220–1; Donna B. Hamilton, *Virgil and 'The Tempest': The Politics of Imitation* (Columbus: Ohio State University Press, 1990), p. 9.
50. Constance Jordan, *Shakespeare's Monarchies: Ruler and Subject in the Romances* (Ithaca, NY and London: Cornell University Press, 1997), p. 150; Strier, ' "I am Power" ', p. 30; Robert Headlam Wells, *Shakespeare on Masculinity* (Cambridge: Cambridge University Press, 2000), pp. 184–5.
51. See David Harris Willson, *King James VI and I* (London: Cape, 1966), p. 26.
52. King James VI and I, *Minor Prose Works*, ed. James Craigie (Edinburgh: Blackwood, 1982), p. 47; *The Political Works*, ed. Charles Howard McIlwain (Cambridge, MA: Harvard University Press, 1918), pp. 11, 272.
53. King James VI and I, *The Poems*, ed. James Craigie, 2 vols (Edinburgh: Blackwood, 1955–8), I, p. 254.
54. *The Poems*, ed. Craigie, II, p. 172; *Political Works*, ed. McIlwain, p. 130.
55. *The windie yeare*, sig. A4ᵛ; *The woefull and lamentable wast* (London, 1608; S.T.C. 4181), sig. B2ʳ.
56. Arthur Golding, *Ovid's 'Metamorphoses'*, ed. W. H. D. Rouse (London: De La More Press, 1904), Book VII, lines 244–89. The liveliest account of the speech's indebtedness is Jonathan Bate, *Shakespeare and Ovid* (Oxford: Clarendon, 1993), pp. 250–5.
57. Benedict, *Curiosity*, p. 248.

58. For earlier dramatic treatments of grave openings and the apocalypse, see William Shakespeare, *Hamlet* (1599–1601), ed. Harold Jenkins (London and New York: Methuen, 1987), I.i.116–18, 120, 123; John Marston, *The Malcontent* (1603), ed. George K. Hunter (Manchester: Manchester University Press, 1975), II.v.128, 130–1.

59. Simpson and Weiner, eds, *The Oxford English Dictionary*, XIII, pp. 811–12.

60. Zakiya Hanafi, *The Monster in the Machine: Magic, Medicine, and the Marvellous in the Time of the Scientific Revolution* (Durham, NC and London: Duke University Press, 2000), p. 83.

61. Heather James, *Shakespeare's Troy: Drama, Politics, and the Translation of Empire* (Cambridge: Cambridge University Press, 1997), p. 218.

62. Corporation of London Records Office, Repertory 15, fo. 414^v.

63. Francis Rous, *Oile of scorpions* (London, 1623; S.T.C. 21344), pp. 166–7.

64. William M. Hamlin, *The Image of America in Montaigne, Spenser, and Shakespeare: Renaissance Ethnography and Literary Reflection* (New York: St Martin's Press, 1995), p. 117.

65. Simpson and Weiner, eds, *The Oxford English Dictionary*, VI, pp. 718–19.

66. Sir Edward Coke, *The first part of the institutes* (London, 1628; S.T.C. 15784), fo. 7^v.

67. Pierre Le Loyer's *A treatise of specters or straunge sights* (London, 1605; S.T.C. 15448) describes a 'monster', an 'elder brother', who successfully petitions for the retention of his 'lawfull portion'; he claims as his defence possession of 'reason and humane discourse' (fos 107^r, 108^v, 109^r). For discussions of this case and others, see Erica Fudge, *Perceiving Animals: Humans and Beasts in Early Modern English Culture* (Basingstoke: Macmillan – now Palgrave Macmillan, 1999), pp. 115–17; Marie-Hélène Huet, *Monstrous Imagination* (Cambridge, MA: Harvard University Press, 1993), pp. 31–3.

68. For a pertinent example, see John Rous, *Diary of John Rous, 1625–1642*, ed. Mary Anne Everett Green, Camden Society, 1st ser., 66 (1856), pp. 84–5.

69. Peter G. Platt, *Reason Diminished: Shakespeare and the Marvellous* (Lincoln, NB and London: University of Nebraska Press, 1997), p. 178.

70. Jeffrey Masten, *Textual Intercourse: Collaboration, Authorship, and Sexualities in Renaissance Drama* (Cambridge: Cambridge University Press, 1997), p. 107.

Chapter 6

1. Ben Jonson, *Bartholomew Fair*, ed. E. A. Horsman (Manchester: Manchester University Press, 1979), III.i.11–12. All further references appear in the text.

2. See, for instance, Richard Burt, *Licensed by Authority: Ben Jonson and the Discourses of Censorship* (Ithaca, NY: Cornell University Press, 1993), p. 81; Richard Dutton, *Ben Jonson: To the First Folio* (Cambridge: Cambridge University Press, 1983), p. 160; James Shapiro, *Rival Playwrights: Marlowe, Jonson, Shakespeare* (New York: Columbia University Press, 1991), p. 155.

3. *The Winter's Tale*, ed. J. H. P. Pafford (London and New York: Methuen, 1981), IV.iv.343.1; *The Tempest*, ed. Stephen Orgel (Oxford and New York: Oxford University Press, 1987), III.iii.21. All further references appear in

the text. A further instance of Jonson's critical construction of *The Tempest* appears in the 1616 Prologue to *Every Man in His Humour*, which was first printed in 1598. 'You, that have so graced monsters,' the Prologue warns, 'may like men' (*Every Man in His Humour*, ed. Martin Seymour-Smith [London: Benn, 1979], 30): appropriating Shakespeare's language, the line plays a variation on the theme of rejecting the 'monstrous' in favour of the 'natural'.

4. Ben Jonson, *The workes* (London, 1616; S.T.C. 14751), title-page.
5. Ben Jonson, *Ben Jonson*, ed. C. H. Herford and Percy and Evelyn Simpson, 11 vols (Oxford: Clarendon, 1925–52), XI, p. 421.
6. Ben Jonson, *The Complete Plays*, ed. G. A. Wilkes, 4 vols (Oxford: Clarendon, 1981–2), I, Second Sounding, 66–7, 69–71.
7. Ben Jonson, *Volpone*, ed. Philip Brockbank (London: Benn, 1973), Epistle, 14–15. All further references appear in the text.
8. Jonson, *Complete Plays*, IV, Chorus to Act III, 31–2.
9. Jonson, *Jonson*, VIII, p. 583. For a 'blot' as a 'blemish or disfigurement', see J. A. Simpson and E. S. C. Weiner, eds, *The Oxford English Dictionary*, 20 vols (Oxford: Clarendon, 1989), II, p. 312.
10. 'I lov'd the man, and doe honour his memory' stated Jonson of Shakespeare in his *Discoveries* (*c.* 1623–5). See Jonson, *Jonson*, VIII, pp. 583–4.
11. The most persuasive studies of the rivalry between the dramatists are James P. Bednarz, *Shakespeare and the Poets' War* (New York: Columbia University Press, 2001); Russ McDonald, *Shakespeare & Jonson/Jonson & Shakespeare* (Brighton: Harvester, 1988); George E. Rowe, *Distinguishing Jonson: Imitation, Rivalry, and the Direction of a Dramatic Career* (Lincoln, NB and London: University of Nebraska Press, 1988).
12. Dutton, *Ben Jonson: To the First Folio*, p. 160.
13. Thomas Cartelli, '*Bartholomew Fair* as Urban Arcadia: Jonson Responds to Shakespeare', *Renaissance Drama*, 14 (1983), pp. 152, 158; Alvin Kernan, 'The Great Fair of the World and the Ocean Island: *Bartholomew Fair* and *The Tempest*', in J. Leeds Barroll, Alexander Leggatt, Richard Hosley and Alvin Kernan, eds, *The Revels History of Drama in English*, 8 vols (London: Methuen, 1975–83), III, p. 458; Scott Cutler Shershow, *Puppets and 'Popular' Culture* (Ithaca, NY and London: Cornell University Press, 1995), p. 91.
14. Stephen Mailloux, 'Interpretation', in Frank Lentricchia and Thomas McLaughlin, eds, *Critical Terms for Literary Study* (Chicago and London: University of Chicago Press, 1990), p. 121.
15. Walter Benjamin, *Illuminations*, tr. Harry Zohn (London: Fontana/Collins, 1973), p. 75.
16. Frances Teague, *The Curious History of 'Bartholomew Fair'* (Lewisburg: Bucknell University Press, 1985), p. 36; Eugene M. Waith, 'The Staging of *Bartholomew Fair*', *Studies in English Literature*, 2 (1962), p. 189.
17. Thomas Coryate, *The Oldcombian banquet* (London, 1611; S.T.C. 5810), sigs P1^{r-v}.
18. Jeffrey Jerome Cohen, 'Monster Culture (Seven Theses)', in Jeffrey Jerome Cohen, ed., *Monster Theory: Reading Culture* (Minneapolis and London: University of Minnesota Press, 1996), p. 7.

19. Jonathan Haynes, *The Social Relations of Jonson's Theatre* (Cambridge: Cambridge University Press, 1992), p. 134; W. Dennis Kay, *Ben Jonson: A Literary Life* (Basingstoke: Macmillan – now Palgrave Macmillan, 1995), p. 21.

20. Audrey Eccles, *Obstetrics and Gynaecology in Tudor and Stuart England* (Kent, Ohio: Kent State University Press, 1982), p. 64.

21. Peter Stallybrass and Allon White, *The Politics and Poetics of Transgression* (London: Methuen, 1986), p. 42.

22. Simpson and Weiner, eds, *Oxford English Dictionary*, V, p. 272.

23. Cartelli briefly points out similarities between Overdo and Prospero ('*Bartholomew Fair* as Urban Arcadia', p. 164), as does Robert N. Watson (*Ben Jonson's Parodic Strategy: Literary Imperialism in the Comedies* [Cambridge, MA: Harvard University Press, 1987], pp. 167–8). By rehearsing ideas of revenge and redemption, however, these critics pass over the 'monstrous' underpinnings of Jonson's 'translation'.

24. Julie Sanders, *Ben Jonson's Theatrical Republics* (Basingstoke: Macmillan – now Palgrave Macmillan, 1998), p. 101.

25. Stallybrass and White, *Politics and Poetics*, p. 22. See also Mikhail Bakhtin, *Rabelais and His World*, tr. Hélène Iswolsky (Cambridge, MA: MIT Press, 1968), pp. 19, 21, 74. For representative 'grotesque' readings of Ursula, see Keith Sturgess, *Jacobean Private Theatre* (London and New York: Routledge & Kegan Paul, 1987), p. 188; Lori Schroeder Haslem, ' "Troubled with the Mother": Longings, Purgings, and the Maternal Body in *Bartholomew Fair* and *The Duchess of Malfi*', *Modern Philology*, 92 (1995), p. 449; Stallybrass and White, *Politics and Poetics*, p. 65.

26. Elizabeth Grosz, 'Intolerable Ambiguity: Freaks as/at the Limit', in Rosemarie Garland Thomson, ed., *Freakery: Cultural Spectacles of the Extraordinary Body* (New York and London: New York University Press, 1996), p. 64; Margrit Shildrick, *Embodying the Monster: Encounters with the Vulnerable Self* (London: Sage, 2002), p. 44.

27. Interestingly, the first references to the display of 'fat' men and women as 'monsters' hail from the latter part of the seventeenth century. See John Evelyn, *Numismata* (London, 1697; Wing E3505), p. 277; [Richard Flecknoe], *The diarium, or journall* (London, 1656; Wing F1212), pp. 44–5; Samuel Jeake, *An Astrological Diary of the Seventeenth Century: Samuel Jeake of Rye, 1652–1699*, ed. Michael Hunter and Annabel Gregory (Oxford: Clarendon, 1988), p. 100.

28. Douglas Bruster, *Drama and the Market in the Age of Shakespeare* (Cambridge: Cambridge University Press, 1992), p. 95.

29. Hyder E. Rollins, ed., *A Pepysian Garland: Black-Letter Broadside Ballads of the Years 1595–1639* (Cambridge, MA: Harvard University Press, 1971), p. 453; Tannakin Skinker, *A certaine relation of a hogfaced gentlewoman* (London, 1640; S.T.C. 22627), sig. B1ʳ.

30. Celia R. Daileader, *Eroticism on the Renaissance Stage: Transcendence, Desire, and the Limits of the Visible* (Cambridge: Cambridge University Press, 1998), p. 68.

31. Henry Cockeram, *The English dictionarie* (London, 1626; S.T.C. 5462), sig. X5ᵛ.

32. David Hillman and Carla Mazzio, 'Introduction: Individual Parts', in David Hillman and Carla Mazzio, eds, *The Body in Parts: Fantasies of Corporeality in Early Modern Europe* (London and New York: Routledge, 1997), pp. xvi–xvii.
33. Barbara Creed, *The Monstrous-Feminine: Film, Feminism, Psychoanalysis* (London and New York: Routledge, 1993), pp. 2, 22, 25, 109.
34. See Timothy Granger, *A most true and marueilous straunge wonder* (London, 1568; S.T.C. 12186); Oteringham, *A most certaine report of a monster borne at Oteringham in Holdernesse* (London, 1595; S.T.C. 18895.5), sig. B1ᵛ; Rochester-upon-Medway City Archives, RCA/A1/1, fos 68–9; *A true report . . . of a mighty sea-monster* (London, 1617; S.T.C. 20892), pp. 10–11.
35. Thomas Rugg, *The Diurnal of Thomas Rugg, 1659–1661*, ed. William L. Sachse (London: Royal Historical Society, 1961), p. xvi.
36. Helkiah Crooke, *A description of the body of man* (London, 1631; S.T.C. 6063), p. 297.
37. Leah S. Marcus, *The Politics of Mirth: Jonson, Herrick, Milton, Marvell, and the Defence of Old Holiday Pastimes* (Chicago and London: University of Chicago Press, 1986), p. 43.
38. Gail Kern Paster, *The Body Embarrassed: Drama and the Disciplines of Shame in Early Modern England* (Ithaca, NY: Cornell University Press, 1993), p. 25; Shannon Miller, 'Consuming Mothers/Consuming Merchants: The Carnivalesque Economy of Jacobean City Comedy', *Modern Language Studies*, 26.2–3 (1996), p. 89.
39. William A. Armstrong, 'Ben Jonson and Jacobean Stagecraft', in John Russell Brown and Bernard Harris, eds, *Jacobean Theatre* (London: Arnold, 1960), p. 54.
40. Simpson and Weiner, eds, *Oxford English Dictionary*, I, p. 34.
41. Jonson, *Jonson*, VIII, p. 582; Teague, *Curious History*, p. 34.
42. Shershow, *Puppets and 'Popular' Culture*, pp. 26, 69, 72.
43. Clare McManus, ' "Defacing the Carcass": Anne of Denmark and Jonson's *The Masque of Blackness*', in Julie Sanders, Kate Chedgzoy and Susan Wiseman, eds, *Refashioning Ben Jonson: Gender, Politics and the Jonsonian Canon* (Basingstoke: Macmillan – now Palgrave Macmillan, 1998), p. 104.
44. Laura Levine, *Men in Women's Clothing: Anti-theatricality and Effeminization, 1579–1642* (Cambridge: Cambridge University Press, 1994), p. 89.
45. Andrew Clark, ed., *The Shirburn Ballads 1585–1616* (Oxford: Clarendon, 1907), pp. 293–4.
46. Rachel Adams, *Sideshow U.S.A.: Freaks and the American Cultural Imagination* (Chicago and London: University of Chicago Press, 2001), p. 210; Andrea Stulman Dennett, *Weird & Wonderful: The Dime Museum in America* (New York and London: New York University Press, 1997), pp. 82–3.
47. Ian Frederick Moulton, *Before Pornography: Erotic Writing in Early Modern England* (Oxford: Oxford University Press, 2000), p. 8.
48. Elizabeth Grosz, "Intolerable Ambiguity', p. 65.
49. Benjamin, *Illuminations*, p. 72; Jacques Derrida, *A Derrida Reader: Between the Blinds*, ed. Peggy Kamuf (Hemel Hempstead: Harvester Wheatsheaf, 1991), pp. 414–15.

50. Don E. Wayne, 'The "exchange of letters": Early modern contradictions and postmodern conundrums', in Ann Bermingham and John Brewer, eds, *The Consumption of Culture, 1600–1800* (London and New York: Routledge, 1995), p. 158.

51. Jonson, *Jonson*, I, p. 134.

52. Kate Chedgzoy, Julie Sanders and Susan Wiseman, 'Introduction: Re-fashioning Ben Jonson', in Sanders, Chedgzoy and Wiseman, eds, *Refashioning Ben Jonson*, p. 13; W. H. Herendeen, 'A New Way to Pay Old Debts: Pretexts to the 1616 Folio', in Jennifer Brady and W. H. Herendeen, eds, *Ben Jonson's 1616 Folio* (Newark: University of Delaware Press, 1991), p. 61; Leah S. Marcus, 'Of Mire and Authorship', in David L. Smith, Richard Strier and David Bevington, eds, *The Theatrical City: Culture, Theatre and Politics in London, 1576–1649* (Cambridge: Cambridge University Press, 1995), p. 170; Teague, *Curious History*, p. 50.

53. Martin Butler, 'Introduction: From *Workes* to Texts', in Martin Butler, ed., *Re-presenting Ben Jonson: Text, History, Performance* (Basingstoke: Macmillan – now Palgrave Macmillan, 1999), p. 11.

54. Timothy Murray, *Theatrical Legitimation: Allegories of Genius in Seventeenth-Century England and France* (Oxford: Oxford University Press, 1987), p. 73.

Epilogue

1. Ben Jonson, *Ben Jonson*, ed. C. H. Herford and Percy and Evelyn Simpson, 11 vols (Oxford: Clarendon, 1925–52), I, p. 211; *Bartholomew Fair*, ed. E. A. Horsman (Manchester: Manchester University Press, 1979), p. xxviii.

2. *Tamburlaine the Great*, in Christopher Marlowe, *The Complete Plays*, ed. Mark Thornton Burnett (London: Everyman, 1999), p. 3.

3. *Mr. William Shakespeares comedies, histories, & tragedies* (London, 1623; S.T.C. 22273), sig. A3^r. All further references appear in the text.

Bibliography

Primary sources: manuscript

Ashmolean Museum
Hope Collection. Jeffrey Hudson file.

Cambridge University Library
MS Ee.5.36. 'A Collection of Prophecies, concerning English and Scotch History', 1623.

Central Library, Kingston-upon-Hull
Archibald E. Trout, 'Some Associations of Hull Fair', manuscript.

Corporation of London Records Office
Repertories of the Court of Aldermen.

Durham Record Office
EP/Du. SN 1/2. Parish register of Durham, St Nicholas, 1540–1705.

Folger Shakespeare Library
MS J.a.1. Dramatic and poetic miscellany, *c.* 1600–*c.* 1620.
MS M.b.7. The second book of history, 1701–22.
MS V.a.339. Medical commonplace book of Joseph Hall, *c.* 1650.
MS V.a.510. Collection of autograph manuscripts by Richard Smith, 1633–1675.
MS V.b.15. Commonplace book on the discovery and exploration of America, *c.* 1650.

Guildhall Library
MS 9234/3. St Botolph without Aldgate, parish clerk's memorandum book, 1590–91.

Houghton Library, Harvard University
fMS Eng 1015. Stephen Batman, 'A Booke of the coppies', 1580–84.

Huntington Library, California
Ellesmere MS. 6174. Letter from Mr Candre to William Southam, 1598.

North Yorkshire County Record Office
PR/MIT 1/1, MIC 2676. Parish register of Middleton Tyas, 1539–1715.

Oxfordshire Archives
PAR 236/1/R1/3. Burial register of the parish of Shipton-under-Wychwood.

Rochester-upon-Medway City Archives
RCA/A1/1. City of Rochester meeting day book, 1623.

Southampton City Archives
D/M 1/3. Letter-book of Samuel Molyneux, 1712–13.

Primary sources: printed

A., G., *No post from heaven*. London, 1643; Wing A8.
Abbot, George, *A briefe description of the whole worlde*. London, 1599; S.T.C. 24.
Ad populum: or, a low-country lecture. London, 1653; Wing A468.
Anglerius, Petrus Martyr, *The decades of the newe worlde or west India*. London, 1555; S.T.C. 645.
Anton, Robert, *The philosophers satyrs*. London, 1616; S.T.C. 686.
Arthur, John, *Deeds against nature, and monsters by kinde*. London, 1614; S.T.C. 809.
At the . . . this present day shall be showne rare dancing on the ropes. London, 1630; S.T.C. 21315.8.
Averell, William, *A meruailous combat of contrarieties*. London, 1588; S.T.C. 981.
——*A wonderfull and straunge newes*. London, 1583; S.T.C. 982.5.
B., H., *The true discripcion of a childe with ruffes*. London, 1566; S.T.C. 1033.
Bacon, Francis, *The Works*, ed. James Spedding, Robert Leslie Ellis and Douglas Denon Heath, 7 vols. London: Longman, 1857–9.
[Ballad describing natural portents]. London, 1580?; S.T.C. 1325.
Barker, John, *The true description of a monsterous chylde*. London, 1564; S.T.C. 1422.
Barrough, Philip, *The methode of physicke*. London, 1583; S.T.C. 1508.
Barthlet, John, *The pedegrewe of heretiques*. London, 1566; S.T.C. 1534.
Bartholomew faire or a variety of fancies. London, 1641; Wing P980.
Basset, Robert, *Curiosities: or the cabinet of nature*. London, 1637; S.T.C. 1557.
Bateman, Stephen, *The doome warning all men to the judgemente*. London, 1581; S.T.C. 1582.
——*The golden booke of the leaden goddes*. London, 1577; S.T.C. 1583.
Bawcutt, N. W., ed., *The Control and Censorship of Caroline Drama: The Records of Sir Henry Herbert, Master of the Revels, 1623–73*. Oxford: Clarendon, 1996.
Beaumont, Francis, *The Knight of the Burning Pestle*, ed. Sheldon P. Zitner. Manchester: Manchester University Press, 1984.
Beaumont, Francis and John Fletcher, *Cupid's Revenge*, in *The Dramatic Works*, ed. Fredson Bowers, 10 vols (Cambridge: Cambridge University Press, 1966–96), II.
Bedford, Thomas, *A true and certaine relation of a strange-birth*. London, 1635; S.T.C. 1791.
Benzoni, Girolamo, *History of the New World*, ed. W. H. Smyth. London: Hakluyt Society, 1857.

Berry, Lloyd E., ed., *The Geneva Bible: A facsimile of the 1560 edition*. Madison, Milwaukee and London: University of Wisconsin Press, 1969.

——*John Stubbs' 'Gaping Gulf' with Letters and Other Relevant Documents*. Charlottesville: University Press of Virginia, 1968.

Blundeville, Thomas, *The theoriques of the seven planets*. London, 1602; S.T.C. 3160.

Boaistuau, Pierre, *Certaine secrete wonders of nature*. London, 1569; S.T.C. 3164.5.

Boemus, Joannes, *The fardle of facions*. London, 1555; S.T.C. 3197.

Bond, Ronald B., ed., *'Certain Sermons or Homilies' (1547) and 'A Homily against Disobedience and Wilful Rebellion' (1570)*. Toronto, Buffalo and London: University of Toronto Press, 1987.

Bourne, Immanuel, *The rainebow, or, a sermon preached at Pauls crosse*. London, 1617; S.T.C. 3418.

A brief narrative of a strange and wonderful old woman that hath a pair of horns. London, 1670; Wing B4610.

Brightman, Thomas, *A revelation of the Apocalyps*. Amsterdam, 1611; S.T.C. 3754.

Brinckmair, L., *The warnings of Germany*. London, 1638; S.T.C. 3758.

Brome, Richard, *The English Moor*, in *The Dramatic Works*, ed. John Pearson, 3 vols. London: Pearson, 1873, II.

B[romhall], T[homas], *A treatise of specters*. London, 1658; Wing B4886.

Browne, Sir Thomas, *Pseudoxia epidemica*. London, 1650; Wing B5160.

Bullein, William, *A dialogue bothe pleasaunte and pietifull, against the feuer pestilence*. London, 1573; S.T.C. 4037.

B[ulwer], J[ohn], *Anthropometamorphosis*. London, 1653; Wing B5461.

Burrough, Edward, *Many strong reasons confounded*. London, 1657; Wing B6011A.

Burton, Robert, *The Anatomy of Melancholy*, ed. Thomas C. Faulkner, Nicolas K. Kiessling and Rhonda L. Blair, 3 vols. Oxford: Clarendon, 1989–94.

Caius, Joannes, *Of Englishe dogges*. London, 1576; S.T.C. 4347.

Calamy, Edmund, *The monster of sinful self-seeking*. London, 1655; Wing C259.

Camden, William, *The History of the Most Renowned and Victorious Elizabeth, Late Queen of England*, ed. Wallace T. MacCaffrey. Chicago and London: University of Chicago Press, 1970.

Cartwright, William, *The Plays and Poems*, ed. G. Blakemore Evans. Madison: University of Wisconsin Press, 1951.

Cavendish, Margaret, *CCXI sociable letters*. London, 1664; Wing N872.

C(hamberlain), R., *Jocabella, or a cabinet of conceits*. London, 1640; S.T.C. 4943.

Chapman, George, *Bussy d'Ambois*, ed. N. S. Brooke. Manchester: Manchester University Press, 1979.

——*Sir Gyles Goosecappe*, in *The Tragedies*, ed. Allan Holaday Cambridge: Brewer, 1987.

Chettle, Henry and John Day, *The Blind Beggar of Bednall Green*, ed. W. Bang. Louvain: Uystpruyst, 1902.

Churchyard, Thomas, *A warning for the wise*. London, 1580; S.T.C. 5259.

Cipriano, Giovanni, *A most strange and wonderfull prophesie vpon this troublesome world*. London, 1595; S.T.C. 5324.

Citois, François, *A true and admirable historie*. London, 1603; S.T.C. 5326.

Clark, Andrew, ed., *The Shirburn Ballads 1585–1616*. Oxford: Clarendon, 1907.

Clarke, Samuel, *A mirrovr or looking-glasse*. London, 1657; Wing C4551.

Cleveland, John, *Poems*. London, 1653; Wing C4689.

Clowes, William, *A briefe and necessarie treatise*. London, 1585; S.T.C. 5448.

Cockeram, Henry, *The English dictionarie*. London, 1626; S.T.C. 5462.

Coke, Sir Edward, *The first part of the institutes*. London, 1628; S.T.C. 15784.

The Compost of Ptholomeus. London, [1540?]; S.T.C. 20480a.

Cooper, Catherine, *A most notable and prodigious historie*. London, 1589; S.T.C. 5678.

Cooper, Thomas, *Thesaurus linguae Romanae & Britannicae*. London, 1565; S.T.C. 5686.

Coryate, Thomas, *The Oldcombian banquet*. London, 1611; S.T.C. 5810.

A courtlie controuersie of Cupids cautels. London, 1578; S.T.C. 5647.

Cowley, Abraham, *Poems*, ed. A. R. Waller. Cambridge: Cambridge University Press, 1905.

Crooke, Helkiah, *A description of the body of man*. London, 1631; S.T.C. 6063.

Crosfield, Thomas, *The Diary*, ed. Frederick S. Boas. London: Milford, 1935.

Crowley, Robert, *Philargyrie of greate Britayne*. London, 1551; S.T.C. 6089.5.

Culpeper, Nicholas, *A directory for midwives*. London, 1651; Wing C7488.

Cuningham, William, *The cosmographical glasse*. London, 1559; S.T.C. 6119.

D., John, *A discription of a monstrous chylde*. London, 1562; S.T.C. 6177.

Davenant, Sir William, *The Shorter Poems*, ed. A. M. Gibbs. Oxford: Clarendon, 1972.

Day, John, *Humour out of Breath*, in *The Works*, ed. Robin Jeffs. London: Holland, 1963.

Dekker, Thomas, *Lanthorne and candle-light*. London, 1609; S.T.C. 6485.

——*The Dramatic Works*, ed. Fredson Bowers, 4 vols. Cambridge: Cambridge University Press, 1953–61.

——*The Non-Dramatic Works*, ed. Alexander B. Grosart, 5 vols. London: Hazel, Watson and Viney, 1884–6.

——*O per se O*. London, 1612; S.T.C. 6487.

Derricke, John, *The Image of Irelande*, ed. John Small. Edinburgh: Black, 1883.

The description of a monstrous pig. London, 1562; S.T.C. 6768.

[Digby, *Sir* Kenelm], *A late discourse made in a solemne assembly*. London, 1658; Wing D1435.

Digby, Sir Kenelm, *Two discourses*. London, 1644; Wing D1448.

The discription of a rare or rather most monstrous fishe. London,1566; S.T.C. 6769.

Doleta, John, *Straunge newes out of Calabria*. London, 1586; S.T.C. 6992.

D'Urfey, Thomas, *Wit and Mirth: or Pills to Purge Melancholy*, 6 vols. London: Tonson, 1719–20.

E., A. B. C. D., *Novembris monstrum*. London, 1641; Wing E3.

Edwards, Thomas, *Gangraena*. London, 1646; Wing G229.

Elderton, William, *The true fourme and shape of a monsterous chyld*. London, 1565; S.T.C. 7565.

Evelyn, John, *The Diary*, ed. E. S. de Beer, 6 vols. Oxford: Clarendon, 1955.

——*Numismata*. London, 1697; Wing E3505.

'Extract of a Letter', *Philosophical Transactions*, 3 June, 26 (1667), pp. 479–80.

Farley, Henry, S^t. *Paules-Church her bill for the parliament*. London, 1621; S.T.C. 10690.

Ferne, Sir John, *The blazon of gentrie*. London, 1586; S.T.C. 10824.

Feuillerat, Albert, ed., *Documents Relating to the Office of the Revels in the Time of Queen Elizabeth*. Louvain: Uystpruyst, 1908.

[Flecknoe, Richard], *The diarium, or journall*. London, 1656; Wing F1212.

Fleming, Abraham, *A bright burning beacon*. London, 1580; S.T.C 11037.

——*A straunge, and terrible wunder*. London, 1577; S.T.C. 11050.

Fliegen, Eva, *The pourtrayture*. London, *c.* 1620?; S.T.C. 11088.3.

Fonteyn, Nicolaas, *The womans doctour*. London, 1652; Wing F1418A.

Forset, Edward, *A comparative discourse of the bodies natural and politique*. London, 1606; S.T.C. 11188.

Foulweather, Adam, *A wonderfull, strange and miraculous, prognostication for this yeer 1591*. London, 1591; S.T.C. 11209.

Fulke, William, *A most pleasant prospect*. London, 1602; S.T.C. 11438.

Fulwood, William, *The shape of .ij. mo[n]sters*. London, 1562; S.T.C. 11485.

G., C., *The minte of deformities*. London, 1600; S.T.C. 11491.

G., I., *The wonder of our times: being a true and exact relation of the body of a mighty giant*. London, 1651; Wing G29.

Galloway, David, ed., *Norwich, 1540–1642*, Records of Early English Drama. Toronto, Buffalo and London: University of Toronto Press, 1984.

Gerardus, Andreas, *The regiment of the pouertie*. London, 1572; S.T.C. 11759.

Glapthone, Henry, *Wit in a Constable*, in *The Plays and Poems*, [ed. R. H. Shepherd], 2 vols. London: Pearson, 1874, I.

Gods handy-worke in wonders. London, 1615; S.T.C. 11926.

Golding, Arthur, *Ovid's 'Metamorphoses'*, ed. W. H. D. Rouse. London: De La More Press, 1904.

Goodcole, Henry, *Natures cruell step-dames*. London, 1637; S.T.C. 12012.

Gorges, Sir Ferdinando, *Sir Ferdinando Gorges and his Province of Maine*, ed. James P. Baxter, 3 vols. Boston: The Prince Society, 1890.

Gosson, Stephen, *The schoole of abuse*. London, 1579; S.T.C. 12097.

Gouge, William, *Of domesticall duties*. London, 1634; S.T.C. 12121.

Goulart, Simon, *Admirable and memorable histories containing the wonders of our time*. London, 1607; S.T.C. 12135.

Grandi, Jacomo, 'An Extract of an Italian Letter', *Philosophical Transactions*, 25 April, 58 (1670), pp. 1188–9.

Granger, Timothy, *A most true and marueilous straunge wonder*. London, 1568; S.T.C. 12186.

Greg, Walter W., ed., *Henslowe Papers*. London: A. H. Bullen, 1907.

Grew, Neremiah, *Mvsaevm regalis societatis*. London, 1681; Wing G1952.

Gurth, Alexander, *Most true and more admirable newes*. London, 1597; S.T.C. 12531.5.

Hakewill, George, *An apologie or declaration of the power*. Oxford, 1635; S.T.C. 12613.

Hakluyt, Richard, ed., *The Principal Navigations, Voyages, Traffiques and Discoveries of the English Nation*, 12 vols. Glasgow: J. MacLehose, 1903–05.

Harington, Sir John, *A Tract on the Succession to the Crown (A.D. 1602)*. London: Roxburghe Club, 1880.

Hartley, T. E., ed., *Proceedings in the Parliaments of Elizabeth I, 1558–1601*, 3 vols. Leicester: Leicester University Press, 1981–1995.

Harvey, Richard, *An astrological discourse vpon the great and notable coniunction*. London, 1583; S.T.C. 12911.

Hayward, Sir John, *Annals of the First Four Years of the Reign of Queen Elizabeth*, Camden Society, 1st ser., 7 (1840).

Herbert, Sir Thomas, *A relation of some yeares travaile*. London, 1634; S.T.C. 13190.

Herring, Francis, *Mischeefes mysterie: or, treasons master-peece, the powder-plot*. London, 1617; S.T.C. 13247.

Heylyn, Peter *Microcosmus*. London, 1621; S.T.C. 13276.

Heywood, Thomas, *The hierarchie of the blessed angells*. London, 1635; S.T.C. 13327.

——*The Silver Age*, in *The Dramatic Works*, ed. R. H. Shepherd, 6 vols. London: Shepherd, 1874, III.

——*The three wonders of this age*. London, 1636; S.T.C. 13365.5.

Highmore, Nathaniel, *The history of generation*. London, 1651; Wing H1969.

Hill, Thomas, *A contemplation of mysteries: contayning the rare effectes of certayne comets*. London, 1574?; S.T.C. 13484.

Hilliard, John, *Fire from heaven*. London, 1613; S.T.C. 13507.

Historia aenigmatica, de gemellis Genoae connatis. London, 1637; S.T.C. 11728.6.

Hitchcock, Robert, *A pollitique platt for the honour of the prince*. London, 1580; S.T.C. 13531.

Hobson, Robert, *The arraignement of the whole creature*. London, 1631; S.T.C. 13538.5.

Hoby, Lady Margaret, *Diary of Lady Margaret Hoby, 1599–1605*, ed. Dorothy M. Meads. London: Routledge, 1930.

Holinshed, Raphael, *Holinshed's Chronicles of England, Scotland and Ireland*, 6 vols. London: Johnson, 1807–8.

Holloway, John, ed., *The Euing Collection of English Broadside Ballads in the Library of the University of Glasgow*. Glasgow: University of Glasgow Press, 1971.

Hooke, Robert, *Micrographia*. London, 1665; Wing H2620.

Humphrey, Laurence, *A view of the Romish hydra confuted in seven sermons*. London, 1588; S.T.C. 13966.

I., R., *The History of Tom Thumb*, ed. Curt F. Buhler. Evanston: Northwestern University Press, 1965.

I., T., *A world of wonders*. London, 1595; S.T.C. 14068.5.

Ingram, R. W., ed., *Coventry*, Records of Early English Drama. Toronto, Buffalo and London: University of Toronto Press, 1981.

James VI and I, King of Scotland and England, *Minor Prose Works*, ed. James Craigie. Edinburgh: Blackwood, 1982.

——*The Poems*, ed. James Craigie, 2 vols. Edinburgh: Blackwood, 1955–8.

——*The Political Works*, ed. Charles Howard McIlwain. Cambridge, MA: Harvard University Press, 1918.

Jeake, Samuel, *An Astrological Diary of the Seventeenth Century: Samuel Jeake of Rye, 1652–1699*, ed. Michael Hunter and Annabel Gregory. Oxford: Clarendon, 1988.

Jewel, John, *The Works*, ed. Rev. John Ayre, Parker Society, 26 (1850).

Joceline, Elizabeth, *The Mother's Legacy to her Unborn Child*, ed. Randall T. Roffen. London: Macmillan, 1894.

Jonson, Ben, *The Alchemist*, in *Three Comedies*, ed. Michael Jamieson. Harmondsworth: Penguin, 1966.

——*Bartholomew Fair*, ed. E. A. Horsman. Manchester: Manchester University Press, 1979.

——*Ben Jonson*, ed. C. H. Herford and Percy and Evelyn Simpson, 11 vols. Oxford: Clarendon, 1925–52.

——*The Complete Plays*, ed. G. A. Wilkes, 4 vols. Oxford: Clarendon, 1981–2.

——*Every Man in His Humour*, ed. Martin Seymour-Smith. London: Benn, 1966.

——*The New Inn*, ed. Michael Hattaway. Manchester: Manchester University Press, 1984.

——*Volpone*, ed. Philip Brockbank. London: Benn, 1973.

——*The workes*. London, 1616; S.T.C. 14751.

Jonston, John, *An history of the wonderful things of nature*. London, 1657; Wing J1017.

Josselin, Ralph, *The Diary, 1616–1683*, ed. Alan Macfarlane. Oxford: Oxford University Press, 1976.

Kenner, Mrs John, *Thou shalt vnderstande*. London, 1553?; S.T.C. 14932.5.

The kingdomes monster vncloaked from Heaven. London, 1643; Wing K587.

Lavater, Lewes, *Of Ghostes and Spirites Walking by Nyght*, ed. J. Dover Wilson and Mary Yardley. Oxford: Oxford University Press, 1929.

Leigh, William, *Strange newes of a prodigious monster*. London, 1613; S.T.C. 15428.

Le Loyer, Pierre, *A treatise of specters or straunge sights*. London, 1605; S.T.C. 15448.

Lemnius, Levinus, *The secret miracles of nature*. London, 1658; Wing L1044.

Leo, John, *A geographical historie of Africa*. London, 1600; S.T.C. 15481.

Le Roy, Louis, *Of the interchangeable course, or variety of things in the whole world*. London, 1594; S.T.C. 15489.

Linschoten, Jan Huygen van, *John Huighen Van Linschoten*. London, 1597; S.T.C. 15691.

Lodge, Thomas, *Wits miserie*. London, 1596; S.T.C. 16677.

Lupton, Donald, *Emblems of rarities*. London, 1636; S.T.C. 16942.

Lupton, Thomas, *A thousand notable things, of sundry sortes*. London, *c.* 1590, S.T.C. 16957.5.

Lycosthenes, Conrad, *Prodigiorum ac ostentorum chronicon*. Basilae: Henricum Petri, 1557.

Lyly, John, *'Gallathea' and 'Midas'*, ed. Anne Begor Lancashire. London: Arnold, 1969.

Machyn, Henry, *The Diary, 1550–1563*, Camden Society, 1st ser., 42 (1848).

Maclure, Millar, ed., *Marlowe: The Critical Heritage, 1588–1896*. London, Boston and Henley: Routledge & Kegan Paul, 1979.

Marlowe, Christopher, *Tamburlaine the Great*, in *The Complete Plays*, ed. Mark Thornton Burnett. London: Everyman, 1999.

The Marriage of Wit and Science, ed. Arthur Brown, Malone Society (1960 [1961]).

Marston, John, *The Malcontent*, ed. George K. Hunter. Manchester: Manchester University Press, 1975.

——*The Poems*, ed. Arnold Davenport. Liverpool: Liverpool University Press, 1961.

Mayne, Jasper, *The City-Match*, in W. C. Hazlitt, ed., *A Select Collection of Old English Plays*, 4th edn, 15 vols. London: Reeves and Turner, 1874–6, XIII.

Mela, Pomponius, *The worke*. London, 1590; S.T.C. 17785.

Melanchthon, Philipp, *Of two wonderful popish monsters*. London, 1579; S.T.C. 17797.

Middleton, Thomas and William Rowley, *The Spanish Gipsy*, in Thomas Middleton, *The Works*, ed. A. H. Bullen, 8 vols. London: Nimmo, 1885–6, VI.

Miller, Henry, *God the protector of Israel*. London, 1641; Wing M2060A.

Mistris Parliament brought to bed. London, 1648; Wing M2281.

Montaigne, Michel de, *The essayes or morall, politike and millitarie discourses*. London, 1603; S.T.C. 18041.

More strange newes: of wonderfull accidents hapning by the late overflowings of waters. London, 1607; S.T.C. 22916.

Morton, John, *The Natural History of Northampton-shire*. London: Knaplock & Wilkin, 1712.

Muenster, Sebastian, *A briefe collection and compendious extract of strau[n]ge and memorable thinges*. London, 1572; S.T.C. 18242.

——*A treatyse of the newe India*. London, 1553; S.T.C. 18244.

Munday, Anthony, *The triumphes of re-united Britania*. London, 1605; S.T.C. 18279.

——*A view of sundry examples*. London, 1580; S.T.C. 18281.

Munster, Sebastian, *Cosmographiae universalis lib. VI*. Basileae: Henrichum Petri, 1554.

A myraculous, and monstrous, but yet most true, discourse. London, 1588; S.T.C. 6910.7.

Nabbes, Thomas, *Covent-Garden*, in *The Works*, ed. A. H. Bullen, 2 vols. London: Wyman, 1887, I.

Nichols, John, ed., *The Progresses and Public Processions of Queen Elizabeth*, 3 vols. London: J. Nichols, 1823.

O' Dogherty, Sir Cahir, *News from Lough-Foyle*. London, 1608; S.T.C. 18784.

'Of the Posture Master', *Philosophical Transactions*, 242, July (1698), p. 262.

Oldenburg, Henry, *The Correspondence*, ed. A. Rupert Hall and Marie Boas Hall, 9 vols. Madison and Milwaukee: University of Wisconsin Press, 1955–73.

An oration militarie to all naturall Englishmen. London, 1588; S.T.C. 18836.5.

Oteringham, *A most certaine report of a monster borne at Oteringham in Holdernesse*. London, 1595; S.T.C. 18895.5.

P., I., *A meruaylous straunge deformed swyne*. London, 1570?; S.T.C. 19071.

Painter, Anthony, *Anthony Paint[er] the blaspheming caryar*. London, 1613; S.T.C. 19120.

Paré, Ambroise, *On Monsters and Marvels*, ed. Janis L. Pallister. Chicago and London: University of Chicago Press, 1982.

——*The workes of that famous chirugion*. London, 1634; S.T.C. 19189.

Parrot, Henry, *The mastive, or young-whelpe of the olde-dogge*. London, 1615; S.T.C. 19333.

Parsons, Robert, *A conference about the next succession to the crowne of Ingland*. London, 1594; S.T.C. 19398.

P[eachum], H[enry], *The worth of a penny*. London, 1641; Wing P949A.

Peedle, Thomas, *The falacie of the great water-drinker discovered*. London, 1650; Wing P1052.

Pepys, Samuel, *The Diary of Samuel Pepys*, ed. Robert Latham and William Matthews, 11 vols. Berkeley: University of California Press, 1970.

Person, David, *Varieties: or, a surveigh of rare and excellent matters*. London, 1635; S.T.C. 19781.

Pet, Edmond, *Lamentable newes, shewing the wonderfull deliverance of maister E. Pet*. London, 1613; S.T.C. 19792.

Platter, Thomas, *Thomas Platter's Travels in England 1599*, tr. Clare Williams. London: Cape, 1937.

Plinus Secundus, Caius, *The historie of the world*. London, 1601; S.T.C. 20029.

Plot, Robert, *The natural history of Stafford-shire*. London, 1686; Wing P2588.

Polemon, John, *The second part of the booke of battailes*. London, 1587; S.T.C. 20090.

Porta, Giambattista della, *Natural magick*. London, 1658; Wing P2982.

Prynne, William, *Histrio-mastix*. London, 1633; S.T.C. 20464.

——*The unlovelinesse of love-lockes*. London, 1628; S.T.C. 20477.

Purchas, Samuel, ed., *Hakluytus Posthumus, or, Purchas His Pilgrimes*, 20 vols. Glasgow: J. MacLehose, 1905–7.

——*Purchas his pilgrim*. London, 1619; S.T.C. 20503.

——*Purchas his pilgrimage*. London, 1613; S.T.C. 20505.

R., C., *The true discripcion of this marueilous straunge fishe*. London, 1569; S.T.C. 20570.

R., I., *A most straunge, and true discourse, of the wonderfull judgement of God*. London, 1600; S.T.C. 20575.

Randolph, Thomas, *Hey for Honesty*, in *The Poetical and Dramatic Works*, ed. W. Carew Hazlitt, 2 vols. London: Reeves and Turner, 1875, II.

Rankins, William, *A mirrour of monsters*. London, 1587; S.T.C. 20699.

Rawlidge, Richard, *A monster late found out and discovered*. London, 1628; S.T.C. 20766.

Rogers, Daniel, *Matrimoniall honovr*. London, 1642; Wing R1797.

Rollins, Hyder E., ed., *An Analytical Index to the Ballad-Entries (1557–1709) in the Registers of the Company of Stationers of London*. Chapel Hill: University of North Carolina Press, 1924.

——*The Pack of Autolycus*. Cambridge, MA: Harvard University Press, 1927.

——*A Pepysian Garland: Black-Letter Broadside Ballads of the Years 1595–1639*. Cambridge, MA: Harvard University Press, 1971.

Rous, Francis, *Oile of scorpions*. London, 1623; S.T.C. 21344.

Rous, John, *Diary of John Rous, 1625–1642*, ed. Mary Anne Everett Green, Camden Society, 1st ser., 66 (1856).

Rueff, Jacob, *The expert midwife*. London, 1637; S.T.C. 21442.

Rugg, Thomas, *The Diurnal of Thomas Rugg, 1659–1661*, ed. William L. Sachse. London: Royal Historical Society, 1961.

Rump: Or an Exact Collection of the Choycest Poems and Songs Relating to the Late Times, 2 vols. London: Privately Published, [1874].

S., E. C., *The government of Ireland under sir John Perrot*. London, 1626; S.T.C. 21490.

Sadler, John, *The sicke womans private looking-glasse*. London, 1636; S.T.C. 21544.

Saltonstall, Wye, *Picturae Loquentes*, ed. C. H. Wilkinson. Oxford: Blackwell, 1946.

Salvianus, *A second and third blast of retrait from plaies and theaters*. London, 1580; S.T.C. 21677.

Sanderson, John, *The Travels of John Sanderson in the Levant, 1584–1602*, ed. Sir William Foster, Hakluyt Society, 2nd ser., 67 (1930 [1931]).

Settle, Dionyse, *A true reporte of the laste voyage into the west and northwest regions*. London, 1577; S.T.C. 22265.

Shakespeare, William, *Anthony and Cleopatra*, ed. Michael Neill. Oxford and New York: Oxford University Press, 1994.
——*The Complete Works*, ed. Stanley Wells and Gary Taylor. Oxford: Clarendon, 1991.
——*Henry VI, Part II*, ed. Ronald Knowles. Walton-on-Thames: Nelson, 1999.
——*Henry VI, Part III*, ed. Andrew S. Cairncross. London and New York, Routledge, 1989.
——*King John*, ed. A. R. Braunmuller. Oxford and New York: Oxford University Press, 1994.
——*King Lear*, ed. R. A. Foakes. London: Thomson, 2000.
——*Macbeth*, ed. Nicholas Brooke. Oxford and New York: Oxford University Press, 1994.
——*The Merchant of Venice*, ed. Jay L. Halio. Oxford and New York: Oxford University Press, 1994.
——*A Midsummer Night's Dream*, ed. Peter Holland. Oxford and New York: Oxford University Press, 1995.
——*Mr. William Shakespeares comedies, histories, & tragedies*. London, 1623; S.T.C. 22273.
——*A New Variorum Edition of Shakespeare: 'Othello'*, ed. Horace Howard Furness. Philadelphia: J. B. Lippincott, 1886.
——*Othello*, ed. E. A. J. Honigmann. Walton-on-Thames: Nelson, 1997.
——*Richard III*, ed. Antony Hammond. London and New York: Routledge, 1990.
——*The Taming of the Shrew*, ed. H. J. Oliver. Oxford and New York: Oxford University Press, 1984.
——*The Tempest*, ed. Frank Kermode. London: Methuen, 1979.
——*The Tempest*, ed. Stephen Orgel. Oxford and New York: Oxford University Press, 1987.
——*The Winter's Tale*, ed. J. H. P. Pafford. London and New York: Methuen, 1981.
[Shakespeare, William and William Rowley], *The Birth of Merlin*, ed. R. J. Stewart and Denise Coffey. Longmead: Element, 1989.
Sharpham, Edward, *The Fleire*, in *The Works*, ed. Christopher Gordon Petter. New York and London: Garland, 1986.
Shirley, James, *Cupid and Death*, in T. J. B. Spenser and Stanley Wells, eds, *A Book of Masques in Honour of Allardyce Nicoll*. Cambridge: Cambridge University Press, 1967, pp. 371–99.
——*The Dramatic Works*, ed. William Gifford and Alexander Dyce, 6 vols. London: Murray, 1833.
Sidney, Sir Philip, *An Apology for Poetry*, ed. Geoffrey Shepherd. Manchester: Manchester University Press, 1973.
——*The Countess of Pembroke's Arcadia (The Old Arcadia)*, ed. Katherine Duncan-Jones. Oxford and New York: Oxford University Press, 1994.
Skinker, Tannakin, *A certaine relation of a hogfaced gentlewoman*. London, 1640; S.T.C. 22627.
Slater, *Master*, *The new-yeeres gift*. London, 1636; S.T.C. 22631.
Smith, Henry, *A preparatiue to mariage*. London, 1591; S.T.C. 22685.
Smith, John, *Travels and Works of Captain John Smith*, ed. Edward Arber and A. G. Bradley, 2 vols. Edinburgh: John Grant, 1910.
Solinus, Caius Julius, *The worthie worke*. London, 1587; S.T.C. 22895a.5.

Somerset, J. Alan B., ed., *Shropshire*, Records of Early English Drama, 2 vols. Toronto, Buffalo and London: University of Toronto Press, 1994.

Spalding, John, *Memorialls of the Trubles in Scotland and in England, 1624–1625*, 2 vols. Aberdeen: Spalding Club, 1850–51.

Spenser, Edmund, *The Faerie Queene*, ed. A. C. Hamilton. London and New York: Longman, 1977.

Sprat, Thomas, *The history of the Royal Society*. London, 1667; Wing S5032.

Stow, John, *The annales of England*. London, 1592; S.T.C. 23334.

—— *The annales of England*. London, 1631; S.T.C. 23340.

Stubbes, Philip, *The anatomie of abuses*. London, 1583; S.T.C. 23376.

Strange ne<w>es. London, [1606]; S.T.C. 4658.

The strange newes. London, 1561; S.T.C. 18507.

Strange newes out of Kent. London, 1609; S.T.C. 14934.

The strange wonder of the world, or the great gyant described. London, 1653; Wing S5922.

The terrible, horrible, monster of the West. London, 1649; Wing T765.

Thevet, André, *The new found worlde, or Antarctike*. London, 1568; S.T.C. 23950.

Tomkis, Thomas, *Albumazar: A Comedy*, ed. Hugh G. Dick. Berkeley and Los Angeles: University of California Press, 1944.

Topsell, Edward, *The historie of foure-footed beastes*. London, 1607; S.T.C. 24123.

—— *The historie of serpents*. London, 1608; S.T.C. 24124.

Torquemada, Antonio de, *The Spanish Mandevile of miracles*. London, 1600; S.T.C. 24135.

Tradescant, John, *Musaeum Tradescantianum*. London, 1656; Wing T2005.

The true discription of two monsterous chyldren. London, 1565; S.T.C. 6774.

The true effigies of the German giant. London, 1660; Wing T2692.

A true relation of the French kinge his goode successe. London, 1592; S.T.C. 13147.

A true report of certaine wonderfull overflowings of waters. London, 1607; S.T.C. 22915.

A true report . . . of a mighty sea-monster. London, 1617; S.T.C. 20892.

Twemlow, J. A., ed., *Liverpool Town Books, 1550–1603*, 2 vols. Liverpool: Liverpool University Press, 1918–35.

Two most remarkable and true histories. London, 1620; S.T.C. 13525.

Twyne, Thomas, *A shorte and pithie discourse, concerning earthquakes*. London, 1580; S.T.C. 24413.

Tymme, Thomas, *A silver watch-bell*. London, 1610; S.T.C. 24424.

Vicars, John, *Prodigies and apparitions*. London, 1642–3; Wing V323.

Vicary, Thomas, *The Anatomie of the Bodie of Man*, ed. F. J. Furnivall and Percy Furnivall. London: Oxford University Press, 1888.

Webbe, Edward, *The rare and most wonderfull things*. London, 1590; S.T.C. 25151.5.

Webster, John, John Ford and Philip Massinger, *The Fair Maid of the Inn*, in John Webster, *The Complete Works*, ed. F. L. Lucas, 4 vols. London: Chatto and Windus, 1927, IV.

Weever, John, *Epigrammes in the oldest cut, and newest fashion*. London, 1599; S.T.C. 25224.

Wentworth, Peter, *A pithie exhortation*. London, 1598; S.T.C. 25245.

Whiteway, William, *William Whiteway of Dorchester: His Diary 1618–1635*, Dorset Record Society, 12 (1991).

Willet, Andrew, *Hexapla in Exodum*. London, 1608; S.T.C. 25686.
——*Hexapla in Leviticum*. London, 1631; S.T.C. 25688.
Williams, Griffith, *Vindiciae regvm; or, the Grand Rebellion*. Oxford, 1643; Wing W2675.
Wilson, Sir Thomas, *The State of England*, ed. F. J. Fisher, Camden Society, 3rd ser., 16 (1936).
The windie yeare. London, 1613; S.T.C. 26092.
Winstanley, William, *The New Help to Discourse*. London: B. H., 1716.
The woefull and lamentable wast. London, 1608; S.T.C. 4181.
A wonder woorth the reading, of a woman in Kent Street. London, 1617; S.T.C. 14935.
The wonders of this windie weather. London, 1613; S.T.C. 25950.

Secondary sources: printed

Adams, Rachel, *Sideshow U.S.A.: Freaks and the American Cultural Imagination*. Chicago and London: University of Chicago Press, 2001.
Adelman, Janet, 'Iago's Alter Ego: Race as Projection in *Othello*', *Shakespeare Quarterly*, 48 (1997), pp. 125–44.
——*Suffocating Mothers: Fantasies of Maternal Origin in Shakespeare's Plays, 'Hamlet' to 'The Tempest'*. New York and London: Routledge, 1992.
Albanese, Denise, *New Science, New World*. Durham, NC and London: Duke University Press, 1996.
Armstrong, William A., 'Ben Jonson and Jacobean Stagecraft', in John Russell Brown and Bernard Harris, eds, *Jacobean Theatre*. London: Arnold, 1960, pp. 43–61.
Aston, Margaret, 'The Fiery Trigon Conjunction: An Elizabethan Astrological Prediction', *Isis*, 61 (1970), pp. 159–87.
Atkins, Sidney H., 'Mr Banks and his Horse', *Notes and Queries*, 167, 21 July (1934), pp. 38–44.
Aubrey, James R., 'Race and the Spectacle of the Monstrous in *Othello*', *Clio*, 22 (1993), pp. 221–38.
Augur, Helen, *The Book of Fairs*. New York: Harcourt, Brace and Company, 1939.
Baker, David J., 'Where is Ireland in *The Tempest*?', in Mark Thornton Burnett and Ramona Wray, eds, *Shakespeare and Ireland: History, Politics, Culture*. Basingstoke: Macmillan – now Palgrave Macmillan, 1997, pp. 68–88.
Bakhtin, Mikhail, *Rabelais and His World*, tr. Hélène Iswolsky. Cambridge, MA: MIT Press, 1968.
Balsiger, Barbara J., 'The *Kunst- und Wunderkammern*: A Catalogue Raisonné of Collecting in Germany, France and England 1565–1750', unpublished PhD thesis, University of Pittsburgh, 1970.
Barber, C. L., *Creating Elizabethan Tragedy: The Theatre of Marlowe and Kyd*. Chicago and London: University of Chicago Press, 1988.
Barish, Jonas, *The Antitheatrical Prejudice*. Berkeley, Los Angeles and London: University of California Press, 1981.
Barker, Francis and Peter Hulme, 'Nymphs and Reapers Heavily Vanish: The Discursive Con-texts of *The Tempest*', in John Drakakis, ed., *Alternative Shakespeares*. London and New York: Methuen, 1985, pp. 191–205.

Bartels, Emily C., '*Othello* and Africa: Postcolonialism Reconsidered', *The William and Mary Quarterly*, 54 (1997), pp. 45–64.

——*Spectacles of Strangeness: Imperialism, Alienation, Marlowe*. Philadelphia: University of Pennsylvania Press, 1993.

Bartolovich, Crystal, ' "Baseless Fabric": London as a World City', in Peter Hulme and William H. Sherman, eds, '*The Tempest' and Its Travels*. London: Reaktion, 2000, pp. 13–26.

Bate, Jonathan, 'Introduction', in Jonathan Bate and Russell Jackson, eds, *Shakespeare: An Illustrated Stage History*. Oxford: Oxford University Press, 1996, pp. 1–9.

——*Shakespeare and Ovid*. Oxford: Clarendon, 1993.

Battenhouse, Roy W., *Marlowe's 'Tamburlaine': A Study in Renaissance Moral Philosophy*. Nashville, TN: Vanderbilt University Press, 1964.

Bednarz, James P., *Shakespeare and the Poets' War*. New York: Columbia University Press, 2001.

Benedict, Barbara M., *Curiosity: A Cultural History of Early Modern Inquiry*. Chicago and London: University of Chicago Press, 2001.

Benjamin, Walter, *Illuminations*, tr. Harry Zohn. London: Fontana/Collins, 1973.

Bevington, David, '*The Tempest* and the Jacobean Court Masque', in David Bevington and Peter Holbrook, eds, *The Politics of the Stuart Court Masque*. Cambridge: Cambridge University Press, 1998, pp. 218–43.

Biester, James, *Lyric Wonder: Rhetoric and Wit in Renaissance English Poetry*. Ithaca, NY and London: Cornell University Press, 1997.

Biow, Douglas, '*Mirabile Dictu': Representations of the Marvellous in Medieval and Renaissance Epic*. Ann Arbor: University of Michigan Press, 1996.

Birch, Thomas, *The History of the Royal Society of London*, 4 vols. London: Millar, 1756–7.

Birringer, Johannes H., *Marlowe's 'Dr Faustus' and 'Tamburlaine': Theological and Theatrical Perspectives*. Frankfurt am Main, Bern and New York: Lang, 1984.

——'Marlowe's Violent Stage: "Mirrors" of Honour in *Tamburlaine*', *ELH*, 51 (1984), pp. 219–39.

Bliss, Matthew, 'Property or Performer?: Animals on the Elizabethan Stage', *Theatre Studies*, 39 (1994), pp. 45–59.

Bompiani, Ginevra, 'The Chimera Herself', in Michael Feher, Ramona Naddaff and Nadia Tazi, eds, *Fragments for a History of the Human Body*, 3 vols. New York: Zone, 1989, I, pp. 364–409.

Bronfen, Elisabeth, *Over Her Dead Body: Death, Femininity and the Aesthetic*. Manchester: Manchester University Press, 1992.

Brotton, Jerry, ' "This Tunis, sir, was Carthage": Contesting Colonialism in *The Tempest*', in Ania Loomba and Martin Orkin, eds, *Post-Colonial Shakespeares*. London and New York: Routledge, 1998, pp. 23–42.

Brown, Eric C., ' "Many a Civil Monster": Shakespeare's Idea of the Centaur', *Shakespeare Survey*, 51 (1998), pp. 175–91.

Brown, Paul, ' "This thing of darkness I acknowledge mine": *The Tempest* and the Discourse of Colonialism', in Jonathan Dollimore and Alan Sinfield, eds, *Political Shakespeare: New Essays in Cultural Materialism*. Manchester: Manchester University Press, 1985, pp. 48–71.

Bruster, Douglas, *Drama and the Market in the Age of Shakespeare*. Cambridge: Cambridge University Press, 1992.
——*Quoting Shakespeare: Form and Culture in Early Modern Drama*. Lincoln, NB and London: University of Nebraska Press, 2000.
Burke, Peter, *Popular Culture in Early Modern Europe*. London: Temple Smith, 1978.
Burnett, Mark Thornton, 'Tamburlaine: An Elizabethan Vagabond', *Studies in Philology*, 84 (1987), pp. 308–23.
——'The "Trusty Servant": A Sixteenth-Century English Emblem', *Emblematica*, 6 (1992), pp. 237–53.
Burt, Richard, *Licensed by Authority: Ben Jonson and the Discourses of Censorship*. Ithaca: Cornell University Press, 1993.
Butler, Martin, 'Introduction: From *Workes* to Texts', in Martin Butler, ed., *Representing Ben Jonson: Text, History, Performance*. Basingstoke: Macmillan – now Palgrave Macmillan, 1999, pp. 1–19.
Callaghan, Dympna, *Shakespeare without Women: Representing Gender and Race on the Renaissance Stage*. London and New York: Routledge, 2000.
Capp, Bernard, *Astrology and the Popular Press: English Almanacs 1500–1800*. London and Boston: Faber, 1979.
Carnegie, David, 'Stabbed through the Arras: The Dramaturgy of Elizabethan Stage Hangings', in Heather Kerr, Robin Eaden and Madge Mitton, eds, *Shakespeare: World Views*. Newark: University of Delaware Press, 1996, pp. 181–99.
Carroll, William C., *Fat King, Lean Beggar: Representations of Poverty in the Age of Shakespeare*. Ithaca, NY and London: Cornell University Press, 1996.
Cartelli, Thomas, '*Bartholomew Fair* as Urban Arcadia: Jonson Responds to Shakespeare', *Renaissance Drama*, 14 (1983), pp. 151–72.
——*Marlowe, Shakespeare, and the Economy of Theatrical Experience*. Philadelphia: University of Pennsylvania Press, 1991.
Cawley, Robert Ralston, 'Shakespeare's Use of the Voyagers in *The Tempest*', *Publications of the Modern Language Association of America*, 41 (1926), pp. 688–726.
Cerasano, S. P., 'The Master of the Bears in Art and Enterprise', *Medieval and Renaissance Drama in England*, 5 (1991), pp. 195–209.
Charnes, Linda, *Notorious Identity: Materializing the Subject in Shakespeare*. Cambridge, MA: Harvard University Press, 1993.
Chedgzoy, Kate, Julie Sanders and Susan Wiseman, 'Introduction: Refashioning Ben Jonson', in Julie Sanders, Kate Chedgzoy and Susan Wiseman, eds, *Refashioning Ben Jonson: Gender, Politics and the Jonsonian Canon*. Basingstoke: Macmillan – now Palgrave Macmillan, 1998, pp. 1–27.
Clare, Janet, 'Marlowe's "theatre of cruelty"', in J. A. Downie and J. T. Parnell, eds, *Constructing Christopher Marlowe*. Cambridge: Cambridge University Press, 2000, pp. 74–87.
Cohen, Jeffrey Jerome, *Of Giants: Sex, Monsters, and the Middle Ages*. Minneapolis: University of Minnesota Press, 1999.
——'Monster Culture (Seven Theses)', in Jeffrey Jerome Cohen, ed., *Monster Theory: Reading Culture*. Minneapolis and London: University of Minnesota Press, 1996, pp. 3–25.
Cornelius, R. M., *Christopher Marlowe's Use of the Bible*. New York, Berne and Frankfurt am Main: Peter Lang, 1984.

Coupe, Laurence, *Myth*. London and New York: Routledge, 1997.

Creed, Barbara, *The Monstrous-Feminine: Film, Feminism, Psychoanalysis*. London and New York: Routledge, 1993.

Cressy, David, *Travesties and Transgressions in Tudor and Stuart England*. Oxford: Oxford University Press, 2000.

Crewe, Jonathan, 'The Theatre of the Idols: Marlowe, Rankins, and Theatrical Images', *Theatre Journal*, 36 (1984), pp. 321–33.

Cropper, Elizabeth, 'On Beautiful Women, Parmigianino, *Petrarchismo*, and the Vernacular Style', *Art Bulletin*, 58 (1976), pp. 374–94.

Crowther, Henry, 'Anthony Payne, the Cornish Giant', *Journal of the Royal Institution of Cornwall*, 10 (1890), pp. 3–7.

Crunelle-Vanrigh, Anny, '"Unmixed with baser '*mater*'": Le Monstre et La Matrice dans *The Tempest*', in Claude Peltrault, ed., *Shakespeare 'La Tempête': Etudes Critiques*. Besançon: Université de Franche-Comté, 1993, pp. 97–113.

Cutts, John P., 'The Ultimate Source of Tamburlaine's White, Red, Black and Death?', *Notes and Queries*, 203 (1958), pp. 146–47.

Daileader, Celia R., *Eroticism on the Renaissance Stage: Transcendence, Desire, and the Limits of the Visible*. Cambridge: Cambridge University Press, 1998.

D'Amico, Jack, *The Moor in English Renaissance Drama*. Tampa: University of South Florida Press, 1991.

Daston, Lorraine and Katharine Park, *Wonders and the Order of Nature, 1150–1750*. New York: Zone Books, 1998.

Davidson, Arnold I., 'The Horror of Monsters', in James J. Sheehan and Morton Sosna, eds, *The Boundaries of Humanity: Humans, Animals, Machines*. Berkeley, Los Angeles and Oxford: University of California Press, 1991, pp. 36–67.

Deats, Sara Munson, *Sex, Gender, and Desire in the Plays of Christopher Marlowe*. Newark: University of Delaware Press, 1997.

Debus, Allen G., *Man and Nature in the Renaissance*. Cambridge: Cambridge University Press, 1978.

Demaray, John G., *Shakespeare and the Spectacles of Strangeness: 'The Tempest' and the Transformation of Renaissance Theatrical Forms*. Pittsburgh: Duquesne University Press, 1998.

Dennett, Andrea Stulman, *Weird & Wonderful: The Dime Museum in America*. New York and London: New York University Press, 1997.

Derrida, Jacques, *A Derrida Reader: Between the Blinds*, ed. Peggy Kamuf. Hemel Hempstead: Harvester Wheatsheaf, 1991.

Diehl, Huston, *Staging Reform, Reforming the Stage: Protestantism and Popular Theatre in Early Modern England*. Ithaca, NY and London: Cornell University Press, 1997.

Dobin, Howard, *Merlin's Disciples: Prophecy, Poetry, and Power in Renaissance England*. Stanford: Stanford University Press, 1990.

Dolan, Frances E., *Dangerous Familiars: Representations of Domestic Crime in England, 1550–1700*. Ithaca and London: Cornell University Press, 1994.

Draper, John, 'Monster Caliban', *Revue de Littérature Comparée*, 40 (1966), pp. 599–605.

Drew-Bear, Annette, *Painted Faces on the Renaissance Stage: The Moral Significance of Face-Painting Conventions*. Lewisburg: Bucknell University Press, 1994.

Dutton, Richard, *Ben Jonson: To the First Folio*. Cambridge: Cambridge University Press, 1983.

Eccles, Audrey, *Obstetrics and Gynaecology in Tudor and Stuart England*. Kent, Ohio: Kent State University Press, 1982.

Falco, Raphael, *Charismatic Authority in Early Modern English Tragedy*. Baltimore and London: The Johns Hopkins University Press, 2000.

Feasey, Lynette and Evelyn, 'Marlowe and the Prophetic Dooms', *Notes and Queries*, 195 (1950), pp. 356–9, 404–7, 419–21.

Findlay, Alison, *Illegitimate Power: Bastards in English Renaissance Drama*. Manchester and New York: Manchester University Press, 1994.

Findlen, Paula, 'Jokes of Nature and Jokes of Knowledge: The Playfulness of Scientific Discourse in Early Modern Europe', *Renaissance Quarterly*, 43 (1990), pp. 292–331.

——'The Museum: Its Classical Etymology and Renaissance Genealogy', *Journal of the History of Collections*, 1 (1989), pp. 59–78.

——*Possessing Nature: Museums, Collecting, and Scientific Culture in Early Modern Italy*. Berkeley, Los Angeles and London: University of California Press, 1994.

Fisher, Philip, *Wonder, the Rainbow, and the Aesthetics of Rare Experience*. Cambridge, MA: Harvard University Press, 1998.

Franssen, Paul, 'A Muddy Mirror', in Nadia Lee and Theo D'haen, eds, *Constellation Caliban: Figurations of a Character*. Amsterdam and Atlanta: Rodopi, 1997, pp. 23–42.

Freeman, Arthur, *Thomas Kyd: Facts and Problems*. Oxford: Clarendon Press, 1967.

Friedman, John Block, *The Monstrous Races in Medieval Art and Thought*. Cambridge, MA and London: Harvard University Press, 1981.

Frost, Thomas, *The Old Showmen and the Old London Fairs*. London: Tinsley, 1874.

Frye, Susan, *Elizabeth I: The Competition for Representation*. New York and Oxford: Oxford University Press, 1993.

Fuchs, Barbara, 'Conquering Islands: Contextualizing *The Tempest*', *Shakespeare Quarterly*, 48 (1997), pp. 45–62.

Fudge, Erica, *Perceiving Animals: Humans and Beasts in Early Modern English Culture*. Basingstoke: Macmillan – now Palgrave Macmillan, 1999.

Fulton, John F., *A Bibliography of the Honourable Robert Boyle*. Oxford: Clarendon, 1961.

Garber, Marjorie, *Shakespeare's Ghost Writers: Literature as uncanny causality*. New York and London: Methuen, 1987.

Giamatti, A. Bartlett, 'Proteus Unbound: Some Versions of the Sea God in the Renaissance', in Peter Demetz, Thomas Greene and Lowry Nelson, eds, *The Disciplines of Criticism: Essays in Literary Theory, Interpretation, and History*. New Haven and London: Yale University Press, 1968, pp. 437–75.

Gillies, John, *Shakespeare and the Geography of Difference*. Cambridge: Cambridge University Press, 1994.

Glare, P. G. W., *Oxford Latin Dictionary*, 2 vols. Oxford: Clarendon, 1983.

Grande, Troni Y., *Marlovian Tragedy: The Play of Dilation*. Lewisburg: Bucknell University Press, 1999.

Greenblatt, Stephen, *Learning to Curse: Essays in Early Modern Culture*. London: Routledge, 1990.

——*Renaissance Self-Fashioning: From More to Shakespeare*. Chicago: Chicago University Press, 1980.

Greene, J., 'Account of a Man with a Child growing out of his Breast', *The Gentleman's Magazine*, 47, December (1777), pp. 482–3.

Griffin, Eric, 'Un-sainting James: Or, *Othello* and the "Spanish Spirits" of Shakespeare's Globe', *Representations*, 62 (1998), pp. 58–99.

Grimal, Pierre, *The Dictionary of Classical Mythology*. Oxford: Blackwell, 1986.

Grosz, Elizabeth, 'Intolerable Ambiguity: Freaks as/at the Limit', in Rosemarie Garland Thomson, ed., *Freakery: Cultural Spectacles of the Extraordinary Body*. New York and London: New York University Press, 1996, pp. 55–66.

Gurr, Andrew, *The Shakespearean Stage 1574–1642*. Cambridge: Cambridge University Press, 1985.

Guy, John, 'The 1590s: The Second Reign of Elizabeth I?', in John Guy, ed., *The Reign of Elizabeth I: Court and Culture in the Last Decade*. Cambridge: Cambridge University Press, 1995, pp. 1–19.

Hackett, Helen, *Virgin Mother, Maiden Queen: Elizabeth I and the Cult of the Virgin Mary*. Basingstoke: Macmillan – now Palgrave Macmillan, 1995.

Hadfield, Andrew, *Literature, Travel, and Colonial Writing in the English Renaissance, 1545–1625*. Oxford: Clarendon, 1998.

Haigh, Christopher, *Elizabeth I*. London and New York: Longman, 1998.

Hall, Kim F., *Things of Darkness: Economies of Race and Gender in Early Modern England*. Ithaca, NY and London: Cornell University Press, 1995.

—— '"Troubling Doubles": Apes, Africans and Blackface in *Mr. Moore's Revels*', in Joyce Green MacDonald, ed., *Race, Ethnicity and Power in the Renaissance*. Teaneck: Fairleigh Dickinson University Press, 1997, pp. 120–44.

Hamilton, Donna B., *Virgil and 'The Tempest': The Politics of Imitation*. Columbus: Ohio State University Press, 1990.

Hamlin, William M., *The Image of America in Montaigne, Spenser, and Shakespeare: Renaissance Ethnography and Literary Reflection*. New York: St Martin's Press, 1995.

Hanafi, Zakiya, *The Monster in the Machine: Magic, Medicine, and the Marvellous in the Time of the Scientific Revolution*. Durham, NC and London: Duke University Press, 2000.

Hankins, John E., 'Caliban the Bestial Man', *Publications of the Modern Language Association of America*, 62 (1947), pp. 793–801.

Hanson, Elizabeth, *Discovering the Subject in Renaissance England*. Cambridge: Cambridge University Press, 1998.

Haslem, Lori Schroeder, '"Troubled with the Mother": Longings, Purgings, and the Maternal Body in *Bartholomew Fair* and *The Duchess of Malfi*', *Modern Philology*, 92 (1995), pp. 438–59.

Haynes, Jonathan, *The Social Relations of Jonson's Theatre*. Cambridge: Cambridge University Press, 1992.

Heninger, S. K., *A Handbook of Renaissance Meterology*. Durham, NC: Duke University Press, 1960.

Herendeen, W. H., 'A New Way to Pay Old Debts: Pretexts to the 1616 Folio', in Jennifer Brady and W. H. Herendeen, eds, *Ben Jonson's 1616 Folio*. Newark: University of Delaware Press, 1991, pp. 38–63.

Hill, Eugene, 'Marlowe's "more Exellent and Admirable methode" of Parody in *Tamburlaine I*', *Renaissance Papers* (1995), pp. 33–46.

Hillman, David and Carla Mazzio, 'Introduction: Individual Parts', in David Hillman and Carla Mazzio, eds, *The Body in Parts: Fantasies of Corporeality in Early Modern Europe*. London and New York: Routledge, 1997, pp. xi–xxix.

Hodgdon, Barbara, *The End Crowns All: Closure and Contradiction in Shakespeare's History*. Princeton, NY: Princeton University Press, 1991.

Holderness, Graham, *Shakespeare: The Histories*. Basingstoke: Macmillan – now Palgrave Macmillan, 2000.

Hoppen, K. Theodore, 'The Early Royal Society', *The British Journal for the History of Science*, 9.1 (1976), pp. 1–24 and 9.3 (1976), pp. 243–73.

Howard, Jean E. and Phyllis Rackin, *Engendering a Nation: A Feminist Account of Shakespeare's English Histories*. London and New York: Routledge, 1997.

Huet, Marie-Hélène, *Monstrous Imagination*. Cambridge, MA: Harvard University Press, 1993.

Hunt, John S., 'Prospero's Empty Grasp', *Shakespeare Studies*, 22 (1994), pp. 277–313.

Hurstfield, J., 'The Succession Struggle in Late Elizabethan England', in S. T. Bindoff, J. Hurstfield and C. H. Williams, eds, *Elizabethan Government and Society: Essays Presented to Sir John Neale*. London: Athlone, 1961, pp. 369–96.

James, Heather, *Shakespeare's Troy: Drama, Politics, and the Translation of Empire*. Cambridge: Cambridge University Press, 1997.

Johnson, James William, 'The Scythian: His Rise and Fall', *Journal of the History of Ideas*, 20 (1959), pp. 250–7.

Jones, Norman, *The Birth of the Elizabethan Age: England in the 1560s*. Oxford: Blackwell, 1993.

Jones, Robert C., *Renewing the Past in Shakespeare's Histories*. Iowa City: University of Iowa Press, 1991.

Jordan, Constance, *Shakespeare's Monarchies: Ruler and Subject in the Romances*. Ithaca, NY and London: Cornell University Press, 1997.

Kastan, David Scott, *Shakespeare after Theory*. London and New York: Routledge, 1999.

Kay, W. Dennis, *Ben Jonson: A Literary Life*. Basingstoke: Macmillan – now Palgrave Macmillan, 1995.

Keller, Evelyn Fox, *Reflections on Gender and Science*. New Haven and London: Yale University Press, 1985.

Kelsall, Malcolm, *Christopher Marlowe*. Leiden: E. J. Brill, 1981.

Kenseth, Joy, ' "A World of Wonders in One Closet Shut" ', in Joy Kenseth, ed., *The Age of the Marvellous*. Hanover: Hood Museum of Art, 1991, pp. 81–101.

Kernan, Alvin, 'The Great Fair of the World and the Ocean Island: *Bartholomew Fair* and *The Tempest*', in J. Leeds Barroll, Alexander Leggatt, Richard Hosley and Alvin Kernan, eds, *The Revels History of Drama in English*, 8 vols. London: Methuen, 1975–83, III, pp. 456–74.

Lefebvre, Henri, *The Production of Space*, tr. Donald Nicholson-Smith. Oxford: Blackwell, 1991.

Lestringant, Frank, *Cannibals: The Discovery and Representation of the Cannibal from Columbus to Jules Verne*. Berkeley and Los Angeles: University of California Press, 1997.

Levin, Carole, *'The Heart and Stomach of a King': Elizabeth I and the Politics of Sex and Power*. Philadelphia: University of Pennsylvania Press, 1994.

Levin, Richard, 'The Contemporary Perception of Marlowe's Tamburlaine', *Medieval and Renaissance Drama in England*, 1 (1984), pp. 51–70.

Levine, Laura, *Men in Women's Clothing: Anti-theatricality and effeminization, 1579–1642*. Cambridge: Cambridge University Press, 1994.

Little, Arthur L., *Shakespeare's Jungle Fever: National-Imperial Re-visions of Race, Rape, and Sacrifice*. Stanford: Stanford University Press, 2000.

The Lives and Portraits of Remarkable Characters, 2 vols. London: Arnett, 1820.

Lupton, Julia Reinhard, 'Creature Caliban', *Shakespeare Quarterly*, 51 (2000), pp. 1–23.

McAdam, Ian, *The Irony of Identity: Self and Imagination in the Drama of Christopher Marlowe*. Newark: University of Delaware Press, 1999.

McDonald, Russ, *Shakespeare & Jonson/Jonson & Shakespeare*. Brighton: Harvester, 1988.

MacGregor, Arthur, 'The Tradescants as Collectors of Rarities', in Arthur MacGregor, ed., *Tradescant's Rarities: Essays on the Foundation of the Ashmolean Museum*. Oxford: Clarendon, 1983, pp. 17–23.

McManus, Clare, ' "Defacing the Carcass": Anne of Denmark and Jonson's *The Masque of Blackness*', in Julie Sanders, Kate Chedgzoy and Susan Wiseman, eds, *Refashioning Ben Jonson: Gender, Politics and the Jonsonian Canon*. Basingstoke: Macmillan – now Palgrave Macmillan, 1998, pp. 93–113.

Mailloux, Stephen, 'Interpretation', in Frank Lentricchia and Thomas McLaughlin, eds, *Critical Terms for Literary Study*. Chicago and London: University of Chicago Press, 1990, pp. 121–34.

Marcus, Leah S., 'Of Mire and Authorship', in David L. Smith, Richard Strier and David Bevington, eds, *The Theatrical City: Culture, Theatre and Politics in London, 1576–1649*. Cambridge: Cambridge University Press, 1995, pp. 170–81.

——*The Politics of Mirth: Jonson, Herrick, Milton, Marvell, and the Defence of Old Holiday Pastimes*. Chicago and London: University of Chicago Press, 1986.

Marienstras, Richard, 'Of a Monstrous Body', in Jean-Marie Maguin and Michèle Willems, eds, *French Essays on Shakespeare and His Contemporaries: 'What would France with Us?'*. Newark: University of Delaware Press, 1995, pp. 153–74.

Marshall, Tristan, '*The Tempest* and the British Imperium in 1611', *The Historical Journal*, 41 (1998), pp. 375–400.

Mason, Jeffrey D., 'Street Fairs: Social Space, Social Performance', *Theatre Journal*, 48 (1996), pp. 301–19.

Masten, Jeffrey, *Textual Intercourse: Collaboration, Authorship, and Sexualities in Renaissance Drama*. Cambridge: Cambridge University Press, 1997.

Matar, Nabil, 'English Accounts of Captivity in North Africa and the Middle East: 1577–1625', *Renaissance Quarterly*, 54 (2001), pp. 553–72.

Maus, Katharine Eisaman, *Inwardness and Theatre in the English Renaissance*. Chicago and London: University of Chicago Press, 1995.

Mauss, Marcel, *The Gift: Forms and Functions of Exchange in Archaic Societies*, tr. Ian Cunnison London: Cohen & West, 1970.

Miller, J. Hillis, 'Narrative', in Frank Lentricchia and Thomas McLaughlin, eds, *Critical Terms for Literary Study*. Chicago and London: University of Chicago Press, 1990, pp. 66–79.

Miller, Shannon, 'Consuming Mothers/Consuming Merchants: The Carnivalesque Economy of Jacobean City Comedy', *Modern Language Studies*, 26.2–3 (1996), pp. 73–97.

Morgan, Jennifer L., ' "Some Could Suckle over Their Shoulder": Male Travellers, Female Bodies, and the Gendering of Racial Ideology', *The William and Mary Quarterly*, 54 (1997), pp. 167–92.

Morley, Henry, *Memoirs of Bartholomew Fair*. London: Warne, 1892.

Moulton, Ian Frederick, *Before Pornography: Erotic Writing in Early Modern England*. Oxford: Oxford University Press, 2000.

——'"A Monster Great Deformed": The Unruly Masculinity of Richard III', *Shakespeare Quarterly*, 47 (1996), pp. 251–68.

Mowat, Barbara A., 'Prospero, Agrippa, and Hocus Pocus', *English Literary Renaissance*, 11 (1981), pp. 281–303.

Murray, Timothy, *Theatrical Legitimation: Allegories of Genius in Seventeenth-Century England and France*. Oxford: Oxford University Press, 1987.

Neale, J. E., *Elizabeth I and Her Parliaments, 1559–1601*, 2 vols. London: Cape, 1969.

Neill, Michael, *Issues of Death: Mortality and Identity in English Renaissance Tragedy*. Oxford: Clarendon, 1997.

——'"Mulattos", "Blacks", and "Indian Moors": *Othello* and Early Modern Constructions of Human Difference', *Shakespeare Quarterly*, 49 (1998), pp. 361–74.

——'Unproper Beds: Race, Adultery and the Hideous in *Othello*', *Shakespeare Quarterly*, 40 (1989), pp. 383–412.

Newman, Karen, *Fashioning Femininity and English Renaissance Drama*. Chicago and London: University of Chicago Press, 1991.

Orgel, Stephen, 'Prospero's Wife', in Margaret W. Ferguson, Maureen Quilligan and Nancy J. Vickers, eds, *Rewriting the Renaissance: The Discourses of Sexual Difference in Early Modern Europe*. Chicago and London: University of Chicago Press, 1986, pp. 50–64.

Park, Katharine and Lorraine J. Daston, 'Unnatural Conceptions: The Study of Monsters in Sixteenth- and Seventeenth-Century France and England', *Past and Present*, 92, August (1981), pp. 20–54.

Parker, Patricia, *Literary Fat Ladies: Rhetoric, Gender, Property*. London: Methuen, 1987.

——*Shakespeare from the Margins: Language, Culture, Context*. Chicago and London: University of Chicago Press, 1996.

Paster, Gail Kern, *The Body Embarrassed: Drama and the Disciplines of Shame in Early Modern England*. Ithaca, NY: Cornell University Press, 1993.

Pechter, Edward, *'Othello' and Interpretive Traditions*. Iowa City: University of Iowa Press, 1999.

Pender, Stephen, 'In the Bodyshop: Human Exhibition in Early Modern England', in Helen Deutsch and Felicity Nussbaum, eds, *'Defects': Engendering the Modern Body*. Ann Arbor: University of Michigan Press, 2000, pp. 95–126.

——'"No Monsters at the Resurrection": Inside some Conjoined Twins', in Jeffrey Jerome Cohen, ed., *Monster Theory: Reading Culture*. Minneapolis and London: University of Minnesota Press, 1996, pp. 143–67.

Phipson, Emma, *The Animal-Lore of Shakspeare's Time*. London: Kegan Paul and Trench, 1883.

Platt, Peter G., *Reason Diminished: Shakespeare and the Marvellous*. Lincoln, NB and London: University of Nebraska Press, 1997.

Polwhele, Richard, *The History of Cornwall*, 7 vols. Dorking: Kohler & Coombes, 1978.

Pomian, Krzysztof, *Collectors and Curiosities: Paris and Venice, 1500–1800*, tr. Elizabeth Wiles-Portier. Cambridge: Polity, 1990.

Porter, Joseph A., 'Complement Extern: Iago's Speech Acts', in Virginia Mason Vaughan and Kent Cartwright, eds, *'Othello': New Perspectives*. Teaneck: Fairleigh Dickinson University Press, 1991, pp. 74–88.

Porter, Roy, 'Introduction', in Stephen Pumfrey, Paolo L. Rossi and Maurice Slawinski, eds, *Science, Culture and Popular Belief in Renaissance Europe.* Manchester: Manchester University Press, 1991, pp. 1–15.

Power, M. J., 'London and the Control of the "Crisis" of the 1590s', *History*, 70 (1985), pp. 371–85.

Prescott, Ann Lake, *Imagining Rabelais in Renaissance England.* New Haven and London: Yale University Press, 1998.

—— 'Rabelaisian (Non) Wonders and Renaissance Polemics', in Peter G. Platt, ed., *Wonders, Marvels, and Monsters in Early Modern Culture.* Newark: University of Delaware Press, 1999, pp. 133–44.

Purcell, Rosamond Wolff and Stephen Jay Gould, *Finders, Keepers: Eight Collectors.* London: Pimlico, 1993.

Purkiss, Diane, 'Producing the Voice, Consuming the Body: Women Prophets of the Seventeenth Century', in Isobel Grundy and Sue Wiseman, eds, *Women, Writing, History, 1640–1740.* London: Batsford, 1992, pp. 139–58.

Quinton, Anthony, *Francis Bacon.* New York: Hing and Wang, 1980.

Roberts, Michael, ' "Waiting upon Chance": English Hiring Fairs and their Meanings from the 14th to the 20th Century', *Journal of Historical Sociology*, 1 (1988), pp. 119–60.

Robson, David, 'Frye, Derrida, Pynchon, and the Apocalyptic Space of Postmodern Fiction', in Richard Dellamora, ed., *Postmodern Apocalypse: Theory and Cultural Practice at the End.* Philadelphia: University of Pennsylvania Press, 1995, pp. 61–78.

Rollins, Hyder E., 'The Black-Letter Broadside Ballad', *Publications of the Modern Language Association of America*, 34 (1919), pp. 258–339.

Rossi, Paulo L., 'Science, Culture and the Dissemination of Learning', in Stephen Pumfrey, Paolo L. Rossi and Maurice Slawinski, eds, *Science, Culture and Popular Belief in Renaissance Europe.* Manchester: Manchester University Press, 1991, pp. 143–75.

Rowe, George E., *Distinguishing Jonson: Imitation, Rivalry, and the Direction of a Dramatic Career.* Lincoln, NB and London: University of Nebraska Press, 1988.

Saenger, Michael Baird, 'The Costumes of Caliban and Ariel Qua Sea-Nymph', *Notes and Queries*, 42 (1995), pp. 334–6.

Sales, Roger, *Christopher Marlowe.* Basingstoke: Macmillan – now Palgrave Macmillan, 1991.

Sanders, Julie, *Ben Jonson's Theatrical Republics.* Basingstoke: Macmillan – now Palgrave Macmillan, 1998.

Schwartz, Hillel, *The Culture of the Copy: Striking Likenesses, Unreasonable Facsimiles.* New York: Zone, 1996.

Schwarzschild, Edward L., 'Death-Defying/Defining Spectacles: Charles Willson Peale as Early American Freak Showman', in Rosemarie Garland Thomson, ed., *Freakery: Cultural Spectacles of the Extraordinary Body.* New York and London: New York University Press, 1996, pp. 82–96.

Shackelford, Jole, 'Seeds with a Mechanical Purpose: Severinus, Semina and Seventeenth-Century Matter Theory', in Allen G. Debus and Michael T. Walton, eds, *Reading the Book of Nature: The Other Side of the Scientific Revolution.* Kirksville: Thomas Jefferson University Press, 1998, pp. 15–44.

Shapin, Steven, *The Scientific Revolution.* Chicago and London: University of Chicago Press, 1996.

Shapiro, James, *Rival Playwrights: Marlowe, Jonson, Shakespeare*. New York: Columbia University Press, 1991.

Shelton, Anthony Alan, 'Cabinets of Transgression: Renaissance Collections and the Incorporation of the New World', in John Elsner and Roger Cardinal, eds, *The Cultures of Collecting*. London: Reaktion, 1994, pp. 177–203.

Shepherd, Simon, *Marlowe and the Politics of Elizabethan Theatre*. Brighton: Harvester, 1986.

Shepherd, Thomas A., *London and Its Environs in the Nineteenth Century*. London: Jones, 1829.

Shershow, Scott Cutler, *Puppets and 'Popular' Culture*. Ithaca, NY and London: Cornell University Press, 1995.

Shesgreen, Sean, *The Criers and Hawkers of London: Engravings and Drawings by Marcellus Laroon*. Stanford: Stanford University Press, 1990.

Shildrick, Margrit, *Embodying the Monster: Encounters with the Vulnerable Self*. London: Sage, 2002.

Simpson, J. A. and E. S. C. Weiner, eds, *The Oxford English Dictionary*, 20 vols. Oxford: Clarendon, 1989.

Skura, Meredith Anne, 'Discourse and the Individual: The Case of Colonialism in *The Tempest*', *Shakespeare Quarterly*, 40 (1989), pp. 42–69.

——*Shakespeare the Actor and the Purposes of Playing*. Chicago and London: University of Chicago Press, 1993.

Smith, Ian, 'Barbarian Errors: Performing Race in Early Modern England', *Shakespeare Quarterly*, 49 (1998), pp. 168–86.

Stallybrass, Peter and Allon White, *The Politics and Poetics of Transgression*. London: Methuen, 1986.

Starks, Lisa S., '"Won with thy words and conquered with thy looks": Sadism, Masochism, and the Masochistic Gaze in *1 Tamburlaine*', in Paul Whitfield White, ed., *Marlowe, History, and Sexuality: New Critical Essays on Christopher Marlowe*. New York: AMS, 1998, pp. 179–93.

Starr, G. A., 'Escape from Barbary: A Seventeenth-Century Genre', *Huntington Library Quarterly*, 29 (1965), pp. 35–62.

Stephens, Walter, *Giants in Those Days: Folklore, Ancient History, and Nationalism*. Lincoln, NB and London: University of Nebraska Press, 1989.

Stewart, Susan, 'Death and Life, in that Order, in the Works of Charles Willson Peale', in Lynne Cooke and Peter Wollen, eds, *Visual Display: Culture Beyond Appearances*. Seattle: Bay Press, 1995, pp. 30–53.

Strickland, Debra Higgs, 'Monsters and Christian Enemies', *History Today*, 50.2 (2000), pp. 45–51.

Strier, Richard, '"I am Power": Normal and Magical Politics in *The Tempest*', in Derek Hirst and Richard Strier, eds, *Writing and Political Engagement in Seventeenth-Century England*. Cambridge: Cambridge University Press, 1999, pp. 10–30.

Sturgess, Keith, *Jacobean Private Theatre*. London and New York: Routledge & Kegan Paul, 1987.

Swann, Marjorie, *Curiosities and Texts: The Culture of Collecting in Early Modern England*. Philadelphia: University of Pennsylvania Press, 2001.

Teague, Frances, *The Curious History of 'Bartholomew Fair'*. Lewisburg: Bucknell University Press, 1985.

Thomson, Rosemarie Garland, *Extraordinary Bodies: Figuring Physical Disability in American Culture and Literature*. New York: Columbia University Press, 1997.

Thurn, David H., 'Sights of Power in *Tamburlaine*', *English Literary Renaissance*, 19 (1989), pp. 3–21.

Torrey, Michael, ' "The plain devil and dissembling looks": Ambivalent Physiognomy and Shakespeare's *Richard III*', *English Literary Renaissance*, 30 (2000), pp. 123–53.

Tromly, Fred B., *Playing with Desire: Christopher Marlowe and the Art of Tantalization*. Toronto, Buffalo and London: University of Toronto Press, 1998.

Underdown, David, *Fire from Heaven: Life in an English Town in the Seventeenth Century*. London: HarperCollins, 1992.

Varley, John Frederick, *Oliver Cromwell's Latter End*. London: Chapman and Hall, [1939].

Vaughan, Alden T., 'Trinculo's Indian: American Natives in Shakespeare's England', in Peter Hulme and William H. Sherman, eds, *'The Tempest' and Its Travels*. London: Reaktion, 2000, pp. 49–59.

Vaughan, Alden T. and Virginia Mason Vaughan, *Shakespeare's Caliban: A Cultural History*. Cambridge: Cambridge University Press, 1993.

Vaughan, Virginia Mason, *'Othello': A Contextual History*. Cambridge: Cambridge University Press, 1994.

Vickers, Nancy, ' "The blazon of sweet beauty's best": Shakespeare's *Lucrece*', in Patricia Parker and Geoffrey Hartman, eds, *Shakespeare and the Question of Theory*. New York and London: Methuen, 1995, pp. 95–115.

Waith, Eugene M., *The Herculean Hero in Marlowe, Chapman, Shakespeare and Dryden*. London: Chatto and Windus, 1962.

——'The Staging of *Bartholomew Fair*', *Studies in English Literature*, 2 (1962), pp. 181–95.

Walford, Cornelius, *Fairs, Past and Present: A Chapter in the History of Commerce*. London: Elliot Stock, 1883.

Waterhouse, Ruth, '*Beowulf* as Palimpsest', in Jeffrey Jerome Cohen, ed., *Monster Theory: Reading Culture*. Minneapolis and London: University of Minnesota Press, 1996, pp. 26–39.

Watterson, William Collins, ' "O monstrous world": Shakespeare's Beast with Two Backs', *The Upstart Crow*, 13 (1993), pp. 79–93.

Watson, Robert N., *Ben Jonson's Parodic Strategy: Literary Imperialism in the Comedies*. Cambridge, MA: Harvard University Press, 1987.

——*Shakespeare and the Hazards of Ambition*. Cambridge, MA: Harvard University Press, 1984.

Watt, Tessa, *Cheap Print and Popular Piety 1550–1640*. Cambridge: Cambridge University Press, 1991.

Wayne, Don E., 'The "exchange of letters": Early Modern Contradictions and Postmodern Conundrums', in Ann Bermingham and John Brewer, eds, *The Consumption of Culture, 1600–1800*. London and New York: Routledge, 1995, pp. 143–65.

Webb, J. Barry, *Shakespeare's Animals: A Guide to the Literal and Figurative Usage*. Hastings: Cornwallis Press, 1996.

Webster, Charles, *From Paracelsus to Newton: Magic and the Making of Modern Science*. Cambridge: Cambridge University Press, 1982.

Welch, Martin, 'The Foundation of the Ashmolean Museum', in Arthur MacGregor, ed., *Tradescant's Rarities: Essays on the Foundation of the Ashmolean Museum*. Oxford: Clarendon, 1983, pp. 40–58.

Weld, Charles Richard, *The History of the Royal Society*, 2 vols. London: Parker, 1858.

Wells, Henry W., *Elizabethan and Jacobean Playwrights*. New York: Columbia University Press, 1939.

Wells, Robert Headlam, *Shakespeare on Masculinity*. Cambridge: Cambridge University Press, 2000.

Whitaker, Katie, 'The Culture of Curiosity', in N. Jardine, J. A. Secord and E. C. Sparry, eds, *Cultures of Natural History*. Cambridge: Cambridge University Press, 1996, pp. 75–90.

Wiles, David, *Shakespeare's Clown: Actor and text in the Elizabethan playhouse*. Cambridge: Cambridge University Press, 1987.

Williams, David, *Deformed Discourse: The Function of the Monster in Mediaeval Thought and Literature*. Exeter: University of Exeter Press, 1996.

Williams, Ethel Carleton, *Anne of Denmark*. Chatham: Mackay, 1970.

Williams, Franklin B., 'Thomas Churchyard's Thunder on the Right', *English Literary Renaissance*, 3 (1973), pp. 380–99.

Williams, Gordon, *A Dictionary of Sexual Language and Imagery in Shakespearean and Stuart Literature*, 3 vols. London: Athlone, 1994.

Willis, Deborah, 'Shakespeare's *Tempest* and the Discourse of Colonialism', *Studies in English Literature*, 29 (1989), pp. 277–89.

Willson, David Harris, *King James VI and I*. London: Cape, 1966.

Wilson, Henry and James Caulfield, *The Book of Wonderful Characters*. London: Hotten, 1869.

Wilson, Richard, 'Visible Bullets: Tamburlaine the Great and Ivan the Terrible', *ELH*, 62 (1995), pp. 47–68.

——'Voyage to Tunis: New History and the Old World of *The Tempest*', *ELH*, 64 (1997), pp. 333–57.

Wood, Edward J., *Giants and Dwarfs*. London: Bentley, 1868.

Yates, Frances A., *Astraea: The Imperial Theme in the Sixteenth Century*. London, Boston, Melbourne and Henley: Ark, 1975.

Zagorin, Perez, *Francis Bacon*. Princeton, NJ: Princeton University Press, 1998.

Zwager, N., *Glimpses of Ben Jonson's London*. Amsterdam: Swets and Zeitlinger, 1926.

Index

Aubrey, James R.   97, 117
audience response   3, 4, 24, 101,
    102, 128, 172, 181
audiences   19, 31, 42, 93, 96, 155,
    156
author, the   142–3, 145, 152–3, 177
autonomy   4

baboons   127
Bacon, Francis   97, 111, 112, 113,
    114, 115, 117
    see also under titles of individual
    works
Baker, David J.   126
Bakhtin, Mikhail   165
balladeers   15
ballads
    general   4, 12, 138
    about 'monsters'   28, 83, 98, 135,
        136, 173
    on Skinker, Tannakin   17, 18
    on Urselin, Barbara   17
banners   14, 16, 18, 53, 161, 180
barbarity   17, 48, 96, 102, 109, 117,
    120
Barbary, King of   99
Barish, Jonas   84
Barnum, Phineas Taylor   12
Bartels, Emily   36, 97
Bartholomew Fair   19, 21, 55, 85
Bartholomew Fair
    arguments in   8
    ending of   174–5
    engagement with Shakespeare in
        154–5, 156–7, 161, 162, 166, 172,
        174, 175
    enormity in   6, 163, 164, 165, 166,
        170, 174
    evasions of   156, 158, 161, 163,
        164, 174, 177
    fairground in   31
    identity in   6
    masque, the, in   158
    Overdo in   163–4
    and *Othello*   157, 163, 166, 167,
        175
    parody in   159–61, 172
    performative occasion of   176
    philosophy in   160–1

pigs in   167, 170
predictive power of   182
publication of   159, 176–8
puppets in   158, 171–4
references to 'monsters' in   154
reproduction in   6
spectacle in   162
stage history of   10
and *The Tempest*   154, 157–8, 163,
    164, 165, 170, 171, 172, 174,
    175
translation in   157, 158, 159, 160,
    163, 164, 166, 169, 171, 172,
    174, 175
Ursula in   158, 164–71
women in   170–1
Bartolovich, Crystal   126
Basilikon Doran   145
basilisk, the   86, 117
Basset, Robert   26
bastardization   51, 71
Bateman, Stephen   43, 84
Battenhouse, Roy W.   59
Bawcutt, N. W.   10
Beale, John   178
bear-baiting   170
Bear Garden, the   11, 20
'bearded ladies'   181
'bearded monsters'   3, 17
bears   11, 17, 169–70
beast of Lerna, the   46
Beaumont, Francis   11
Beaumont, Francis, and John Fletcher
    52
Bedford, Thomas   26
belief   7, 113
Benedict, Barbara M.   133, 147
Benjamin, Walter   157, 175
Best, George   100
bestiality   25, 99, 148, 205 (n. 14)
Biester, James   37
bills   13, 16, 186 (n. 28)
binary arrangements   28, 105, 109,
    123
Biow, Douglas   131
bird-like child, a   30
Birringer, Johannes H.   52
Birth of Merlin, The   1, 3, 17, 53
birthmarks   118